Dedicated to the memory of
HUBERT GRAY
who loved the outdoors

Kananaskis Country

A guide to hiking, skiing equestrian & bike trails

by Gillean Daffern

SECOND EDITION

Rocky Mountain Books
Calgary

ACKNOWLEDGMENTS

There are many people who have helped me in the quest for information: Rick Moyse, Ron Andrews, Eric Kuhn, Jim Ridley, Rod Jaeger, Bob Wood, Jim Murphy, Glen Naylor, Pat Ronald, Laurie Powell, Dianne Meili, Isomay Ballachey, Randolf Freeman, Gill Ford, Dave Zvevick, Ken McKyle, Dianne Pachal, Dave Higgins, Brian Prior, Maryalice Stewart, C.W. Sadleir, Dick Mackie, Jack Carter, Tony Forster, Wally Drew and John Cartwright.

Most of the trips were undertaken in the company of my husband, Tony, without whose encouragement and help in numerous ways this book would never have been finished. Special thanks are also due to Michelle Condie and Neil Daffern who had the onerous task of transposing topo maps into metric. I am also grateful to those people who searched their slide and photo collections for cover photographs and in-text illustrations: Alf Skrastins, Leon Kubbernus, Don Hollingshead, Ross Goodwin, Ron Chemney, Robin and Marion White and Henry Leparskas.

The list of credits would not be complete without a special acknowledgment to Don Cockerton of the Alberta Forest Service who went out of his way to provide up-to-date information. Thanks Don!

Front cover photo: Three Isle Lake, looking towards Mount Worthington
— Leon Kubbernus

Back cover photo: Mount Kidd makes an impressive backdrop to the Kananaskis Country golf course ski trails.

Frontispiece: Crossing the avalanche path en route to Lawson Lake and North Kananaskis Pass. In the background is Mount Lyautey and The Forks of the Kananaskis River.

First edition 1979
Second edition 1985

Published by Rocky Mountain Books
106 Wimbledon Crescent, Calgary, Alberta
Printed and bound in Canada by
Hignell Printing Limited, Manitoba

ISBN 0-9690038-5-4

CONTENTS

KANANASKIS COUNTRY

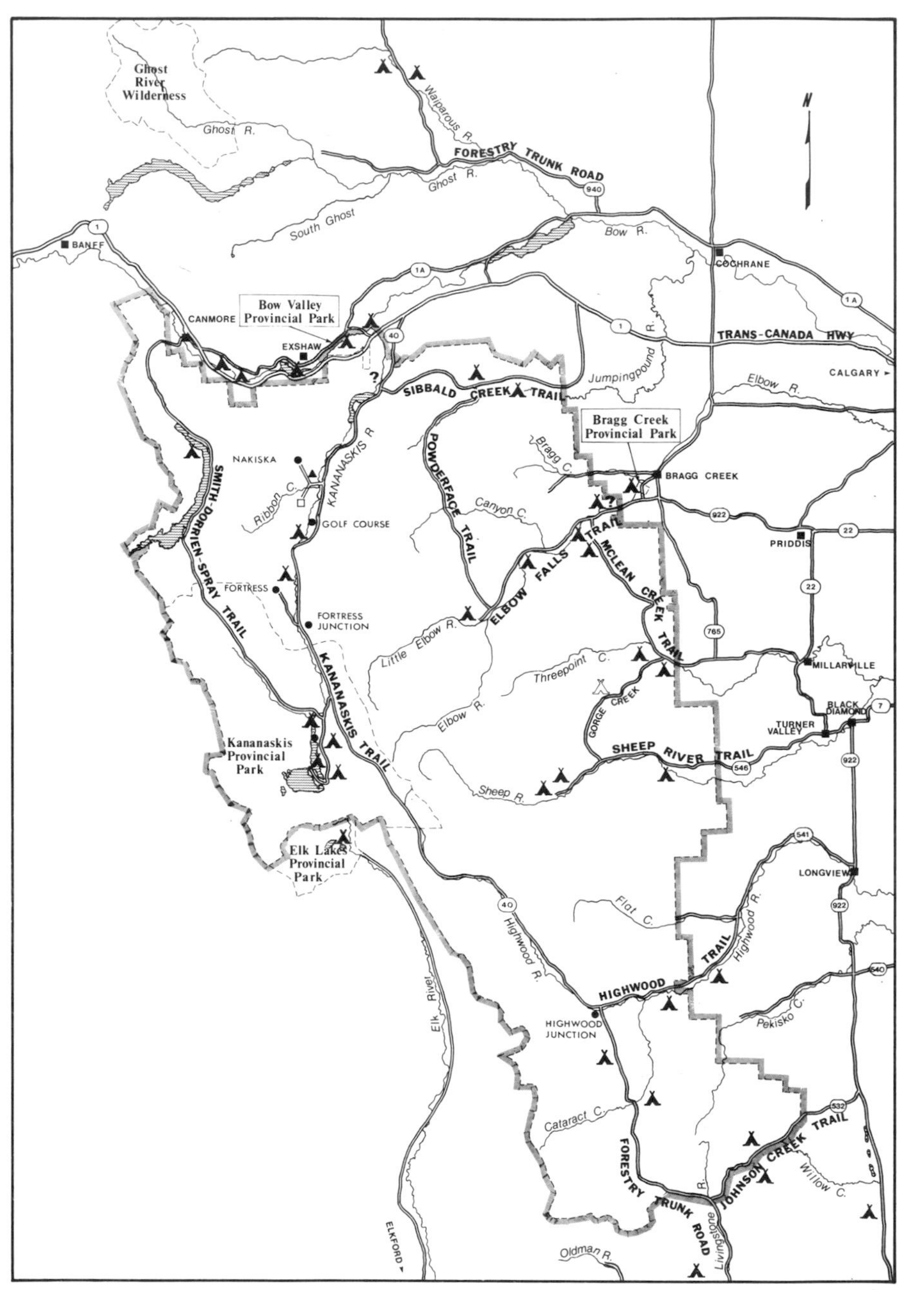

INTRODUCTION TO KANANASKIS COUNTRY

In 1858, explorer John Palliser named the pass he was about to cross, *"Kananaskis Pass, after the name of an Indian, of whom there is a legend, giving an account of his most wonderful recovery from the blow of an axe which had stunned but had failed to kill him, and the river which flows through this gorge also bears his name".* Today, the pass, the lakes below it, and the river flowing north towards the Bow River form the heart of Kananaskis Country, a provincial recreation area established on October 7th, 1977 to "alleviate congestion in National Parks, and to provide greater recreation opportunities for Albertans".

The area's original 3,200 square kilometres was enlarged in 1982, and now encompasses over 4,000 square kilometres of mountains and forests on the eastern slopes of the Canadian Rockies including the core area of Kananaskis Provincial Park and the headwaters of the Highwood, Sheep, Elbow and Jumpingpound Rivers. The area is bounded on the west by Banff National Park and the Alberta—British Columbia boundary, and on the east by the Bow Crow forest reserve boundary. The practical limit of Kananaskis Country to the north and south is Highway 1A, and Johnson Creek Trail (Hwy. 532) coupled with Forestry Trunk Road 940. In this edition I have also included the adjoining areas of The Ghost, and Elk Lakes Provincial Park in British Columbia which are usually accessed from Kananskis Country.

There are 2 distinct scenic zones. In the west, bordering the Great Divide, are high peaks of glacier-worn sedimentary rock carved into cirques and mantled with glaciers which, together with melting winter snowpack, give rise to boisterous streams and spectacular waterfalls. Glacial debris carried down to densely- forested valley bottoms colors large valley lakes an intense shade of blue/green. Once the sole dominion of the grizzly, this area has become a playground for adventurous, experienced hikers who can expect steep mountain trails and unpredictable mountain weather with snow a possibility at any time of year. Heavy winter snowfall, which makes this zone so attractive to the cross- country skier, keeps summer trails closed until July.

At the other extreme, the eastern boundary of Kananaskis Country is a friendly landscape of rolling foothills bristling here and there with little sandstone outscrops. Fire-succession pine forest covers northern slopes. On south slopes, the coniferous trees are replaced by a montage of aspen forest and prairie which increases proportionately to the pine forest the further south you go. Cattle graze in pastoral valleys each one with its own chain of beaver ponds. This zone has been extensively explored during the search for natural resources and is cross-crossed with cutlines and exploration roads, some of which have found new use in recreational trails. Because snow fall is generally minimal, hiking and horseback riding are possible almost all the year round.

In between these 2 zones lies the transitional zone which has characteristics of both: sharp rock peaks, high grassy ridges home to large flocks of sheep, deep gorges, and seasonal streams attesting to the zone's dry climate, lying as it does in the rainshadow of the highest mountains. Some of the best trails leading to the finest viewpoints are found in this middle zone.

TRAILS

The official trails, maintained by Alberta Parks and Recreation and the Great Divide Trail Association are all signed at trailheads and junctions. Many are new trails built by the Alberta Forest Service since 1978, some are historic trails which have been upgraded, and the rest are an amalgamation of exploration roads, logging roads and cutlines. At the time of publication, official trails in the West Highwood can be counted on the fingers of one hand, and there are none at all in the East Highwood, Flat Creek and The Livingstone area. Unsigned, unofficial routes follow pack trails, exploration roads, logging roads and cutlines, and sometimes no trails at all. In this edition, several new ridge walks have been included which run the gamut from hands in pocket walks along grassy hogbacks to strenuous climbs entailing the odd pitch of scrambling where the hands are used mainly for balance.

Trails are classified into hiking, skiing, equestrian and biking trails. Hiking trails are further divided; half-day hike means just that with a hiking time not exceeding 3 hours even for a very slow party, a day hike lasts between 5 - 6 hours, a long day hike can extend to 10 hours, and backpack involves overnight camping. Times will differ from person to person and can be estimated from the distance and height gain given under each trail heading and from your own assessment of your physical fitness.

Naismith's Rule is the simplest method of estimating time:
Adults 5 km/h and 1/2 hour for every 300 m of height gain.
Youth Group 4 km/h and 1 hour for every 450 m of height gain.

Remember, this rule applies to hiking time only and assumes that you are fit, the terrain is easy and the weather is good. Times should be modified to include rest stops, difficult terrain and bad weather. Skiing times are almost impossible to estimate as so much depends on snow conditions; an easy half-day trip can take a whole day if you have to break trail through 50 cm of bottomless snow.

I have not attempted to grade hiking trails. Some trails may be rougher or steeper than others but involve only hiking unless otherwise indicated in the trail description. Ridge walks are difficult to categorize. For example, Mist Ridge is mainly a walk with one pitch of easy scrambling, wheras the Aster Lake to Three Isle Lake traverse has no scrambling but demands a steady foot and a head for heights if you are to make it through safely. Ski trails have been given easy, intermediate and difficult ratings. This reflects technical difficulty and takes no account of snow conditions which can raise or lower the grading on any given day.

The work "bike" under the trail heading indicates that the trail, though not necessarily **ALL** of the trail, is suitable for mountain biking. Very often, you will want to cycle part of the way then carry on on foot to the ridge top or pass. Fire roads, logging roads, exploration roads and cutlines all make good bike routes, Odlum Creek logging road being the prime example. The use of a bike on foot trails and equestrian trails (soft and sometimes muddy) is discouraged.

GENERAL INFORMATION

ACCESS

Access roads and roads within Kananaskis Country are shown on the road map on page 2. At the time of publication, the following roads are closed between December 1st and June 15th (opening dates may vary according to weather and road conditions):

- Kananaskis Trail (Hwy. 40) between Kananaskis Lakes Trail and Highwood Junction.
- Elbow Falls Trail (Hwy. 66) west of Elbow Falls
- Sheep River Trail (SR 546) west of Sandy McNabb recreation area.
- Powderface Trail.
- McLean Creek Trail.
- Gorge Creek Trail.
- Forestry Trunk Road 940 between Cataract Creek Campground and Wilkinson Summit.

FACILITIES

Total visitor services are available in the fringe towns of Canmore, Cochrane, Bragg Creek, Black Diamond, Turner Valley and Longview. Dead Man's Flat, Exshaw, Seebe, and Millarville offer partial services.

GAS

- Fortress Junction (all year round)
- Highwood Junction (summer only)

GROCERIES AND CAMPING SUPPLIES

- Fortress Junction (all year round)
- Boulton Trading Post (all year round, weekends only in winter and off-season)
- Highwood Junction (summer only)

RESTAURANTS AND FAST FOOD OUTLETS

- Fortress Junction (all year round)
- Boulton Trading Post (all year round, weekends only in winter and off season)
- Kananaskis Country Golf Course (summer, winter only)
- Fortress Mountain ski area (winter only)
- Nakiska ski area (winter only)

ACCOMMODATION

- William Watson Lodge (all year round, handicapped and senior citizens only)
- Fortress Mountain ski area (winter only)
- Ribbon Creek Youth Hostel (all year round)
- Ribbon Creek Alpine Village (all year round, due to be in operation by 1988)

INFORMATION CENTRES

- Canmore, Provincial Building
- Barrier Lake on Kananaskis Trail (Hwy. 40)
- Kananaskis Park Visitor Centre on Kananaskis Lakes Trail
- Gooseberry on Elbow Falls Trail (Hwy. 66)
- Bow Valley Park Visitor Centre off Highway 1X

- Spray District Office on Smith-Dorrien – Spray Trail
- Highwood Junction (summer only)

PUBLIC TELEPHONES

- At all information centres
- Barrier Lake day-use area
- Elbow Ranger Station
- Eau Claire campground
- Fortress Junction
- Fortress Mountain ski area
- Jumpingpound Ranger Station
- Kananaskis Country Golf Course
- Kananaskis Experiment Station
- Lac des Arcs Campground
- McLean Creek campground
- Mount Kidd Recreational Vehicle Park
- Nakiska ski area
- Pocaterra parking lot
- Ribbon Creek parking lot
- Sheep River Ranger Station
- Wasootch Creek day-use area
- West Bragg Creek parking lot
- William Watson Lodge

USEFUL TELEPHONE NUMBERS

- Travel Alberta toll free 1-800-222-6501
- Kananaskis Advisory Committee 297-3362
- Alberta Recreation and Parks, Canmore 678-5508
- Alberta Forest Service, Calgary 239-0004
- Fish & Wildlife, Calgary 297-6423
- Bow Valley Provincial Park Visitor Centre 673-3663
- Kananaskis Provincial Park 591-7222
- Gooseberry Travel Information Centre 949-4261
- Barrier Lake Travel Information Centre 673-3985
- William Watson Lodge 591-7227
- Fortress Ski Area 591-7108
- Kananaskis Country Golf Course 591-7070
- Kananaskis Ranger Station 591-7155
- Elbow Ranger Station 949-3754
- Turner Valley Ranger Station 933-4381
- Highwood Ranger Station 558-2240
- Jumpingpound Ranger Station 932-5575
- Ghost Ranger Station 932-5668

IN CASE OF EMERGENCY PHONE:

- Kananaskis Provincial Park Ranger Office 591-7222
- Elbow Ranger Station 949-3754
- Bow Valley Provincial Park Office 673-3663
- R.C.M.P. Canmore - dial 0 and ask for 678-5516
- R.C.M.P. Cochrane - dial 0 and ask for 932-2211 or your nearest R.C.M.P. Office.

Devils Head from Margaret Lake.

1 MOCKINGBIRD LOOKOUT — Map 1

Day hike, intermediate ski
Equestrian, bike
Distance 3.2 km
Height gain 365 m
Maximum elevation 1933 m
Topo map 82 O/6 Lake Minnewanka

Access: Forestry Trunk Road 940. 13.9 km north of the forest boundary, turn west onto a dirt road signed "Waiperous Creek Valley". Drive for 3 km past Camp Mockingbird to a junction. Keep right. 0.7 km after crossing a bridge over a small stream, park at the bottom of the fire road to your right.

Its short length and proximity to campgrounds makes the trail to Mockingbird Lookout a popular one with school and youth groups. It's also an excellent intermediate ski trail, one of the few trails in the area closed to snowmobiles. Be aware, though, that the road along Waiparous Creek between Highway 940 and the fire road is not plowed. This means an extra 4.1 km of skiing each way.

Walk up the fire road. Beyond the gate, the road winds through dense pine forest onto the south ridge of the hill where it levels a little and follows the ridge line along to lush summit meadows. The present lookout, built in the 1973-74 seasons, replaced the old box-like structure which had stood on this spot for over 20 years. In turn, the first Mockingbird Lookout superseded the one on nearby Blackrock Mountain which was abandoned in 1952. If you look S.W. across Waiperous Creek you will see a solitary mountain closer in than the Front Ranges and about 600 m higher than Mockingbird. This is Blackrock Mountain, and the pimple on top is the old lookout (see route #5). To its right, the rock obelisk of Devils Head is unmistakable.

The bare mountains around the head of the Red Deer River are just visible to the north. Closer in, the eyes travel over hectares of forest through which wind the Burnt Timber, Fallen Timber and Little Red Deer rivers and all their tributaries. A little north of east the eye is stayed by large areas of open ground near the edge of the forest. These are the Greasy Plains, a name with a Tolkienesque ring to it signifying marsh and moulding vegetation. In reality, the Greasy Plains on Grease Creek were named by explorer James Hector who called them "Pre de Graisse" after the black birch or Grease Wood which grows along the creek bed. They were a well-known feature of the Indian trail between Morley and the Red Deer River. Right of the plains and beyond diminishing waves of forested ridges - Salter, Keystone, Swanson and Wildcat - you can see a few of Calgary's skyscrapers. Completing the 360 degree panorama is the view to the south. The dominant feature here is Moose Mountain whose summit is occupied by the next lookout in the chain running south to the U.S. border.

2 WAIPAROUS CREEK — Map 1

Backpack, equestrian, bike
Distance 18 km
Height gain 580 m
Maximum elevation 2135 m
Topo map 82 O/6 Lake Minnewanka

Access: Forestry Trunk Road 940. 13.9 km north of the forest boundary, turn west onto a dirt road signed "Waiparous Creek Valley". Drive for 3 km past Camp Mockingbird to a junction. Turn left onto a rougher road which is passable for another 4 km to the end of the red-dashed line shown on the topo map. At the foot of a deeply-trenched hill navigable only by all terrain vehicles, turn left into a parking area.

The North Ghost or Waiparous Creek (meaning Crow Scalp in Stoney) is the most accessible of the three Ghost Rivers: an exploration road, and later on a cutline, take you easily into the head of the valley. Walking along a road is hardly an aesthetic experience. Moreover, this road is a very popular one with trail bikers, particularly the section to the Margaret Lake turnoff for which I've suggested alternative routes wherever possible. However, don't let this put you off going up Waiparous Creek; the rock scenery is superb and it's easy enough to get off the beaten track. Six fords are problematical at runoff, particularly the first one which is unavoidable.

The road climbs up then down a 50 m hill. If you don't fancy this start you can scrabble along the river bank and pick up a cutline in the trees beyond which leads back to the road. At the bottom of the hill turn right or if you've arrived via the river bank, cross the road onto a cutline which offers a quieter and softer alternative for the next 3 km. Route finding is easy; wherever it touches the road simply follow the yellow snowmobile signs. Near the end of the third and longest straight, turn left - still obeying the snowmobile signs - onto a grassy track which returns you to the road just a short distance from the Margaret Lake turnoff. Across the river, Devils Head mountain is a mirror image of its other more familiar side. To its right, the castellated mountain may be the Castle Rock shown on the 1930 map of the Bow River Provincial Forest.

At the road junction turn left and wade the river a little downstream of the ford which has some deep holes. The road crosses a major S.W. - N.E. cutline then curves round a river bend, fading out temporarily where the stream from Castle Rock cirque enters the Waiparous. At the next ford, the road is joined by another road coming in from the S.W. - N.E. cutline on your left. Recross the creek and follow the road over a low forested ridge to the third crossing at the confluence of the Waiparous with its north fork. Except at runoff, it's possible for hikers to edge along the south bank between the last two fords. Watch for a cairn and survey marker en route.

The north fork is bounded on the west by a 300 metre rock prow, facade for a remarkable line of cliffs extending half way along the valley, and on the east side by two ruinous mountains almost totally crumbled into orange screes. The main valley is no less interesting. The road winds past a popular camping spot by the side of a small waterfall, then, reversing the S-bend, travels beneath a long curved wall of grey stones - a perfect example of a concave river bank left high and dry above the river's present shoreline. High above, a cliff rivaling that of the north fork, sends forth long shadows. On windy days, water seeping over the edge drifts in a fine spray across black- streaked walls. Cross the creek and climb steeply over a side ridge below the prow to another creek crossing, the final one. Both crossings can be avoided by an unsuspected traverse along the south bank.

A gloomy stretch of road, often muddy from rills running off the hillside, ends at a viewpoint overlooking a free-falling waterfall across the valley. Zigzag down to the valley floor, cross a major side creek, and arrive at a road junction. Equestrians should take the road to the left which wastes no time in climbing to get above the upcoming canyon. Those on foot can continue along the river bank to where the road apparently ends at a campsite, then climb a well-trodden trail up the bank to a continuation of the road above. Both routes join above the canyon 0.2 km farther on. Clearings in trees to the right indicate the entry point into meadows above the river's initial plunge into the chasm, a delightful spot which is usually the culmination of a trip up the Waiparous. The road continues on for almost another kilometre.

UPPER WAIPAROUS CREEK Although it can't be seen from the end of the road, a cutline does in fact carry on to the meadows at the very end of the valley. To get to the start of it, descend the bank and wade the river, aiming for the left-hand bank of the side stream sporting a single waterfall half glimpsed from the road's end. The cutline, which climbs high above the Waiparous (closeted once more in a gorge), merits a rating of difficult on the cutline scale. Serpentine in nature, it has an annoying habit of traversing steep sidehills on the slant and, in addition, is clogged with windfall requiring lengthy detours at many points. Two deeply-cut side streams may be difficult to cross during their tumultuous headlong rush to join the Waiparous at runoff.

The spectacular cliffs of Waiparous Creek's north fork.

3 MARGARET LAKE — Map 1

Day hike, equestrian, bike
Distance 8.4 km
Height gain 185 m
Maximum elevation 1725 m
Topo map 82 O/6 Lake Minnewanka

Access: Forestry Trunk Road 940. 13.9 km north of the forest boundary, turn west onto a dirt road signed "Waiparous Creek Valley". Drive for 3 km past Camp Mockingbird to a junction. Turn left onto a rougher road which is passable for another 4 km to the end of the red-dashed line shown on the topo map. At the foot of a deeply-trenched hill, navigable only by all terrain vehicles, turn left into a parking area.

This gem of a lake has the misfortune to lie smack in the middle of an all-terrain vehicle land use area. Right now, the only route is along roller-coaster cutlines and exploration roads shared with noisy trailbikes. Deadfall in the forest deters shortcutting.

Follow Waiparous Creek trail (#2) to the road junction at the first ford. Walk along the right-hand road to a major S.W. - N.E. cutline and turn right. This cutline is one of the worst kind; if you're not climbing up or down, then you're pussy- footing it around side-to-side puddles gouged out of soft clay. Near the junction of road and cutline, a bypass road on the left cuts out the first steep hill. Many hills later turn second left onto the signed snowmobile trail, and follow it over a hill into a dip. The lake lies on the left-hand side - a sudden blue opening in the pines. All the most spectacular peaks of the Ghost are lined up as backdrop; a grand sight which overpowers your initial repugnance at the mess made by all-terrain vehicles driving to the water's edge. Quieter spots can be found along the north bank where glades slope down to the lake at sunbathing angle.

4 NORTH GHOST SKI TRAILS — Map 1

5 km of trails
Topo map 82 O/6 Lake Minnewanka

Access: Forestry Trunk Road 940. 12.9 km north of the forest boundary, turn left towards the North Ghost Campground. From the parking lot, ski across the bridge into the campground.

The trails, groomed and packed, follow campground loops on either side of the centre road. These are excellent trails for beginner skiers; the terrain is generally flat with a few gentle hills on the upper loops. The highest road to the right leads to a large meadow with picnic shelter.

5 BLACKROCK MOUNTAIN LOOKOUT — Map 1

Day hike
9 km from camping spot
Height gain 925 m
Maximum elevation 2462 m
Topo map 82 O/6 Lake Minnewanka

Access: Forestry Trunk Road 940. At the Bar Cee Ranch 25.4 km north of Highway 1A, turn west and drive for another 15.6 km along the Ghost River Road. Ignore all lesser roads to the right. The sensible place to park is at the camping spot above the steep hill leading down to the Ghost River. Depending on conditions and type of vehicle - you need good clearance - you can drive a further 3.5 km. If you think the distance gained is worth the risk, descend the hill to a 4-way junction. Go straight and cross the dry stony creekbed which was once the Ghost River and is still subject to flash floods which periodically wipe out the road at this point. Head up-valley past huts owned by Trans- Alta Utilities. At the next island of vegetation park at the junction with a rougher road making a beeline for Blackrock Mountain.

Although the lookout was superseded in 1952 by Mockingbird to the east, the pack trail to the summit is still in fair shape even after 30 years of neglect. It takes a daring line up the south slopes of the mountain causing you at many points on the ascent to wonder where it can possibly go next.

The road enters forest and arrives at the derelict linesman's cabin where you can register your climb at the trail survey box and fill up your water bottles from the nearby side creek which is always running. Continue up the road to an unsigned junction where many people have gone astray in the past. You **must** turn left here onto the lookout trail which makes a long sweep to the left before switchbacking up to timberline meadows; at every right-hand bend you meet the old telephone line snaking down the hillside. Above treeline, the trail makes a final zig onto a broad ridge, then heads straight for the cliffs girdling the mountain.

On screes below the cliff the trail has largely disintegrated, so head up whichever route looks easiest to you (a left to right line is easiest), and rejoin the built-up trail at the cliff base. The telephone wire rises dizzily overhead. Traverse left and when it seems that some desperate manoeuvre must be made, a break suddenly appears in the cliff and the trail sweeps through into an uptilted scree basin. Slits in the cliffs and fissures in the ground invite exploration. The telephone line reappears over the cliff edge and is strung on a line of tripods rising over the edge of the basin onto the plateau. Flat and grassy, and isolated on three sides by overhanging cliffs, this "lost world" is surely the most surprising feature of Blackrock Mountain. To the west Devils Head mountain sticks up like a lonely sentinel above a similar tableland. The summit is still a long way off, a pimple at the end of the plateau which gradually grows in stature as you approach. En route, the amateur botanist will have a field day identifying many uncommon species of alpines including the campanula uniflora (dwarf harebell) and the intriguing townsendia condensata which looks like a giant-sized fleabane stuck in the ground up to its head.

Two cairns signal the trail's final ascent up the tapering scree ridge where you zigzag from side to side between the sunny southern cliff and the icy northern precipice. High up, the distance lessens to less than 6 steps in either direction and suddenly you arrive at the mauvais pas, a 2 metre-wide rock ridge which even the most timorous hiker can cross without fear - as long as the infamous west wind isn't gusting. The few metres of easy ground following leads to a summit a little larger than a helicopter landing pad, in the middle of which, and tethered by cables, stands the 56 year-old lookout.

The final bastion of Blackrock Mtn. from the plateau. Route zigzags up the left-hand skyline.

Devils Head from the final zigzags. This photo well illustrates Blackrock Mtn.'s aloofness from the main body of the Front Range.

6 GHOST RIVER — Maps 1 & 2

Day hike, backpack, equestrian
22.5 km to Spectral Creek junction
Height gain 320 m
Maximum elevation 1860 m
Topo map 82 O/6 Lake Minnewanka

Access: Forestry Trunk Road 940. At Bar Cee Ranch, 25.4 km north of Highway 1A, turn west and drive for another 15.6 km along the Ghost River Road. Ignore all lesser roads to the right. The sensible place to park is at the camping spot above the steep hill leading down to the Ghost River. Depending on conditions and type of vehicle - you need good clearance - you can drive a further 6.7 km to a ford beyond Blackrock Mountain. So, assuming you're willing to take the risk and there are enough four-wheel drive vehicles around to bail you out, descend the hill to a 4-way junction. Go straight and cross the dry stony creekbed which was once the Ghost River before the waters were channeled into a canal and diverted to the Lake Minnewanka drainage. The road heads up-valley past huts owned by Trans-Alta Utilities and eventually crosses a bridge over the canal to the west bank. Park at the first ford. On the north bank a vegetated exploration road steers for the gap between Blackrock Mountain and Bastion Wall.

Despite the exploration roads, the cutlines and the trail bikes, the Ghost River still retains an aura of untouched wilderness. It is a spectacular valley, reaching far back into the heart of the Palliser Range; a very long day's journey indeed to the meadows below Mount Oliver. The upper half of the valley is Wilderness Area administered by Alberta Recreation and Parks under statutory authority of the "Wilderness Areas Ecological Reserves and Natural Areas Act" of 1981. This means that horses (including pack animals) and all motorized vehicles must stay outside the boundaries. Hunting, trapping and fishing are prohibited.

Most backpackers use the valley as part of a popular 3-day loop starting and ending at the camping spot on the Ghost River Road. The route follows the Ghost River to Spectral Creek, climbs to Aylmer Pass at the Banff National Park boundary, descends to Lake Minnewanka (side visit to Aylmer lookout) and returns to the starting point via the north shore trail along lake Minnewanka and Devils Gap. For backpackers wishing to get off the beaten track there are innumerable side valleys to explore. From the head of Spectral Creek an easy pass leads into Stony Creek, where you can join the network of remote trails described in "The Canadian Rockies Trail Guide" under the heading "the Front Ranges".

The route follow the exploration road along alluvial flats all the way, crossing back and forth across the river 12 times. Since the river rarely rises above knee height, even at maximum runoff, fording is less of a problem than a nuisance. By the judicious use of game trails, you can cut the fords down to 2. For instance, the first 4 can be bypassed by a trail varying from good to barely adequate on the south bank. One kilometre past the 5th crossing, a cliff dipping into the river forces you to wade to the north bank (large pile of stones) and pick up the road just east of a major tributary. (Map ref. 200864) This is the last view you have of Devils Head Mountain, which for the first half of the route has played peek-a-boo above a succession of walls and box canyons.

The Ghost River Wilderness boundary lies a kilometre west of the tributary at the narrows. Again, the next 6 river crossings can be eliminated by sometimes easy and sometimes frustrating progress along the north bank where the grass grows unusually long and green below trees charred in the 1970 fire. At the 4th (9th overall) crossing, the so-called Paradise trail heads south to a boundary marker on the low point of the ridge connecting Mounts Costigan and Aylmer (map ref. 156815). There is no real trail, only the occasional blaze to guide you through a hellish mixture of muskeg and deadfall. It is debatable whether the birds-eye view of Lake Minnewanka is worth the trouble.

Turning north-west now, the valley floor widens. All through this section, excavations along the river bank indicate the presence of grizzlies digging for hedysarum roots. To the layman, hedysarums are indistinguishable from the more common vetches, but there is one foolproof way of telling them apart. Look carefully at the pods. Vetches have a single fat pod, wheras the fruit of the hedysarum is flat and jointed, looking rather like a string of one-cent pieces.

When you finally draw level with Mount Aylmer, which has been in view for many hours, you must ford the Ghost at the crossing upstream of the confluence with Spectral Creek. Fifteen minutes walking brings you to an important junction with the Aylmer Pass trail to the left.

UPPER GHOST Although an old packers' trail runs along the east bank between Spectral Creek and a point just north of Spirit Creek, such is its nebulous nature that most backpackers prefer to use the well-defined cutline, river crossings and all, which takes you all the way to the meadows below Mount Oliver. Offshoots serve the 3 major tributaries to the east. Note that the Spirit Creek cutline branches off nearly one kilometre south of the confluence at map ref. 104921.

7 SPECTRAL CREEK TO AYLMER PASS — Map 2

Backpack
Distance 7 km
Height gain 440 m
Maximum elevation 2300 m
Topo map 82 O/6 Lake Minnewanka

Access: Ghost River trail (#6)

The route is marked incorrectly on both the topo map and the Ghost River Wilderness pamphlet. The cutline - for this is what you follow as far as the forks - intersects all the windings of the creek; sometimes it IS the creek. A wet spruce forest, deadfall and willow brush put paid to any idea of circumnavigation. Where fallen trees have blocked a long stretch along the north bank, detour right on a blazed trail which is probably a remnant of the original pack trail. NOTE: Be wary of grizzlies between the Ghost River and the forks; don't plan on setting up camp anywhere along this section.

The cutline fords the river to the south bank one last time, then ends in a mishmash of undergrowth at the river's edge. In between these two points, and well marked by a cairn and flagging, the trail to Aylmer Pass takes off between two blazed trees. It rises effortlessly to timberline, then cuts across to the mouth of the pass. Benches on either side of the waterfalls provide one or two flat tent sites sheltered from the wind's blast. Aylmer pass is long and narrow, a rolling carpet of tough bearberry, juniper and heather mats on which the passage of many feet has made little impression. Somewhere between timberline and the top of the pass, which is identified by the Banff National Park boundary sign, you are likely to be mobbed by the area's famous bighorn sheep who tend to regard all humans as potential saltlicks. Have the camera ready.

From Aylmer Pass looking down the south fork of Spectral Creek towards Brock Ridge (left) and Apparition Mtn. (right). — Alf Skrastins.

SIDE TRIPS If you have a day or even two to spare, a side trip to the headwaters of Spectral Creek is well worth the effort. Slightly upstream of the aforementioned waterfalls, a good game trail leads around into the spongy south fork. In early summer, the little lake in the cirque is edged with alpine buttercups, greening and blooming as the snowbanks melt.

The pass to the north at map ref. 059884 is an easy route over to the west fork. From its highest point you can wander along Brock Ridge to a cairn and viewpoint about 100 m below the summit. At the head of the west fork a gap in the encircling mountains allows access into and out of the Stony Creek drainage for backpackers and grizzlies. Blue-tinted Spectral Lakes, source of the north fork and a worthy destination rivaling Aylmer Pass, are most easily reached by contouring at treeline round the intervening ridge from west fork meadows.

Although the Ghost River Wilderness pamphlet map marks a trail connecting the west fork meadows to the cutline at the forks, I have been unable to find it. In its stead you can probably make use of a sheep trail which traverses the north and east slopes of Brock Ridge at treeline, then descends to the south fork from where it is a relatively easy pull up to the Aylmer Pass trail.

8 DEVILS GAP AND GHOST LAKES — Map 3

Day hike, equestrian, bike
7.8 km from camping spot
Height loss 105 m
Maximum elevation 1585 m
Topo map 82 O/6 Lake Minnewanka

Access: Forestry Trunk Road 940. At Bar Cee Ranch, 25.4 km north of Highway 1A, turn west and drive for another 15.6 km along the Ghost River Road. Ignore all lesser roads to the right. Park at the camping spot above the steep hill leading down to the Ghost River.

This spectacular break in the Front Ranges between the Ghost River and Lake Minnewanka has been used as a gateway to the mountains for centuries. Early explorers - the first recorded visit was by Sir George Simpson passed this way following a well-established Indian Trail between Morley and the Bow River in the vicinity of the present-day Canmore. Conversely, the gap also brought marauding Kootenai Indians from British Columbia into the Prairies to hunt Buffalo. Fierce battles with the Blackfoot, who eventually drove the Kootenai back into the mountains, and frequent skirmishes between the warring factions of the Plains Indians are the basis of an Indian legend which tells of a ghost seen going up and down the river, picking up the skulls of the dead who had been killed by the Cree. It is well documented that there are many Indian graves along the riverbank. According to Sir James Hector, the woods atop Deadman Hill in the angle between the Ghost and the Bow rivers are one vast burial ground.

To help you get in the appropriate mood for this "ghostly" hike, pick a dull brooding day in late fall when the wind rattles the brown leaves on the aspens and the mountains seem withdrawn from life, waiting patiently shoulder to shoulder for the first snow.

Walk down the hill to the Ghost River valley. Go left then straight at two 4-way junctions. You should now be heading across the white polished stones of the old riverbed towards the Gap, accompanied on your right by a line of upraised rubble hiding the canal diverting water from the upper Ghost to the Lake Minnewanka drainage. Keep left at a junction on the far side. Close to the Banff National Park boundary the road slumps and should be circumvented by a trail to the right which starts behind the blank signboard. En route, I suggest that you take a 15 minute diversion across the canal to Ghost Lodge, formerly Royal Mounted Police Post No. 7. Above it rises Phantom Crag, a popular cliff with rock climbers who, in keeping with the spirit of the valley, have given the climbs names like Banshee, The Wraith and Rattling Corner.

The trail rejoins the road at the boundary cairn. Keep left, following not so much the road but a smoother trail winding about it. Be alert for an unsuspected junction with a wide stony track to left which is the trail proper. For the next kilometre, however, you have a choice of routes and I'd strongly advise, for the outward journey anyway, following the original track down to First Ghost Lake. Winds, blasting through the gap, have scattered sand all through the forest hereabouts. It emanates from a small area of dunes and wadis bordering the lake, which is not a lake at all but a dried up bed of caked mud. Head for the talus slopes at the S.W. corner of the lake where a path leads up to the main trail. The crag above the junction bears an uncanny resemblance to El Capitan in Yosemite National Park, but is only half the height.

Unlike what is shown on the topo map, the trail climbs over the 1500 m contour and crosses the mouth of a spectacular canyon en route to the south shore of second Ghost Lake. Cliffs on either side of the gap reach their greatest height in this area and are particularly impressive on squally days when mists lift and part momentarily to reveal tantalizing outlines of ridges nearly 1000 m overhead.

The Devils Gap trail comes to an end at an unmarked junction midway between the second and third Ghost Lakes. To the right, the north shore trail along Lake Minnewanka fords the channel; straight ahead, the historic Carrot Creek trail edges along the south bank of third Ghost Lake.

If you want more exercise it's worth following the latter trail for a further 2 km to Lake Minnewanka. Before the two dams were built in 1912 and 1941 the surface of the lake was lower by 28 m and, in fact, didn't exist at all in this place. It had as many names as water levels: Devil's Lake, Cannibal Lake and Peechee Lake after Sir George Simpson's guide. Finally in 1888 it was officially designated Lake Minnewanka, "Lake of the Water Spirit", and the name Peechee transferred to the mountain facing you across the water.

Ghost Lodge

Alpine meadows above Ghost Pass. Astral Lake is just out of sight in the valley bottom to right.

9 THE SOUTH GHOST — Map 3

Backpack, equestrian
Distance 23 km
Height gain 807 m
Maximum elevation 2210 m
Topo map 82 O/3 Canmore

Access: Forest Trunk Road 940. At Bar Cee Ranch 25.4 km north of Highway 1A, turn west and drive for about 7.5 km along the Ghost River Road to an intersecting cutline. Turn left and park on the bank top.

The most important thing to know about the South Ghost River is that there IS no river. The water emerges from the ground in only three spots: a stretch of about 500 m in the meadows below Astral lake which re-appears 2.5 km lower down in the vicinity of the hunters camp,and a long 2 km stretch west of the confluence with the Ghost River. In between the confluence and the hunter's camp there is 17 km of virtual desert, so plan your camping trip accordingly.

From the top of the bank, hike down either the steep cutline or the trail which starts farther left and merges with the cutline just before a T-junction. Turn right and follow the old road down to the Ghost River which must be waded to the continuation of the road on the other bank. Head downstream then cut across to the South Ghost River near the confluence. Although the going is fast and easy along gravel flats imprinted here and there with remnants of road, nearly half the day will have slipped by before you draw level with the mountains. As you pass by Orient Peak to your right, look for the free-standing arch on the ridge of rotten teeth descending towards the creek. At the bottom of this ridge, pick up much longer sections of road on the north bank. The road is well established by the time you enter the inner valley between the portals of End Mountain and a look alike Devils Head on the right which rises sheer from the creekbed. 500 m farther on the road crosses to the south bank.

When the road recrosses to the north bank and ends, the valley changes character. Gone are the gravel flats. In its place is a narrow V-shaped valley filled with spruce and traversed by a pack trail which crosses back and forth across the creek bed 4 times before arriving at the hunters camp. Directly opposite, a sheep trail climbs a side valley towards Exshaw Pass. Cross the stream twice in quick succession. By the time you reach the mouth of a large tributary to the north - a distance of only 1 km from the hunters camp - the creek is already dry. The beautiful campsite by the creek junction is serviced by water 5 minutes walk away up the tributary.

So far, the route has been relatively flat and easy, but now the hard work begins. The trail first gains height up the west bank of the tributary then settles into a rising traverse 150 m above the gorge of the South Ghost. Leveling off at treeline, it follows the contours of the mountain around a buttress, and in and out of a shallow cirque and finally dissipates at the Banff Park boundary behind a clump of spruce trees. Traverse intervening hillside into a narrow defile which is South Ghost Pass. The desired view can be obtained by climbing the hillside south of the pass onto large tracts of alpine meadows.

Astral Lake, source of the South Ghost River, lies so well- hidden in a fold of the hills that sunlight brightens the surface for only a few hours each day. To get to the camping spot below the lake, descend to creek level from the end of the trail and follow it up to flat meadows near a small waterfall - source of the distant water music heard from the trail near the pass.

TO CARROT CREEK From the pass it is possible to descend the east fork of Carrot Creek (faint trail) to the main Carrot Creek trail. From here you have the option of either descending to the Trans-Canada Highway or of climbing over the timbered pass to Lake Minnewanka and returning via Ghost Lakes and Devils Gap to the Ghost River Road. See also route #8 and the Carrot Creek trail description in The Canadian Rockies Trail Guide.

TO COUGAR CREEK There are two ways of achieving this, but first of all you have to get to map ref. 195710 on the boundary ridge either by way of the pass or, if camping below Astral lake, via grassy slopes above the west shoreline.

ROUTE 1, an easy bad weather route, is suitable for less experienced backpackers who feel uncomfortable humping a heavy backpack along narrow ridges, which is what route 2 is all about. Descend a little way towards the south fork of Carrot Creek, then veer left onto a good sheep trail which runs along a shallow bench below a talus slope. When the bench gives out, descend at the edge of scree into the head of the valley. You've lost a lot of height (280 m) and must regain it all plus another 40 m during the climb up the grassy ramp to the Carrot/Cougar col (2454 m). NOTE: this is not the lowest gap shown on the topo map, but a slightly higher one to the east at map ref, 186691.

ROUTE 2 follows a sheep trail along the boundary ridge to the Carrot/Cougar col. From the map reference point, turn south and ascend a grassy summit with cairn. As you walk down the other side you can peruse the next section of route to the second summit. The steep bit through cliff bands looks a bit intimidating; if you didn't know that it goes you might well turn back at this point and follow route 1. Be assured that it's one of those places which looks more difficult than it really is. Close up you discover that the sheep have trodden out big indentations in the brown rubble to form a kind of winding staircase near the right-hand edge where the going is firmer. Don't bother to climb to the summit. From the flat shoulder above the step, traverse the west slope to the col between second and third summits. The vertiginous view into Cougar Creek causes instant recoil to the near side of the ridge which suddenly seems much less steep than previously. Still the sheep trail continues, climbing up red screes towards the third and highest summit (2637 m) but at the last minute traversing around the right side to gain a col beyond. This is where you and the trail part company. Turn N.W. and descend the broad hogsback to the Carrot/Cougar Creek col, a not unwelcome return to the feel of soft grass underfoot and the resinous scents of juniper and pine wafting up from the valley below. See route #10 Cougar Creek: North-west fork to Carrot/Cougar col.

10 COUGAR CREEK — Maps 3 & 4

Day hike, backpack
10.5 km to Carrot/Cougar col
Maximum elevation 2450 m
Topo map 82 O/3 Canmore

Mountain avens cover the stony creekbed of Cougar Creek.

Access: Elk Run Industrial Park Access Road via Highway 1A. Park opposite the west bank at Cougar Creek.

Winding deep into the heart of the Fairholme Range, Cougar Creek — shown as Gorge Creek on early maps — offers the hiker everything from a half hour's stroll to a weekend backpack up the N.W. fork. NOTE: Water in the main fork is non-existent past the 4 km mark.

Walk up the gravel road to the rock dam at the entrance to the gorge. Clamber over, aiming for the east bank of the creek where a faint trail, crossing and recrossing the stream, can be followed to its terminus just past the first fork to the east. Although there is no trail beyond this point the going is just as easy along the flat stony creekbed cushioned with yellow mountain avens, and the rock scenery is even more impressive, particularly as you near the head of the main valley — a very wild spot indeed. Pass the wide mouth of the N.W. fork. In another 2 km the valley makes a right-angled turn to the N.W. and ends under steep scree slopes criss-crossed with sheep tracks which offer a route of sorts over to the South Ghost.

NORTH-WEST FORK TO CARROT/COUGAR COL The flat valley floor soon steepens into a creekbed strewn with boulders apparently rolled down from the rockslide which blocks the valley at mid- point. The welcome appearance of water signals the beginning of a laborious section which only seems long. Fight your way through willow bushes arching over the stream to the bottom of the first waterfall. Turn it on the left-hand side. At the top, and before a second fall, it is perhaps easier to switch to the right-hand bank; either way, the routes involves some steep sidehill bashing. Gradually you emerge out of the depths into a smooth green bowl curving up to the boundary ridge with Banff National Park. It can be crossed almost anywhere into Carrot Creek. The usual route, though, is the Carrot/Cougar col (map ref. 186691) reached by a small stream identified at its confluence in the basin by outcroppings of white rock. See route #9 for descriptions of routes into Carrot Creek and the South Ghost.

11 GRASSI LAKES — Map 4

Half-day hike
2 km one way
Height gain 244 m
Maximum elevation 1670 m
Topo map 82 O/3 Canmore

Access: Smith-Dorrien—Spray Trail. 5.2 km west of the bridge over the Bow River at Canmore, turn left onto a road signposted "Spray Residences". Park on the bank of Rundle Reservoir almost opposite the first road to the right which is the private access road to the pentstocks.

This picturesque valley, containing 2 exquisite lakes and Indian pictographs of some importance, has been cruelly abused. The gorge at the upper end — the historic Whiteman Gap through which the Red River settlers travelled en route to British Coloumbia — has been dammed; the pentstocks, pipeline and powerlines are background to every view and as an additional insult cars, beer bottles and other unwanted junk have been thrown over the cliff from the road above. Fortunately, since becoming part of the Kananaskis Country, the junk is carted away at regular intervals.

Thirty years before construction of the Spray Plant in 1951, Lawrence Grassi built a trail connecting the mineral springs at Canmore with the lakes which were called Twin Lakes at that time. Nowadays, only the upper half of the trail remains in its entirety. The stamp of Grassi — best known for his meticulous trail building at Lake O'Hara — is still evident in the carefully modulated grade, the stone staircases, the wooden ladder, handrails and resting benches at viewpoints.

A few metres up the pentstock access road, an old sign tacked to a tree on the left-hand side indicates the start of Grassi's trail. It wanders through forest, then climbs more steeply (this is where the staircase and ladder come in useful) to open slopes giving fine views of the 100 m waterfall below the lakes. Cross the access road to the lakes which lie one above the other and are renowned for their clarity and bright aquamarine color. The cliffs above are remnants of a coral reef, pockmarked and riddled with small caves identified as prehistoric rock shelters.

Climb a short scree slope into the upper gorge. Facing you at head height on the first large boulder you come to are 4 pictographs of human figures and caribou believed painted by ancestors of the Kootenay Indians over a thousand years ago. A waterfall, popular with ice climbers, splashes down the wall on the left. Pick your way through a maze of boulders to a more recent trail which climbs to the dam. Winds funneling through Whiteman Gap continually ruffle the dark green waters of the reservoir.

12 CANMORE NORDIC CENTRE — Map 4

50 km plus of intermediate and difficult trails
Topo map 82 O/3 Canmore

Access: **Smith-Dorrien—Spray Trail (Hwy.) 4.1 km west of the bridge over the Bow River at Canmore. Recreational trail system also accessible from the terminus of Three Sisters Drive north in Canmore.**

At the time of publication, the Canmore Nordic Centre — venue of the 1988 Winter Olympics — is still being built in preparation for the official 1986/87 opening. The sketch map shows the approximate location of 32 km of cross-country trails, 17.5 km of biathalon trails, and several kilometres of recreational trails whose alignment is likely to change slightly as construction progresses. Conceived primarily for the racer, the 3 to 5 metre-wide trails will wind through dense forest about Walker #3 coal mine and, in order to accommodate the required lengths in what is really a very small area, will require cross- over points with bridges. They will be open to tourers who may find the less convoluted Georgetown and Canmore to Banff recreational trails more to their liking. Because snow conditions are generally marginal around the stadium areas, natural snow will be augmented by snow-making equipment.

Facilities will include a day lodge with cafetaria, 2 stadiums, a biathalon shooting range, and 2.5 km of lighted trail for night skiing. Summer activities will include hiking, the most obvious destination being Georgetown where hikers can potter about the foundations of the company mining town which flourished between the years of 1912 and 1915.

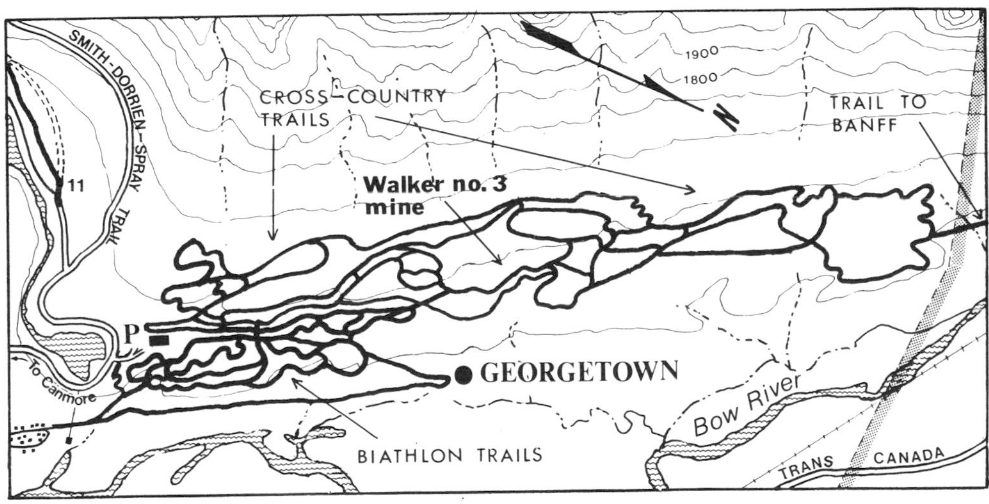

13 THREE SISTERS CREEK — Map 4

Day hike
Distance 5 km
Height gain 310 km
Maximum elevation 1615 m
Topo map 82 O/3 Canmore

Chinaman's Peak from the upper valley.

Access: Trans-Canada Highway at Bow River Campground.

Man's influence on the scenery of Three Sisters Creek goes back 80 years to the logging industry. Relics of that era and more recent changes brought about by Canmore Coal Mines can be seen at various locations along the trail.

Walk up the campground road to the Trans-Canada Highway. Almost opposite, on the west side of the highway, you'll see an old entrance into Canmore Mines which has been blocked off by a pile of slag. Climb onto this road and follow it across a smaller road, a powerline and another road — all in quick succession — to the main Canmore Mines road which is wide, smooth and unmistakable. Turn right. The road recrosses the powerline at a railway line, then after an long uneventful stretch, crosses the powerline a third time to a wide stony river bed which used to be Three Sisters Creek. Don't follow the trail along the bank. Instead, walk a bit further along the road before turning left onto Three Sisters Creek exploration road which crosses a double powerline right-of-way (a different powerline to the one crossed previously) and the diversionary stream.

A twenty minute walk through sombre spruce forest brings you to a rock and concrete dam, now in disrepair, and a scattering of log flumes. The road switches to the south bank to avoid unstable mud slopes and arrives at a small waterfall marking the boundary of a major fault system. Here the road has collapsed into the creek and you must scramble up wet slabs covered with coal detritus if you wish to hike the final kilometre to the road's end at two rotting log cabins. Faint trails aid further exploration of the valley and its tributaries.

If you want to vary the return route, descend the exploration road to the main Canmore Mines road, then simply follow the creekbed over 2 railway lines and a small road to the Bow River. A trail along the riverbank passes underneath the bridge carrying the Trans-Canada Highway and returns you to your starting point at Bow River Campground.

14 STEWART CREEK — Map 4

Day hike
Distance 6 km
Height gain 310 m
Maximum elevation 1615 m
Topo map 82 O/3 Canmore

Access: **Trans-Canada Highway at Bow River Campground.**

This foray into Canmore Mine's land takes you into a valley between The Three Sisters and Wind Ridge where strong hikers have the option of ascending to Wind Ridge.

Walk up the campground road to the Trans-Canada Highway. Almost opposite, on the west side of the highway, you'll see an old entrance into Canmore Mines which has been blocked off by a pile of slag. Climb onto this road and follow it across a smaller road, a powerline and another road — all in quick succession — to the main Canmore Mines road which is wide, smooth and unmistakable.

Turn left. Shortly after crossing another powerline right-of- way turn second right into a road signed "Landfill". Arriving at the gate of the landfill site, formerly a strip mine and before that Dry Lake (a depository for the waters of Stewart Creek),turn right and climb onto the narrow-gauge railway which runs almost from one end of the mine lands to the other. Grassed over, with only a few sleepers remaining (in this section anyway), the railbed would make an excellent trail to points of interest such as the old stone Lamp House at Echo Mines which is already designated a historic building.

Walk left along the railbed, disregarding the first creek and intersecting road you come to. This is Fall Creek, not to be mistaken for Stewart Creek which is the second stream along. A little way east of Stewart Creek turn right at a 4-way junction onto the Stewart Creek exploration road. At the apex of the alluvial fan spilling out of the defile, the road crosses the creek — the sweet cloying smell comes from silver willows in the creekbed — then turns left and heads up the west bank of the valley to a concrete dam and water flume. The road crosses back and forth across the stream a few times, finally settling on the east bank for a long stretch. Just below the forks the road crosses to the west bank for the last time and chokes up with deadfall.

When the road was on the east bank you may have noticed a trail heading up a shallow scoop into the trees. This is the start of a very steep sheep trail onto Wind Ridge; you can see it quite plainly climbing the grass ridge below the summit. If you elect to ascend to the ridge by this route you have the option of descending by the normal route (#15) to the 4-way road junction, but instead of turning right as you would normally do, go straight downhill keeping right at every junction until you reach the Canmore Mines road. Turn left and rejoin your outgoing route near the landfill site.

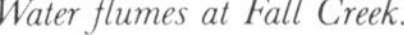

Water flumes at Fall Creek.

The castellated appearance of Wind Ridge is well seen in this view taken S. W. of the summit. Pigeon Mtn. in background.

15 WIND RIDGE — Map 4

Day hike
Distance 7.6 km
Height gain 810 m
Maximum elevation 2180 m
Topo map 82 O/3 Canmore

Access: Trans-Canada Highway. From Dead Man Flat interchange, drive to Pigeon Mountain parking lot. The trail is the exploration road leaving the far top corner of the parking lot.

From Dead Man Flat, the dark timbered mass of Wind Ridge looks an uninteresting proposition. On the other side of the mountain, though, hidden from view, grassy slopes provide a beautiful route to the summit. Swept by warm chinook winds, these sun-facing slopes are often in condition by mid April when surrounding mountains are still snowbound. An exploration road to timberline takes all the hassle out of the ascent. The same road can be followed into West Wind Creek.

Follow the road across the powerline right-of-way. Just after a large opening, the route temporarily enters private land whose owners request that hikers keep to the roads, refrain from littering, lighting fires and camping on their property. Cross Pigeon Creek to a T-junction with the Collembola exploration road. Turn right and cross West Wind Creek on a plank to the main West Wind Creek exploration road which has come in from Dead Man Flat. Turn left. After a gate keep straight at the junction with the Canmore Mines road to right, and straight thereafter, ignoring all minor roads to right and all roads to the left crossing the creek. Eventually the road bends to the north and should be followed past all intersections, a grove of douglas fir trees and a coal seam to a 4-way junction at the top of the hill. Traverse left along a road which tapers out on the east end of the ridge. This is the logical spot to rest awhile and look across at Windtower, and Wind Mountain which is often mistaken for Mount Lougheed. Named by James Hector during the Palliser expedition of 1858, it was apparently climbed by Bourgeau in search of botanical samples, although it is unclear if he reached the summit.

Cliff bands across the south face give the ridge a castellated appearance from down below. A good sheep trail leads to the bottom of the lowest band which looks tricky but is easily negotiated by means of a diagonal ledge liberally supplied with footholds and jughandles. The trail continues on to a shale shoulder — brief respite — then climbs more steeply to the the summit area where a geodetic survey marker distinguishes the highest point.

If you wish to make the circuit with West Wind Creek, carry on along the ridge which is easy and enjoyable. The only potential difficulty, the cliff bands below the summit, can be bypassed on the right side. Arriving at a col overrun by north slope spruce trees, descend steep grass on the south side into West Wind Creek. The terrain funnels you into a deep creekbed which you must escape from by following any of numerous sheep trails traversing left onto gentler hillsides. From this direction the valley trail is difficult to pick up. I suggest you head slightly left and enter forest to the left of a small rise flagged with a few wind-tattered trees. Search for a well-blazed tree.

WEST WIND CREEK Shortly after the exploration road bends to the north and begins climbing, blazed trees on the left-hand side indicate the start of a kilometer-long trail to the big meadow. Pick up another narrower trail at the far right-hand corner of the meadow (blaze) and follow it through two smaller openings and mixed forest into the head of the valley. All along the trail aspen trees exhibit many scars from teeth and claw marks. Veer right and emerge onto open slopes below Wind Ridge, a grand viewpoint for Windtower and West Wind Pass alias "Passage aux Bicyclettes" after preliminary plans for Kananaskis Country showed a bicycle path traversing the pass. The exposed trail winding up between cliff bands is best left to the sheep.

Wind Ridge from West Wind Creek.

16 SKOGAN PASS — Maps 4 & 5

Day hike, intermediate ski
Equestrian, bike
Distance 19 km to Ribbon Creek
Height gain 655 m
Height loss 625 m
Maximum elevation 2073 m
Topo map 82 O/3 Canmore
82 J/14 Spray Lake Reservoir

Access: 1. Trans-Canada Highway. From Dead Man Flat interchange drive to Pigeon Mountain parking lot. The trail is the exploration road leaving the far top corner of the parking lot.
Access: 2. Kananaskis Trail (Hwy. 40) at Ribbon Creek parking lot or Nakiska ski area parking lot.

The pass has long been used as a route between the Kananaskis valley and the Bow Corridor. A trail crossing what was then known as Pigeon Pass because of its proximity to Pigeon Mountain is shown on George Dawson's map of 1886 as an old Indian trail. Presumably, it was this same trail which was widened by the Forest Service in 1936 in order to carry the telephone line linking Dead Man Flat ranger cabin to the boundary cabin at the mouth of Ribbon Creek. Since then, most signs of the trail have been obliterated by the road into the Marmot Basin project area and by the powerline right-of-way and the road serving it which is now the new trail. In 1972, when Don Gardner was reconnoitering for the Ribbon Creek ski trails, the name Skogan Pass came into being. Translated from the Norwegian it means a magic forest with elves and trolls.

Turn left up the powerline right-of-way, utilizing wherever possible the road's detours into the forest. About halfway to the pass, above a dip, the road once more turns aside into the forest (cairn) and makes long zigzags gaining height. Pass Pigeon Mountain trail on the left. A kink in the road at a side creek signals the start of a traverse across pristine meadows which should be savoured in full because never again does the route escape the clutches of the logging and power industries. Shortly after passing two geologically interesting slumps on the uphill slope, the road winds to the right and arrives at Skogan Pass, a vague spot in the trees which is determined solely by the downhill inclination of the road in front of you. Whilst you're there take a 5-minute detour onto the summit of the powerline right-of-way; the view through the powerlines is quite good.

The road descends and crosses the powerline, then swings right around the head of Lorette Creek, entering the northern boundary of the Marmot Basin Project at a gate. Climb uphill to a junction with the powerline right-of-way and the Marmot Cabin Meteorological Station road on the right. When coming from the opposite direction people often get confused at this point, thinking they are at the pass (it's the same height) or they wander off up the wrong road.

Descend the road which winds about the powerline right-of-way. At the bottom of the hill, the road breaks away through a narrow avenue of mature spruce into a large cutblock where you have your first real view of the mountains about Ribbon Creek. Wooden tripods on the right-hand side of the road used to carry the telephone line between ranger stations. Pass High Level ski trail on the left and, 0.9 km lower down, Sunburst ski trail at the powerline right-of-way. This is a parting of the ways for equestrians who must follow the powerline trail all the way down to the Kananaskis Valley. It joins the main Ribbon Creek – Barrier Lake powerline access road (#44) just north of Marmot Creek.

Those on foot or on ski should continue winding down the road to Marmot Creek bridge. Keep left at the junction with Marmot Creek road immediately following and arrive at Marmot Basin road, now an access route to the on-hill restaurant and upper slopes of Nakiska ski resort. Here you have the option of either following the road downhill to the base lodge, or of turning left after a few metres onto a new trail which winds pleasantly around the perimeter of the ski area; offshoots to right lead back to the lodge and parking lot. Keep right at a major junction with Troll Falls trail, cross the ski area access road and descend to Ribbon Creek, gained half-way between the hostel (left) and Ribbon Creek parking lot (right).

17 PIGEON MOUNTAIN — Map 4

Day hike
Distance 8 km
Height gain 990 m
Maximum elevation 2394 m
Topo map 82 O/3 Canmore

Access: Via Skogan Pass trail (#16.)

Pic des Pigeon, named for the obvious reason by the Palliser Expedition of 1858, stands at the bend of the Bow River above Dead Man Flat. It is an easy and popular ascent along an unofficial, unsigned trail to a superb viewpoint.

Follow the Skogan Pass trail for 5 km. Just before a kink in the road where it crosses a side stream, turn left up a well-trodden trail marked by a cairn. It climbs to the top of a triangular grass spur — a prominent Pigeon Mountain landmark, then settles into a rising traverse below the orange crags and screes of the S.E. summit, aiming for the low point between this top and the higher summit to the N.W. Sheep and elk are often spotted in the vicinity. From the col it's an easy walk up grass laced with scree to the summit. It is best to return the same way; although there is reputed to be a trail connecting the summit to the old Pigeon Mountain ski area, I have been unable to find it.

From the traverse, looking back towards Skogan Pass and Mt. Collembola.

Negotiating the Red Pinnacles.

18 MOUNT ALLAN CENTENNIAL TRAIL FROM THE TRANS-CANADA HIGHWAY — Map 4

Long day hike
11 km to summit
19 km to Ribbon Creek
Height gain 1400 m
Maximum elevation 2819 m
Topo map 82 O/3 Canmore
82 J/14 Spray Lakes Reservoir

Access: Trans-Canada Highway. From Dead Man Flat interchange drive to the Pigeon Mountain parking lot. The trail is the exploration road leaving the far top corner of the parking lot.

Mount Allan is named after John Allan, founder of the Geology Department of the University of Alberta and consultant to Calgary Power during construction of the dams at Kananaskis Lakes. Recently the name has acquired a certain notoriety arising from the controversial choice of the mountain as a venue for alpine skiing events during the 1988 Winter Olympics. Its other claim to fame,and one which brooks no argument, is the Centennial Trail, a marvellous high-level route traversing the mountain from north to south which has the distinction of being the highest hiking trail in the Canadian Rockies.

The north ridge route described below calls for an early start and a reasonable level of fitness if you wish to make it to the summit and back again before dark. Apart from the initial section, which may at some future date be rerouted, the trail is marked throughout by orange markers on trees and orange paint splodges on rocks. The traverse of Mount Allan from the Trans- Canada highway to Ribbon Creek or vice versa is a very long day indeed and requires vehicles at both ends. For information on the southern portion of the route turn to trail #71.

Follow the road across the powerline right-of-way. Just after a large clearing, the road temporarily enters private land whose owners request that hikers keep to the roads, refrain from littering, lighting fires and camping on their property. Cross Pigeon Creek (last water) to a T-junction with the Collembola exploration road. As can be seen by the sudden appearance of orange trail markers, you are back on the original route from Dead Man Flat which is rarely used nowadays. Turn left up the road, following the markers. The first right-hand bend signals the end of private land and the start of a tedious uphill climb to the road's end at treeline. A trail carries on to the lip of the cirque between Mounts Allan and Collembola (cairns and poles), then makes short steep zigzags up a grassy scoop onto the north ridge of Mount Allan. Walk up to the foot of the black rockband. To get around this impasse, the trail traverses exposed grass ledges on the east side which can be tricky, even dangerous, when snow-covered early and late in the season. Scramble up to a large cairn on the ridge. The long easy section following is terminated by a row of red pinnacles straddling the ridgeline and dipping down the western flank. Slip through a gap on the west side and regain the ridge by any of numerous trails climbing the rocky slope. Clumps of nodding saxifrages, instantly distinguishable from the more common variety by crimson bulbils on the stem, grow in tiny pockets of soil among the boulders. Arriving at a false summit, you discover that the real summit is still half a kilometre distant across a slight dip — a final upheaval of orange screes served by a trail which, in the way of all sheep trails, traverses right around the upper slopes to the S.E. ridge byond. Branch off at the appropriate place and climb to the summit.

The view from the cairn is a little disappointing; the panorama you might expect from a 2800 m peak is severely limited by the proximity of Mounts Lougheed and Collembola. Nevertheless, another window has opened up to the south disclosing the Ship Mountains about Ribbon and Galatea Creeks, and best of all, from the point of view of the hot thirsty hiker, the emerald green tarn under Mount Sparrowhawk which sparkles tantalizingly under the midday sun.

JUBILEE LAKES As a destination, the seasonal ponds in the cirque between Mount Collembola and the north ridge of Mount Allan are hardly worth the effort of the long walk in. The cirque has more important usages. From the farthest pond, you'll notice that the north ridge of Mount Allan is easily accessible via a steep grass slope; should the need arise it offers an easy escape route off the ridge in sudden storm. Similarly, a reasonable slope leads to the col between the 2 summits of Mount Collembola. Besides acting as an escape route, it can be used as an alternative ascent route to the highest summit, one which misses out the exposed rock step.

The final rise to the summit. Route 19 follows left-hand skyline.

19 MOUNT COLLEMBOLA TRAVERSE — Map 4

Long day hike
12 km from Pigeon Mountain parking lot to Mount Allan
Height gain 1646 m to Mount Allan
Height loss 253 m
Maximum elevation 2819 m
Topo map 82 J/14 Spray Lakes Reservoir

Climbing the east ridge of Mt. Allan. The traverse of the twin peaks of Mt. Collembola (behind) looks deceptively easy from this direction.

Access: Trans-Canada Highway. Via Mount Allan Centennial Trail (#18)

The traverse of the two summits of Mount Collembola is a much more serious undertaking than the traverse of Mount Allan; there are route finding difficulties and several unavoidable sections of exposed scrambling. The name Collembola, by the way, refers to Springtails, in particular the sixteen-eyed snowflea which is found in abundance on the surface of melting snow below treeline. The most primative of insects, the springtails are also very ancient, with fossil records going back more than 400 million years to the Devonian period.

The route leaves Mount Allan Centennial trail at the end of the Collembola exploration road. Climb the ridge in front of you, being careful not to divert onto game trails bearing right and eventually downward towards Jubilee Lakes. The ridge levels off below a slanting rock band shielding the highest summit (2767 m). Scramble up the exposed left edge.

From the summit cairn, walk down easy grass and shale to the gap between the two summits where a similar rock band forces a traverse along grassy ledges on the east side. When the step leans back a little, look for a marker stick half-way up the rocks and clamber up to it. A further 8 m of slabs with good holds leads to easy ground around the lower summit (2728 m). If you want, you can avoid this pitch by traversing all the way round the east face to the S.W. ridge beyond the summit. All difficulties at an end, descend broad slopes of black lichen-covered rocks, then grass, to the Collembola/Allan col. From here it's an easy but tedious ascent up bright orange rocks and shales of the east face to the summit of Mount Allan. The route tops out at the cairn.

20 EAST WIND POND — Map 4

Day hike
Distance 9.5 km
Height gain 825 m
Maximum elevation 2195
Topo Map 82 O/3 Canmore
82 J/14 Spray Lakes Reservoir

Access: Trans-Canada Highway from Mount Allan Centennial Trail (#18).

Unmarked on the topo map and hidden by a fold of the hills from the eye of the ridge walker on Mount Allan, East Wind Pond remained undetected by the vast majority of hikers until 1972 when Harry Connolly's much publisized attempts to reach the lake were splashed across the pages of the Calgary Herald together with a color photograph taken on the successful trip. Impossibly steep slopes and impenetrable bush needn't be your experience; there is, in fact, a quite reasonable route to the lake which requires the minimum of bushwacking.

Follow the Mount Allan Centennial Trail up the Collembola exploration road. Quite high up the ridge turn right (second right after gaining the road) onto an exploration road which takes you gently downwards into Wind Creek. Stay on the road, ignoring overgrown offshoots to right and left. Not long after you cross the creek to the west bank, the road for all practical purposes ends at a T-junction.

A good trail carries on up the creek, but even this peters out after a while and you're left to make your own way through untracked forest with deadfall to meadows under the shadow of Mount Lougheed. Leave the creek at the point where it turns S.E. towards its source on the colorful slopes of Mount Allan and head off in the opposite direction towards the col between the 3107 m summit of Mount Lougheed and a grassy knoll to its N.W.; an easy climb once you tear yourself loose from the clutches of head-high willow bushes on the lower slopes.

The lake, actually a composite of several deep springs joined one to another like the florets in the centre of a daisy, lies in the secluded valley beyond the col. It's an easy descent down meadows patched with spruce and larch to the lakeshore. If you dip your hand into the water you will find the upper layers quite tepid and teeming with tiny red freshwater shrimps.

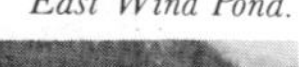
East Wind Pond.

21 GROTTO CANYON — Map 4

Half-day hike
Distance 2.5 km
Height gain 180 m
Topo map 82 O/3 Canmore

Access: Highway 1A at Grotto Mountain day use area.

Grotto Canyon is well known for its imposing rock scenery and Indian pictographs. The route is signed.

The trail follows the powerline right-of-way, then, at the arrow, turns right and runs alongside the stony creekbed into the canyon. Watch for a white arrow carved in the wall to the right; it supposedly points at the wall opposite where the eagle-eyed will discern faint red ochre figures of Indian warriors dancing across the smooth slab about 2 m up from the ground.

At the T-junction you will notice that any water in Grotto Creek comes from a waterfall in the right-hand cleft. A huge chockstone precludes all but the most determined explorer from going any further in that direction. Grotto Creek to the left is completely dry and very narrow, with walls reaching their greatest height in this section. In winter, water dripping down the right-hand wall is transformed into two ice pillars known to waterfall ice climbers as His and Hers. Beyond this point, the canyon opens out into meadows and forest. If you want to make a day of it, follow a fainter trail past the hoodoos into the heart of the valley.

Grotto Canyon near the petroglyphs.

Upper Exshaw Creek looking towards Exshaw Pass, the farthest right of the 2 gaps — Alf Skrastins.

22 EXSHAW CREEK — Maps 3 & 5

Long day hike
12.5 km to pass
Height gain 840 m
Maximum elevation 2210 m
Topo map 82 O/3 Canmore

Access: Highway 1A at Exshaw. Turn north onto road immediately east of the bridge over Exshaw Creek. Keep left and park at road's end. Cross the footbridge over the river.

Exshaw creek is the long valley extending north from the village of Exshaw. It can be followed as far as time permits or used as a backpackers' route into the South Ghost. The trail, unofficial and unsigned, fades away long before the pass is reached.

NOTE: The first kilometre along the road is showered with rocks when blasting is in progress, so either hike the trail on a Sunday or phone the cement plant at 673-3815 for their blasting schedule. Although it is possible to follow the creek bank to the dam it involves some dangerous manoeuvring to get onto the east end of the dam wall and is not recommended.

Walk along the access road signed "Blasting Keep Out". Above the dam transfer onto a trail which crosses the creek many times on good logs during the first few kilometres. Shortly after passing through a camping area on the west bank you arrive at the mouth of large tributary, a climbers' access route to shapely Mount Fable which has been in view for the last few kilometres. Its grassy alluvial fan is an obvious lunch spot or turning back point if you just want a short day.

The trail, which has been following the west bank for some time, crosses under the cliffs of Fable's east buttress to the east bank and gradually peters out. Carry on up the creekbed between slopes almost denuded of trees. After such a long approach the final pull to the pass is a backbreaker, but I think you'll agree that the view back down Exshaw Creek is well worth the effort. The valley on the north side of the pass is not the best way into the South Ghost. What you must do is traverse in a north-westerly direction to a higher pass at map ref. 238698, then, using sheep trails, descend the east slopes of the new valley directly to the hunters camp.

23 HEART CREEK INTERPRETIVE TRAIL — Map 5

Half-day hike
Circuit 3 km
Topo map 82 O/3 Canmore

Access: Trans-Canada Highway. At the Lac des Arcs interchange drive to the Heart Creek parking lot on the south side of the highway.

The Heart Creek trail is short interesting and popular. Since the first edition of this book was printed, the trail has been improved with the construction in 1982 of 7 log bridges over the stream. Note, too, that the new parking lot is located 0.7 km west of the creek near the Lac des Arcs interchange.

Walk along the trail under the powerline to Heart Creek trail junction at the sign. Crossing and recrossing the stream 7 times, you follow a winding course between high rock gates introducing each new turn of the valley floor. The trail ends below a vertical step in the creekbed and within earshot of a waterfall hidden by a tight twist in the canyon wall. At low water, the determined hiker can scramble along greasy rocks and jammed logs to the base of the fall.

If you wish to go farther into the valley use a rough trail starting in trees to the left of the rock step. (Don't confuse it with a muddy rake below the ascending cliff line.) This trail climbs above the rock step, then drops to the creekbed a little way above the waterfall. Walk up the creekbed to a right-angled bend to the east where the trail, reappearing, enters forest and can be followed for some distance towards the head of the valley.

24 HEART MOUNTAIN — Map 5

Day hike
Circuit 10.5 km
Height gain 870 m
Maximum elevation 2135 m
Topo map 82/O3 Canmore

Access: Trans-Canada Highway. At the Lac des Arcs interchange, drive to the Heart Creek parking lot on the south side of the highway.

The mountain gets its name from the plunging syncline formation on the upper slopes which has the appearance of a heart when viewed from across the Bow Valley. Its rocky north-west ridge, is one of those hikes where experience and conditioning decide how high you should climb. Many people quit half-way up, some reach the summit ridge and a few go on to complete the circuit. I highly recommend the latter course; nowhere are there difficulties comparable to those of the ascent route.

From the parking lot, follow the access trail for 0.7 km to Heart Creek trail junction at the sign. The trail up the ridge is obvious. After a short moderately steep section the trail flattens out, but this doesn't last long and soon you're following a tenuous line up scree and broken rock above cliffs dropping away into Heart Creek. Slabs at one point can be avoided by a detour into the trees. When the ridge flattens out you must transfer onto the upper ridge to your left. In the past many people have gone wrong at this point, hence the false trail up the bench. Climb 4 m of vertical rock on good hand and foot holds to a small cairn. The upper ridge, easy at first, steepens into slabs which the climber, no doubt, will greet with enthusiasm. Most of you however, will elect to follow the trail into the security of the yellow scree gully to the left. When the gully steepens into loose broken rocks escape to a small tree on the gully's right-hand edge and emerge onto easier ground above the slabs. All difficulties at an end, walk up to the first summit where you are greeted most incongruously by broad meadows and trees.

The trail continues over 2 minor humps. Below a third hump the ridge turns east and narrows to a stony ramp above cliffbands on both sides — a suitably impressive approach to the highest summit. Don't forget to sign the summit register in the cairn. Descend broad grass slopes to a gap, then, regaining all the lost altitude, climb to another cairned summit which offers an even better view of Barrier Lake. Traverse across to the further top marking the culmination of another north-west ridge — your descent route. Contrary to its appearance from the Trans-Canada Highway this ridge is broad and easy, and apart from the initial talus slope, set at a much gentler angle than the ascent route. As you reach treeline so the traces of man's passage strengthen into a trail which can be followed all the way down to the powerline right-of-way near the highway. Walk left to a side stream and follow it downstream a few metres until you reach Quaite Creek trail. A left turn will return you to your starting point at the parking lot.

Heart Mtn. Ascent route follows upper right-hand ridge.

25 QUAITE CREEK TO JEWELL PASS — Map 5

Day hike, intermediate ski, bike
Distance 7 km
Height gain 290 m
Maximum elevation 1630 m
Topo map 82 O/3 Canmore

Access: Trans-Canada Highway. At the Lac des Arcs interchange, drive to the Heart Creek parking lot on the south side of the highway. Because the connecting trail between Lac des Arcs and Quaite Creek rarely has snow, skiers must park on the shoulder of the Trans-Canada Highway opposite the Loader Peak sign.

This is a popular trail with youth groups looking for sheltered trails and a backcountry campground not too far from civilization. The valley accumulates and holds snow very well, so don't be put off by a lack of the white fluffy stuff at the highway.

Follow the trail across Heart Creek and the lower slopes of Heart Mountain. Despite the constant background noise from the Trans-Canada Highway, this is a surprisingly pleasant section through aspen forest harboring the elegant blue columbine. Arriving at Quaite Creek, turn right and follow the logging road through the narrows to the mill site, now a huge meadow. The 20-site back-country campground with fire pits, picnic tables and water pump is located to the left of the road at the edge of the trees.

A few metres on, in a flurry of red squares on trees, the road divides. Both branches lead to Jewell Pass (the skier can take advantage of this and make a circuit), but the right-hand or (west) branch which crosses Quaite Creek is the official route and also the shorter. It climbs quite steeply, eventually leveling out near the pass which is identified by a 4-way trail junction and more red squares on trees. Views are restricted to treed hillsides rising above nearby treetops. Prairie View trail (#43) and the trail to Barrier Lake (#42) turn off to the right. The unmarked road straight ahead is the eastern branch of the Quaite Creek Road at the mill site. Skiers descending this way should be aware that a little way down, the route makes a dog-leg to the right onto a seemingly more minor road.

Quaite Creek looking towards Barrier Lake Lookout (right). The campground is just out of sight to left.

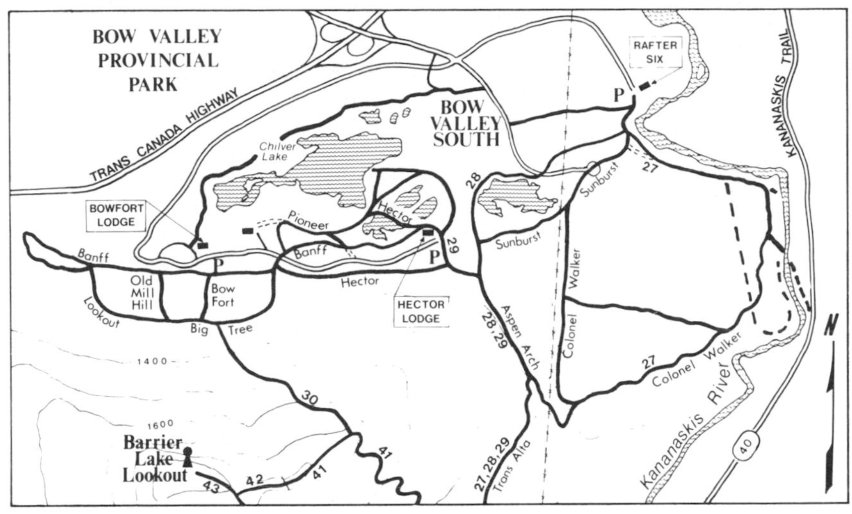

26 YAMNUSKA CENTRE & RAFTER SIX TRAILS — Map 5

Half-day & day hikes,
Easy & intermediate ski, equestrian
Topo map 82 O/3 Canmore

Access: Trans-Canada Highway at Seebe Interchange. Follow signs to: 1) Yamnuska Centre. Park in the visitors parking lot opposite the Beaufort Lodge or drive to the end of the road at Hector Lodge and park in the semi-circular road to the right. 2) Rafter Six Guest Ranch. Park outside the lodge gates. 3) Bow Valley Provincial Park South overflow campground.

Rafter Six guest ranch, the southern portion of Bow Valley Provincial Park and Yamnuska Centre lie adjacent to one another south of the Trans-Canada Highway across from Bow Valley Provincial Park. Despite boundary fences, a network of trails roam indiscriminately, passing through gaps or gateways from one property to another and for this reason are more easily considered as one unit. The major trails, those leading out of the area, are described separately under routes #27, #28, #29 & #30. For every trail shown on the sketchmap there are dozens of smaller ones to discover. Ski trails double as hiking and equestrian trails and vice versa. Unfortunately, this is a low snowfall area and there aren't many weekends throughout the winter when the ski trails are in condition.

Yamnuska Centre and Camp Hector have no facilities open to the general public other than the use of parking lots. Right now, entry into Bow Provincial Park South is limited to times when the overflow campground is in use. For a little while in 1983 when 16,000 Scouts attended the World Jamboree, it became the biggest campground in the world.

Rafter Six guest ranch throws out the welcome mat to day visitors; and what could be better after a day in the saddle or on skis to return to the lodge for some home cooking or apres ski relaxation in the lounge? The ranch has a colorful history dating back to the eighteen hundreds when Colonel James Walker ran his horses there while supervising the first logging operation west of Winnipeg across the valley at Kananaskis. When Alvin Guinn (of Guinn's Pass) took over ownership from Soapy Smith, Rafter Six became a guest ranch and also a popular movie-making location for adventure films such as Grizzly Adams, Wilderness Family, Little Big Man, Across the Great Divide etc. Moving with the times, present owners Stan and Gloria Cowley are encouraging cross-country skiers and weekend campers (with or without horses) who for a modest fee are entitled to use of the facilities including the heated outdoor swimming pool. For more information phone the ranch at (403) 673-3622.

27 BARRIER LAKE VIA THE RIVER ROAD — Map 5

Day hike, easy ski
Equestrian
Distance 9 km
Height gain 152 m
Topo map 82 O/3 Canmore

Access: Trans-Canada Highway. At the Seebe interchange follow signs to Rafter Six Guest Ranch.

The trail starts to the right of the lodge as you face it and runs through the campground meadow into trees at the far end where it reasserts itself and climbs over an esker to the boundary fence with Bow Valley Provincial Park. Don't go through the gate. The trail passes through a gap in the barbed-wire fence to left and joins the River Road on the bank of the Kananaskis River. Turn left up the road. Shortly after a gate you have the option of taking a shortcut to right and will have to weigh up the relative merits of a pleasant forest trail with those of a point of historical interest which occurs at the second side road to the left. What you are looking at here is a remnant of the very first road built in the Kananaskis Valley. Constructed in 1934, it ran between Seebe and the Kananaskis Forest Experiment Station which at that time was a camp for the unemployed. If you follow it, you'll come to the old bridge over the Kananaskis River and another remnant of road, almost completely grassed over, climbing the far bank to Kananaskis Trail. The bridge stringers have pretty well gone now, but the abutments, protected by metal gabions, still stand firm.

River Road now swings away from the river, climbing a little. The shortcut trail comes in from the right opposite a trail to left. At a white post, a trail to right joins a road under the powerline at a gate. After a gap of perhaps 1 km, keep left at the junction with the powerline access road, intersect the powerline right-of-way, then swing north — badly off direction — and join route #28 at a road junction. Turn left along the road signed Trans-Alta ski trail. After a long, uneventful stretch you pass Pigeon Lookout fire road to right, and a few minutes later arrive at the junction with route #44 (left, straight). Turn left downhill and follow the road across the dam to Barrier Dam day-use area on Kananaskis Trail.

28 BARRIER LAKE FROM BOW VALLEY PROVINCIAL PARK SOUTH — Map 5

Day hike
Distance 7 km
Height gain 122 m
Topo map 82 O/3 Canmore

Access: **Trans-Canada Highway. At the Seebe interchange follow signs to Bow Valley Provincial Park South. Park in the overflow campground.**

Walk down the park road to a large unnamed lake at a left-hand bend. If Bow Valley Provincial Park South is closed, the same point can be reached from Rafter Six Guest Ranch (see map). Turn right onto a trail which skirts the shoreline to a log cabin picturesquely situated on a promentory. Take a close look inside; tree stumps in the living room should tell you that this is no ordinary cabin. It was, in fact, built specifically for the movies and in its heyday, before sun and wind bleached its timbers, appeared in films such as "The River of No Return" starring Marilyn Monroe. The remains of a jetty ends in deep green sedges some distance from open water. Continue along the shore to the far end of the lake and join a road which swings left following the open ridge between the lake and the boundary fence with Camp Hector. Route #29 comes in from the right after the gate. At the top of the hill the road straightens and runs through a gap in the hills to the T-junction with the River Road. Keep right and follow route #27 to Barrier Lake.

The original 1934 road bridge over the Kananaskis River.

29 BARRIER LAKE FROM HECTOR LODGE — Map 5

Day hike, easy ski
Distance 5.5 km
Height gain 122 m
Topo map 82 O/3 Canmore

Access: Trans-Canada Highway. At the Seebe interchange follow signs to Yamnuska Centre. Drive to Hector Lodge and park in a semi-circular road to the right.

Beyond the parking lot the road splays into three short stubs. Follow the centre stub onto a trail which crosses the meadow to the tepee area. In the trees join Hector Ski trail at a sign reading "To Barrier Lake" and follow it uphill to the road in the S.W. corner of Bow Valley Provincial Park. Turn right onto route #28 which in turn joins route #27 at the T-junction with the River Road.

30 PIGEON LOOKOUT FIRE ROAD FROM YAMNUSKA CENTRE — Map 5

Day hike
Distance 3 km
Height gain 460 m
Maximum elevation 1800 m
Topo map 82 O/3 Canmore

Access: Trans-Canada Highway. At the Seebe interchange follow signs to Yamnuska Centre. Use the visitors parking lot opposite Beaufort Lodge. The trail starts by the signboard.

This steep forest trail is not maintained and is kept open only by the passage of students from Yamnuska Centre who use it as a shortcut to Barrier Lake Lookout. Apart from its directness, the trail has little else to recommend it.

Follow Bowfort ski trail uphill to the junction with Big Tree ski trail. Turn left and in a few minutes turn right onto an unsigned trail which wends left to the bottom of a ridge, then climbs direct to Pigeon Lookout fire road which is gained 0.5 km below the lookout site.

Movie Cabin seen from route #28.

BOW VALLEY PROVINCIAL PARK — Map 5

Half-day hikes
Topo map 82 O/3 Canmore

Western wood lilies.

Access: Highway 1X, accessible from either Highway 1A or the Trans-Canada Highway at Seebe interchange.

The park lies on a plain of the Bow River at the foot of the mountains. During the last glacial retreat the valley was spread with a thin layer of gravel inwash which resulted in the great variety of land forms you see today: kames and eskers, lakes, a mosaic of aspen and spruce forest, and large flat meadows where the grass grows barely above your insoles.

Apart from the amenities of 2 campgrounds, 4 day-use areas and a visitor centre, the park has 8 short trails which are especially suited to senior citizens, couples with young children and school or youth groups who want to learn about the area's unique landscape. Park naturalists give guided walks or you can go by yourself. Brochures are available at trailheads and from the Visitor Centre.

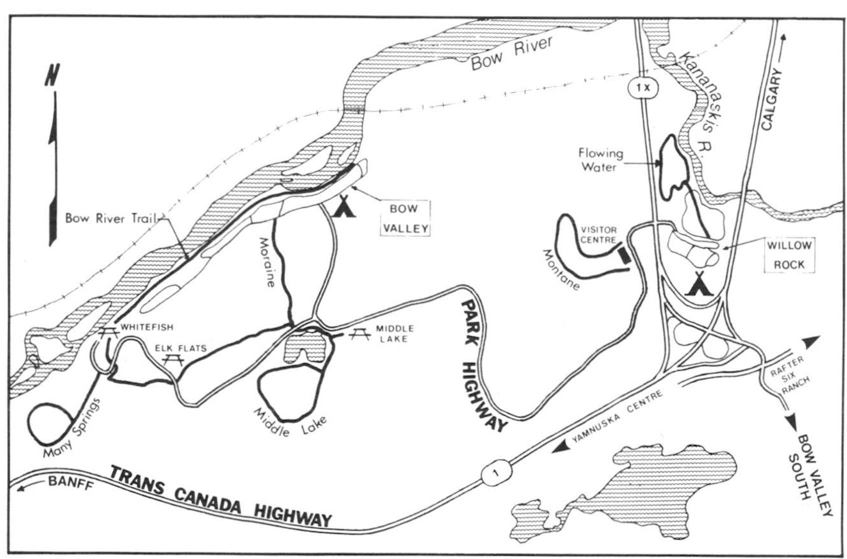

31 FLOWING WATER INTERPRETIVE TRAIL

Distance 2.0 km

Access: Willow Rock campground.

A signboard near site #87 on the campground road marks the official start of the loop. Keep right at a junction a little way in, staying close to the bank of the Kananaskis River which in winter is fringed with ice curtains from seepages. The trail crosses a rust-colored stream containing traces of iron, then climbs onto a dry ridge where a seat offers a welcome rest and a view over the lower Kananaskis Valley. Now on the homeward stretch, the trail descends to a large beaver pond whose teeming insect life contrasts strangely with dead drowned trees used as observation posts by swallows. The water has flooded the forest beyond the pond and the final section of trail must be negotiated by boadwalk. A little after the spruce tree (#10 in the brochure), watch for a large clump of yellow lady slipper on the left; it can be recognized by a bulbous lower lip which is inflated almost to bursting point. Arriving at the trail junction, turn right and walk back to the campground road.

32 MONTANE INTERPRETIVE TRAIL

Distance 2.2 km

Access: Visitor Centre. Walk round the verandah to the trail sign at the far side of the building.

Initial meadows of creamy camas lilies give way to drier grasslands carpeted with tough bearberry and juniper mats. Cross the powerline right-of-way, and climb onto the top of an esker, a snakelike ridge of gravel deposited by a meltwater stream deep within a glacier and left behind when the ice sheet melted. Drop down into a remnant of douglas fir forest, recross the powerline and return through mixed forest to the Visitor Centre parking lot.

33 MIDDLE LAKE INTERPRETIVE TRAIL

Distance 2.5 km

Access: Middle Lake day-use area.

Come to Middle Lake in early summer, late June to early July time, when the meadow between the parking lot and the lake is one big prairie flower garden. Western wood lilies grow in such profusion you must tread a careful path down to the signboard and trail junction. Turn left here and walk along the east shore of the lake, watching as you go for Barrow's golden eye and ring necked ducks among the rushes. At the next junction the brochure suggests you walk the loop in a clockwise direction, so head off into a checkered forest of aspen and spruce. Three-quarters of the way around, at trail stop #10 in the brochure, watch for stumps of douglas fir trees logged at the turn of the century by the Eau Claire logging company. Just a little farther on, claw- shaped scars on aspen bark advertise the presence of black bears in the park. The trail comes out into the open at the lake's southern shore where two seats are ideally placed for a few minutes of quiet contemplation before your return to the outward loop which lies only a few metres away at the S.E. corner of the lake.

Middle Lake.

34 MORAINE INTERPRETIVE TRAIL

Distance 1.5 km

Access: Bow Valley Campground. The trail starts from the right-hand side of the ampitheater.

After crossing the powerline right-of-way, the trail winds round hummocks and moist leafy hollows onto a ridge of old moraine which is followed all the way to the park road. On the west side of the ridge creeping junipers, bearberries, kinnickinick and stunted aspens bent almost double testify to the strong chinook winds which blow through the gap. A few metres after passing the trail to Elk Flats day-use area on the right, the trail crosses the park road and follows the north shore of Middle Lake to the junction with Middle Lake trail at the signboard. If you have time, Middle Lake trail is a logical extension.

35 ELK FLATS TRAIL

Distance 1.7 km

Access: via Moraine trail.

The trail branches off Moraine trail near Middle Lake and journeys to Elk Flats day-use area on the park road. It's a useful little trail which enables the hiker to join up several interpretive trails in one afternoon.

36 BOW RIVER INTERPRETIVE TRAIL

Distance 2.0 km

Access: Bow Valley campground. The trail starts across the road from campsite #A 22, but can be accessed from any campsite facing the river.

The trail, which parallels the campground road along the river bank, is used mainly by anglers and by campers wanting an evening stroll before turning in for the night. It offers good views across the Bow River to the well known climbers' mountain Yamnuska, which, so the sign tells us, was formed when a slab of hard limestone fractured along a weak area called the McConnell Fault and was thrust over the top of softer sandstones. If you have binoculars you can distinguish the fault line near the bottom of the cliff. Although the trail officially ends near Whitefish day-use area, an unofficial trail carries on along the river bank to the sand dunes.

37 WHITEFISH ACCESS TRAIL

Distance 1.2 km

Access: Whitefish day-use area. The trail starts at the far end of the parking lot beyond the barrier.

The trail immediately turns right and climbs the bank. After crossing the park road, it wends right towards Many Springs parking lot, but a few metres short of the lot turns left and climbs over a timbered ridge to the park road opposite Elk Flats day-use area.

38 MANY SPRINGS INTERPRETIVE TRAIL

Distance 1.6 km

Access: Many Springs parking lot on the road to Whitefish day- use area.

A short distance from the parking lot, the trail makes a loop around Many Springs basin. Turn right here and when you come to the powerline right-of-way, follow it downhill to the bridge over Many Springs Creek which flows into small deep ponds seen from the viewing platform a little farther along the trail.

Recross the powerline and make your way around the perimeter of the basin to the springs at the east end where it is suggested you keep to the boardwalk. Out on the calcareous flats, elephant heads and beautiful purple butterworts grow in profusion. Any fly or mosquito venturing onto the leaves of the butterwort is in for a nasty surprise. The scientific name for the plant is "Pinguicula" meaning fat and refers to the glandular hairs on the leaves' upper surface which secrete a greasy, sticky fluid thus trapping the insect whose frantic struggles cause the margin of the leaves to roll over them and begin dispersing preserving and digestive acids. In one to three days when the leaves slowly unroll, all that is left of the unfortunte insect is a hard black granule of its chitinous parts.

The trail now leaves this fascinating arena of death and returns you to your starting point through mixed forest and dry meadows of red windflowers, western wood lilies and pale comandras.

The hiker's route takes you close to the edge of a sandstone escarpment where there is a grand view of the Bow Valley.

39 YAMNUSKA RIDGE — Map 5

Day hike, equestrian
Distance 3.5 km
Height gain 436 m
Maximum elevation 1798 m
Topo map 82 O/3 Canmore

Access: Highway 1A. 2.1 km east of 1X Highway turn north onto the quarry road and drive to a parking area in meadows before a gate.

This very popular trail takes you to a superlative viewpoint on the open ridge east of Mount John Laurie which is more commonly known as Yamnuska — Wall of Stone. It's the ideal early season hike; although the snow still lies deep on the Front Ranges to the west, the blooming of the prairie crocus in the meadows and the drumming of the grouse in the forest tell you that spring has arrived at Yamnuska. Unfortunately, spring also brings that unwanted hitchhiker, the wood tick, which seems particularly voracious in this area. Water is available at the bottom level of the quarry where a small spring has been tapped.

Walk up the road to the quarry. For the next little while equestrians and hikers follow different trails.

Hikers: From the first left-hand bend, a climber's trail leads to the middle level of the quarry, turns right and wanders along the top of a sandstone escarpment for half a kilometre. Matted alpines — saxifrages, sandworts and stonecrops — find toeholds on sloping pavements between the trees and the cliff edge. The view is already impressive and there is a great temptation to sit here awhile on the rocks listening to the chat of nearby climbers and the occasional more distant calls filtering down from the great cliff of Yamnuska above. When the escarpment starts to break down, the trail swings inland and joins the horse trail.

Equestrians: Follow the road all the way into the upper level, then transfer onto a trail which climbs the bank about halfway along. Keep right of the big rock. After half a kilometre of level going through mixed forest watch for the hikers' trail coming in from the right.

After crossing a dry gully, the trail and its many variants turns uphill. Three-quarters of the way up the slope, it levels off across open ground allowing a birds-eye view of the Bow Valley. Who would have thought from the highway that there were so many lakes and ponds sprinkled about the forest? At a second opening, above a short connecting climb through aspens, the trail divides. Most people climb direct to the ridge-top trail. Equestrians should follow the right-hand trail which takes a gentler line and arrives at the ridge-top trail at the boundary fence with Morley Indian Reservation.

If you want to extend the trip, walk west along the ridge towards Yamnuska. After a short steep step keep left at a junction with Loggers Valley trail at a barbed-wire fence. The trail ends at the base of cliffs at a T-junction with the climber's descent route from the summit. The right-hand trail which starts off up an awkward gully, is feasible for scramblers but is not recommended; there is a very real danger of hikers inadvertently kicking down loose rubble onto the heads of climbers below.

40 LOGGERS (C.M.C.) VALLEY — Map 5

Day hike, equestrian
Distance 3 km
Circuit 10.5 km
Height loss 168 m
Topo map 82 O/3 Canmore

Access: Yamnuska Ridge (#39). From the ridge-top trail.

The valley at the back of Yamnuska, actually the south fork of Old Fort Creek, can only be approached from Yamnuska Ridge. Note: hikers and equestrians take different routes for the initial kilometre.

Hikers: At the aforementioned junction, pass through the gap in the barbed wire fence to the north side of the ridge. The trail, faint at first, crosses open ground then zigzags down through forest to a logging road.

Equestrians: From the eastern boundary of the ridge-top trail, pass through a gate into the Stoney Indian Reservation. Turn left, slip back inside the boundary fence now on the north side of the ridge-top fence, and descend the track alongside the boundary fence to a logging road. Follow it leftwards to the junction with the hiking trail at the remains of a log cabin.

Both routes descend the road, deeply trenched by rivulets from melting snow, to the valley bottom. The water pools in the flats by the side of a cabin rebuilt by the Calgary Mountain Club who use it as a base for climbs in the area. Flounder through to a trail on the bank top, turn left and descend to the stream where you can either continue along a trail on the south bank or cross the creek on a log to a drier road on the north bank; either way, trail and road can be followed upstream to a point level with two cliffs known as Bilbo Buttress and Frodo Buttress separated by a large area of gullies called The Runes.

Strong hikers have the option of returning to the parking lot via the col to the west of Yamnuska. When level with the col, strike out across the swampy heart of the valley into a side creek where game trails facilitate the approach to the col. Keep left near the top and pick up a climbers' trail descending from the summit of Yamnuska. Still following the trail, contour around the base of the cliff until you come to the central scree bowl, then drop down scree to the upper level of the quarry.

41 PIGEON LOOKOUT FIRE ROAD — Map 5

Day hike, intermediate ski
Distance 5 km
Height gain 421 m
Maximum elevation 1798 m
Topo map 82 O/3 Canmore

Access: Kananaskis Trail (Hwy. 40) at Barrier dam day-use area.

The viewpoint at the site of Pigeon Lookout is a popular destination despite a mundane approach via the fire road. Conversely, the road makes an excellent ski trail requiring little snow cover.

Follow the road across Barrier Lake dam and up the hill to a T-junction. Turn right, then almost immediately left onto Pigeon Lookout fire road which is gated. The road winds uphill, closeted in trees until it reaches the environs of the lookout where sloping meadows facing south and a view of Barrier Lake encourage a well deserved rest.

The white-painted lookout, which for 24 years had been a familiar landmark from the Kananaskis Valley, was removed in the fall of 1984 and taken down to the Forest Experiment Station. (Handicapped by a restricted field of vision, it had been superseded in 1983 by Barrier Lake Lookout on the summit of the mountain). The wheel had turned full circle for the lookout tower which first saw service as a guard tower at the Experiment Station's P.O.W. camp in the early 1940's.

Alternative Route: A few metres before the fire road gate, a well-trodden trail leaves the road on the left-hand side. It follows the route of the old telephone line; you can still see remnants of wire and the odd insulator post high on the trail. Because of its excessive steepness I suggest you reserve this trail for the descent. At the top end, it leaves the fire road about 400 m down from the viewpoint, and is marked by tree blazes.

Barrier Lake and Mt. Baldy from the site of Pigeon Lookout.

42 JEWELL PASS FROM BARRIER LAKE — Map 5

Day hike
Distance 7.1 km
Height gain 250 m
Maximum elevation 1630 m
Topo map 82 O/3 Canmore

Access: Kananaskis Trail (Hwy. 40) at Barrier dam day-use area.

The trail up Jewell Creek is best used in conjunction with route #25, or as part of an excellent one-day circuit incorporating Prairie View (#43) and Pigeon Lookout Fire Road (# 41) trails. Since the first edition of this book was published, the trail has been improved and is signed at all junctions.

Walk across Barrier Lake dam, keeping an eye out for two resident bluebirds. At the powerline right-of-way turn left and follow the rough road to a junction with the powerline access road coming in from the north. Turn left here and walk for 1.4 km to a trail sign on the right-hand side of the road. (If the water level is sufficiently low, you can reach the same point by walking along the sands and shingles of the shoreline — a much pleasanter route which invites dawdling. From a large bay, continue along a trail under the powerline (route #44) to the aforementioned powerline access road, turn left and watch for the trail sign on the right-hand side of the road after 0.75 km.)

Go right. The improved portion of the trail crosses the powerline right-of-way and follows the bank top (last view) into the confines of Jewell Creek. Pale blue clematis and pale pink venus slipper orchids brighten the dimness of the forest floor. And if you're there at the right time — June usually — look for tasty morell mushrooms growing by the trailside. At the forks, detour left to 10 metre-high Jewell Falls. Although the falls are a big disappointment in mid summer when the streams are almost dry, it's a pleasant enough spot for rest and refreshment before the final rise to the pass. The trail follows the right- hand fork, bridges it twice, then leaves the creek and heads across flat ground to the dead-end of a very overgrown logging road which is followed to Jewell Pass.

The view from Barrier Lake lookout of the Canmore Corridor near Exshaw: Quaite Creek (bottom left), Grotto Mtn. (top left), Exshaw Creek and Mt. Fable (top right).

43 PRAIRIE VIEW TRAIL — Map 5

Day hike
Distance 3.5 km
Height gain from Jewell Pass 366 m
Height gain from Pigeon Lookout 198 m
Maximum elevation 1996 m
Topo map 82 O/3 Canmore

Access 1: From Jewell Pass via trails #25 or #42.
Access 2: Via Pigeon Lookout Fire Road (#41)

This useful trail linking Jewell Pass to Pigeon Lookout fire road on the other side of the mountain, enables the hiker to make a circuit from Barrier Lake incorporating Jewell Pass (#42), Prairie View (#43) and Pigeon Lookout Fire Road trails which are best hiked in that order if you wish to take advantage of the surprise view. From the highest point, a spur trail leads to Barrier Lake Lookout — a popular destination with campers in Quaite Creek.

From Jewell Pass the narrow trail starts off by paralleling trail #42 a way, then begins a slow climb to a gap on the S.W. ridge of the unnamed mountain. The sudden emergence from closed-in pine forest to an airy ledge above a cliff is as surprising as the sudden view which encompasses a large portion of the upper Kananaskis Valley and the prairies beyond Chiniki Lake. The view is even better higher up the trail, so rather than linger in this spot, head left up the ridge, keeping an eye out as you go for fat marmots sunning themselves on exposed ledges. Cross a deep fissure at the point indicated by bits of red flagging. At the television repeater station the trail divides, the right- hand trail descending a spur ridge to the start of route #41 (a fire road) at the site of Pigeon Lookout. The fainter trail to left climbs another 137 m to the summit of the mountain which has been occupied since 1983 by Barrier Lake Lookout. The extra effort is well worthwhile, for the view to north and west, hitherto hidden by the bulk of the mountain, is breathtaking.

44 STONEY TRAIL — Maps 5 & 6

Day hike, equestrian
Easy ski, bike
Distance 17 km
Height gain 79 m
Topo map 82 0/3 Canmore
82 J/14 Spray Lake Reservoir

Access: 1. Kananaskis Trail (Hwy. 40) at Barrier dam day-use area.
Access: 2. Kananaskis Trail at Ribbon Creek parking lot.

This is primarily an equestrian trail which follows the powerline access road up the west side of Kananaskis Valley from Barrier Lake to Ribbon Creek.

Cross Barrier Lake dam. At the powerline turn left and follow the right-of-way without deviation to a large bay. Continue along a trail under the powerline to the powerline access road which has come in from the north and serves as access from route #27, #28 and #29. Turn left here and arrive at the reservoir for a second time. Across the narrows you get a good view of Mount Baldy, previously known as Barrier Mountain, Mount Baldy and Barrier Mountain in that order. The Indians called it Sleeping Buffalo Mountain because of its striking resemblance to the animal when viewed in profile from their camp to the north; the rump, the shoulders and massive craggy head are easily made out as you drive along the Kananaskis Trail to the Barrier dam trailhead.

Shortly after passing Jewell Pass trail to the right, you cross Jewell Creek and embark on a long straight stretch to the end of the reservoir. Look for a picnic shelter, lonely on an island, which dates back to pre-reservoir times, 1936 to be exact, when the original forestry trunk road was built through the valley. The road now turns S.W., passing close under Mount Lorette's south ridge, a popular beginners rock climb. At Lorette Creek, make a wide detour round beaver ponds. Two kilometres short of Ribbon Creek, the Skogan Pass powerline cum equestrian trail (#16) comes in from the right. Cross Marmot Creek soon after. Arriving in the proximity of Nakiska ski area access road, equestrians are encouraged to cross the road and follow the powerline right-of-way to its very end at Ribbon Creek access road just east of Ribbon Creek Youth Hostel. Cross, and make your way up to the parking lot.

45 LUSK PASS TRAIL — Maps 5 & 21

Day hike, difficult ski
Equestrian
Distance 9 km
Height gain 350 m
Maximum elevation 1740 m
Topo map 82 O/3 Canmore
82 O/2 Jumpingpound Creek
82 J/15 Bragg Creek

Access: 1. Sibbald Creek Trail (SR 968) at Stony Creek day-use area.
Access: 2. Powderface Trail at Cox Hill parking lot.

This forest trail is actually an old road still marked in red on the topo map, but now completely grassed over. It's used mainly by equestrians as a link between the upper Kananaskis Valley and the equestrian trails of the Jumpingpound.

Follow the trail by the side of the cutblock onto the road connecting Kananaskis Forest Experiment Station with a gravel pit. Turn left, and when you reach the gravel pit, transfer onto a short trail which takes you to the truncated end of the Lusk Creek road.

For the first 2.5 km, the road rises step-like through three experimental plots. Pass a road to the right leading to the Old Mill Road below the fire road. Descend a hill to another trail junction; this time the narrower road to the right, though in close proximity to the other one, climbs uphill to Barrier Pass trail. Keep left and climb over a small rise to an ill-defined junction in a patch of grass. You must turn left here and cross Lusk Creek.

The road now travels along the east bank of Lusk Creek, eventually turning away and climbing much more steeply up a side valley towards the pass. A small meadow, an anomoly in a tight forest of matchstick pines, marks the summit. The short descent trail to Powderface Trail (Hwy.) follows the drainage out of the meadow, ultimately crossing a branch of Jumpingpound Creek a few metres from the Cox Hill parking lot.

Lusk Pass trail between connecting roads to Old Mill Road. As you can see by the sign, this section of road is part of the Forest Experiment Station ski trail system.

46 BALDY PASS FROM THE NORTH — Map 5

Day hike, intermediate ski
Distance 10 km
Height gain 549 m
Maximum elevation 1900 m
Topo map 82 O/3 Canmore
82 J/14 Spray Lakes Reservoir

Access: Sibbald Creek Trail (SR 968) at Stony Creek day-use area.

In summer, unless you're interested in learning about reforestation, route #50 is the shorter and more interesting trail to Baldy Pass. In winter, the situation is reversed when avalanche slopes along a deep V-shaped valley make the southern route potentially hazardous. Although snow cover may be light at the trailhead, chinook winds blasting over the pass from the south deposit such masses of snow into upper Lusk Creek that trail breaking can be a real chore.

Follow the trail by the side of the cutblock onto the road connecting Kananaskis Forest Experiment Station with a gravel pit. Turn right, then almost immediately left onto the Old Mill Road. As you will see by the sign, this road is part of the "Lusk Creek Tour of logging and reforestation areas." After you've put many windings of the road behind you, you reach a junction at the edge of a large cutblock. The Lusk Creek Tour route turns off to the left. Keep right here and a few minutes later, turn left at a T-junction with a fire road. Keep right at the next junction identified by a hut. Still on the Old Mill Road descend slightly to Lusk Creek.

Just after the crossing the road divides. Abandon the Old Mill Road to right in favour of the Baldy Pass Road to left which climbs much more gently uphill. It intersects the Old Mill Road higher up the creek, then winds ever more steeply towards the pass through a mature spruce forest. The last half kilometre is along a trail. From the cairn on the open ridge descend 50 vertical metres to the pass.

47 KANANASKIS FOREST EXPERIMENT STATION SKI TRAILS — Map 5

Easy, intermediate and difficult ski
15 km of trails
Topo map 82 0/3 Canmore

Access: Sibbald Creek Trail at Stony Creek day-use area.

The interlocking logging roads of the Forest Experiment Station, including Lusk Pass and Baldy Pass trails, make excellent ski trails when there is sufficient snow. The trails are unofficial, unsigned, and used mainly by employees of the Experiment Station.

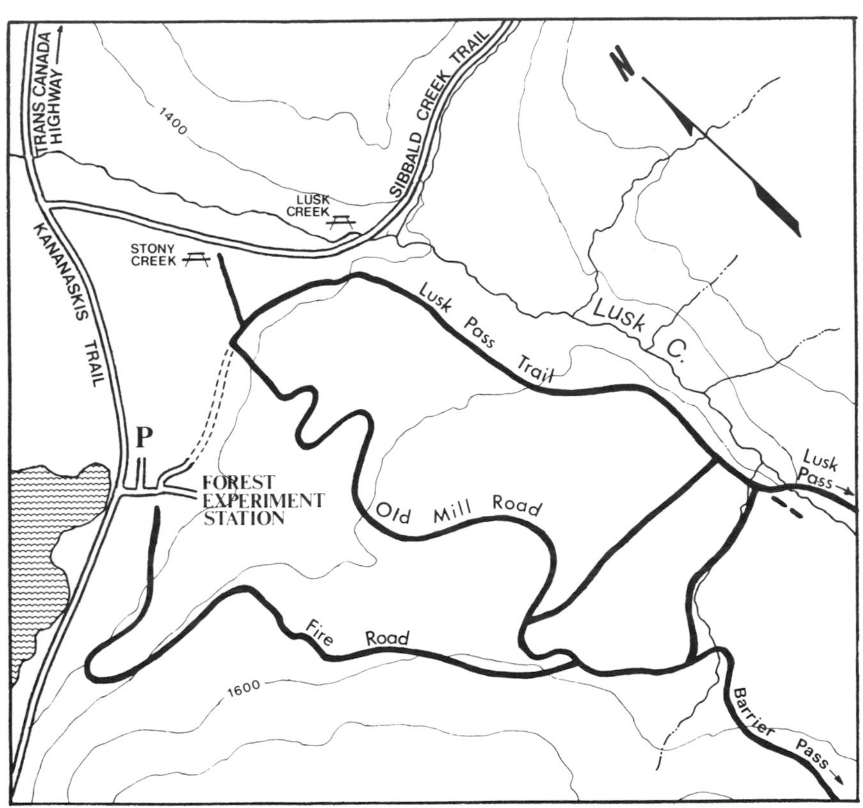

48 FOREST MANAGEMENT INTERPRETIVE TRAIL — Map 5

Distance 2.3 km
Topo map 82 O/3 Canmore

Access: **Kananaskis Trail (Hwy. 40) At Kananaskis Forest Experiment Station turn first left into a parking lot. Walk through to the Colonel's Cabin Visitor Centre which is open in summer from 10:00 a.m. to 4:30 p.m. weekdays, and from 10:00 a.m. to 6:00 p.m. at weekends. Brochures are available.**

This self-guiding interpretive trail is laid out in two loops shaped like the figure 8. The first and longest loop, with spur trails to a lookout and a viewpoint deck, introduces you to the trees and vegetation of the forest, shows you how fire has affected wild life habitat and allows you to use various meteorological instruments and a stream gauge used in watershed research at the Marmot Basin project area. The second loop focuses entirely on forest management. There are exhibits of soils, thinning, pruning, logging and reforestation by planting and by seed.

Stop off at the visitor centre which was built in 1935, one year after the Dominion Forest Service set up the Kananaskis Forest Experiment Station. Not much research was done until 1947; for the first two years the Department of National Defence operated the station as a relief camp for unemployed and at the outbreak of World War II it became prisoner of war camp #130. It was during this time that the log cabin housing the camp commander became known as the Colonel's Cabin. (The ornate iron work on the door handle is believed to have been the work of a P.O.W. named Fritz.) The prisoners — mostly German merchant seamen — were put to work cutting wood for Kovach Coal mines and clearing land in preparation for Barrier Lake; a few were allowed to climb Mount Baldy provided they stayed on the trail and promised not to escape.

After the war ended, the station reverted to its original purpose. The guard tower was incorporated in Pigeon Lookout and the barracks moved up the Banff-Jasper Highway to become Youth Hostels. In 1975 the cabin became a visitor centre, focal point for the interpretive trail designed to give the growing number of tourists to the valley an insight into forest management. If you want to learn more about the history of the Kananaskis Forest Experiment Station I suggest you read Ruth Oltman's book "The Valley of Rumours - the Kananaskis".

Colonel's Cabin with Baldy Mtn. in the background.

49 PAINTBRUSH — Map 5

Half-day hike
Distance 1 km
Topo map 82 0/3 Canmore

Looking south along Barrier Lake.

Access: Kananaskis Trail (Hwy 40) at Barrier Lake day-use area. Drive to the upper parking lot.

Each picnic site is connected to a major trail which leads to the upper parking lot. From the upper parking lot, the trail climbs a few steps then zigzags through aspen woodlands harboring the red paintbrush onto a rocky knoll overlooking Highway 40. Despite its lowly height above the road, the hill is a surprisingly good viewpoint for Barrier Lake and the upper Kananaskis Valley, especially in fall when aspen groves make splashes of bright color in the dark coniferous forest.

50 BALDY PASS FROM THE SOUTH — Map 5

Day hike
5 km to pass
Height gain 490 m
Maximum elevation 1900 m
Topo map 82 J/14 Spray Lakes Reservoir

Access: Kananaskis Trail (Hwy. 40). 10.3 km south of Kananaskis Country boundary, turn west into the Baldy Pass parking lot. The trail starts at a sign on the opposite side of the highway.

This trail is the usual summer hiking route to Baldy pass. Water can't be relied on, so fill up your water bottles at O'Shaugnessy Falls. In winter, because of a steep avalanche slope near the pass, it is advisable to use the longer route from Sibbald Creek Trail (#46).

The trail follows the edge of a cutblock past a logging road on the left to a 4-way junction in the trees marked with several large red squares. (The road straight ahead leads to Porcupine Creek and Wasootch Creek parking lot.) Turn left and follow the road into the valley confines where it gradually narrows to trail width. At the mouth of a wide side creek spewing stones, it crosses to the right-hand bank of the main creek and begins climbing through mossy spruce forest. A steep, potentially dangerous avalanche slope is crossed 5 minutes before the pass is reached.

Barely rising above the trees, the pass offers only marginally interesting views; it pays to wander up the ridges on either side a bit. To reach the northern terminus of the trail at Sibbald Creek Trail (SR 968), walk about 100 m up the stony ridge to the south until a small cairn alerts you to the start of the trail down the forested east slope.

En route to Baldy Pass from the south — Neil Daffern. ➤

51 PORCUPINE CREEK — Maps 5 & 19

Day hike
1.5 km to forks
6.5 km to canyon
Height gain 421 m to canyon
Maximum elevation 1829 canyon
Topo map 82 J/14 Spray Lakes Reservoir

Access: Kananaskis Trail (Hwy. 40). Park at Porcupine Creek bridge 11.3 km south of the Kananaskis Country boundary. The valley is also accessible from Wasootch Creek or Baldy Pass parking lots (see trails #53 and #50).

Because of easy terrain near the highway and a beckoning trail Porcupine Creek is a popular valley with hikers wanting to get off the beaten track. There are no trails beyond the forks where the going gets rough.

A gravel road on the east bank of the stream ends in about 400 m at a T-junction with the Wasootch Creek to Baldy Pass trail (# 53). A faint trail takes over for the short distance to the forks where you have a choice of routes.

The south fork is the longest and least interesting branch of Porcupine Creek. Gravel banks carpeted in yellow avens typify the dry valleys of the eastern slopes. At runoff, numerous creek crossings are forced on the hiker by alternating rock walls dipping into the stream. The east fork is distinguished by a magnificent canyon located in the first major fork to the left. Perpendicular rock walls topped by wafer-thin ridges winging upwards to unseen summits rise above spongy banks of bright green moss and bubbling springs.

East fork of Porcupine Creek.

Wasootch Creek. Wasootch slabs to left, Wasootch Tower to right.

52 WASOOTCH CREEK — Maps 5 & 19

Day hike, easy ski
7.3 km to forks
Height gain 365 m
Topo map 82 J/14 Spray Lakes Reservoir

Access: Kananaskis Trail (Hwy. 40). 11.9 km south of Kananaskis Country boundary, turn east into the Wasootch Creek parking lot.

The word Wasootch, derived from the Stoney Indian word "wazi" meaning one, denotes "uniqueness, solitariness" and is thought to be connected with Wasootch Tower which is a valley landmark. The valley has a long association with native people; during clearing for the present highway, archeologists salvaged over 5,000 artifacts dating back to 4,500 B.C.

It is not a good early season ski trip. If you wish to preserve the bases of your skis wait until the boulders in the creek bed are covered up by several snowfalls.

The valley trail leads to Wasootch Slabs, a popular practice cliff with climbers. The Canadian army conducted mountain warfare training on these cliff during the 1950's, and it is they who painted the large white letters at the bottom of various slabs for identification purposes. The rock outlier on the opposite side of the valley is Wasootch Tower, a sacred place if the origin of the name Wasootch is to be believed.

Although there is no trail beyond this point, walking is very easy along the flat wide gravel bed. Water is intermittent, often disappearing underground for long stretches at a time. At the forks the scenery changes; the valley narrows and the trees close in. Stream hopping becomes the norm if you are going all the way to the head of the valley.

53 WASOOTCH CREEK TO BALDY PASS TRAIL — Map 5

Half-day hike, easy ski
Distance 3 km
Topo map 82 J/14 Spray Lakes Reservoir

Access: Kananaskis Trail (Hwy. 40). 11.9 km south of the Kananaskis Country boundary, turn east into Wasootch Creek parking lot. The trail starts by the sign in the picnic area.

This is a connecting trail joining Wasootch Creek parking lot to Baldy Pass trail (#50) via Porcupine Creek. Hikers bound for waterless Baldy Pass can pick up water from either Porcupine Creek or from three side creeks which cross the logging road a kilometre before the Baldy Pass trail junction.

After rounding the end of Wasootch Ridge, the trail joins an old right-of-way which climbs over a timbered side hill into Porcupine Creek. Branch right on alluvial flats and cross the log bridge over Porcupine Creek to a logging road on the far bank. Turn right at the next three junctions with overgrown roads. Shortly after the last one, you reach the Baldy Pass trail at a 4-way junction well-marked with red squares and arrows. Turn right for Baldy Pass. (The road straight ahead leads to Baldy Pass parking lot on Hwy. 40.)

54 WASOOTCH RIDGE — Map 5 & 19

Day hike
7 km to summit
Height gain 945 m
Maximum elevation 2323 m
Topo map 82 J/14 Spray Lakes Reservoir

Access: Kananaskis Trail (Hwy. 40) 11.9 km south of Kananaskis Country boundary, turn east into Wasootch Creek parking lot.

The long ridge dividing Wasootch and Porcupine Creeks is for experienced hikers only. It is more difficult than Mount Allan, but easier than the ridge between Aster and Three Isle Lakes; that is, if you follow the ridge in its entirety. Most people don't, being content to make their objective either the big cairn or the first grassy summit before the scrambling begins. Once you are on the ridge, there is no easy way off; you must either complete the ridge or return by the same route. There is no designated trail.

From the parking lot there are several rough paths climbing the steep hillside; all more or less converge on the ridge above Wasootch Slabs. Remnants of a trail can be followed for the next kilometre up a longer, less steep step which leads to a long almost level section ending at the big cairn. After this, the ridge narrows, dipping below treeline with many ups and downs not apparent from the topo map. Finally, it shakes free of the trees and rises in a graceful curve to a grassy summit which is the end of the road for most people. The ridge beyond should only be tackled by experienced hikers who enjoy scrambling and a little exposure.

The upcoming fin of rock is best turned on the Porcupine Creek side; it requires a few feet of scrambling to get down onto the talus slope below the rib. Unless you are a purist, miss out the next minor summit as well by a traverse on the Wasootch Creek side. An easy section through trees ends at a viewpoint. Although the ridge ahead looks formidable, be assured that the route I am about to describe, albeit a convoluted one, gets you to the summit without resorting to mountaineering tactics. Start off by scrambling along the first easy bit of ridge. When it zigs left, descend to steep scree slopes on the Wasootch Creek side and traverse under the rock wall until it's possible to climb up an easy scree chute (use the right-hand side) to a deep notch invisible from the viewpoint and which is the key to the whole ascent. Now on the Porcupine Creek side, contour below the rock crest and regain the ridge above all difficulties. An easy scree slope leads to the highest summit.

If you don't want to return the same way, drop down into Wasootch Creek from the col beyond the summit. Sections of runnable scree and dirt facilitate progress down an unpleasant slope of slatey rocks and bushes. This lands you in the N.W. fork of Wasootch Creek about a kilometre away from the main branch. Walk back down Wasootch Creek to the parking lot

sootch Ridge at the big cairn. Most ridge walkers turn back at the top slightly to the right of the cairn.

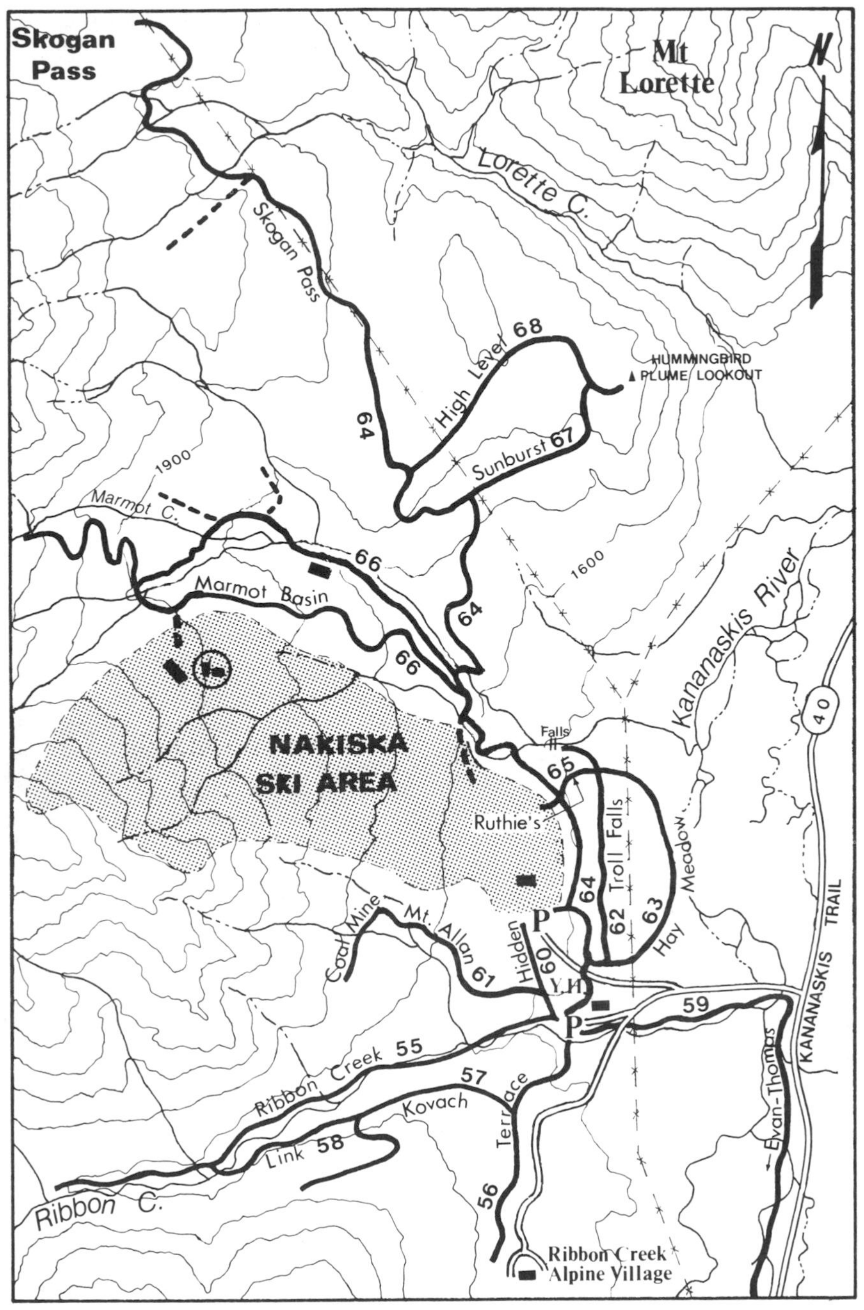
Skogan Pass
Mt Lorette
Lorette C.
Skogan Pass
High Level 68
HUMMINGBIRD PLUME LOOKOUT
64
Sunburst 67
1900
Marmot C.
66
Marmot Basin
1600
64
66
Kananaskis River
40
NAKISKA SKI AREA
Falls
65
Ruthie's
Troll Falls
Meadow
64
62
63
Hay
P
Coal Mine
Mt. Allan 61
Hidden 60
Y.H.
KANANASKIS TRAIL
59
P
Ribbon Creek 55
57
Kovach
Terrace
Link 58
Evan-Thomas
56
Ribbon C.
Ribbon Creek Alpine Village

RIBBON CREEK SKI TRAILS — Maps 5 & 6

41.2 km of trails
Topo map 82 J/14 Spray Lakes Reservoir

Access: Kananaskis Trail (Hwy. 40) at Ribbon Creek. Depending on the trail you wish to ski, park at the Nakiska ski resort parking lot, the Ribbon Creek parking lot, or the alpine village parking lot.

During the next two years, while construction of the Nakiska ski resort is going on, the cross-country ski trails will be in a state of flux. Some of the existing trails will disappear: Stump Meadow, the lower half of Skogan Pass, the upper half of Ruthie's, the upper half of Hidden, most of Coal Mine and all of Timber. New trails will be added; specifically, a new beginning to the Skogan Pass trail, a connector to Marmot Basin road and a new trail up Marmot Creek. The sketch map shows the area as it will look after construction is finished. Inevitably, there will be some minor changes in route and kilometrage, and the names I have used will no doubt be different in some cases. For latest information on the progress of new trails, drop in at Barrier Lake information centre.

55 RIBBON CREEK

Easy
3.5 km to the forks

This is a very popular trail with beginners and families with small children who are looking for something short and easy, yet interesting.

As it follows the windings of the summer route through the gorge, the trail gains height almost imperceptably; it is only on the return run — one long glide — that the 180 m height gain from the parking lot to the confluence of Ribbon Creek with its north fork becomes apparent. Because of possible avalanche danger, the trail beyond the forks is not recommended. NOTE: in mid winter, this sunless valley can be very cold.

56 TERRACE

Easy
Distance 1.5 km

Terrace is a connecting trail between Ribbon Creek parking lot and the alpine village. Until the village is built, the trail is closed beyond Kovach trail junction. The hill between the bench top and Ribbon Creek may be a little hairy for absolute beginners.

57 KOVACH

Difficult
Distance 1.6 km

The trail is named after the old mining settlement which once stood on the bank of Ribbon Creek in the vicinity of the parking lot. It starts off easily enough from Terrace trail. The difficult section occurs after the junction with Link trail and consists of steep hills with right-angled bends leading to a very fine viewpoint at road's end.

58 LINK

Difficult
Distance 0.8 km

As the name implies, this trail links Terrace and Kovach trails with Ribbon Creek trail near the forks. If you want to take advantage of the downhill, ski the trail from the Kovach trail end — the fast run down through mature spruce forest to the bridge over Ribbon Creek is an exercise in agility. The short stretch up the bank to Ribbon Creek trail is steep and can be awkward if icy, definitely a difficult section if skied in reverse direction.

59 EVAN-THOMAS

Easy
Distance 5 km

Evan-Thomas is a uniformly flat trail using, in part, the bike path which connects with the ski trails at Kananaskis Country Golf Course. Be prepared to take your skis off and walk across both the alpine village access road and the bridge over the Kananaskis River.

60 HIDDEN

Intermediate
Distance 1.2 km

This trail connects Ribbon Creek parking lot with Nakiska ski resort parking lot.

61 MOUNT ALLAN TO COAL MINE

Intermediate
Distance 2.5 km

This steep winding trail follows the summer hiking trail and the mine access road to Mine Scar. Watch for bighorn sheep feeding in the meadow. A fast fun descent!

62 TROLL FALLS

Intermediate
Distance 1.8 km

Troll Falls trail was the first trail cut specifically for skiers at Ribbon Creek. Built by Don Gardner in 1972 at the request of the Hostel Association, it began life as a narrow winding trail very different in character to the present bulldozed swath cut by the park's trail crew in 1982 and in 1985. Its rolling terrain makes it a little harder to ski than Hay Meadow trail with which it is often combined. At the 4-way junction with Ruthie's and Hay Meadow trails a spur trail leads to frozen Troll Falls which should on no account be missed.

63 HAY MEADOW

Easy
Distance 1.2 km

Used by logging ponies at the turn of the century as pasture, the flat meadows and aspen groves of Hay Meadow trail are ideal for the novice skier. If you want to avoid the intermediate access via Troll Falls trail, I suggest that you either head north across Nakiska Ski resort access road from the hostel, or use the N-S powerline right-of-way slightly to the east.

Troll Falls.

Marmot Basin Loop in Marmot Creek; the easy section.

64 SKOGAN PASS

Intermediate
10.3 km to the pass

The longest trail in the system (20.6 km return with a 625 m height gain) requires an early start if you are to reach the pass. The lower third skirts the base of Nakiska Ski resort and has some steep hills that upgrade to difficult in icy conditions. After crossing Marmot Creek, the route follows the powerline access road through forest and cutblocks, and is obvious until you arrive at a junction with the Marmot Cabin meteorological station access road. A sign is badly needed at this point to guide you onto the right-hand trail which **descends** to the northern boundary of the Marmot Basin project before making the final climb to the pass at the powerline right-of-way. If you are going through to Dead Man Flat, see Skogan Pass #16.

65 RUTHIE'S

Intermediate
Distance 0.3 km

The top half of the trail will be expropriated by the ski area. The steep lower half connects the new Skogan Pass trail to Troll Falls trail at the 4-way junction.

66 MARMOT BASIN LOOP

Difficult
Distance 7.5 km

This scenic trail is for proficient skiers who can handle both a long uphill trek into the larch zone and a continuous steep descent with some tight corners. Snow conditions are usually excellent. Rather than return to the parking lot via Skogan Pass trail, you have the option of transferring to the downhill slopes. Here's a chance for experienced skiers to show off their prowess at the end of the day.

Important At the time of publication, the Marmot Basin road, which is the west leg of the loop, is closed to skiers and is likely to remain so until all construction on the upper part of the mountain is finished. An on-hill restaurant, due to be built within half a kilometre of the loop's highest point, is bound to prove popular with cross-country skiers.

67 SUNBURST

Difficult
Distance 1.1 km

Although the most direct route to Hummingbird Plume lookout, only a masochist will get enjoyment out of the constant herringboning and side-stepping. Use High Level trail for the ascent and reserve this trail for a fast fun descent.

68 HIGH LEVEL

Intermediate
Distance 2.9 km

High Level offers by far the easiest route to the Hummingbird Plume lookout. After crossing the powerline, the trail climbs through spruce forest to what is probably the high point on the whole trail. A totally unexpected descent brings you to the junction with Sunburst trail. Keep left here and wind gradually upwards again to the top of Hummingbird Plume Hill. "Lookout" is a rather grandiose name for a run-down shack which doesn't appear to be worth a second glance. But take a closer look inside; on the walls are inscribed the names of German prisoners of war who worked in the area salvaging timber burned in the 1936 fire. At that time there really was a view from the lookout. Now the pines have grown too high and you have to walk right to the edge of a 500 m cliff before you can get that same view of the Kananaskis valley.

Skogan Pass trail near Nakiska ski resort.

69 TROLL FALLS — Map 6

Half day hike
Distance 2.1 km
Topo map 82 J/14 Spray Lakes Reservoir

Access: Kananaskis Trail (Hwy. 40) at Ribbon Creek parking lot.

The trail starts from the north side of the parking lot and in 0.5 km crosses the ski resort access road to a T-junction. Go right, then, at the bottom of the hill, turn left onto the wide rolling track built to road width, a far cry from the old narrow, twisting trail through the aspens which many of us remember with pleasure. After the next 4-way junction with Ruthie's and Hay Meadow ski trails, the trail reverts to original width for the final 0.3 km alongside Marmot Creek. Troll Falls leaps over the edge of hard bedrock into a small gloomy recess where it's hard to escape spray and branches and get an unobstructed photograph at the same time.

70 MARMOT BASIN — Map 6

Day hike
Distance 7.5 km
Height gain 850 m
Maximum elevation 2320 m
Topo map 82 J/14 Spray Lakes Reservoir

Access: Kananaskis Trail (Hwy. 40) at either Ribbon Creek parking lot or Nakiska ski resort parking lot.

The roads and trails through the Marmot Basin Project area offer quick access to timberline meadows below Mounts Allan and Collembola. You can, if you want, climb both these peaks from Marmot Basin; there are no trails but the terrain is easy enough. Conversely, Marmot Basin offers refuge to hikers caught in bad weather on the ridges.

Get onto Skogan Pass trail (#16) and follow it for 2.5 km or 1.5 km (depending on your starting point) to gravelled Marmot Basin access road. In another 0.1 km, at a road junction, you have a choice of routes, but the usual route continues along Marmot Basin road which turns left uphill. It's a long steep climb into the spruce zone.

Disregard Mine Scar exploration road to left near the junction and various minor roads to left and right. When the road forks close to Nakiska ski resort's on-hill restaurant, turn right onto the older road which dips to Twin Creeks and ends in a clearing. Carry on along a trail starting from the top right-hand corner of the clearing. It zigzags briefly into Marmot Basin — jumping off point for a smaller trail which can be followed up valley past an aluminum hut and an assortment of meteorological instruments to meadows below the Collembola/Allan col — then swings away and zigzags some more up a ridge to timberline larches. From a cluster of meteorological instruments which can be spotted from the ridge tops — shiny beacons signifying the end of the trail — you're just an easy traverse away from the S.E. ridge of Mount Allan.

Passageway between the pinnacles.

71 MOUNT ALLAN CENTENNIAL TRAIL FROM RIBBON CREEK — Map 6

Long-day hike
11 km to summit
19 km to Trans-Canada Highway
Height gain 1400 m
Maximum elevation 2819 m
Topo map 82 J/14 Spray Lakes Reservoir

Access: Kananaskis Trail (Hwy. 40) at Ribbon Creek parking lot.

It was 1966. The next year was Canada's centennial and in recognition of this fact the Rocky Mountain Ramblers, spearheaded by Wally Drew, decided to build a trail up the long S.E. ridge of Mount Allan to the summit and down the equally long north ridge to Dead Man Flat on the Trans-Canada Highway. It would be the highest trail ever built in the Canadian Rockies. The work took three summer seasons to complete and culminated in a champagne ceremony at the summit where a large wooden sign was erected. It didn't stand there for long; within three months the picas had chewed away the supporting poles and the sign had fallen. In 1983, a more substantial bronze plaque was placed half-way along the ridge at the conglomerate rock pinnacles known as The Rock Garden. Kananaskis Country has now taken over the maintenance of the trail, repainting orange markers on trees and paint splodges on rocks, and erecting signs at questionable junctions low down in the forest.

View form near summit of Mt. Allan looking back along the S.E. ridge to Olympic Summit at top left.

A short way up Hidden ski trail, turn left onto the Mount Allan Centennial Trail. Keep left at all major intersections until you arrive on the lowest of 3 exploration roads leading to Mine Scar where you should turn right. Within a few metres, turn left again onto a trail which shortcuts through intervening forest to the middle and upper roads; the intricacies of the route are well signed. Now walk left along the upper road for 0.4 km and turn up the second road to your right — identifiable by an orange arrow — which leads to the top of the Mine Scar. Shortly after intersecting a grassed road, watch for where the Centennial Trail turns uphill. Thirty minutes walking should see you at this final junction.

A short uphill climb through aspens brings you to the open slopes of the mountain. The sight of the trail crawling upwards, climbing 610 m in less than 2 km is discouraging, but the grassy rib it follows has its compensations in the marvellous views which unfold, and in the summer's succession of flowers ending in late August with a blue color scheme of asters and long-stemmed harebells. Take a breather on the shoulder, then zigzag some more up a shale slope to the apex of three grassy ribs — the start of the S.E. ridge proper.

The upcoming rock step looks imposing but is easily turned on the north side by a series of broad ledges and a gully which calls for hands in a few places. Having expended much energy in reaching the grassy hogsback pretentiously called Olympic Summit, it is disconcerting to discover that the main summit looks as far away as ever. But persevere; the angle has eased off and the most scenic part of the route is yet to come. This is where the trail winds through The Rock Garden, itself only a prelude to a more spectacular passage between the rocky ridge crest and a row of 25 metre high conglomerate pinnacles. Some interesting scrambling following paint splodges brings you to a narrowing of the ridge where you can either go over the tops or keep to the trail on the south slope. The final rise is best taken direct; a solid stone staircase is preferable anytime to the loose yellow scree of the south face which is where some people go.

72 MINE SCAR — Map 6

Half-day hike
Distance 3 km
Height gain 259 m
Maximum elevation 1737 m
Topo map 82 J/14 Spray Lakes Reservoir

Access: Kananaskis Trail (Hwy. 40) at Ribbon Creek parking lot. Via Mount Allan Centennial Trail (#71).

Mine Scar can be reached by following any of the 3 mine roads crossed by the Centennial Trail; they all lead to different levels of the mine. Now a lush meadow and celebrated viewpoint overlooking the Kananaskis Valley, it is a near perfect example of reclamation. Nearly 40 years ago it was the site of a thriving coal mine owned and operated by the Kananaskis Exploration and Development Company, an ugly, noisy place served by a road from the village of Kovach on the north bank of Ribbon Creek. Nowadays, little remains of the village which stretched from the present-day parking lot to a point east of the N-S powerline. When you get back down to valley bottom, search the trees north of the hostel for stone steps and the foundations of a verandah. Across the river from the parking lot (site of the mine office building) are the remains of bunkhouses used by Calgary Power personnel during the clearing of the powerline right-of-way between Kananaskis Lakes and Ribbon Creek.

73 MOUNT KIDD LOOKOUT — Map 6

Day hike
Distance 3 km
Height gain 564 m
Maximum elevation 2103 m
Topo map 82 J/14 Spray Lakes Reservoir

Access: Kananaskis Trail (Hwy. 40) at Ribbon Creek Alpine Village.

A lookout suddenly appeared on the grassy north buttress of Mount Kidd in the summer of 1982. Since a lookout acts like a magnet to hikers, especially one in full view of an alpine village, construction is due to begin in the summer of 1985 on a tourist trail which will start behind the alpine village and follow a line up the N.E. ridge between north face forest and east face meadows.

In the meantime, I suggest you walk south along Terrace trail (#74) to the first side stream you come to where a faint flagged trail on the north bank can be followed upstream to the base of steep slopes. Choose from three grassy ribs. It's a steep climb whichever route you choose, and you'll be glad to reach the lookout which presents a superb panorama of surrounding mountains and valleys. If you want more exercise, walk along the grassy ridge top to the cliffs of Mount Kidd, keeping a sharp eye out as you go for the bighorn sheep which inhabit the mountain. The occasional grizzly has been spotted by the lookout, no doubt the same one reported on Terrace trail from time to time.

Mt. Kidd Lookout offers a good view of the upper Kananaskis Valley. Shadowy peak to left is Mt. Lorette.

74 TERRACE TRAIL — Map 6

Day hike
Distance 10.5 km
Topo map 82 J/14 Spray Lakes Reservoir

The Wedge.

Access: 1. Kananaskis Trail (Hwy. 40) at Ribbon Creek parking lot or Ribbon Creek Alpine Village.
Access: 2. Kananaskis Trail (Hwy. 40) at Galatea Creek parking lot. Via Galatea Creek trail (#78).

Terrace trail follows terraces of the Kananaskis River beween Ribbon Creek and Galatea Creek with access trails en route to Ribbon Creek Alpine Village and Kananaskis Country Golf Course. Except in the vicinity of the alpine village, which at the time of publication is not yet built, the trail is signed and marked with red triangles throughout.

From Ribbon Creek parking lot the portion of trail shared with skiers crosses the log bridge over Ribbon Creek and winds up the bank to a junction with Kovach ski trail. Right now, the next section of trail to the alpine village is not built, so I suggest you get onto the village access road which lies just a few metres to your left and follow it to its end where you can pick up a dirt road leading to the village site. Now find the gravelled road leading to a water storage reservoir on the hillside behind the village. Where the road bends to the right, keep straight (red marker on a tree) along an older road now completely grassed over. 1 km from the village, at the point where the road makes a right-angled bend to the left, transfer onto a narrow trail carrying on in the same direction as before. (The road winds down to the 15th hole on the west bank of the Kananaskis River and will be used mainly in winter as a route to and from the Kananaskis Country Golf Course ski trails.

Finally free of roads and junctions, the trail follows river terraces below the east face of Mount Kidd which acts like a giant reflector, throwing the sun's heat back down onto dry hillsides of pine, aspen and scrub. During spring melt, waterfalls leaping down gullies in the cliffs fill small streams crossing the trail. To your left, a chain of beaver ponds mark the western boundary of the golf course. Cross two wide stony creekbeds which are almost always dry, the second one coming 15 minutes before the trail joins Galatea Creek trail at the footbridge over Galatea Creek.

75 RIBBON CREEK — Map 6

Day hike, backpack
Intermediate ski, bike
11 km to Ribbon Falls
13 km to Ribbon Lake
Height gain 350 m Ribbon Falls
Height gain 594 m Ribbon Lake
Maximum elevation 2073 m
Topo map 82 J/14 Spray Lakes Reservoir

Access: Kananaskis Trail (Hwy. 40) at Ribbon Creek parking lot.

Ribbon Creek trail follows a spectacular valley hemmed in by the cliffs of Mounts Kidd and Bogart. At the 10 km mark, cliffbands give rise to 2 spectacular waterfalls and cause difficulty to the hiker bound for Ribbon Lake. If exposed, strenuous scrambling with a heavy pack doesn't appeal to you, use alternative trails such as Guinn's Pass trail (#77) or Buller Pass trail (#89) as access to the upper valley.

The new trail up the section of Ribbon Creek between the parking lot and the north fork is a vast improvement over the old one which at one point involved a desperate traverse high above the river. Now, 2 log bridges expedite progress. At 2.5 km, in an area of spruce forest affectionately called Toad Forest by early hostellers, watch for Link trail coming in from the left. This trail feeds in from Terrace trail near Ribbon Creek Alpine Village, a future alternative starting point.

Cross North Ribbon Creek bridge and pass within the space of 2 km the remains of 3 log cabins, legacy of the Eau Claire logging operation which operated in this valley from 1886 to the beginning of the Second World War. Shortly after the last cabin, the trail enters Dipper Canyon, a delightful section of river with cataracts and quiet deep pools which can be a little tricky for skiers. The rest of the route is a gradual climb across the runout zones of large avalanche slopes to the 20 site back- country campground located below Ribbon Falls. At times of high avalanche hazard, skiers should be prepared to make Dipper Canyon their turnaround point.

RIBBON LAKE **Warning:** The trail beyond the falls is very much more difficult, even dangerous. Hikers with heavy packs, particularly women who have less arm strength than men, will have difficulty pulling themselves up the chains. The safeguard of a correctly-used climbing rope would not be out of place.

From the campground, the trail zigzags up the steep north bank and crosses the head of a gully onto a large scree slope within sight of the upper falls. Walk across to the bottom of the headwall. With the help of a chain, climb a moderately-angled corner until level with a large ledge on the left which is your next objective. Take care traversing 3 m of intervening slab which is becoming very slick. Now walk along the ledge to a second chain and heave yourself up 5 m of difficult rock, bulging in the middle, onto easier ground above. Wend right, then left onto a long horizontal ledge protected with a third chain which acts as a handrail. This ledge traverses above the highest point of the headwall and a fall from here is likely to be fatal. Don't relax your vigilance on easier ground beyond; the rocks are very smooth and greasy and a slip from here could send you perhaps not over the edge but to the very brink, hanging on to a few bushes like the hero of a 1920 Harold Lloyd movie. Continue up minor rock steps to Ribbon Lake. On topping out, the trail winds around the north shoreline to the campground sited at the western end. Look for springs bubbling out of circular depressions in the lake bottom; the continually shifting marl has a mesmerizing effect.

Headwall below Ribbon Lake. Hiker is half-way up the second chain pitch — Tony Daffern.

76 NORTH RIBBON CREEK — Map 6

Day hike
7 km to First Lake
Height gain 732 m to Third Lake
Maximum elevation 2210 m
Topo map 82 J/14 Spray Lakes Reservoir

First waterfall.

Access: Kananaskis Trail (Hwy. 40) at Ribbon Creek parking lot.

If the trail up the north fork was upgraded, there is no doubt it would become as popular as the trail to Ribbon Falls. Fortunately, or unfortunately, depending on your point of view, the trail is still in a fairly primitive state and you must put a little effort into reaching the valley's secluded lakes and waterfalls. The route is not signed or marked in any way.

Follow Ribbon Creek trail (#75) for 3.5 km. About 350 m before it crosses the north fork bridge, a pile of stones and tree roots on the right marks the entrance to the north fork trail — a grassed-over road at this point. The road quickly narrows into a rough trail which at times traverses 30 m above the stream. Care is needed at points where it is slipping down the shale banks. After this rough preliminary section, the trail settles down for a long, easy stretch along the river bank with occasional forays through head-high willow brush. Join a small remnant of logging road which disappears just as mysteriously as it appeared about 0.2 km before you reach the mouth of a canyon. Start climbing up the steep north bank. A little way up, a spur trail to left leads to First Waterfall — a popular lunch spot out of the wind. Back on the trail again, continue climbing to a junction with a climbers' access trail leading into the valley between Mounts Sparrowhawk and Lougheed. Go left here, traversing above the canyon and a second 30 m high waterfall — difficult to view satisfactorily without endangering yourself — to First Lake. Bogart Tower stands sentinel above the south shore. To its left, a waterfall tumbles down from Third Lake.

The trail continues around the north shore past camping spots, crosses North Ribbon Creek in a mishmash of willows (be thankful for a trail), and turns up the south bank of the creek. When the trail peters out on flat ground above the cataract, climb left- hand slopes to an intersecting sheep trail which takes you to the bench top. Note the cairn for the return journey. From here you can either follow the scree trail seen climbing the scree slope above the bench — a good route if you intend to miss out Second Lake and climb directly to Third Lake (better used on the descent perhaps), or head off into the trees where a very faint trail leads to the east shore of Second Lake. The unusual clarity of its emerald green water coupled with its magnificent setting under Mounts Sparrowhawk makes this lake one of the prettiest in Kananaskis Country.

Third Lake, hidden in a cirque behind Bogart Tower, is much more difficult to reach; contour lines on the map are deceptively wide apart and give no indication that the way is blocked by a cliff. Certainly the longest and questionably easiest route makes a wide sweep to the right up talus slopes, then cuts left across the bench top. Most people, though, use the sheep trail (continuation of the trail mentioned earlier) which traverses below the cliff (cairns), then splits and climbs up various gullies at the cliff's lowest point. The second gully from the left is easiest. Above the rock, all trails converge and as one climb a steep, vegetated slope to a hanging valley. Using worn patches of grass guide, head for a break in the rocky rib connecting Bogart Tower to Mount Bogart. Descend to its lowest point at the foot of Bogart Tower where you'll find a trail of sorts descending to Third Lake's north shore. By the time you get there, the afternoon shadow cast by high rock walls will have spread its pall over the scene, silhouetting the little spruce- lined promentory against the still-glowing cliffs of Mount Bogart.

77 GUINN'S PASS — Map 6

Backpack
Distance 3.25 km
Height gain 259 m from upper Ribbon Creek
Height gain 457 m from Galatea Creek
Maximum elevation 2423 m
Topo map 82 J/14 Spray Lakes Reservoir

Access: **This connecting trail between upper Ribbon Creek and Galatea Creek may be accessed from Buller Pass (#89), Ribbon Lake (#75) or Galatea Creek (#78) trails.**

The trail leaves Buller Pass trail at the springs in upper Ribbon Creek. It climbs into a barren valley holding a shallow pond, then, after a few zigzags to gain height, traverses easy- angled talus slopes to the pass (cairn). If you have time, wander out along the ridge to the east for a birds-eye view of Ribbon Lake.

No greater contrast between the two sides of a pass could be imagined. On the south side you wind down steeper slopes of close-cropped turf starred with blue speedwell and smelling of sheep. At timberline, the trail crosses over the beginnings of a stream, loses height rapidly down a talus slope, then returns to the stream, now closeted in a deep gully which becomes a suffocating furnace at midday when the sun strikes full on the white stones. Follow this gully all the way down to Galatea Creek, bridge the creek and join route #78 approximately 0.8 km from Lillian Lake. Backpackers tackling the pass in reverse direction should aim to put the gully behind them early in the day before the sun gets too far around.

78 GALATEA CREEK TO LILLIAN LAKE — Map 6

Day hike, backpack
Distance 6 km
Height gain 259 m
Maximum elevation 1737 m
Topo map 82 J/14 Spray Lakes Reservoir

Access: Kananaskis Trail (Hwy. 40) at Galatea Creek parking lot.

It wasn't so long ago when the hike up Galatea Creek was fraught with difficulty and uncertainty. In the early morning, low water levels in the Kananaskis River would entice hikers to cross to the trail. On returning in the late afternoon, they would sometimes find the river a raging torrent after the opening up of the sluice gates at Pocaterra Dam. Quite a few people spent the night trapped on the west bank in sight of the road and their cars.

But all that is in the past. Sturdy log bridges have replaced the greasy logs, the trail has been cleared, widened and straightened, and a suspension bridge built over the Kananaskis River. As a result, Lillian Lake is now one of the most popular destinations in Kananaskis Country. On hot summer weekends, the environs of the lake takes on an almost festive atmosphere from the mingling of campers and day visitors who are fishing, socializing, even swimming in translucent apple-green waters shallow enough to retain a little of the sun's warmth.

Descend the old road to the suspension bridge over the Kananaskis River. On the west bank, the trail crosses Galatea Creek to the junction with Terrace trail and turns left. The next 4 river crossings come in quick succession, the trail finally electing to stay on the north bank where it traverses the steep lower slopes of a wide avalanche path which automatically puts this trail out of bounds for skiers. Near the end of the open hillside, the trail crosses to the south bank, but not for long. A few metres downstream of the forks, it recrosses to the north bank and enters the densely-forested N.W. fork of Galatea Creek through a lush avenue of cow parsleys and red paintbrushes. A bridged crossing of the stream 0.5 km from the forks heralds the start of the final climb — which is rather grim for the heavily laden. 0.8 km beyond the Guinn's Pass trail turnoff in the bottom of an avalanche gully, the trail levels, recrosses to the north bank at the outlet and follows the indentations of the shoreline around to the 20 site back-country campground which is located at the lake's N.W. corner.

GALATEA LAKES The once hard-to-find trail to the upper lakes has become a lot clearer in recent years. It starts behind campsite #11 and climbs a steep scrubby slope to the left of the forest edge. At the top of the steep bit, cross a small stream to a talus slope of fragmented fossils which leads to the first lake set in a deep bowl. The second lake, lying in the shadow of a mountain known to climbers as "The Tower", can be reached by a trail around the north shore of the first lake. Note the hole in the ridge between "The Tower" and its S.E. buttress.

Hiker is descending the south side of Guinn's Pass into Galatea Creek. The 2 most prominent peaks are The Fortress (left) and Mt. Galatea (right).

Lillian Lake.

79 KANANASKIS COUNTRY GOLF COURSE SKI TRAILS — Map 6

10.7 km of easy ski trails
Topo map 82 J/14 Spray Lakes Reservoir

Access: Kananaskis Trail (Hwy. 40) at Kananaskis Country Golf Course. The trails can also be reached by ski from Ribbon Creek Alpine Village via an unofficial, intermediate trail, from Ribbon Creek parking lot via Evan-Thomas trail, and from Mount Kidd Recreational Vehicle Park and Wedge Pond day-use area via the bike path.

These are excellent trails for beginners or families with young children. When you feel like a break, visit the licenced cafeteria in the clubhouse; opening hours are from 10:30 am to 5:30 pm on weekends and holidays only. Skiers with packed lunches are also welcome. Right now, the facilities open for business just after Christmas through to the end of the ski season.

The trails are packed, trackset, and, as you might expect, very flat with the exception of the loop west of the Kananaskis River which has some mild hills at the south end allowing exceptional views of the surrounding mountains. By mid afternoon, Mount Kidd spreads a cold shadow over the fairways, signalling a return to the clubhouse for apres-ski refreshments before the journey home.

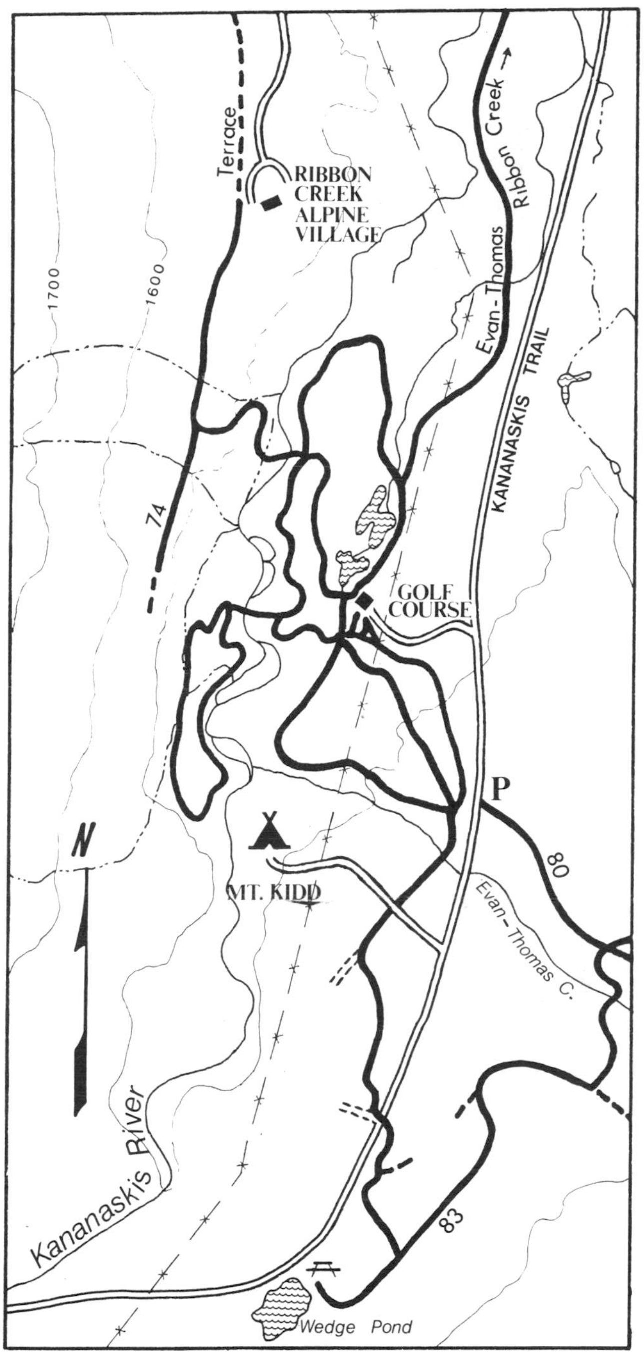
Terrace
RIBBON
CREEK
ALPINE
VILLAGE
Ribbon Creek
Evan-Thomas
KANANASKIS TRAIL
1700
1600
74
GOLF
COURSE
P
80
N
MT. KIDD
Evan-Thomas C.
Kananaskis River
83
Wedge Pond

80 EVAN-THOMAS CREEK — Map 6

Long-day hike, backpack
Intermediate ski, equestrian, bike
14 km to pass
Height gain 760 m
Maximum elevation 2180 m
Topo map 82 J/14 Spray Lakes Reservoir

Access: Kananaskis Trail (Hwy. 40) at Evan-Thomas Creek parking lot 0.4 km north of the bridge over Evan-Thomas Creek. Wedge Pond is an alternative starting point (see #83).

The exploration road up Evan-Thomas Creek can be used in a variety of ways: as a means of getting into alpine country around Evan-Thomas Pass, as a long-distance trail to the Little Elbow River or as a jumping-off point for other routes, such as Old Baldy. In winter, the road is an extremely popular ski trail which, in general, holds the snow very well. The challenge is to get to the pass and back before dark.

From the end of the parking lot walk through to the exploration road. Turn left and begin a gentle climb through lodgepole pine forest. At a 4-way junction with the trail from Wedge Pond (right), go left or straight — it doesn't matter which because both roads join a little farther on. Twice the road climbs high above the gorge before finally dropping down to valley bottom. 7 km from the trailhead, a large side stream issuing from the unnamed creek north of Fisher Peak signals the departure point for backpackers bound for upper Canyon Creek. This stream rarely freezes over and can pose a real problem for skiers.

Cross to the west bank of Evan-Thomas Creek and arrive at a road junction. (The road to the right climbs to within 1 km of the Evan-Thomas Creek and Rocky Creek watershed, then turns south and ends on open slopes.) Keep left, recross the creek and climb unnecessarily high before descending once more to creek level. Cross the runout zone of a large avalanche slope at the head of the valley. You can now see two low gaps in the watershed ridge in front of you. The road climbs towards the left-hand one and passes 50 m above the gap, just a few steps away from the talus slopes of the mountain to the east. Skiers will enjoy powder skiing in the open spruce forest around the pass.

Evan-Thomas Creek below final rise to pass. In the background is the 3008 m peak between the north and west forks of the Little Elbow River.

Looking south from Old Baldy's summit. Identifiable peaks include Mt. James Walker (left), The Fortress (centre), Mt Galatea (right) and Fortress Ridge (#86) (right centre).

81 OLD BALDY — Map 6

Day hike
6.5 km to summit
Height gain 885 m
Maximum elevation 2400 m
Topo map 82 J/14 Spray Lakes Reservoir

Access: Kananaskis Lakes Trail (Hwy. 40). Via Evan-Thomas Creek trail (#80)

Known as Old Baldy and not to be confused with Mount Baldy further north, this western outlier of Mount McDougall is well worth climbing for the superlative view. Unfortunately, there is no satisfactory route to the summit; the bare upper slopes are guarded on all sides by a young lodgepole forest clogged with deadfall, willow and alder brush. Of all the possible routes, this one is the most interesting. Since the first edition of the guide was published there is the beginnings of a trail appearing through the worst of the bush.

Follow Evan-Thomas Creek trail to the 4-way junction. You must turn left here. Arriving at a side stream, leave the exploration road and bushwack along the near bank of the creek into the V- shaped valley arising from the west slopes of Mount McDougall. Were it not for head-high willows and alders choking the creek bottom, progress would be easy, but as it is, you have to traverse first on one hillside and then on the other, a very frustrating form of progress which finally ends at a creek junction. The right-hand branch, which carries most of the water, empties into the confluence in a series of picturesque waterfalls and pools.

Follow the left-hand creek to a small unmarked lake filling a saucer-shaped depression under scree slopes. Sheltered from winds, this cirque is a good lunch spot. From the west end of the lake, climb steep grass to the ridge between Old Baldy and the summit marked on the topo map as being 8945′ high. As you stroll westward towards your objective's grassy summit, the mountains rise up one-by-one until finally a breathtaking panorama is revealed extending from Mount Joffre — the white fang in the south — to Mount Aylmer and the mountains of The Ghost.

82 WEDGE POND FISHING TRAIL — Map 6

Half-day hike
Circuit 1 km
Topo map 82 J/14 Spray Lakes Reservoir

Access: Kananaskis Trail (Hwy. 40) at Wedge Pond day-use area.

Remember Wedge Pond as it used to be? a smaller shallower lake, a gleam of prussian blue glimpsed from the highway, overhung by trees and fringed with sedges which when parted revealed jellied blobs of green frog spawn.

In 1982 the lake was drained, the silt carted away and used for topsoil for the nearby Kananaskis Country golf course. Eventually the hole, larger and deeper than before, was filled, only this time the water was an opaque shade of grey with a slight green cast to it. The stocking of the lake with rainbow trout, the building of a car park and a circular trail around the lake completed the project.

The first thing you notice is the ugly mud shore, so hardpacked and eroded it will take decades before the vegetation is re- established. Thankfully, the lake's glorious views can't be altered. If you walk the trail in a clockwise direction, the backdrop changes from Fortresses Mountain and its entourage to spectacular Mount Kidd, to Old Baldy and Mount McDougall far off to the north and finally to The Wedge and Limestone Mountain so close in that their distinctive shapes are reduced to meaningless pieces of forest and rock.

At the S.W. corner of the lake, a wide track leads in a few minutes to the old Kananaskis Valley road. If you want to extend the walk by an hour or two, turn left and follow the road past an intersection to the powerline right-of-way. Climb up the right-of-way do an intersecting trail which has arisen from a half circle remnant of old road near the highway and follow it uphill onto the open slopes of The Wedge's N.W. ridge — a remarkable viewpoint which only gets better the higher you climb.

Scenic Wedge Pond with The Fortress (left) and Fortress Ridge (left to centre) as backdrop. Galatea Creek to right.

83 WEDGE POND TO EVAN-THOMAS CREEK TRAIL — Map 6

Half-day hike
Easy ski with one intermediate hill
Equestrian, bike
Distance 3 km
Height gain 50 m
Topo map 82 J/14 Spray Lakes Reservoir

Access: **Kananaskis Trail (Hwy. 40) at Wedge Pond day-use area.**

The old road gives unaesthetic hiking. Conversely, it makes an excellent cross-country ski trail for novice skiers who just want a short ski to the end of the trail and back. The trail is groomed and there are markers throughout so you don't get lost.

At the end of the parking lot turn left and follow an old exploration road for a straight flat kilometre. Keep right at the junction with the bike path/cross-country ski trail to Mount Kidd Recreational Vehicle Park. Not long after crossing a meadow allowing unobstructed views in all directions, the road bends right and climbs gently to a T-junction. Turn left, and descend to Evan-Thomas Creek. Ford the stream. The road climb the west bank (one intermediate hill) and joins Evan-Thomas Creek trail at the 4-way junction.

84 EAU CLAIRE INTERPRETIVE TRAIL — Map 6

Half-day hike
Distance 1.5 km
Topo map 82 J/14 Spray Lakes Reservoir

Access: **Kananaskis Trail (Hwy. 40) at Eau Claire campground. The trail starts between sites 48 & 49.**

The campground is built on the site of a lumber camp established by Eau Claire and Bow River Company during the late eighteen hundreds and which was still operating, although to a reduced extent, in the years prior to the Second World War. Trees logged during the winter were hauled on horse-drawn sleds to the banks of the Kananaskis River to await the spring runoff. Incredibly, the log drive north to the Bow River and then west to Eau Claire sawmill in the centre of Calgary took two months to complete.

As you walk around this forest trail, you'll notice the inordinate amount of charred deadfall lying around — the result of the disasterous 1936 fire believed started by early tourists at Kananaskis Lakes. The fire heralded the swan-song for Eau Claire in the valley. Already hard hit by the depression, they were now reduced to salvaging burned timber for mine props, posts and rails. All the trees hereabouts have grown up since that time; the lodgepole pines first of all, and now young spruce are growing in their shade. In another 50 years the forest will once again be dominated by the spruce tree, the myriad plants and shrubs of today replaced by a soft carpet of moss and spruce needles.

85 FORTRESS LAKE — Map 6

Day hike
4 km one way
Height gain 380 m
Maximum elevation 2164 m
Topo map 82 J/14 Spray Lakes Reservoir

Access: Kananaskis Trail (Hwy. 40) at Fortress Mountain ski area. Start behind the lodge.

This is a short strenuous hike through Fortress downhill ski area to an inky-blue lake tucked under the eastern cliffs of The Fortress. The trail is unofficial and unsigned.

Walk up the maintenance road alongside the curved T-bar to the ridge top. Depending on your level of fitness, two ways present themselves in getting to the top of Farside double chairlift on Fortress Ridge opposite. You can either plunge 153 m to the chairlift's base in the valley below, then toil up 320 m of maintenance road to the ridge top or, more sensibly perhaps, follow another maintenance road which winds laboriously all the way around the head of the valley to the same place.

From the upper terminal of Farside double chairlift, head S.W. to a dip in the ridge holding a small pond. A good game trail more or less follows the stream issuing from the pond down shale and treed slopes to valley bottom. Turn left up a valley trail leading to the lake shore. A wide-angle lens — the wider the better — is necessary if you wish to get both the lake and the mountains in the picture. It's worth bringing binoculars along too; mountain goats are often seen wandering along east-face ledges on The Fortress in search of delicacies.

The view from Fortress Ridge of Fortress Lake below the rock peaks of The Fortress and "Gusty Peak".

Fortress Ridge; looking back at third top from col below fourth summit. Route bypasses rock step via a gully on the left-hand side.

86 FORTRESS RIDGE — Map 6

Day hike
4 km one way
Height gain 625 m
Maximum elevation 2362 m
Topo map 82 J/14 Spray Lakes Reservoir

Access: Kananaskis Trail (Hwy. 40) at Fortress Mountain ski area. Start behind the lodge.

The ridge extending N.E. from The Fortress ends at a superlative viewpoint overlooking the Kananaskis Valley. There is no trail, nor is one needed for the route is obvious and the going easy at first. Later, it becomes more difficult and may not be suitable for novice hikers.

Follow Fortress Lake trail (#85) to the upper terminal of Farside double chairlift. Walk N.E. along the broad grassy ridge to a summit striped with forgetmenots and creamy androsace growing in moist runnels. After the next grassy bump, for convenience called the second summit because it is separated from the first by a definite col, a rocky descent of 120 m brings you to the lowest point of the ridge which is identified by larches spilling over from the east slope. Now climb a long grass slope to the third top. Suddenly, the ridge narrows and the hitherto friendly slopes on either side steepen into cliffbands. A difficult rock step immediately above the third col is best avoided by a scramble down a grassy gully on the east side. From the col, it's a steep but straightforward climb to the fourth and final summit.

From your "island in the sky" you can see most of the Kananaskis Valley, from Mount Baldy and the golf course — spread out like a map below you — to the serrated summits of the Opal range to the south. Look up Galatea Creek (none of the lakes are visible) and pick out the trail winding up to Guinn's Pass. Of all the mountains in the Kananaskis Range, formerly called the Ship Mountains on account of the large number of summits named after ships engaged in the Battle of Jutland, none is more impressive than The Fortress which from this ridge is seen to its best advantage.

87 GOAT CREEK

Easy ski
Distance 18 km
Height loss 300 m
Topo maps 82 O/4 Banff
82 O/3 Canmore

Access: Smith-Dorrien—Spray Trail at Whiteman Gap. 9.5 km from the bridge over the Bow River at Canmore turn right into a parking lot with trail sign.

The trail between Whiteman Gap and Banff Springs Golf Course is gently downhill most of the way. Fast skiers can ski to Banff for lunch (add on extra kilometrage to the restaurant of your choice), then work it off on the return trip.

Cross the creek and get onto the Goat Creek logging road. Follow it for 1.9 km, keeping right where other trails join in until the Banff National Park boundary is reached. After another 7.2 km, the road crosses to the left (west) bank on a good bridge and winds down steeper hills to the bridge over the Spray River. A few minutes uphill work leads to an important junction with the Spray fire road. Turn right (north) for Banff. 6.5 km from Banff join the popular Spray River loop trail at the picnic area. Go either way. The fire road to the left journeys past the Hostel to Banff Springs Hotel; the usual route crosses four-mile bridge over the Spray River and enters the Golf Course near the parking lot. See also "Ski Trails in the Canadian Rockies" by Rick Kunelius.

Looking back up Goat Creek trail towards the northern outlier of Chinaman's Peak — Alf Skrastins.

Spray Lake Reservoir from the environs of West Wind Pass.

88 WEST WIND PASS — Map 4

Day hike
Distance 3 km
Height gain 381 m
Maximum elevation 2088 m
Topo map 82 J/4 Spray Lakes Reservoir

Access: Smith-Dorrien—Spray Trail 4.8 km south of the Spray District Office at Three Sisters dam.

A trail, which has come into being by the passage of many feet over the years, leads up Spurling Creek to the pass between Windtower and an unnamed mountain to the north. The Provincial Park trail crew have flagged the route, but don't intend to upgrade the trail. There is no water.

Two creeks close together cause confusion at the start. Oddly enough, the right-hand one with the copious water and the good trail on the left bank is the wrong one; it only leads to springs a little way in. Follow flagging up the west side of the dry left-hand creek, where long grasses obscure the trail's climb onto the bank top. The trail, much clearer now, stays on the bank for the lower third of the route, then moves away onto steeper hillsides in the middle and upper sections. Again, there are some puzzling spots where the trail disappears on patches of open ground, but if you keep going in the same general direction you'll always come upon the continuation of the trail in the trees. Watch for small cairns.

A steeper section precedes your arrival at the pass which is flat and open. Limestone slabs make stepping stones across turf starred with tiny *gentiara prostrata* whose deep blue color mirrors that of the summer sky overhead. On the Wind Creek side, the ground drops away as if sliced by a knife. Growing in a crevice at the very edge of the precipice is a solitary larch tree, just a young sapling, which by some fortuitous quirk of the wind is the first of its kind in this valley.

Notice the proliferation of sheep trails crossing the hillsides between the pass and Wind Ridge. One such trail leads down from the north end of the pass (cairns) through cliff bands into West Wind Creek. Climbers use it as access to the base of Windtower; hikers should leave it well alone.

Buller Creek.

89 BULLER PASS — Map 7

Long day hike, backpack
10 km to Ribbon Lake
Height gain 671 m
Maximum elevation 2484 m
Topo map 82 J/4 Spray Lakes Reservoir

Access: Smith-Dorrien—Spray Trail at Buller Mountain day-use area. The trail starts on the east side of the highway opposite the entrance to the day-use area.

Although the Buller Pass trail is used mainly by backpackers travelling to Ribbon Lake, the south pass — an exceptionally fine viewpoint — is within range of the fit day hiker. The present trail, which was built in 1981, supercedes the old route across the north pass.

Straightaway the trail bridges the outlet from Buller Pond and makes a beeline for Buller Creek. It crosses to the north bank and climbs steadily up-valley to a brief levelling off in a grove of huge engleman's spruce. Cross to the south bank and zigzag up a step in the valley floor to a riverside meadow — an ideal spot for lunch and the last reasonable place to refill the water bottles this side of the pass. A little farther upstream Buller Creek pours over a lip of hard bedrock into a blue foaming bowl rimmed with concentric rock ledges.

Shortly after the trail crosses the dry south fork you arrive at an unmarked junction with the North Buller Pass trail. Turn right up the south fork. In just half a kilometre the scenario changes dramatically from forest to grassland speckled with a few larch trees. Good campsites can be found adjacent to intermittent upwellings of the stream. At the head of the valley, the hitherto flat valley floor rises up in a steep wall of stones below the pass. The trail gains height up the left side, then makes a long traverse to the right above an area of slabs in mid wall to flatter ground at the pass which is identified by a large cairn. Zigzag down the east side boulder slope to a grassy draw. Turn right and follow the draw to the brink of a drop-off where you'll see an unofficial trail to right shortcutting along the top of the slope to Guinn's Pass trail. Part way down the slope, where Ribbon Creek bursts out of the hillside, you join Guinn's Pass trail proper at the trail sign.

Keep left, descending all the way to the bottom of the hill. The trail crosses Ribbon Creek by a narrow plank, then winds through alternating spruce forest and lush smelly meadows thick with yellow columbines, a mellow color scheme supplanted in the height of summer by the dazzling white of perfumed valerians and the crimsons and pinks of variegated paintbrushes. You arrive at the south shore of Ribbon Lake and the back-country campground simultaneously.

Buller Pass, looking towards Ribbon Lake and Mt. Kidd. ►

NORTH BULLER PASS The original north fork route, marked with blue paint splodges, can still be followed by the observant hiker. It could be integrated with South Buller Pass trail to make a loop or used as an alternative way out from Ribbon Lake.

Almost at once the trail disappears on open ground at the mouth of the south fork. It picks up in the trees on the other side and continues for another kilometre before crossing to the north bank below a box canyon with waterfall. Walk up stony ground to the base of the headwall. The reappearing trail climbs a steep ribbon of grass to the left, then cuts right across a scree slope to the pass. Follow blue-painted rocks down shelving meadows veering right into a shallow draw between a knoll on the left and the unnamed peak separating the two passes on the right. The route joins South Buller Pass trail low down near the drop-off. If you are making for South Buller Pass, it makes sense to traverse right before you get too far down the draw.

90 WATRIDGE SKI TRAILS — Map 7

15 km of intermediate and difficult trails
Topo map 82 J/14 Spray Lakes Reservoir

Access: Smith-Dorrien—Spray Trail (Hwy). 11.4 km south of Spray District Office at Three Sisters dam, or 6.2 km north of Mud Lake parking lot, turn west onto the Watridge logging road. Drive for 5.3 km to the end of the plowed road at a parking lot in a clearing. NOTE: The Watridge logging road will be plowed on a second priority basis.

In the summer and fall of 1984, the Foothills Nordic Ski Club, under the direction of Tony Daffern whose idea it was, and with help from Provincial and Federal job creation programmes, built 15 km of trails between Watridge logging road and Spray Lake Reservoir. The trails are conceived primarily as an early season training area for racers and as a late season race venue when Canmore Nordic Centre is closed. Except on race days, the trails are open to the non-racing public who also have the option of touring along dozens of untracked logging roads made accessible by the plowing of the Watridge logging road. The trails' location close to the Great Divide ensures regular snowfalls and a ski season extending from mid November to early May.

3, 5, 7.5, 10 and 15 km loops winding though mature forest and cutblocks are color-coded for easy identification – orange, blue, green, violet and red. Trails are 4 m wide, double track set and marked with hazard warnings, kilometre signs, and directional signs at junctions throughout. Three-metre wide bridges are in place across Watridge and Maruschka Creeks. Because of the trails' challenging nature – there are many technically difficult hills and bends especially on the 5 and 7.5 km loops – it is advised that tourers be strong intermediate skiers. **Please note that the trails were designed to be skied in one direction and have been signed accordingly (see sketchmap).**

The 15 km loop.

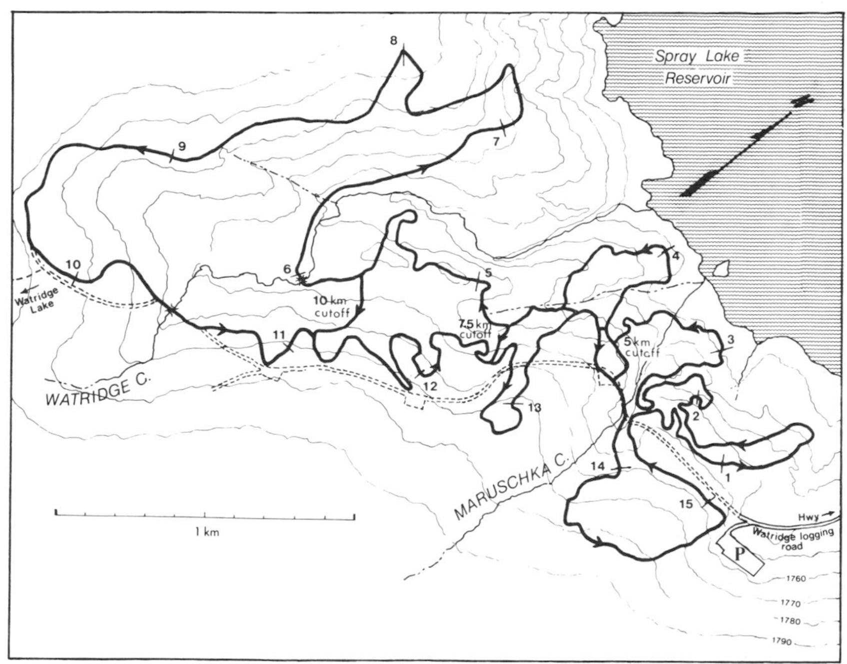

91 KARST TRAIL & WATRIDGE LAKE — Map 7

Half-day hike
3.9 km to lake
4.7 km to spring
Topo map 82 J/14 Spray Lakes Reservoir

Access: Smith-Dorrien—Spray trail. 11.4 km south of Spray District Office at Three Sisters dam, or 6.2 km north of Mud Lake parking lot, turn west onto the Watridge logging road. Keep right at all intersections until you get to the parking lot.

This large pale green body of water is renowned for the size and quantity of its cutthroat trout. Fishermen note: portage of canoes and collapsible rubber dinghies is possible along the short easy access trail. At the lake the mountain silence is broken by the continual background roar from Karst Spring, one of the largest of its type in North America. In 1983 a trail was built from the east end of the lake to the spring and there are plans to erect interpretive signs en-route.

Keep on walking along the logging road. Turn right at the next junction and descend to Watridge Creek which is now spanned by a 3 metre-wide bridge. In a few meters turn left and keep left at another junction a little farther on. When the present road also begins to swing round to the right, turn left onto a forest trail which leads to the east shore of Watridge Lake. This is the jumping off point for the muddy anglers' trail along the north shoreline which is also the route to Mount Assiniboine Provincial Park.

If you are going on to Karst Spring cross the outlet on boardwalk. As you do so it must surely strike you as odd that wheras the outlet is little more than a trickle, the Watridge Creek you crossed earlier was a wide rushing stream. The mystery is resolved at the end of the trail where you discover that the real source of Watridge Creek — unmarked on the topo map — is a spring gliding out of a gloomy recess on Shark Mountain and thundering in cascades down the mountainside. It's at its most spectacular during early summer; in fall and winter the rate of flow slackens somewhat and reveals boulders carpeted in bright green moss.

One can only speculate where the water comes from. From the valley between Mount Shark and Tent Ridge perhaps, though the snow-fed rivulets which vanish into the ground of the cirque most likely reappear lower down as the main valley stream. Or could it be that this is the resurgence from 2 deep lakes sited in the basin west of Commonwealth Pass? A lake's water supply could well explain the spring's almost constant rate of flow throughout the year. Nevertheless, it boggles the mind to think of a subterranean stream coursing through stoney labyrinths, changing valley and slope, and passing under Mount Shark for a distance of 6 km before rising again at Karst Spring.

Karst Spring at its source.

Watridge Lake looking towards Cone Mtn.

92 SPRAY VALLEY, BRYANT CREEK AND MOUNT ASSINIBOINE — Map 7

Backpack, intermediate ski
6.7 km to Bryant Creek trail
Height loss 85 m
Topo map 82 J/14 Spray Lakes Reservoir

Access: **Smith-Dorrien—Spray Trail. 11.4 km south of Spray District Office at Three Sisters dam, or 6.2 km north of Mud Lake parking lot, turn west onto Watridge logging road. Keep right at all intersections until you get to the parking lot.**

Now that the road along the west shore of Spray Reservoir is closed to traffic beyond Spray Lakes West campground, this trail has become the normal access route to Bryant Creek and Mount Assiniboine Provincial Park.

Follow #91 to the east shore of Watridge Lake (2.2 km). Hike along the north shoreline trail to the lake's west end and transfer onto a blazed trail which descends to the Spray River. Cross the footbridge to a junction. Turn left for White Man Pass, Spray Pass, Palliser Pass and Leman Lake. Turn right for Mount Assiniboine Provincial Park and the Bryant Creek trail which is joined a few metres after the bridged crossing of Bryant Creek. See also "The Canadian Rockies Trail Guide" for information on all these routes.

SKIERS NOTE: Although many people use the trail as winter access to Bryant creek and Mount Assiniboine Provincial Park, this route has several drawbacks of which the plowing of the Watridge logging road on a secondary basis is the most serious. There have also been instances of tourers getting lost in the convolutions of the racing trails. The safest route starts from Buller Mountain day-use area on the Smith-Dorrien – Spray Trail (Hwy.). A new trail leaves the N.E. corner of the parking lot and descends through 1 km of forest to Spray Lake Reservoir at the outlet with Smuts Creek (map ref. 151370) from where it is an easy ski across the lake to Bryant Creek.

93 MARUSCHKA LAKE — Map 7

Half-day, day hike
2.5 km to lake
Height loss to lake 76 m
Height gain to valley head 183 m
Maximum elevation 1996 m
Topo map 82 J/14 Spray Lakes Reservoir

Access: Smith-Dorrien—Spray Trail. 11.4 km south of the Spray District Office at Three Sisters Dam, and 6.2 km north of Mud Lake parking lot, turn west onto the Watridge Logging Road. 2 km from the junction, turn left up a side road and follow it for 1.7 km (keep right at junction in 1.3 km) to a clearing. Since the first edition of this book was published, the road beyond has been partially covered with slash and is impassible to motorized vehicles.

This exceptionally beautiful sheet of green water lies well- hidden in the valley between Tent Ridge and Mount Shark. Large cutblocks, which come uncomfortably close to ruining the setting, provide easy access which may in future years be superceded by a new trail from Watridge parking lot. In the meantime, keep walking along the logging road to its end in the second cutblock. Because of impenetrable slash on continuing roads, it's easiest to head straight for Maruschka Creek, which is within earshot, and from here pick up a good game trail on the bank which can be followed for 0.5 km upstream to the lakeshore.

If you want more exercise, the disappearing and reappearing streams of the upper valley are worth exploring. Waves of recessional moraines covered wth grass and boulders give rise to a typical knob-and-kettle topography which makes progress up valley very frustrating, since half your time is spent in descending into sinkholes. Here and there, the stream surfaces in tiny blue pools at the bottom of sinks and are called David Lake, Kirsten Tarns and Summer Lakes in order of altitude. The last two named gradually disappear as the summer progresses and the water table becomes lower.

Maruschka Lake, looking towards Mt. Smuts.

94 COMMONWEALTH CREEK — Map 7

Day hike
8 km to pass
Height gain 460 m
Maximum elevation 2330 m
Topo map 82 J/14 Spray Lakes Reservoir

Lower lake from pass. Upper lake is located on the terrace below the true boundary ridge with Banff National Park.

Access: Smith-Dorrien—Spray Trail. 11.4 km south of Spray District Office, or 6.2 km north of Mud Lake parking lot, turn west onto Watridge logging road. Park at the entrance to the first side road to the left.

Although Commonwealth Creek (formerly Smuts Creek) has no established trail, the valley is open and the going easy. Like its neighbour to the north, Burstall Creek, it is the gateway to some fine alpine country worthy of more than one day's visit.

Walk south along the logging road. At a road junction beyond Tryst Creek, keep straight on along another road rehabilitated with slash. From its end at Commonwealth Creek, bushwack upstream for 15 minutes to the open valley. En route, you'll notice a side stream coming in from the south. If you only want a half-day trip, I suggest you follow it to a forest-rimmed lake below Commonwealth Peak called Commonwealth Lake, but still referred to as Lost Lake by many people.

In the open, an excellent elk trail follows the north perimeter of swampy meadows past a succession of beaver ponds. It can be followed far up valley to flat ground below the diminutive north glacier of Mount Birdwood. Begin climbing to the pass. It's far less arduous if you start a little way back before the trail's end where the gradient is less steep. Angle left to timberline larches below talus slopes, then climb over easy grass and scree to the pass between Mount Smuts and Mount Birdwood which rises like the thin blade of a knife to your left.

Meadows, disturbed here and there by Spray River grizzlies, slope gently down to a large sunken valley occupied by two lakes and rimmed, except to the south, by a ridge only a little lower than the named summits. The higher lake, frozen for 9 month of the year, is joined by a cord of white water to the larger lower lake whose waters sink into the ground to join some vast underground drainage system. A trail can be followed beside the stream to the upper lake and from there to a pass higher than the one you crossed previously; a very fine vantage point indeed for the west face of Mount Birdwood.

95 TRYST LAKE — Map 7

Day hike
Distance 3 km
Height gain 260 m
Maximum elevation 2150 m
Topo map 82 J/14 Spray Lakes Reservoir

Access: Smith-Dorrien—Spray Trail. 11.4 km south of Spray District Office, or 6.2 km north of Mud Lake parking lot, turn west onto Watridge logging road. Park at the entrance to the first side road to the left.

A typical cirque lake lying beneath a peak shaped like a clenched fist, Tryst Lake is an excellent choice for a short hike in fall when the larches are changing colour. The trail is unofficial and unsigned.

Walk south along the logging road for 1.6 km. Fifty metres before the small stream issuing from Tryst Lake and at the edge of an extensive clearcut, search for a faint game trail in the trees to the right. Follow it as best you can to the stream in the runout zone of an avalanche slope. Pick up a muddy elk trail on the far bank and follow it up the steep draw to lakeside meadows.

96 HOGARTH LAKES — Map 7

Half-day hike, easy ski
Distance 2.5 km to third lake
Topo map 82 J/14 Spray Lakes Reservoir

Access: Smith-Dorrien—Spray Trail at Mud Lake parking lot.

Logging roads give easy access to a string of three good fishing lakes named after Scottish forest ranger James Hogarth. Unlike neighbouring lakes which are muddied by silt, the Hogarth Lakes are remarkable for their translucent green color shading to cream in the shallows.

Cross Mud Lake dam. On flat ground after the dam, French Creek, diverted from its natural course (Smith-Dorrien Creek) by means of canals and culverts, flows into Mud Lake. No picture postcard view, aptly-named Mud Lake is a receptacle for all the glacial debris carried down from the Robertson and French glaciers.

Follow the Burstall Pass trail. At the bottom of the first hill, turn right onto the unsigned Hogarth Lakes logging road. In another kilometre the road fords Burstall Creek then splinters into secondary roads to left and right. The major road wanders along the west shoreline of all three lakes, then — and this is only of interest to skiers who want to make a loop — doubles back between the lakes and Mud Lake and rejoins the logging road at the creek crossing.

Looking towards Burstall Pass from the traverse between the 2 passes. Notice the tracks of the normal winter route at bottom right of the photo.

97 BURSTALL PASS — Map 7

Day hike, intermediate ski
Distance 8 km
Height gain 472 m
Maximum elevation 2380 m
Topo map 82 J/14 Spray Lakes Reservoir
82 J/11 Kananaskis Lakes

Access: Smith-Dorrien—Spray Trail at Mud Lake parking lot.

Burstall Pass trail takes you quickly and easily into superb alpine country straddling the Great Divide. Backpackers travelling to the upper Spray Valley, departure point for the historic Palliser, Spray and Whiteman passes, may use this trail in preference to or in conjunction with route #91.

In winter, Burstall Pass is an excellent ski destination, superior even to the popular Robertson Glacier trip. If you stick to the summer route, avalanche danger is minimal. The route is signed throughout.

Cross Mud Lake dam and turn left up the hill to the intersection with French Creek logging road. Turn right and walk for 3 km to the end of the Burstall Creek logging road at the mill site. An enjoyable ski trail, its summer tedium can be relieved by frequent visits to the three Burstall Lakes which are never more than a few minutes walk away. From the clearing, a trail carries on, winding down the bank to a large dryas flat criss-crossed with braided streams. Guided by signs, cross the flat to its N.W. corner where the trail enters trees to the left of a wide avalanche slope.

Climb the timbered headwall. Although the trail has been cleared and widened, skiers must still resort to side-stepping and herringboning up this section. (Skiers note: the gully which the trail crosses at the top of the headwall is the preferred route of descent. This fun run emerges near the bottom of the aforementioned avalanche slope so should only be skied in stable snow conditions).

The trail crosses a long flat meadow below avalanche slopes, then starts climbing gently through sub-alpine meadows with scattered islands of spruce. At last timber, the trail leaves the valley and climbs onto the long bumpy ridge to the west; a complicated terrain confounded further by a deep sink hole on the west side of the pass proper. Day hikers can reach a better viewpoint by traversing around the south side of the sinkhole to a grassy shoulder, then walking due south until the peacock blues and greens of historic Leman Lake come into view. See the "Canadian Rockies Trail Guide" for a description of the route into the Spray Valley.

SOUTH BURSTALL PASS (2484 m) This slightly higher pass at map ref. 155226 (82 J/11) is easily gained from Burstall Creek; just walk up the obvious draw to the flat area of fissured pavements where you'll find a tall cairn marking the exact location of the pass. It is a viewpoint sans parallel for the glaciated north face of Mount Sir Douglas, Palliser Pass and the Royal Group. Behind your back the four dogtooth Mountains — Mount Smuts, Mount Birdwood, "Pig's Tail", and Commonwealth Peak — are lined up four abreast. For the finest view, one incorporating components from both passes, I suggest you climb the intervening scree ridge — an easy ascent from this direction. An oblique terrace connecting the 2 passes makes possible a circuit which should on no account be missed by skiers looking for new telemarking slopes to conquer.

From the Banff Park side of the sinkhole there is a grand view of Leman Lake and Spray Pass.

Robertson/Sir Douglas Col from Haig Glacier — Tony Daffern.

98 ROBERTSON GLACIER — Map 7

Day hike
Easy or intermediate ski
Distance 10 km to col
Height gain 985 m to col
Maximum elevation 2890 m at col
Topo map 82 J/14 Spray Lakes Reservoir
82 J/11 Kananaskis Lakes

Access: Smith-Dorrien—Spray Trail at Mud Lake parking lot.

In summer, it's not uncommon to see skimpily-dressed hikers striding along the trail carrying skis, poles and boots. Robertson Glacier is, after all, the most accessible glacier in this part of the Rockies and, most important, relatively free from crevasses. The majority of winter skiers end their trip at treeline (an easy ski trip), some carry on to the toe of the glacier (intermediate with potential avalanche danger) and a very few reach the Robertson/Sir Douglas col. NOTE: The area socks- in badly when chinook winds are blowing.

Follow the Burstall Pass trail (#97) to the dryas flats. Instead of crossing the flats, keep to the edge of the trees and swing south into the long thin valley between "Piggy Plus" and "Whistling Ridge". After the last trees, the valley narrows to a V-shaped trough filled with glacial rubble, an unpleasant stretch best negotiated by taking a line 30 m up on the east slope. In winter this section of the the route is vulnerable to avalanches from both sides of the valley, so be prepared to turn back if an extreme avalanche hazard warning is in effect, if it is snowing and blowing heavily or has done so in past few days, or if there has been a recent sudden rise in temperature. Once you reach the toe of the glacier all avalanche danger is past. Confined between cathedral-like walls, the glacier rises in white waves each one steeper than the last to the Robertson/Sir Douglas col. Continual down-drafts tend to crust the snow surface.

The steep slope down to the Haig Glacier, easy scree in summer, is a thoroughly nasty convex avalanche slope in winter and should be left alone by inexperienced, ill-equipped parties. French Creek (#99) is a much safer alternative on and off the Haig Icefield.

99 FRENCH CREEK — Map 7

Day hike, intermediate ski
9 km to col
Height gain 863 m
Maximum elevation 2768 m at col
Topo map 82 J/14 Spray Lakes Reservoir
82 J/11 Kananaskis Lakes

Access: Smith-Dorrien—Spray Trail at Mud Lake parking lot.

Lack of a good trail will deter all but the most ardent hiker from reaching French Glacier at the head of this wild valley. However, this doesn't seem to faze downhill and cross-country skiers who seem willing to endure almost anything in the quest for snow.

Strangely enough, the route is easier in winter when snow covers the moraines and willow brush, and nearly every weekend now sees parties of fit, strong tourers starting out for, but not always reaching, the Haig Glacier. Only skiers with mountaineering experience and avalanche know-how should attempt the French Creek-Robertson Glacier circuit. The problem lies with the convex avalanche slope between the Robertson and Haig glaciers. (see also #98)

Follow signs to Burstall Pass. At the top of the first hill beyond the dam keep straight on along the French Creek logging road. Go left at the next intersection and immediately afterwards straight, thereafter keeping left on the major road which ultimately crosses French Creek (collapsed bridge). On the east bank follow the road uphill to another river crossing above the first waterfall. Do not cross the creek. Stay on the east bank, following a strip of grass between river willows and forest where the going is easiest. The second waterfall occurs at a junction with a tributary to the east. In summer, use the steep elk trail gouged out of moss and mud to the left of the fall. Skiers must side-step up the tributary to level ground, then follow a flagged trail to right which leads back into French Creek. After another flat section by the stream you arrive at the third waterfall. Again, a flagged trail detours to the left. The last diversion occurs at the bend where the valley turns S.E., and is one which skiers should take particular note of because messing around below the avalanche slopes of "Piggy Plus" isn't too healthy. Climb diagonally up the left bank (in effect, you are cutting off the corner) onto a forested ridge with scanty patches of meadow marking the demarcation line between vegetation and moraine. From here, the easiest way onto French Glacier, summer or winter, is up the draw in the centre of the lateral moraine. From the highest point descend slightly to the base of the ice.

The French Glacier, really a little bit of the Haig Icefield spilled over into the trough between Mounts Robertson and French, is much more interesting in winter when a metre of powder snow covers the moraines and you can pretend the ice extends right down to treeline. The col is farther away than you think and has the annoying knack of appearing to stay the same distance away the higher you climb. You can measure your progress by looking behind you now and then; the scene is growing in magnificence and soon you are looking over the tops of Mount Burstall and "Piggy Plus" to Commonwealth Peak and Mount Birdwood which from this direction resembles a monstrous black beak. Just after you pass the pinnacle, keep left to avoid a deep moat under Mount Robertson. Suddenly, mountains begin to stick up above the horizon; you have arrived on the Haig Glacier.

April powder on French Glacier moraines. Mt. Robertson is the spectacular mountain in the background. ►

Chester Lake.

100 CHESTER LAKE — Map 7

Day hike, intermediate ski
Distance 5.5 km
Height gain 310 m
Maximum elevation 2220 m
Topo map 82 J/14 Spray Lakes Reservoir

Access: Smith-Dorrien—Spray Trail at Chester Lake parking lot. Start from the ski sign at the upper edge of the lot.

On hot summer weekends the meadows around the lake are crowded with tents whose occupants are either fishing or exploring the upper valleys. Lately, it has also become a popular winter trip for skiers wanting a challenging downhill run.

Logging roads still make up half of the route. Turn second left across Chester Creek then turn right, keep left, keep right, turn left, turn right, turn left, go straight; you are, in fact taking every uphill option which presents itself until you get to a 5-way junction. Go right here. Keep left up a hill and come to a junction at a right-hand bend with a minor road straight ahead which is being touted as an easier exit route for skiers out of the meadows. The summer route follows the major road around to the right and embarks on a long traverse past the former parking lot to the start of the trail on the left-hand side (sign). The trail climbs through spruce forest, a narrow twisting trail very difficult to ski well on the descent, then levels off in sheltered flower meadows preceding the larch belt at the lakeshore. At the outlet, the trail turns left and divides soon after.

UPPER CHESTER CREEK Follow the lakeshore trail past the trail to Three Lakes valley on the left. Climb through trees to a meadow at treeline then continue up a stony draw to the top of a terminal moraine. From the end of the trail a more barren scene can hardly be imagined. Brown rocks of all sizes and shapes are piled up in great heaps on the narrow valley floor. Nearer at hand, meadows as immaculate as manicured city lawns border the infant Chester Creek which sees daylight for perhaps 50 m before sinking into the ground below a permanent snow bank.

THREE LAKES VALLEY From the lakeshore trail, turn left onto a trail which climbs over an intervening ridge of larches and boulders to the valley north of Chester Creek. Walk upstream to a little emerald green tarn whose damp shores are beautified by clouds of silky white cotton grass. As you climb the grassy headwall above the tarn, watch for tufts of coarse white goat hair snagged on cinquefoil bushes and rough boulders knobbly with fossilized horn coral. On hot days you can usually spot the goats feeding on delicacies growing in wet slanting gullies shaded from the sun. Lakes two and three — shallow ponds filling rock basins — are of little interest; often the third lake is completely dried-up by September.

RUMMEL LAKE In many people's opinion this little lake, which was named in 1984 after Elizabeth Rummel, surpasses Chester Lake in both color and setting. There is no trail; usually hikers have followed logging roads in from the Smith-Dorrien — Spray trail and then struck out along Rummel Creek in the footsteps of grizzlies who seem inordinately fond of the area. A better way, with the minimum of bushwacking and thus with less chance of unexpected bear encounters, starts from Chester Lake trail a half kilometer below the lake. Head across to Three Lakes valley, cross the creek and climb about 100 m of hillside to a prominent gap (Map ref. 201304) between a low forested hill to the left and the main mass of Mount Galatea to the right. Descend the open meadows of an unnamed creek until it's possible to contour round the base of steep slopes towards the lake.

Three Lakes Valley looking west across Smith-Dorrien Valley into French Creek. Glaciated peaks are Mt. French, Mt. Robertson and Mt. Sir Douglas.

101 HEADWALL LAKES — Maps 6 & 7

Day hike
Intermediate ski to end of road
Distance 7.4 km
Height gain 472 m
Maximum elevation 2332 m
Topo map 82 J/14 Spray Lakes Reservoir

Access: Smith-Dorrien—Spray Trail at Chester Lake parking lot. Start from the ski sign at the south side of the lot.

Headwall Creek has been overshadowed by its better known neighbour to the north, Chester Creek. Yet it is perhaps the finest valley on the east side of the highway, containing within its boundaries a microcosm of all components of mountain scenery: lakes, waterfalls, meadows, talus slope and limestone pavements.

Since the Smith-Dorrien ski trails came into being, the initial route through a maze of logging roads has been considerably simplified; you simply follow the appropriate color-coded ski markers. Start off on blue loop. In 1 km you turn left up a major road signed with blue/yellow markers and arrive in 0.8 km at a junction with blue loop to left. Keep right, following yellow markers up a long, diagonal hill to a logged area on a ridge, the hub of logging roads fanning out to the north and east. Stay on the yellow color-coded road (lowest one) which eventually fords Headwall Creek and climbs a steep hill to the edge of a cutblock on the left. Leave the road here and search the edge of the cutblock for the start of what is becoming with use a very good trail through forest to the first meadow.

After the next belt of trees, particularly dense thickets of engleman's spruce are best avoided by a traverse along the base of talus slopes. Scramble up a short headwall onto a karst pavement and arrive at the first lake. The second lake, much more dramatically situated in a rock-girt bowl, is easily gained by walking up the grassy headwall to the left of the tumbling stream.

Lower Headwall Lake.

Cirque lake in the N.E. fork of James Walker Creek. Mt. Murray in the background.

102 JAMES WALKER CREEK — Maps 6 & 7

Day hike
Intermediate ski to end of road
Distance 5 km
Height gain 274 m
Maximum elevation 2118 m
Topo map 82 J/14 Spray Lakes Reservoir
82 J/11 Kananaskis Lakes

Access: Smith-Dorrien—Spray Trail at the Sawmill day-use area.

A good logging road leads to within 1.5 km of a small lake. Once there, you're well placed for further exploration of twin upper valleys divided by the ridge of Mount James Walker.

From the parking lot, walk in an easterly direction to a gated trail which is the main James Walker Creek logging road. A little way in, the road splits temporarily at the big rock; go either way. Keep right at a major road junction above a long steep hill. Still following the James Walker Creek logging road, walk past overgrown roads peeling off to left and right to end at the bottom of an avalanche slope. A game trail carries on, rather vague where it crosses the avalanche slope, but becoming clear once it enters forest. It emerges below bumpy meadows identifiable as an old rock fall, then follows the right-hand edge of the forest all the way to the lakeshore. Shallow waters deepen to shades of blue below north shore talus slopes.

UPPER VALLEYS Walk round to the inlet stream. A game trail follows the east bank as far as a split in the creek below an avalanche slope where it disappears in willow brush. Pick your own line up the forested headwall; a route west of the major stream is probably easiest. The creek divides half-way up the slope, each stream falling in cascades from its respective valley. The left-hand finger valley is the largest, a stony wasteland pock-marked with stagnant pools. Conversely, the right-hand branch holds an interesting tarn whose effluent feeds meadows extending to the very rim of the headwall.

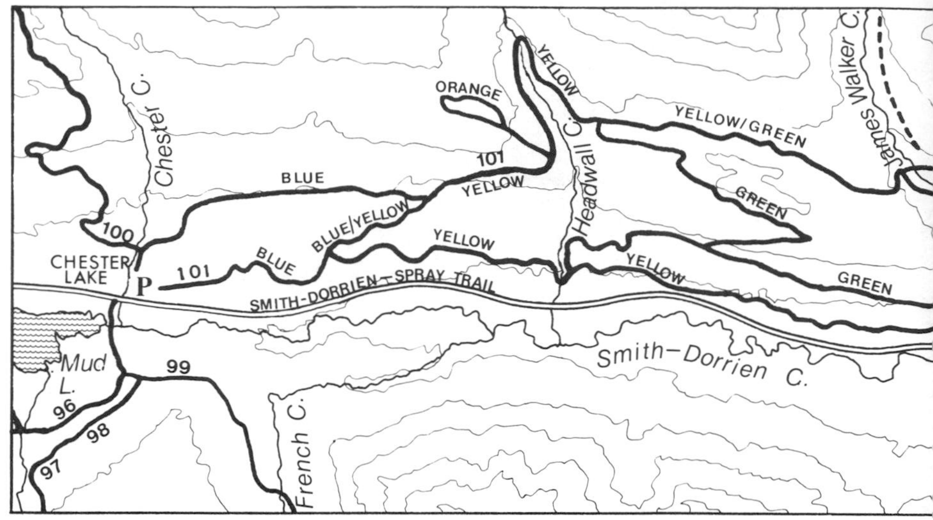

103 SMITH-DORRIEN SKI TRAILS — Map 7

Intermediate, difficult ski
32 km of trails
Topo map 82 J/14 Spray Lake Reservoir

Access: **1. Smith-Dorrien—Spray trail at Sawmill day-use area.**
Access: **2. Smith-Dorrien—Spray Trail at Chester Lake parking lot.**

In the summer of 1984, work began on clearing more logging roads in the Smith-Dorrien valley. The reasons where two-fold; first, to provide skiers with suitable touring terrain — the 5 km and 10 km loops cleared the previous year by members of the Foothills Nordic Ski Club in order to host a race were anything but easy — and second, to connect the network of logging roads at James Walker Creek with those at Headwall Creek and Chester Creek. Over the next 5 years, there are plans to extend the trail system to the Rummel Creek logging roads, the Hogarth Lakes logging roads and the Watridge Ski trails.

As you can see from the sketchmap, there are 2 starting points and numerous ways in which the trails can be combined to make loops. Suggested loops and connecting trails are color-coded with round markers on trees: Yellow (12.5 km), Green (8.9 km), Red (6.4 km), Blue (3.9 km) and Orange (1.5 km). The largest possible loop around the outside of the system measures 18.5 km. In addition to the packed trails, there are dozens of other roads much to numerous and complicated to be shown on the sketchmap which the tourer can explore.

With the possible exception of Blue loop, and short lengths of Red and Yellow loops near Sawmill day-use area, the Smith-Dorrien ski trails are not really suitable for beginner skiers; all loops have intermediate and occasionally difficult sections somewhere along their lengths. Trail brochures (available at the trailheads) give you some idea of the degree of difficulty to be expected. Running through open spruce forest and cutblocks in the lower reaches of James Walker, Headwall and Chester Creeks, the trails offer superb views of the Spray Mountains on the opposite side of the valley. A snowfall exceeding that of Elk Pass ensures a six-month ski season beginning in early November.

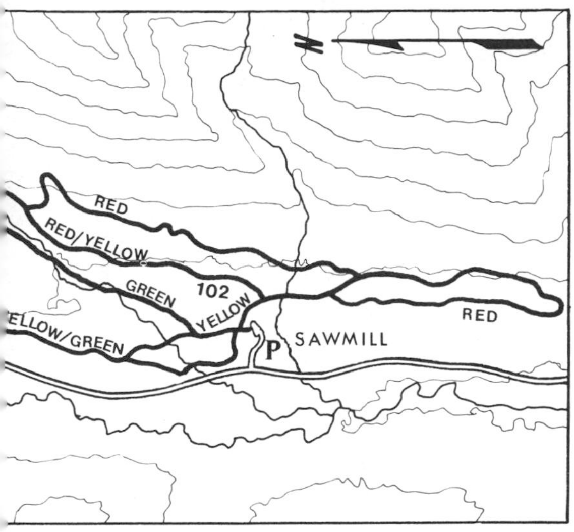

Blue-yellow Loop looking towards Mt. Birdwood and Commonwealth Peak.

Warspite Lake.

104 BLACK PRINCE CIRQUE INTERPRETIVE TRAIL — Map 8

Half-day hike
Intermediate ski
Circuit 4.3 km
Height gain 130 m
Topo map 82 J/11 Kananaskis Lakes

Access: Smith-Dorrien—Spray Trail at Black Prince day- use area. The trail starts behind the garbage disposal unit.

The trail crosses the logging road, heads upstream to a bridge over Smith-Dorrien Creek, then doubles back to the logging road now on the west bank. Follow the road up the hill to the cutblock. When the road starts to bend to the left, turn right onto a new trail which descends into Warspite Creek. At the bottom of the hill the trail loops; go either way.

In the mature forest of the valley floor, the ground is carpeted with the delicate green fronds of the grouse-berry, also known as the red huckle berry. The red berries are tart but edible. Masses of gooseberry and blackcurrent bushes grow on more open ground, as does the bracted honeysuckle whose inky- black berries, instantly distinguishable from other berries by gaudy crimson bracts, may look luscious but taste vile. The Indians claimed that if you ate enough they would send you crazy.

Warspite Lake, at trail's end is contained within a jumble of boulders sprouting the occasional spruce tree. There is no visible outlet, but if you listen carefully, you can hear escaping water gurgling deep down beneath the trail on the eastern shore. Shallow waters, less than half a metre deep, mirror boulder islands flecked with white lichen. In summer, strong sunlight activates algae covering the rocks of the lakėbed and turns the lake a brilliant emerald-green color.

105 GYPSUM MINE TRAIL — Map 8

Day hike, intermediate ski
Distance 7.5 km
Height gain 470 m
Maximum elevation 2130 m
Topo map 82 J/11 Kananaskis Lakes

Access: **Smith-Dorrien—Spray Trail at Peninsula day-use area. In winter, park in Canyon Parking lot and ski across the lake to the intersection of the mine road with Smith-Dorrien Creek.**

The old road winding up the north ridge of Mount Invincible leads to an abandoned gypsum mine which was operated by the Alberta Gypsum Company for a few short years in the late 1960's. The road is excellent for skiing; however, skiers should be aware that for a stretch of about a kilometre it crosses potential avalanche slopes and should be left alone whenever avalanche hazard is high or extreme.

The road, gated and unsigned, starts from the far end of the parking lot. Walk downhill past side roads to Smith-Dorrien Creek. Now that the bridge has been removed, further progress is determined solely by the height and turbulence of Smith-Dorrien Creek; don't count on hiking this trail during early summer. Turn right at the next junction. (The overgrown trail to the left was the first attempt at getting a road to the gypsum deposit. See #155 for more recent usage.)

The road traverses steep avalanche slopes — don't linger — then switchbacks up the north ridge through open forest allowing unrestricted views of the Smith-Dorrien valley. There are two obvious shortcuts, but only the first one is worth taking. Shortly after the right-hand bend where you can look along the valley to your objective, the road levels and runs in a straight line along the ridge top to the mine.

106 PENINSULA TRAILS —Maps 8 & 9

Very short trails
Topo map 82 J/11 Kananaskis Lakes

Access: **Smith-Dorrien—Spray Trail at Peninsula day-use area. The gravelled trail starts from the hiking sign.**

The trails of the peninsula lead to good fishing spots and incomparable vistas down the length of Lower Kananaskis Lake. The main trail keeps an almost straight line to land's end. Four little loops branch off from the trail, each following a bulge of the eastern shoreline through dense thickets of alder, willow, buffalo berry, honeysuckle and raspberry bushes.

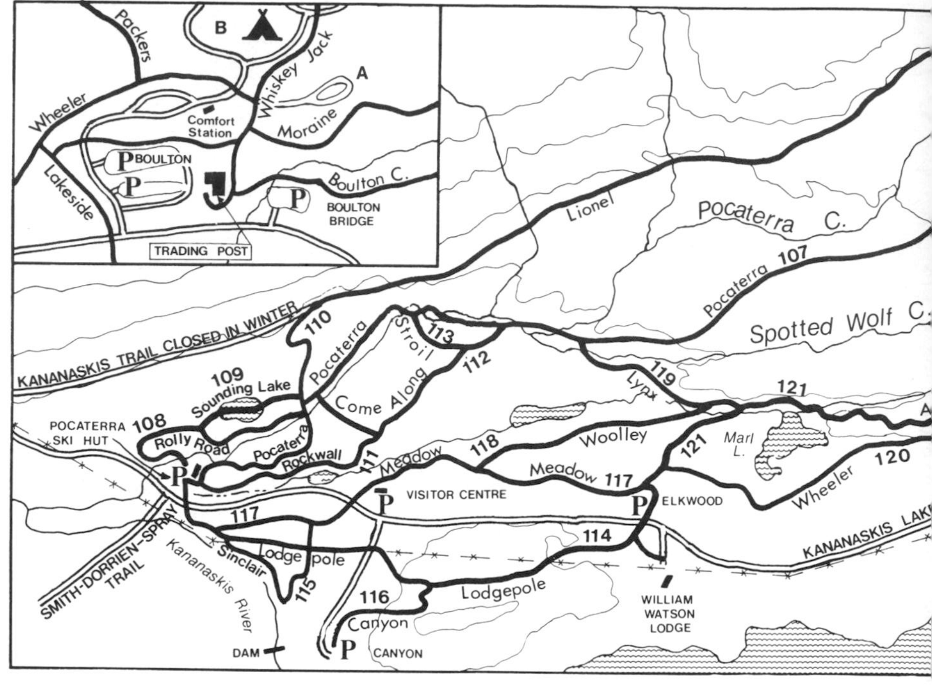

KANANASKIS PROVINCIAL PARK SKI TRAILS — Map 9

88 km of trails
Topo map 82 J/11 Kananaskis Lakes

Access: Kananaskis Lakes Trail (Hwy.). There are 9 access points from the park road: Pocaterra Ski Hut, Kananaskis Visitor Centre, Canyon, Elkwood, William Watson Lodge, Boulton, Boulton Bridge, Elk Pass and Upper Lake.

In 1980, under Don Gardner's direction, a network of cross- country ski trails was laid out using existing fire roads, powerline access roads and old packers' trails. Today, with the cutting of completely new trails, the total trail length has been expanded to nearly 90 km. Because the area lies on the Great Divide good snow is guaranteed. This fact, coupled with easy access and many facilities has made the Kananaskis Provincial Park the ultimate playground in the Canadian Rockies for recreational skiers who want groomed and trackset trails. Trail maps are available from information centres and parking lot trailheads. NOTE: Provincial Park regulations require dogs to be leashed, not only for the safety of skiers but for the safety of the dogs themselves; lost dogs make meals for hungry coyotes.

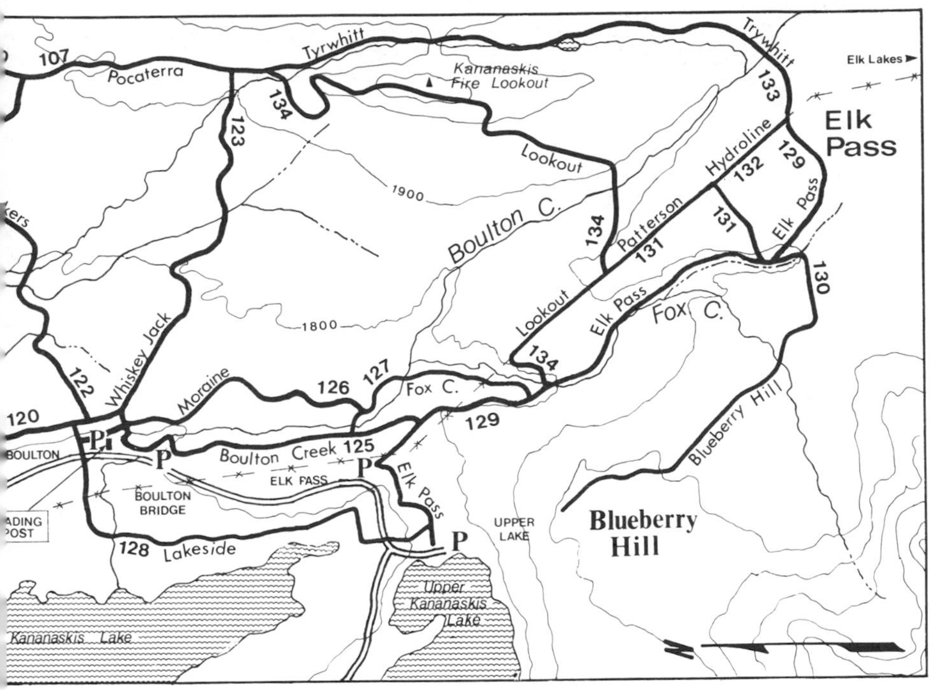

Four of the access points offer something more than parking lots and toilets like ice boxes. Pocaterra Ski Hut, a log cabin overlooking the "meadows" — actually beaver ponds in summer — has an information desk, a large eating and meeting area and indoor toilets. It's open seven days a week from 9:00 a.m. to 5:00 p.m. during winter months only. A public telephone is located behind the building near the parking lot access road.

A little farther along the park road, Kananaskis Visitor Centre is open seven days a week all year round. An information desk, a voluntary self-registration book for skiers leaving on multi-day trips, a public telephone and fully-equipped washrooms are the least of its amenities. On cold days, comfortable couches in the lounge and a blazing fire are much appreciated during lunch breaks. Or, you can tour the interpretive and photographic exhibits and watch a slide show in the theatre.

The Boulton Trading Post at Boulton parking lot is the only grocery store and restaurant in the park. During winter months it opens on weekends and holidays between the hours of 9:00 am and 6:00 pm. Nearby, loop "B" of Boulton campground remains open during winter months for overnight camping.

William Watson Lodge is available for handicapped skiers and senior citizens at very reasonable rates. Four duplexes sleep a total of 40 persons and are equipped with baths, showers and kitchens. The main lodge has a lounge with fireplace, library and laundry room. For more information and reservations — accepted up to 4 months in advance — phone (403) 591-7227 or write to Kananaskis Provincial Park, General Delivery, Seebe, Alberta, T0L 1X0.

Pocaterra Ski Hut.

107 POCATERRA

Easy
Distance 10 km

This long, popular trail which stretches from Pocaterra Ski Hut to Whiskey Jack trail connects with nine other trails, six of which branch off within the first 3.4 km as the trail winds about Pocaterra Creek through meadows and willowy muskegs. Beyond the junction with Lynx trail in the last meadow, the trail enters mature forest, at the same time beginning a steady climb with a few fast hills to Kananaskis Lookout fire road. This relatively level stretch along the fire road at the base of the mountains is nearly always cold and windy.

108 ROLLY ROAD

Intermediate
Distance 1.5 km

The trail starts behind the signboard at Pocaterra parking lot. Straightway, it crosses Pocaterra Creek and joins the Kananakis walk-in group campground access road at the bottom of an intermediate hill. From here on, the rolling nature of the terrain exemplifies the trail's name.

109 SOUNDING LAKE

Easy
Distance 0.7 km

Half-way along Rolly Road trail, skiers have the option of an easier alternative. The Sounding Lake trail crosses a small frozen lake and finishes with a short downhill run to the 4-way junction at Kananaskis walk-in group campground.

110 LIONEL

Distance 7.2 km
Easy

Lionel is the easiest and least pleasing of all the ski trails in the park. It leaves Sounding Lake trail 100 m east of the 4- way junction at Kananaskis walk-in group campground and winds uphill onto Highway 40. 5.5 km later it leaves the highway at Kananaskis Lookout fire road and climbs to a junction with Pocaterra trail. Best skied in reverse direction in fast, icy conditions.

111 ROCKWALL

Intermediate
Distance 1 km

Most of the trail follows a long flat meadow (marsh and lakes) below the Rockwall. The intermediate section lies between the meadow and Come Along trail on the ridge top. When skied in reverse direction early and late in the season, beware of the long runout across the meadow; skiers have been known to sink in up to their ankles in water.

112 COME ALONG

Intermediate
Distance 1.6 km

This narrow trail along a timbered ridge top is a more challenging alternative to Pocaterra trail.

113 STROIL

Difficult
Distance 0.4 m

A steep connecting link between Pocaterra and Come Along trails which offers a fast fun descent.

114 LODGEPOLE

Easy with one intermediate hill
Distance 4 km

This trail connects Elkwood parking lot and nearby William Watson Lodge with Meadow trail close to Pocaterra parking lot. It is bisected by Canyon campground access road into two dissimilar sections: an undulating trail winding through pine forest and small clearings south of the road, and, north of the road, a straight flat trail which follows the power line right- of-way and ends with a steep intermediate hill above Meadow trail.

115 SINCLAIR

Intermediate
Distance 2 km

Sinclair is a semi-circular trail which connects Canyon parking lot to Lodgepole and Meadow trails. The north leg is a narrow winding trail with awkward hills — quite a difficult section to ski well. In direct contrast, the other half of the trail (formerly Canyon Link) makes use of a wide campground road whose long hills are easily handled.

116 CANYON

Easy
Distance 1.4 km

This pleasant, double-trackset trail joins Canyon parking lot to Lodgepole trail. Half a kilometre from the parking lot a clay pit site allows a spectacular view of the Opal Range and the Kananaskis Valley. Aim to be there in the late afternoon when the west face of the Opals catches fire from the westering sun.

117 MEADOW

Intermediate
Distance 5.3 km

This trail connects Pocaterra parking lot to Elkwood parking lot via the Kananaskis Visitor Centre. It divides naturally into three sections. Both end sections are tight, twisting forest trails demanding quick reflexes on corners. The middle section between Woolley trail and Kananaskis Visitor Centre is flat and open and attracts hordes of beginners who enjoy skiing on meadows within sight of a comfortable lounge.

118 WOOLLEY

Intermediate
Distance 2.3 km

A narrow winding trail which connects Meadow trail to Lynx and Amos trails without passing through Elkwood parking lot. Exciting hills at either end contrast with the flat middle section which winds around the perimeter of meadows and ponds allowing views of the Opal Range. Can you spot frozen Opal Falls?

Meeting on Meadow trail.

119 LYNX

Intermediate
Distance 1.7 km

A roller coaster trail which climbs up and down a succession of timbered ridges between Pocaterra trail and the junction of Woolley and Amos trails in a large meadow. The small creek which is followed for a short distance below the meadow runs into a succession of lakes and beaver ponds below the Rockwall.

120 WHEELER

Easy
Distance 4.7 km

Connects Elkwood parking lot with Amos, Lakeside, Packers and Whiskey Jack trails in the vicinity of Boulton parking lot. This wide, double-trackset trail, a bike path in summer, is an excellent beginners' trail. Gentle hills at either end add spice to the flat middle section along the ridge top. Close to Elkwood parking lot, the trail passes within a few metres of Elkwood Amphitheater which offers shelter on days when the snow is sheeting down.

121 AMOS

Easy
Distance 2.4 km

This enjoyable trail is named after Paul Amos, Stoney Indian guide and blood brother to George Pocaterra. Often skied as part of a loop with Wheeler, its narrow width and undulating nature requires a little more expertise from beginners.

122 PACKERS

Intermediate
Distance 3.1 km

Long before there were roads in the Kananaskis Valley, this trail was part of the pack trail between Highwood Pass and the Kananaskis Lakes. Nowadays, it is used as a link between Wheeler trail at Boulton campground access road and Pocaterra trail 100 m higher up the slope. Taken in either direction it's a hard trail to ski really well, particularly when icy later in the season. The small area of flat meadow near Pocaterra trail is uncharacteristic of the rest of the trail which has sharp bends and steep awkward hills.

123 WHISKEY JACK

Intermediate
Distance 4.3 km

Starting from Boulton and Boulton Bridge parking lots, Whiskey Jack offers the quickest route from any parking lot to the Kananaskis fire lookout. Most often, though, it's combined with Tyrwhitt, Elk Pass, Fox Creek and Boulton Creek trails to make a popular 18 km loop. Steep hills alternate with gentler sections. The celebrated S-bend half-way along the trail requires caution, particularly when it gets icy later in the season. A fun run downhill.

124 BOULTON PARKING LOT CONNECTING TRAIL

Easy
Distance 0.5 km

This useful trail connects skiers parked at the upper level of Boulton parking lot to Lakeside and Whiskey Jack trails. See sketchmap.

125 BOULTON CREEK

Easy
Distance 2.5 km

A narrow forest trail following the windings of Boulton Creek between Boulton Bridge parking lot and the Elk Pass trail. Dippers are usually seen on open stretches of water. Often skied in conjunction with Moraine trail.

126 MORAINE

Intermediate
Distance 2.4 km

Moraine is a delightful trail best skied from the Fox Creek trail end if you want to take advantage of longer downhills. Baseball Diamond Meadow near the junction with Whiskey Jack trail serves as a lesson area.

127 FOX CREEK

Intermediate
Distance 1.6 km

This very narrow forest trail is most often used as access between Boulton Bridge parking lot and the popular Elk Pass trail. If skied in the downhill direction, two awkward hills close to Elk Pass trail will faze beginners.

128 LAKESIDE

Intermediate
Distance 3 km

For most of its length, Lakeside is a wide double-trackset trail following the bike path between Boulton parking lot and Upper Lake parking lot via Lakeview campground. It leaves the bike path at the most southerly crossing of the park road, crosses a meadow — fine view of Blueberry Hill — and climbs to a junction with Elk Pass trail 0.2 km east of Upper Lake parking lot.

Elk Pass trail showing the open forest of upper Fox Creek. ►

Blueberry Hill, looking out over upper Kananaskis Lake towards Mt. Putnik (centre).

129 ELK PASS

Intermediate
Distance 7.0 km

Elk Pass on the British Columbia boundary is the most popular destination in the park. It is not the environs of the pass, but rather the character of the trail itself coupled with consistantly excellent snow conditions which draw skiers back to Elk Pass time after time. The return run down the meadows of Fox Creek is memorable.

The trail actually starts from Upper Lake parking lot, but most people join the route at Elk Pass parking lot 0.9 km farther along the trail. From this point on, it follows the double- trackset powerline access road all the way. A sign and padlocked gate across the trail marks the Great Divide.

130 BLUEBERRY HILL

Difficult
Distance 3.2 km

This challenging spur of the Elk Pass trail leads to a superlative viewpoint overlooking both Kananaskis Lakes. Pick a fine day for this trip. The difficulties of some sections of trail are not readily appreciated during the ascent. It is only on the descent, when gathering speed at an alarming rate down a tight twisting trail — skis rooted in tracks — that you realise why this trail has a difficult rating. Wipe-outs and near misses with trees is usual. The narrow draw is particularly hard to ski down without plowing up the banks to a standstill. Many beginners take off their skis and walk this section. Plans for cutting a trail down the north slope of Blueberry Hill to Upper Kananaskis Lake in order to make a circuit seem to have been abandoned.

131 PATTERSON

Intermediate
Distance 1.6 km

Named after Raymond Patterson, rancher in The Highwood during the 1920's and author of several bestselling books, this trail utilizes both the powerline right-of-way between Lookout trail and Hydroline and the delightful powerline access road which leaves Elk Pass trail in the meadows of upper Fox Creek.

132 HYDROLINE LINKAGE

Easy
Distance 1.1 km

This trail, which connects Patterson trail to Elk Pass, follows a line of posts along the powerline right-of-way. On windy days the tracks drift in badly.

133 TYRWHITT

Intermediate
Distance 4.5 km

Trywhitt connects Pocaterra trail to Elk Pass. The highest continuous trail in the park, it holds the snow well until May. The dominant feature of the trail is Tyrwhitt meadows, a favorite spot with grizzlies wandering over East Elk Pass from the Elk Valley during summer months. There's a steep uphill climb between Boulton Creek and the powerline right-of-way at Elk Pass. The previously difficult section was widened in 1982 and is now quite reasonable.

134 LOOKOUT TRAIL

Difficult
Distance 6.8 km

The usual route of ascent to Kananaskis fire lookout starts from the junction with Whiskey Jack and Tyrwhitt trails. Intermediate zig-zags give way to a long traverse below the ridge line, an apparently flat section on the ascent which can be very fast on the downhill. Picnic tables against the south wall of the lookout offer a shelter and a grand view of Kananaskis Lakes while you eat your lunch.

The route to the lookout from Elk Pass trail is rated the most difficult trail in the park and is most often used as an ascent route; the descent requires lots of snow to slow you down! The bridge over Boulton Creek marks the start of the serious climbing. Be prepared to do a lot of herringboning and a pitch or two of side-stepping. In certain conditions, clouds of warm air lolling about in the depths of the Elk Valley spill over the divide and frost the spruce trees along the ridge line.

135 KING CREEK CANYON — Map 9

Half-day hike
2.5 km to end of canyon
Topo map 82 J/11 Kananaskis Lakes

Access: Kananaskis Trail (Hwy. 40) at King Creek day-use area.

This trail leads climbers, hikers and the occasional grizzly through the canyon to the forks at the foot of Mount Blane. In winter, frozen seepages on the south wall are popular with aspiring waterfall-ice climbers.

Right from the start the trail is forced back and forth across the creek by vertical canyon walls. Log bridges facilitate progress for the first kilometre, but after this you must resort to paddling during runoff, or, when rocks and logs are uncovered by receding waters later in the season, play the game of getting to the end of the canyon without getting your feet wet. At trail's end you can either walk up the north fork to a 2222 m col between King Creek Ridge and Mount Hood, or you can follow the south fork with similar ease to a 2332 m gap between Mounts Jerram and Wintour. Both valleys are open and the going easy.

King Creek canyon at sunset.

The view of the south Opals from the summit: Mt. Elpoca above figure, Mt. Wintour to right of King Creek, Elk Pass at top right.

136 KING CREEK RIDGE — Map 9

Day hike
Distance 3.5 km
Height gain 731 m
Maximum elevation 2423 m
Topo map 82 J/11 Kananaskis Lakes

Access: **Kananaskis Trail (Hwy. 40) at King Creek day-use area.**

King Creek Ridge is the grassy ridge north of King Creek. Despite lack of a trail, it's an easy ascent offering panoramic views of the Kananaskis valley and a close-up look at the west wall of the Opal Range.

Cross King Creek to the segment of old road on the north bank. To the left of the cliffs, a steep trail with many variants winds up a disorderly slope of scree, rocks and trees — definitely the worst part of the whole route — to open hillsides above. Although the trail peters out in the grass, small cairns at irregular intervals guide you up the slope to the south end of the summit ridge. Turn north and walk up a comfortably-wide grassy staircase to the summit cairn. There are actually 2 summits of equal height 200 m apart; the farthest one, however, requires a few metres of exposed scrambling so isn't often visited.

On the west side, cliffs plunge 800 m to the valley floor; you feel as if you're standing on the tip of some ocean headland, only here you are looking out across an immense sea of conifers filling the lower Kananaskis Valley. Behind your back are the magnificent Opals which have been your companions all the way up the ridge. Virtually all of the first ascents were made during the 1950's. One of the last peaks to fall was The Blade, an impressive gendarme on the south ridge of Mount Blane which can be seen to better advantage from lower down the ridge. To the south, across King Creek canyon, the mountain shaped like the final flourish of a soft ice cream cone is Mount Wintour, named after Captain C. Wintour who lost his life in the Battle of Jutland in 1916. Its narrow north ridge (seen head on) is frequently used as a training ground for beginner mountaineers.

137 SOUNDING LAKE LOOP — Map 9

Half-day hike, bike
1.5 km to campground
Topo map 82 J/11 Kananaskis Lakes

Access: Kananaskis Lakes Trail (Hwy.) at Pocaterra parking lot.

This trail is the usual route to Kananaskis walk-in group campground. One vehicle carrying tents, food and other paraphernalia is allowed in along Rolly Road; campers must walk either along Rolly Road trail or Pocaterra trail. NOTE: This campground is closed in winter.

The trail starts behind the parking sign at the far end of the parking lot. Straightway, it bridges Pocaterra creek and joins Rolly Road a few metres in from Kananaskis Lakes Trail. Turn right and follow the road to the campground situated at the T-junction with Pocaterra trail.

En route, make a 5-minute diversion to Sounding Lake at the ski trail sign. Unless you're willing to do a bit of wading, you're not going to get those scenic photographs of Mounts Gap, Tyhrwitt, Wintour and the rest of the Opal Range reflected in still waters, for surrounding the lake is a floating carpet of aquatic plants which quiver like some gigantic green waterbed every time you set foot on it. Apparently firm islands of bunch grass sink under the water then bob upwards like corks as you pass.

If you want to extend the walk a bit, turn left at the T-junction and follow Pocaterra trail across numerous bridged crossings of the creek to meadows at the confluence with Spotted Wolf Creek. Watch for moose in willow thickets on either side of the trail. Back at the campground, return to your starting point via Pocaterra trail which delivers you to Pocaterra Ski Hut adjoining the parking lot.

138 CANYON INTERPRETIVE TRAIL — Map 9

Half-day hike
Distance 1 km
Topo map 82 J/11 Kananaskis Lakes

Access: Kananaskis Lakes Trail (Hwy.) at Canyon campground. The trail starts a little way past the campground register box on the access road to leading to "C" loop. Brochures are available from the visitor centre.

The outward stretch is an uneventful descent through mixed forest to a bridge over the river bed. The small amount of flowing water is mere seepage from Pocaterra Dam; the Kananaskis River itself is harnessed in the pipe seen from trail stop #6 at the top of the far bank. From the pipeline you descend a long stairway into the canyon proper. As you walk up the old river bed, everything you see reminds you of the once proud river: the smooth walls scoured by churning rocks, the undercutting produced by the full force of the current swirling around an outside bend; even the gravel of the canyon floor is the result of large rocks grinding one against the other as they were rolled along. Near the end of the trail you pass several small rock pools colored green from algae which is only growing there because the stream is so shallow and so slow moving. After you've crossed the last bridge, either return to your starting point via a steep trail up the bank or follow a more gradual trail farther right onto "B" loop.

139 ROCKWALL — Map 9

Half-day hike
Distance 0.5 km
Topo map 82 J/11 Kananaskis Lakes

Access: **Kananaskis Lakes Trail (Hwy.) at the Visitor Centre parking lot.**

The trail starts from the left-hand side of the building at the hiking sign and in 15 minutes or less takes you to the edge of the Rockwall, a 3 km-long escarpment above a chain of lakes and beaver ponds. I recommend your visiting the trail around sunset when a higher rock wall, the Opal Range, glows like a wall of fire along the eastern rim of the Kananaskis Valley.

140 LOWER LAKE TRAIL — Map 9

Half-day hike
Distance 3.5 km
Height gain 33 m
Topo map 82 J/11 Kananaskis Lakes

Access: **1. Kananaskis Lakes Trail (Hwy.) at Canyon day-use area. The trail starts from the parking lot by the boat launch.**
Access: **2. Kananaskis Lakes Trail (Hwy.) at Elkwood parking lot.**
Access: **3. Kananaskis Lakes Trail (Hwy.) at William Watson Lodge.**

From Canyon day-use area, the trail passes through the walk-in picnic area en route to the promontory marking the boundary of this sheltered backwater. Leave the anglers and boaters behind as you turn south into the wind, and travel down the length of the lake to an area of meadows and mud flats at the mouth of a small stream. Follow the stream up a damp valley harboring a stand of mature spruce with a rich understory of cow parsley. When you meet the asphalted trails for the handicapped at the top of the hill, keep left, right and straight on. Cross the powerline right-of-way and join the main access trail between William Watson Lodge and Elkwood amphitheater which in turn joins Lodgepole bike path. Turn right and follow the bike path for the last few metres to the park road crossing opposite Elkwood parking lot.

141 MARL LAKE — Map 9

Half-day hike
Distance 1.6 km
Topo map 82 J/11 Kananaskis Lakes

Marl Lake, looking towards Mts. Foch and Sarrail.

Access: Kananaskis Lakes Trail (Hwy.) at Elkwood campground or Elkwood parking lot.

From the parking lot, follow the trail past the amphitheater (keep left at all junctions) to "B" loop. Cross the road twice between sites #52 and #53, and #45 and #46. Keep left at junctions with trails coming in from "C" and "D" loops and arrive at the trailhead where you can pick up brochures. The quickest and simplest way is from "D" loop between sites # 114 and #115. There is such a confusion of connecting trails between various campground loops and between the loops and the trailhead, I suggest you get hold of a campground map.

The interpretive trail splits into a loop almost straightway. Keep left, following a dry strip of forest between fens whose rich grasses are forage for elk, moose and deer all year round. After a brief section through lodgepole pine forest, the trail descends to the lakeshore. The delicate pale-green color of the water is due in part to the coating of marl on the lake bottom. Looks almost like sand doesn't it? Marl is an interesting phenomenon. What happens is that stream water seeping through the limestone rock of the valley floor dissolves the calcium which is then carried into the lake. Because the lake is shallow and therefore relatively warm, it encourages the growth of algae which uses water to produce food. Most of the calcium isn't used and is released back into the water in the form of a greyish- colored powder known as marl. Eventually, the lake will silt up and become just another fen like those you passed earlier.

At trail stop #8 the trail turns away from the lake and returns you to the trailhead through forest and clearings allowing views at trail stops #9 and #10 of the Opal Range.

142 BOULTON CREEK INTERPRETIVE TRAIL — Map 9

Half-day hike
Distance 3 km
Topo map 82 J/11 Kananaskis Lakes

Access: Kananaskis Lakes Trail (Hwy.) at Boulton Bridge parking lot. The trail starts behind the trail sign.

Cross the footbridge over Boulton Creek and walk up boardwalk onto the bench above the parking lot. Turn right. The trail passes in front of the old patrol cabin used by the Department of Fish and Wildlife before Pocaterra Dam was built (the smaller cabin behind was the garage), and arrives at the south edge of Baseball Diamond Meadow. Join Moraine ski trail which continues along the bench close "A" loop of Boulton campground. The area between the Patrol Cabin and the first viewpoint above Boulton Creek has been the site of several archaeological finds; artifacts, including rock flakes and spear points found in the meadows between trail stops #1 & #2 indicate this was an important work area used by Indians over 8,000 years ago.

When the bench starts to lose form, the trail leaves Moraine ski trail which you discover is not a summer trail at all beyond this point, and zigzags steeply down the hillside to a bridge over Boulton Creek. A few metres on it joins Boulton Creek ski trail which **is** a summer trail and can be followed all the way back down to the parking lot. En route, beaver dams and dippers are the main attractions.

143 KANANASKIS FIRE LOOKOUT — Map 9

Day hike, bike
Distance 6 km Height gain 430 m Maximum elevation 2125 m
Topo map 82 J/11 Kananaskis Lakes

Access: Kananaskis Lakes Trail (Hwy.) at Boulton parking lot or Boulton campground.

Of all 3 possible routes to the lookout, this one which follows Whiskey Jack and Lookout ski trails is the most popular. Start off along a wide track which leaves the upper level of the parking lot near its entrance. Arriving at Whiskey Jack ski trail opposite Baseball Diamond Meadow, turn left and climb the hill. Cross the campground access road leading to "A" loop, and a little farther on, after another hill, cross the campgound access road between "C" and "D" loops. Make sure you follow trail signs for Whiskey Jack ski trail.

After this, it's a straightforward climb with no junctions to the Kananaskis Lookout fire road at the headwaters of Spotted Wolf Creek which you have crossed twice already. Turn right at the triangular patch of meadow and follow the fire road as it switchbacks up the north ridge of the lookout hill to summit meadows. The lookout, built in 1974, is the second one on the site. Despite its lowly altitude, it is sufficiently high above the surrounding country to allow a tremendous view of forests, lakes and mountains. Watch for the resident porcupine.

144 WEST ELK PASS — Map 9

Day hike, bike
Distance 5.8 km
Height gain 213 m
Maximum elevation 1905 m
Topo map 82 J/11 Kananaskis Lakes

Access: Kananaskis Lakes Trail (Hwy.) at Elk Pass parking lot.

The summer trail follows the Elk Pass ski route to within 1 kilometre of West Elk Pass. (This final kilometre may not be suitable for mountain bikers.) Start off along the powerline access road which climbs over a high ridge into Fox Creek. Immediately after the bridged crossing of the creek, keep right at a junction with a road climbing to the powerline (Lookout ski trail). The road, much narrower now and grassed over, follows the east bank of the noisy stream. You discover that the main volume of water comes from a tributary half-way up the valley; thereafter, the stream quietens in a deep slow-moving channel overhung by 6 m high willow bushes. On a stretch of cordoroy road, keep right at a junction with another powerline access road (Patterson ski trail) which leaves the valley at the point where it is opening out into wet meadows and beaver ponds. About a hundred metres beyond the junction with Blueberry Hill ski trail and before the road bends left and starts climbing to Elk Pass, turn right onto a narrow foot trail signposted "Elk Lake Trail".

It crosses the soggy meadow and travels on only slightly drier ground to the west of it to the Alberta — British Columbia boundary which is marked by an information board and a cutline cleared by the Boundary Commission in 1916. A little way up the cutline to the west you will find monument "M1" — the letter "M" designating Elk Pass and the letter "1" showing it's the monument nearest the lowest summit of a pass. Designed by A. O. Wheeler, it's basically a truncated concrete pyramid, 20 inches high with a brass reference plate bolted to the side. Other monuments are located higher up the cutline.

145 FOX LAKE — Map 9

Day hike
Distance 6.8 km
1 km from West Elk Pass
Height gain 253 m
Maximum elevation 1945 m
Topo map 82 J/11 Kananaskis Lakes

Access: Via West Elk Pass trail (#144) at West Elk Pass.

Fox Lake can easily be visited on the same day as West Elk Pass. NOTE TO BACKPACKERS: If you leave packs unattended at the boundary, make sure you hang them out of reach of the infamous Elk Pass porcupines.

Head up the cutline, past "1M" boundary marker and the trail to Upper Elk Lake. Cross a broad band of wet meadows to the continuation of the cutline on the other side. Climb the first short steep hill. About half-way between the top of the hill and "2M" boundary marker, turn left onto a narrow trail between blazed trees which leads gently downwards to the north shore of Fox Lake. The green water is shallow and the shoreline muddy and imprinted with animal tracks.

View of West Elk Pass and Fox Lake from Frozen Lake trail.

146 FROZEN LAKE — Map 9

Day hike
Distance 7.8 km
2 km from West Elk Pass
Height gain 497 m
Maximum elevation 2188 m
Topo map 82 J/11 Kananaskis Lakes

Access: Via West Elk Pass trail (#144) at West Elk Pass.

This is a much more strenuous extension to the West Elk Pass day hike than Fox Lake. True to its name, the lake remains frozen for about 9 months of the year, so plan your visit from mid July on. This unofficial, unsigned trail requires good route-finding ability. NOTE TO BACKPACKERS: If you leave packs unattended at the boundary, make sure you hang them out of reach of the infamous Elk Pass porcupines.

Follow Fox Lake trail (#145) to where it branches off the cutline. Keep on walking up the cutline which from this point on becomes very overgrown with willow bush. A little past "2M" boundary marker, climb a second longer hill using either the cutline or a trail on the left-hand side which rejoins the end of the cutline in the vicinity of "4M" boundary marker.

From here on, the trail is somewhat sketchy. You should pass a small cairn, and at one point be on a well-defined trail which veers right to some flagging on a tree. Make a left turn here. After some metres of more gentle climbing, the trail traverses towards the lake, utilizing at first a broad bench between rock bands and later, rougher slopes of scrub and scree allowing panoramic views of the Elk Pass area. From trail's end, walk up larch meadows to the lake.

Cradled in the precipitous arms of Mount Fox, its still, dark surface unruffled by any wind, Frozen Lake is an awesome sight. Unless you are willing to scramble up one of the arms, it's an extremely difficult lake to photograph; I recommend you take along a wide-angle lens.

Upper Elk Lake — Alf Skrastins.

ELK LAKES PROVINCIAL PARK

Access: 1. From Alberta. Drive to Kananaskis Provincial Park. Park at Elk Pass parking lot on Kananaskis Lakes Trail and follow route #144 to West Elk Pass. Skiers should use route # 129 to Elk Pass at the powerline. See also routes #147, #148 and #149.
Access: 2. From British Columbia. From Michel on Highway 3, turn north and drive for 35 km to the village of Elkford. At the first stop sign, turn left onto Boivin Road, right onto Fording Drive, left onto Corbin Road and finally right onto Galbraith Road which takes you to the end of the pavement. Continue along the gravelled road now called the Elk River Road. 44 km north of Elkford, you cross the Elk River and join the Kananaskis powerline access road on the east bank; it is still another 43 km from the crossing to the Park on a deteriorating road. Park at the designated spot and walk another 400 m to the Park entrance which is located on the left-hand side of the road opposite the Phillips cabins.

The components of all that is finest in mountain scenery — spectacular rock peaks, glaciers and above all, lakes and waterfalls are concentrated in a little area of 61 sq km at the head of the Elk River.

There are certain regulations you should know about. 1. Horses and motorized vehicles are not permitted on trails. 2. The headwaters of Petain and Nivelle Creeks excluded, camping is restricted to 3 locations: the Park Headquarters, Lower Elk Lake and Petain Creek at the west end of Upper Elk Lake. Firepits and firewood are provided. 3. Fishing limit is 8 fish per day per person and, of course, you must have a valid British Columbia angling licence. Brochures are available at Kananaskis Visitor Centre and at British Columbia information bureaus.

147 WEST ELK PASS TO PARK ENTRANCE — Map 9

Long day hike, backpack
4 km from pass
Height loss 177 m
Topo map 82 J/11 Kananaskis Lakes

Access: Via West Elk Pass trail #144.

This is the usual summer approach to Elk Lakes from Kananaskis Provincial Park. From the information board on the Alberta — British Columbia boundary, the trail initially keeps to the west edge of the longitudinal meadow. It crosses the infant Elkan Creek and about a kilometre further on draws close to the bank of that creek which by now has plunged into a deep valley called Canon Creek on the boundary maps of 1917. Wind down the hill and at the bottom recross Elkan Creek on a notched log. Many- buttressed Mount Aosta is seen in all its gothic splendor across the Elk Valley meadows. Keep an eye on what's beneath your feet, though, for the lovely meadows are swamps. Guided by trodden-down grasses, teeter from one island of security to another, aiming for higher ground with trees on the far side. The trail reasserts itself here and joins the valley trail at a signpost half a kilometre west of the park entrance.

148 WEST ELK PASS TO UPPER ELK LAKE — Map 9

Long day hike, backpack
3.5 km from pass
Height loss 152 m
Topo map 82 J/11 Kananaskis Lakes

Access: Via West Elk Pass trail (#144).

This rough forest trail has no virtue other than directness to the Petain Creek area. From the information board on West Elk Pass, walk west up the cutline towards Mount Fox. A few metres beyond the "M1" boundary marker, turn left onto a newly-cut trail which traverses the forested flank of Mount Fox towards the Elk Valley. A talus slope signals your imminent arrival at the bridge over the Elk River a few metres downstream of Upper Elk Lake. Join routes #150 and #151 on the S.W. bank.

Information board at West Elk Pass.

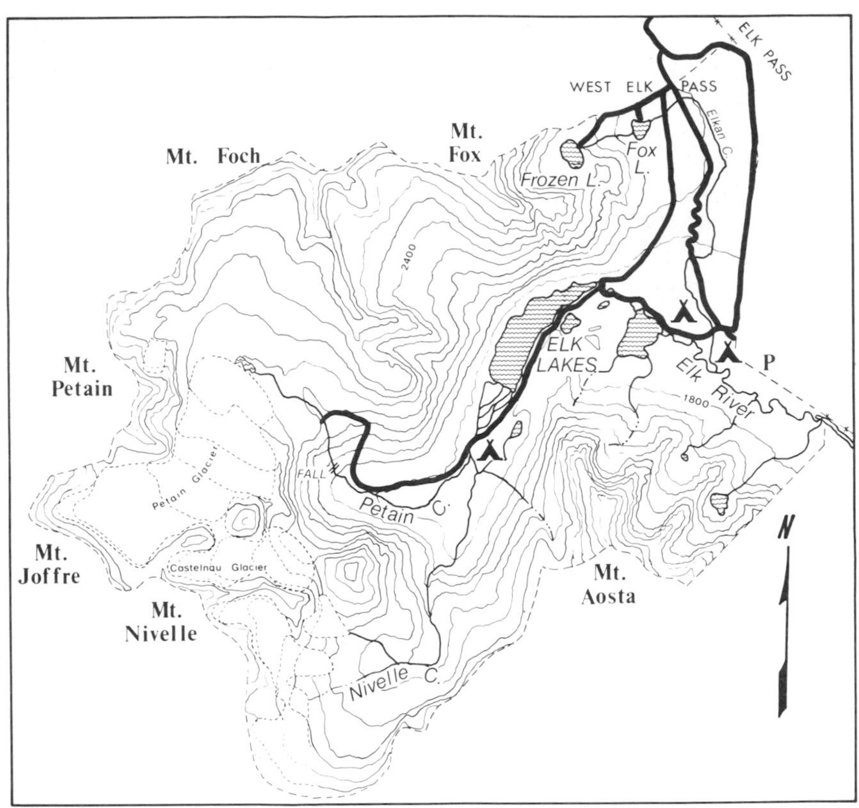

149 ELK PASS TO PARK ENTRANCE — Map 9

Intermediate ski
4 km to park entrance
Height loss 238 m
Topo map 82 J/11 Kananaskis Lakes

Access: **Via Elk Pass ski trail (#129) to Elk Pass at the powerline.**

In winter, the powerline right-of-way is the usual approach to Elk Lakes which are fast becoming a popular destination with day skiers from Kananaskis Provincial Park. The distance from Elk Pass parking lot on Kananaskis Lakes Trail to Upper Elk Lake and return is approximately 26.5 km.

Leave the groomed ski trails at Elk Pass and head south along the powerline right-of-way past the old caboose. The gradient is moderate throughout apart from one steepish hill which can be avoided on the return trip by a detour up the access road. The right-of-way levels in a big meadow and joins the Elk River Road at the Park entrance opposite the Phillips cabins. If going on to Elk Lakes, follow the alternative start to route #150.

Lower Elk Lakes. Castelnau Glacier is partly visible above the forested ridge.

150 LOWER AND UPPER ELK LAKES — Map 9

Day hike from park entrance
1.6 km to Lower Lake
3.2 km to Upper Lake
Height gain 25 m
Topo map 82 J/11 Kananaskis Lakes

This trail is ideally suited to families wishing to introduce their youngsters to the art of mountain camping. FISHERMEN NOTE: the portage of canoes and rubber dinghies is easy to Lower Elk Lake.

There are 2 starts to this trail. The main trail passes through the Park Headquarters and campground en route to a bridge over an unnamed side creek. The alternative route starts from the end of the Elk Valley Road (signposted "No motorized vehicles"), and follows the edge of the meadow to the aforementioned bridge where it joins the main trail.

Directly after the creek crossing, you arrive at the junction with West Elk Pass trail to the right. Elkan Creek and its damp meadows are crossed on boadwalk a few minutes later. Reentering forest, the trail follows the windings of the Elk River which near its source is a rushing glacier-fed stream emanating updrafts of ice-cold air. Near its effluence, a spur trail to right leads to Lower Lake campground on the bank top.

Lower Elk Lake is a quiet body of water, sheltered from mountain winds by a high wall of forest secreting tiny lakes. Sticking up above the trees are the pale gray peaks of the French Military Group and a splash of white which is Castelnau Glacier. The trail continues along its north shore, again resorting to boadwalk at the beaver ponds half-way along. Arriving at the N.W. corner of the lake, cross the Elk River in a series of single-log bridges to a junction on the south bank, turn right (the trail to the left is an anglers trail) and follow the windings of the river upstream to another trail junction at the mouth of Upper Elk Lake with route #148 signposted "Elk Pass and Fox Lake".

Upper Elk Lake is long and fiord-like, squeezed between steep forest to the left and precipitous slabby slopes to the right which in places rise over a thousand metres to the summits. Often the tops are obscured in layers of cloud, and mists trailing across sodden flanks hide the starting points of dozens of new rills bursting into life after a day of rain,

151 PETAIN WATERFALL AND CIRQUE — Map 9

Day hike from park entrance
6.4 km to waterfall
8.4 km to cirque
Height gain to waterfall 131 m
Height gain to cirque 558 m
Maximum elevation at rim of cirque 2286 m
Topo map 82 J/11 Kananaskis Lakes

Access: Via #150 to Upper Elk Lake.

Walk along the shoreline trail to the far end of Upper Elk Lake. The trail continues along a gravel outwash plain crisscrossed by braided streams to Petain Creek back-country campground. Cross the bridge, and follow much of the same type of terrain along the west bank into a band of mature spruce. The trail emerges onto open ground below the headwall where you are in full sight of Lower, Middle and Upper Petain Falls. Leave the trail here and make your own way across meadows covered in golden avalanche lilies in spring to the river bank below the lowest and most spectacular falls. Don't cross the creek; the snout of the Castelnau Glacier overhangs the talus slope like the Sword of Damocles. Pieces of ice break off regularly with loud bangs which scare the hell out of you.

If you are thinking of carrying on into Petain Cirque, be warned that the going is relentlessly steep. Lower down, branches across the trail are a bit of a nuisance, but higher up, after the gully crossing, you'll be glad to haul yourself up with anything at hand — branches, roots, even prickly gooseberry bushes. Three-quarters of the way up the slope, the trail climbs a grassy buttress (mild scrambling), then heads up a stony draw between bushes for a few metres before branching left towards a small cairn marking the beginning of a long traverse to the left. All of the trail above treeline is indistinct and it's a good idea to look behind you now and again to take careful note of landmarks in preparation for the return journey. Arriving at the final rock band, the trail dips slightly to the base of a rib bisected by a large ledge and topped by a cairn which offers the non-climber a not too difficult passage into the cirque. Alternatively, ascend easier or more difficult routes to right and left.

The northern half of the cirque is virtually ice free and you can wander about at will, climbing to a height of 2700 m if you want to from where you can look across at Petain Glacier which fills the other half of the cirque. Although you seem very close to the encircling ridges, it's best to leave them alone; all the mountains in the French Military Group have incredibly loose rock and even simple climbs like Castelnau have been described as "the most frightening climb I've ever been on".

Lower Petain Falls.

The view over Lower kananaskis Lake from the summit platform.

152 CANADIAN MOUNT EVEREST EXPEDITION INTERPRETIVE TRAIL — Map 9

Half-day hike
Distance 2.4 km
Height gain 122 m
Topo map 82 J/11 Kananaskis Lakes

Access: Kananaskis Lakes Trail (Hwy.) at White Spruce parking lot.

In 1984, Interlakes interpretive trail was renamed in honour of the first ascent of Mount Everest by Canadians. As you zigzag upwards through the trees, so you read the story of the expedition's triumphs and tribulations, their arrival on the highest summit of the world coinciding with your own arrival on a modest hill overlooking Upper and Lower Kananaskis Lakes. From the viewing platform, the trail returns to the parking lot via the open west leg of the loop. Stop for a few moments at strategically-placed seats and try to envisage what this country, once the traditional hunting grounds of the Kootenay Indians, used to look like before the dams were built.

The lake was much smaller then, the right-hand half of it divided into bays by peninsulas and 4 large, forested islands resembling black bristle tops. There were also 3 smaller islets, one of which lies submerged in the bay off Upper Lake Dam. A little below that, in the vicinity of White Spruce parking lot, Twin Falls lie buried under tons of rubble.

It was the year 1914 when M.C. Hendry of the Water Power branch of the Federal Government submitted a report assessing the storage possibilities of the Kananaskis Lakes. He had personal reservations about the scheme and amended his report with the words, "the beauty of the lake in its natural state and the extreme probability of its becoming a summer resort in the near future should not be lost sight of". It was another 63 years before his prophecy was to come true, and in the meantime, in the 1930's, Calgary Power built a log dam at the Upper Lake. By the 1950's the scenery of the lake was irretrievably changed. Lower Kananaskis Lake was dammed and a plant and pentstock built below the canyon of the Kananaskis River, Interlakes plant and pentstock was built below where North Interlakes parking lot is now, a powerline and access road ran north to Barrier Lake and south over Elk Pass to British Columbia, and worst of all, the old log dam was replaced by a new earth dam which raised water levels in the Upper Lake to such an extent, it submerged all the islands which gave the lake its unique beauty. George Pocaterra, who fought Calgary Power unsuccessfully, was moved to write, "the most beautiful mountain scenery in the world as far as I am concerned was at these lakes, but now is completely spoiled by the power dams, the drowning of these marvelously beautiful islands and exquisitely curving beaches, the cutting down of centuries old trees, and the drying up of the Twin Falls between the two lakes, and the falls below the lakes".

153 UPPER LAKE TRAIL — Maps 8 & 9

Day hike
Distance 16.4 km
Topo map 82 J/11 Kananaskis Lakes

Access: **1. Kananaskis Lakes Trail (Hwy.) at North Interlakes parking lot.**
Access: **2. Kananaskis Lakes Trail (Hwy.) at Upper Lake day-use area**
Access: **3. Kananaskis Lakes Trail (Hwy.) at White Spruce parking lot.**

The north, south and east shore trails, each totally different in character, can be joined to make a full day circumnavigation of the lake. They also serve as access to trails leading to Rawson Lake, Aster Lake and the North and South Kananaskis Passes.

NORTH SHORE. 4.9 km From North Interlakes parking lot follow Three Isle Lake trail for 1.3 km. Turn left at the sign onto a soft forest trail which parallels the shoreline within sound of the slap of waves on gravel beaches. Half-way along, the trail climbs into the blinding glare of a large boulder field where craftily constructed steps facilitate passage across its humps and hollows. While still in the boulder field, now disguised by a sparse covering of vegetation and trees, you arrive at the junction with the spur trail to North Point back- country campground. 20 campsites scattered down the length of the peninsula are ideally suited to campers arriving by canoe. Continue on past a stony basin half-filled with viridian green water so still and clear it looks like glass. Five minutes later, the trail contours round the head of a deep inlet and turns up the east bank of the Kananaskis River, at this point a very boisterous stream which culminates in Kananaskis Falls a few metres downstream of the bridge. At the T-junction with Lyautey trail on the west bank, turn left.

North shore trail.

SOUTH SHORE. 7.9 km The south shore section is hilly to begin with and lies so deep in the forest it is without views unless you count Mount Lyautey's cliffs glimpsed from time to time above the treetops. 2 km from the bridge, cross a semi-open draw which leads to Hidden Lake and ultimately Aster Lake. (see route #161). Not long after this, the trail drops to the lakeshore and stays there for the rest of the way to Upper Lake day-use area; bridged crossings of Rawson Creek and Sarrail Creek (waterfall) tell you that you're almost there. Walk through the picnic area onto the trail which runs along the dam top. At the far end, opposite the access road from White Spruce day-use area, turn left and begin the final segment of the route along the east shore, the last segment to be built.

EAST SHORE. 3.6 km The east shore is characterized by headlands and the half-moon curve of bays. When strong west winds send waves racing across the lake to break with a thump on the shore it's easy to imagine yourself by some inlet of the ocean. Heightening that impression are terraces of shingle and sand shaped into patterns by wind and fluctuating water levels. In early summer, the lowest water levels expose the bleached bones of the drowned forest; offshore islets are once again seen as headlands of the former shoreline. The deeply indented bay half-way along and just north of the treed island joined to the mainland by a causeway of mares tails was once the site of a small lake. Further north, the low islet lying half a kilometre offshore is all that's left of a proud promentory, and half a kilometre further out there used to be a narrow boat-shaped island whose few trees were so arranged to resemble the masts of a sailing ship. On windy days, the dash of spray against the rocks gave the illusion that it was the island itself that was moving. But Schooner Island has gone now, and so have Pegasus, Cressy and Hague Islands — all drowned when the dam was built. With a feeling of regret that you are unable to see the lake in its former magnificence round the final headland and arrive back at your starting point.

154 RAWSON LAKE — Map 8

Day hike
4.5 km to lake
Height gain 320 m
Maximum elevation 2025 m
Topo map 82 J/11 Kananaskis Lakes

Access: Kananaskis Lakes Trail (Hwy.) at Upper Lake day-use area.

Since construction of Upper Lake trail, this beautiful green lake under Mount Sarrail has become much more accessible. You leave the south shore section of Upper Lake trail at the second major creek crossing and head up the left-hand bank of Rawson Creek on what is now a fairly good trail beaten out of mud and moss. The angle eases a short way before you reach the lakeshore. Fishing is not allowed.

155 MOUNT INDEFATIGABLE TRAIL — Map 8

Day hike
3.8 km to end of trail
Height gain to end of trail 482 m
Height gain to outlier 802 m
Maximum elevation outlier 2514 m
Topo map 82 J/11 Kananaskis Lakes

Access: **Kananaskis Lakes Trail (Hwy.) at North Interlakes parking lot.**

If you had to choose only one trail in Kananaskis Provincial Park, this should be the one; the views of Upper and Lower Kananaskis Lakes are unparalleled and will have you reaching for your camera at every twist and turn in the trail. The gruelling climb up the avalanche gully described in the first edition of this guide has been replaced by a brand new trail which follows the edge of the escarpment to the east. At trail's end, strong hikers have the option of carrying on to the summit of Mount Indefatigable's N.E. outlier. Carry water with you.

Cross North Interlakes Dam to the fire road. A few steps after the gate, turn right and start climbing, first through drafty pine forest then much more steeply up the bright rocks and dusty shales of the escarpment - a superlative viewpoint. When sufficient sweat has been wrung from your brow, the trail eases off and traverses into the grassy gully to the left, then swings back again onto the open bench above the escarpment. As you follow the trail up the bench, so Upper Kananaskis Lake falls astern behind the south ridge of Mount Indefatigable and Lower Kananaskis Lake comes into prominence. From the final viewpoint, which looks north towards Smith-Dorrien Creek, the trail turns into the forest and ends in clearings gilded with glacier lilies.

N.E. OUTLIER OF MOUNT INDEFATIGABLE Walk uphill to the larch belt below a general steepening of the upper mountain and tag onto any good game trail traversing right into the cirque at map ref. 300124. From the seasonal pond, head north up grass slopes covered in mid summer by long-stemmned fleabanes which blur to a purple haze on hillsides dropping away to the edge of the escarpment. Gain the right-hand ridge of the outlier and climb easily to the summit — an airy spot on the edge of the escarpment which attains its greatest height below the cairn.

TO PENINSULA PARKING LOT This alternative descent route is much less interesting than the ascent route, has no trail initially, involves a difficult river crossing and requires a second car to get you back to your starting point. If you feel like giving it a whirl, start from the col between the outlier and Mount Indefatigable and descend shale and grass to 2 diminutive tarns lying in the cirque between Mounts Indefatigable and Invincible. The headwall below the cirque is most easily tackled from the first pond. Push your way through a narrow band of trees onto a talus slope and descend the left-hand edge of it onto semi-open ground. After almost 120 m of height loss, you should emerge onto the old gypsum mine exploration road midway between a large clearing and the outlet stream from the second pond. Turn right. Join Gypsum Mine trail (#105) at the base of the hill and follow it across Smith-Dorrien Creek to Peninsula parking lot.

156 LYAUTEY — Map 8

Day hike, backpack
Distance 3.1 km
Height gain 31 m
Topo map 82 J/11 Kananaskis Lakes

Access: 1. Via Upper Lake trail (#153)
Access: 2. Via Three Isle Lake trail (#157)

Coupled with the north shore section of Upper Lake trail, Lyautey is often used as an alternative start to Three Isle Lake trail. The distance is actually slightly less and the scenery incomparably finer.

Upstream of the junction with Upper Lake trail the Kananaskis River is very much quieter, welling over its banks into the neighbouring forest and necessitating the use of boadwalks and bridges. Sandbars herald your arrival onto a somewhat drier area covered with low-lying willow bushes allowing a 360 degree view of the surrounding mountains. The trail, which has been gradually moving away from the river, climbs across an avalanche slope onto a forested ridge then descends to the junction with Three Isle Lake trail.

157 THREE ISLE LAKE & SOUTH KANANASKIS PASS — Map 8

Long day hike, backpack
Easy ski, bike
8.3 km to forks
11.9 km to lake
13.6 km to pass
Height gain to pass 610 m
Maximum elevation 2306 m
Topo map 82 J/11 Kananaskis Lakes

Access: **Kananaskis Lakes Trail (Hwy.) at North Interlakes parking lot.**

Three Isle Lake is probably the most popular destination of all the routes radiating out from Upper kananaskis Lake. Although you can hike there and back in one day, it is far better to backpack in for a weekend and spend 2 half days exploring the surrounding high country. Skiing is safe and enjoyable to the last large trees at the base of the headwall. Going further is not recommended; on occasions, huge avalanches sweep the headwall from top to bottom.

Cross North Interlakes Dam and follow the fire road along the north shore of upper Kananaskis Lake. In 1.3 km, Upper Lake trail turns off to the left. (Combined with Lyautey trail, it offers a slightly shorter alternative route to the 6.7 km mark.) After several kilometres of tedious road walking, watch for where the trail leaves the left-hand side of the fire road at a creek crossing. Cross the bridge and walk softly under a cool canopy of climax forest to the Upper Kananaskis River which is spanned by a fine log bridge. In a few moments, Lyautey trail comes in from the left.

South Kananaskis Pass and the meadows of upper Beatty Creek. The mountain through the notch is Mt. Munro.

The trail stays within earshot of the noisy river, emerging from the trees at one point onto the bottom of a talus slope where you get your first view of the headwall below Three Isle Lake. A little farther on, a wonderfully clear, deep spring bridged by the trail is the best place to fill up the waterbottles. 7.3 km from the trailhead, you arrive at the forks under Mount Putnik, a popular lunch stop. Campsites are located to either side of the trail leading to Lawson Lake.

You, however, must turn left at the trail junction and climb steadily up Three Isle Creek through isolated stands of douglas fir to the base of the headwall where the river makes a right- angled bend to the south towards the glaciers of Mount Northover. Most of the height gain occurs in the next 0.8 km as the trail switchbacks up the headwall, neglecting grass and forest to the right in favor of scree and rock bands at left centre. Nevertheless, the going is quite easy, even for the loaded-down backpacker, and soon you are descending to Three Isle Lake and the back-country campground.

The trail continues along the north shore to the west end of the lake, then climbs to South Kananaskis Pass sited at the demarcation line of Alberta forest and British Columbia meadow. The prominent cairn on the hillside to the west was built by the Boundary Survey in 1916. It's worth clambering up there for a birds-eye view of the lake, and once there you may as well continue on much more easily to a minor 2820 m summit 1.5 km N.W. of Mount Worthington — a superlative viewpoint for the Royal Group and Palliser Pass. Morning light is best for photographs.

158 UPPER KANANASKIS RIVER VIEWPOINT — Map 8

Day hike
8.5 km one way
Height gain 500 m
Maximum elevation 2225 m
Topo map 82 J/11 Kananaskis Lakes

Access: Kananaskis Lakes Trail (Hwy.) at North Interlakes parking lot.

This hike takes you to a high ridge overlooking the forks of Upper Kananaskis River and Three Isle Creek. It is one of the best viewpoints in the Park: the Mount Lyautey massif looks most spectacular from this angle and you can trace almost all of the North Kananaskis Pass route from start to finish. Because the route involves careful navigation (there is no formal signposted trail), this trip should only be undertaken by experienced hikers.

Follow Three Isle Lake trail (#157) to the creek crossing where the trail leaves the fire road. Cross the creek and continue along the fire road to its end at the bottom of a steep firebreak. Climb the break to a meadow. From a cairn at the meadows top left-hand corner, a trail heads left to the edge of a steep bank — cairn and blazed trees — then turns uphill and ends at treeline on an avalanche slope. Memorize this spot for the return journey.

Using fragmented game trails, traverse left across mixed grass and scree slopes until you are able to drop down a little into an open creekbed. The complicated topography of knolls and sinks hereabouts is best handled by heading west up the creek to a low point in the ridge overlooking Upper Kananaskis Valley, then climbing south along the ridge line to the viewpoint at map ref. 256114. The large cairn was built by the Boundary Survey in 1916 when the ridge was used as camera station "Lyautey North".

Early morning at Three Isle Lake. South Kananaskis Pass is low gap to right.

View from Upper Kananaskis River Viewpoint of Upper Kananaskis Lake.

159 LAWSON LAKE & NORTH KANANASKIS PASS — Map 8

Backpack
15.2 km to Turbine Canyon
17.4 km to pass
Height gain 655 m
Maximum elevation 2360 m
Topo map 82 J/11 Kananaskis Lakes

Access: Kananaskis Lakes Trail (Hwy.) at North Interlakes parking lot.

"Mackiptoon's secret pass" had its first recorded visit in 1854 by James Sinclair who led a group of Red River immigrants over the divide into the Columbia Valley. 250 head of cattle had so much difficulty, they had to be shot and some of the meat used to make pemmican. Four years later, Captain John Palliser, who learned of the route from Sinclair, crossed the pass in search of a southern trade route across the Rockies. It was soon to be abandoned when Kicking Horse Pass to the north was discovered by his colleague Sir James Hector that same summer; nevertheless, Palliser thought the pass important enough to be named on his map of 1863.

Fifty eight years were to elapse before the pass was again investigated, this time by the Boundary Commission who determined once and for all that the pass had no commercial value and so no monument survey was ever made. So much snow had fallen that July of 1916 it took many attempts before R. W. Cautley alone and on snowshoes was able to reach the pass. After the 1930's the old trail fell into disuse and has only recently been reestablished under the Provincial Parks administration.

Follow Three Isle Lake trail (#157) to the Forks. Keep right. After 20 minutes walk along the riverbank, during which time you pass Forks back-country campground, start climbing up and across a wide steep avalanche slope covered in head-high willows and alders which have a permanent downhill lean from the weight of the winter snowpack. Reenter forest and arrive after a bit more climbing at a bridge over the stream issuing from the cirque between Mounts Putnik and Beatty, a pleasant spot for recuperation before tackling the final set of switchbacks onto the open bench. Ahead, the Haig Glacier comes into view between mountains shaped like battleships. Wander on through forest at the edge of the meadow to larch-fringed Lawson Lake — a very popular camping spot, but don't expect to eat trout for breakfast.

The trail travels along the west shoreline, then descends past the ranger cabin to Maude Brook. On the north bank, a spur trail to the right leads past Turbine Canyon back-country campground to the dizzying brink of Turbine Canyon itself where Maude brook and a stream from Haig Glacier moraines join and drop perpendicularly into a deep gorge which can be jumped across in one or two places as it twists its way down 330 m of hillside to the Upper Kananaskis River. The safest viewpoints are from a faint trail along the south bank.

From Maude Brook bridge, the trail turns left, climbing slowly between alternating meadows and forest below Beatty Glacier to a knoll overlooking Maude Lake. Walter D. Wilcox, who visited the area in 1901, thought it was "a desolate lake surrounded by bare cliffs and the awful solitude of that half-way belt which has neither the beauty of the green valleys nor the grandeur of the great snow-fields". Even today, the setting may be a little too bleak for some campers' tastes, but the fishing is great, and if you have binoculars handy you can often spot goats on the slopes of Mount Maude. North Kananaskis Pass is in sight now and all you have to do is follow the west shoreline around to the N.W. corner where a line of cairns leads you into the windswept passage between Mounts Maude and Beatty.

HAIG GLACIER From the east end of Turbine Canyon back- country campground, a climbers' trail follows the west bank of the creek issuing from Haig Glacier moraines. It drops to the creekbed beyond a small canyon, then, when progress seems likely to be barred by a waterfall, climbs steep grass slopes on the west side to the edge of the terminal moraine. A line of small cairns guide you **downhill** into the stony head of the creek where the trail ends. On the moraine to your right, a mysterious circular wall of large rocks invites speculation that it may have been built by the Boundary Survey 68 years ago.

Walk past milky tarns and mounds of white bedrock. Unlike what is shown on the topo map, the glacier has retreated and is now locked behind high rock walls penetrated only by the gorge cut by the glacial stream. Below the wall, the waters slow down and make plaited patterns across an alluvial flat, then gathering together and picking up speed, pass under a rock arch and shoot out into space above a 300 m cliff.

To get onto the glacier you must cross the stream and climb the obvious ramp of jumbled rocks abutting against the wall. Work your way left across parallel ridges towards the highest point on the skyline from where it's an easy step down onto the ice. Although the Haig glacier is comparatively safe, you should be properly equipped if travelling through to the Robertson and French Glaciers.

The bleak environs of Maude Lake. Beatty Glacier to right — Alf Skrastins.

160 THREE ISLE LAKE TO NORTH KANANASKIS PASS — Map 8

Backpack
Distance 10.5 km
Height gain 655 m
Height loss 610 m
Maximum elevation 2360 m
Topo map 82 J/11 Kananaskis Lakes

Access: 1. Via Three Isle Lake trail at South Kananaskis Pass (#157).
Access: 2. Via Lawson Lake trail at North Kananaskis Pass (#159).

It is possible to traverse from South to North Kananaskis Pass (or vice versa if preferred) without dropping all the way down to the Palliser River. Except for one short section on the shoulder of Mount Beatty, there are good trails throughout.

From South Kananaskis Pass walk down the meadows of Beatty Creek to Beatty Lake, a blue gem lying close to the edge of the escarpment. After crossing the outlet, the trail turns right down a dry canyon bed suddenly bereft of Beatty Creek which has drained underground and won't be see light of day until its emergence 260 m lower down. Suddenly, the nice safe canyon you've been following disgorges onto a steep, expoed scree slope down which the trail picks a tenuous line into the middle reaches of Beatty Creek. Rockfalls have dammed this section of valley creating small blue lakes between boulders and sink holes.

On the brink of a second, even steeper escarpment (which, believe it or not, was recently downclimbed by a mad mountain biker), search for a rough trail ascending the hillside to your right (north) onto the flat shoulder of the mountain west of Mount Beatty (map ref. 178133). It doesn't matter if you can't find the trail; the shoulder is obvious and once gained, the terrain funnels you to the escarpment edge where you join a remnant of old trail dating back to 1926. Openings in the trees allow spectacular views of Palliser Pass and the Royal Group.

The descent to Leroy Creek is the worst part of the whole route; you are almost certain to lose the old trail in some of the worst willow bush I've ever encountered. There seems to be a bit of a new trail developing which bears right (east) to an avalanche slope offering a more reasonable descent to the creek. Cross to the north bank. There you can pick up a good trail heading upstream. Arriving at a trail junction at the big bend, turn right, recross the creek, and begin the slow, gradual climb through mature forest away from Leroy Creek.

As soon as you've crossed the tributary arising from North Kananaskis Pass, the trail steepens and with hardly a switchback to ease those aching calf muscles, heads straight for the pass up mixed grass and talus slopes. Near the top, the trail crosses the creek to the south bank. Nowadays this stream bed carries hardly more than a trickle of water and is never a problem to cross, but in Palliser's time, before landslides blocked Maude Lake's exit to the west, the white rushing water and waterfalls must have been a fine sight as well as an obstacle of some proportion. North Kananaskis Pass is a bleak spot, wide open to the west wind, so without further ado, follow a line of cairns down to Maude Lake and pick up route #159.

Warrior Mtn. from Aster Lake — Alf Skrastins.

161 ASTER LAKE — Map 8

Backpack
11 km from trailhead
Height gain 580 m
Maximum elevation 2290
Topo map 82 J/11 Kananaskis Lakes

Access: **Kananaskis Lakes Trail (Hwy.) at Upper Lake day-use area.**

The undeveloped trail into the high glacial valley under Mount Joffre is for experienced backpackers only; expect steep slopes, sketchy trails and navigating problems. In winter, a good knowledge of avalanche hazard evaluation is essential; several parties of ski mountaineers bound for Mount Joffre have been avalanched on the talus slopes above Hidden Lake.

Follow the south shore of Upper Lake trail for 5 km . Before this trail was built, access from the shoreline to Hidden Lake was described by Walter D. Wilcox in 1902 as "an hour of the most difficult bush work I have ever seen". Nowadays, the Upper Lake trail intersects the the old route midway between the 2 lakes, thereby cutting out some onerous bushwacking. The other half of the route along a partly open draw is much easier. Hidden lake belongs to the bathtub variety and you'd better hope that the water is sufficiently low to allow you to skirt along the east shore to its far end where a trail starts between 2 blazed trees. Climb steeply to timberline. From a cairn, look across at Fossil Falls which is still too distant to photograph satisfactorily without a telephoto lens.

You have now arrived at the most difficult part of the route; the ascent of the headwall. Start off by climbing diagonally upwards towards the cliffs of Mount Sarrail. The trail, regaining definition, contours a bit around the base of the cliff, passes below a waterfall falling free from the east glacier, climbs some more to the right of the fall, and finishes with a sensational traverse above rockbands. On easy ground now wend your way between rocks and trees to a long thin pond, sometimes dry, where the trail peters out. Aim for Aster Creek at map ref. 274047. Because you are walking against the grain of the country, this last stretch takes longer than you might think and has on occasion given parties going in the reverse direction a serious route-finding problem. The scenery around the forks is exceptionally beautiful: glaciers make an dazzling backdrop for lush flower meadows among the spruce trees, and to your right, Aster Creek drops in a series of steps to the ultimate drop-off at Fossil Falls. Many backpackers elect to camp here rather than at Aster Lake itself where, not surprisingly, campsites are few and exposed to katabatic winds blowing off the Mangin Glacier.

With many a detour to admire the cascades, make your way slowly up the south bank of Aster Creek to Aster Lake which you discover with a faint feeling of disappointment is a sprawling unphotogenic body of water. Glacial silt deposited by the braided streams of the dryas flat at the west end has colored the water an opaque shade of gray. Its setting, however, is undeniably superb, lying as it does at the hub of half a dozen high alpine valleys which invite further exploration. One of the most rewarding forays is to the high col N. W. of Warrior Mountain from where you get a close-in view of that curious peak Waka Namb'e which translated means Great Spirit Thumb or Hand of God. Shaped like a clenched fist, it overhangs Joffre Creek 1200 m below.

162 ASTER LAKE TO THREE ISLE LAKE — Map 8

Backpack
Distance 10.5 km
Height gain 620 m
Maximum elevation 2845 m
Topo map 82 J/11 Kananaskis Lakes

Access: 1. Via terminus of Aster Lake trail (#161)
Access: 2. Via Three Isle Lake trail (#157)

This route takes a magnificent line along the ridgepole of the Great Divide. Although there is no actual scrambling, mountaineering skills are a definite asset: you should have good balance — difficult with a heavy pack — and a liking for exposure if you are to enjoy the experience.

If you are equipped for glacier travel, the passage between Mount Northover and Mount Lyautey offers a reasonable alternative route to Three Isle Creek below Three Isle Lake. But don't attempt this route in winter; the avalanche danger in upper Three Isle Creek is unacceptable.

Starting from the east end of Aster Lake, follow the north shore trail to Aster Creek which is the jumping-off point for the alternative route to Three Isle Creek outlined above. Round the south buttress of Mount Northover and climb up the narrow scree valley behind it, bearing right near the top to gain a col at map ref. 252041. Walk into British Columbia, at this point a bleak hanging valley holding two tarns. From the second tarn, climb back up to the Great Divide via snow-patched scree slopes leading to the col immediately west of Mount Northover.

The Great Divide from route #162. At 3450 m, Mt Joffre is the highest peak between Mt. Assiniboine and the U.S. border — Alf Skrastins.

An alternative route presents itself here. However, it requires careful navigation in poor visibility and the use of ice axe and crampons to deal with exposed ice later in the season. In brief, it descends the neve in a N.N.W. direction to a pass at map ref. 238061, then follows the unnamed valley to the N.W. down to Three Isle Lake.

The usual route climbs onto the ridge to the west. For 3 km you walk a tightrope of scree between the neve of Northover Glacier and slopes plunging over 1200 m into Joffre Creek. At first, the rounded ridge and the thickness of the ice buffers the drops on either side, but this comfortable style of progress changes half-way along when both sides meet in a sharp point. Look out if you dare across the gulf of the Palliser River to Mount King George and the rest of the Royal Group. To the north, bulky Mount Sir Douglas rises above a tangle of lower peaks. Likewise, the scene to the south is dominated by the white fang of Mount Joffre, at 3450 m the highest mountain between the U.S. border and Mount Assiniboine.

All too soon the glorious ridge comes to an end. Drop down a path gouged out of scree to the col at map ref. 221065. Look back one last time at the Royal Group framed between Defender and Onslow, then turn north and glissade down yellow scree slopes to the flat valley floor where you join the alternate route. The unnamed stream, which rises like Three Isle Creek and Aster Creek from the glaciers of Mount Northover, flows into Three Isle Lake half-way along the south shore.

This photo clearly shows the changeover from rounded ridge to relative knife edge. Onslow Mtn. and the Royal Group make an impressive backdrop — Tony Daffern.

Elbow Lake in the height of summer.

163 ELBOW LAKE — MAP 9

Half-day hike
Intermediate ski
Equestrian, bike
Distance 1.3 km
Height gain 150 m
Maximum elevation 2105 m
Topo map 82 J/11 Kananaskis Lakes

Access: **Kananaskis Trail (Hwy. 40) at Elbow Pass day-use area. NOTE: At the time of publication this section of Highway 40 is closed between December 1st and June 15th.**

This scenic blue lake is one of the most popular destinations in the Provincial Park; reputedly, the fishing is excellent. The trailhead also serves as the jumping-off point for backpackers and equestrians wanting fast access into the upper reaches of the Elbow and Sheep Rivers. Snow lies deep on the trail during winter months but because this section of Highway 40 is closed between December 1st and June 15th, you must start your ski trip from Boulton parking lot on Kananaskis Trail and ski up Whiskey Jack, Pocaterra and Lionel ski trails to the highway. Total kilometrage to the lake and back is 25.8 km.

The trail, a former all-terrain vehicle road, switchbacks up a low forested ridge to the south shore of the lake and a junction with Big Elbow trail which is really a continuation of the road. The narrow trail to right leads to the 20 site back-country campground, then continues on around the east shore to wet meadows where it peters out just a few metres short of Big Elbow trail on the Provincial Park boundary.

Second summit from traverse below third summit.

164 POCATERRA RIDGE — Maps 9 & 10

Day hike
6.5 km to Little Highwood Pass
Height gain 1036 m
Maximum elevation 2667 m
Topo map 82 J/11 Kananaskis Lakes

Access: Kananaskis Trail (Hwy. 40) at Little Highwood day-use area. NOTE: At the time of publication this section of Highway 40 is closed between December 1st and June 15th.

This beautiful ridge with 4 well-defined summits lies on the west side of Highway 40 between the Valleyview Trail junction and Highwood Pass. Mainly because it lacks a trail, the traverse is considered more difficult than the S.E. ridge of Mount Allan, but easier than the Mount Collembola traverse with no rock steps to worry about. Usually hiked in combination with route #166.

Wade through willow brush on the south side of the highway to Pocaterra Creek. Cross, using fallen trees or the beaver dam if you can locate it. Bearing right all the time, head uphill through masses of menziesia bushes which gradually thin out as you climb higher up the ridge into the coal belt which, you notice, also occurs at the same elevation on the ridge between Gap and Elpoca Mountains across the valley. Emerge from the trees onto a wide, grassy ridge with rocky outcrops bejeweled with clumps of alpine cinquefoil. Though beautiful and the sort of place one wishes could be transferred at a wave of the wand to the rock garden back home, it doesn't compare with the actual summit (cairn, surveyors bench mark) whose S.W. slopes are packed with an incredible array of flowers mostly of the blue shades.

When you can drag yourself away from this delectable spot descend to the lowest point on the ridge where larch trees, spilling over the gap from either side, make a soft carpet of yellow needles. An intersecting game trail offers an escape route into the unnamed valley to the west where you can pick up route #166. After one brief sortie above treeline, the ridge finally shakes off the last of the larches and climbs a steepening and narrowing ridge to a second summit capped with an elegant cairn of brown rocks. A grassy, concave ridge leads down to the gap beyond. The third summit is from either direction a very easy ascent which, if you are not a purist, can be missed out altogether by traversing to the gap between summits #3 and 4. Instruments along the way have been measuring the slope's creep for the last few years. The grassy avalanche gully east of the gap offers an easy way down to the highway should you wish to escape at this point.

The ridge ahead looks a little fearsome but is really very easy. Start off by walking along the east side of the horizontal ridge, then switch over to "the sidewalk" on the west side about half-way along. The cockscomb of rock is bypassed on the east side by a bench which requires care in one or two places. In time, this loose section will become easier as the passage of many feet stamp the scree and shale into a path. The bench, as is usually the way in the Canadian Rockies, slants up to the ridge beyond the rock and is followed by a broad shale slope leading to the first of summit #4's three tops. As you cross from one top to another, eventually attaining the highest summit of Pocaterra Ridge, it becomes apparent that the formidable-looking rock bands seen from down below and which may have caused you some apprehension are merely north face facades.

At the summit several descent routes present themselves. If you are making for Highwood Pass parking lot it's easiest to drop down the grassy south ridge into Pocaterra Creek and pick up route #166. Otherwise, descend the steep, stony west ridge to Little Highwood Pass and return to your starting point via the north leg of route #166.

165 HIGHWOOD PASS MEADOWS — Maps 9 & 10

Half-day hike
Distance 0.5 km
Maximum elevation 2206 m
Topo map 82 J/10 Mount Rae

Access: Kananaskis Trail (Hwy. 40) at Highwood Pass parking lot. NOTE: At the time of publication, this section of Highway 40 is closed between December 1st and June 15th.

From the signboard at the north end of the parking lot follow the trail out into the meadow. Because of its proximity to the highway, this sub-alpine meadow and its inhabitants have been thoroughly "researched"; some of the ground squirrels you see running about wear earrings and other less whimsical types of identification tags. Turn left onto board-walk at the trail junction and walk past interpretive signs to viewing platforms tastefully hidden within clumps of spruce trees. Some of the large trees hereabouts are over 350 years old which gives you some idea of the harshness of winter at this altitude. The farthest platform overlooks a meltwater channel with small sink holes.

Alpine anenomies grace the shore of Rockfall Lake.

166 LITTLE HIGHWOOD PASS — Maps 9 & 10

Day hike
3.5 km to pass
9 km to Little Highwood day-use area
Height gain 335 m
Maximum elevation 2545 m
Topo maps 82 J/10 Mount Rae
82 J/11 Kananaskis Lakes

Access: 1. Kananaskis Trail (Hwy. 40) at Highwood Pass parking lot.
Access: 2. Kananaskis Trail (Hwy. 40) at Little Highwood day-use area. NOTE: At the time of publication, this section of Highway 40 is closed between December 1st and June 15th.

The name is confusing to people since Little Highwood Pass does not lie either within or on the boundary of the Highwood River drainage. It's located between 2 forks of Pocaterra Creek; a high col, snowbound until August, separating "Pocaterra Ridge" from the backbone of the Elk Range. If going right through, you'll need vehicles at both ends, of course. Most people climb to the pass and back from the Highwood Pass end which is an easy ascent despite lack of a proper trail. In fall, photowandering among the larches of Pocaterra Creek is a popular pastime.

Start off along Highwood Pass Meadows interpretive trail. When it veers right, follow the meltwater channel in front of you to a large rock at the bottleneck. This signals the start of a good game trail which climbs over the forested ridge into Pocaterra valley at a tiny reflecting pond among the larches. Walk up the edge of talus slopes (one or two cairns) to a steepening of the ground where you can pick up a remnant of trail heading towards the creek. Follow the stream well into Tyrwhitt cirque, cross to the north bank, and head due north up a stony draw patterned with lingering snow banks to the pass. Look back across Tyrwhitt cirque to "Grizzly Col" and an unusual rock arch half-way down Mount Tyrwhitt's east ridge.

Views in all other directions are nonexistent, so without further ado descend into the unnamed branch of Pocaterra Creek via the shallow gully at the demarcation line of grey and brown rocks. Cross fans of neve to the east bank of a stream where a ribbon of meadow provides a fast, easy descent route among snowy drifts of alpine anemonies. Half-way down the valley you arrive at Rockfall Lake which was formed when a large portion of the ridge to the west slid and piled up in great mounds across the valley floor and half-way up "Pocaterra Ridge". Pick your way around the west shore and descend debris into a miniature "Valley of the Rocks". Tiny blue pools mark the northerly limit of easy travel and although you are less than a kilometre from your destination, it's best not to become emeshed in some dreadful willow bush surrounding the resurgent creek. Rather, traverse right onto the more open slopes of "Pocaterra Ridge", veering right all the time so as to arrive at Highway 40 opposite Little Highwood day-use area.

Extensive alpine meadows at the head of the second valley. Route climbs right-hand slopes to summit at centre right.

167 TYRWHITT LOOP — Maps 9 & 10

Long-day hike
12 km round trip
Height gain 885 m
Maximum elevation 2697 m
Topo map 82 J/10 Mount Rae
82 J/11 Kananaskis Lakes

Access: Kananaskis Trail (Hwy. 40) at Highwood Pass parking lot.

When you look at the route on a topo map, the loop seems contrived with little point to it. What you don't see are the magnificent meadows and larch forests of the two valleys which can be visited in no other way. Added to this is the satisfaction of crossing a pass and climbing a summit all in the same trip. Compared with neighboring route #166 Little Highwood Pass, Tyrwhitt Loop is a much more strenuous hike with two distinct gains in altitude — the last one coming late in the day when you are tired. Beyond the first few kilometres shared with route #166, there are no trails.

Start off along Highwood Pass Meadows interpretive trail. When it veers right, follow the meltwater channel in front of you to a large rock at the bottleneck. This signals the start of a good game trail which climbs over the forested ridge to your left into Pocaterra Creek at a tiny reflecting pond among the larches. Walk up the edge of talus slopes (one or two cairns) to a steepening of the ground where you can pick up a remnant of trail heading towards the stream; before reaching the stream, however, turn left up a grassy draw leading into Tyrwhitt cirque. As you pick your way among the boulders, veering left all the while, stop and look up at the arch on Mount Tyrwhitt's east ridge. Now climb the steep loose scree slope to the col between Mount Tyrwhitt and its eastern outlier. From "Grizzly" col, experienced scramblers can climb past the arch to the summit of Mount Tyrwhitt — a superlative viewpoint. On the east side of the col, a beautiful grassy ridge bearing S.E. offers an alternative to the valley route, but do remember to drop off the end of the ridge in a southerly direction; any attempt to shortcut into the valley to the east will land you in trouble.

From the col, the normal route heads down what is normally easy-angled snow slopes to meadows holding a lake and tiny blue pond eyes. Just below the level of the lake, traverse the ridge to left at larch line. Round the S.E. end of it and, homeward bound now, traverse back along its east slopes into a new tributary of Storm Creek. Emerge from the larches into lush emerald-green meadows watered by rivulets issuing from melting snow gullies.

A return to your starting point involves an ascent of 305 m to an unnamed summit at map ref. 423057 (82 J/10 Mount Rae). You can gain its grassy S.E. ridge almost anywhere along its length, but the usual route is a grass and shale slope topping out at the saddle immediately below the highest point. You'll want to linger awhile by the summit cairn — a superb ringside seat for the Misty Range opposite — before heading on down the north ridge of the mountain to the parking lot. The first few metres of exposed scrambling above the northern precipice can be avoided by much easier routes starting from a bit lower down the S.E. ridge. High on the mountain, piece together bits of trail on the west side of the ridge which lead you onto the grassy middle and lower sections where the angle eases off somewhat. At treeline, either continue in the same line until you strike the game trail you followed that morning, or make a beeline for the parking lot.

The descent route to Highwood Pass follows a rough trail down the left-hand ridge.

168 PTARMIGAN CIRQUE — Maps 9 & 10

Half-day hike
Distance 2.5 km
Height gain 229 m
Maximum elevation 2438 m
Topo map 82 J/10 Mount Rae

Access: Kananaskis Trail (Hwy.40) at Highwood Pass parking lot. NOTE: At the time of publication, this section of Highway 40 is closed from December 1st to June 15th.

This circuit trail gets you quickly into beautiful alpine meadows in the cirque between Mounts Rae and Arethusa. Bighorn sheep are often seen in the vicinity as well as the occasional grizzly.

Pick up a brochure at the trailhead and start out towards the meadows. At the junction, fork right onto Ptarmigan Cirque trail which crosses the highway and winds uphill through an open forest of spruce and fir to a trail junction. The brochure suggests that you walk the circuit in a clockwise direcion, so head left, topping out into flat meadows at the next bend. The trail rambles past boulders bearing fossilized horn coral to the turnaround point. If you leave the trail here, and climb higher into the cirque, you'll find much better fossils in the sunken boulder basin under Mount Rae. From this close in, the highest mountain east of Highway 40 resembles a monumental slag pile. It was named by James Hector after Dr. John Rae who is perhaps best known for his part in organizing the final two expeditions in search of Franklin's ill-fated expedition to find the North-West Passage.

Back on the official trail, cross the stream and begin the homeward journey along the top of a lateral moraine. It is the perfect place to look for white-tailed ptarmigan; these large brown and white birds with feathery pantaloons blend so perfectly with the rocks they are almost impossible to detect when standing still. Notice how the flowers of the boulder field are quite different from those growing in the meadows. Here, you'll find cushion plants like the brilliant pink moss campion growing side by side with succulents like the thick-rooted spring beauty. Both types of plants share a long taproot — often half a metre in length — which is both an anchor and a probe looking for moisture deep within the rockpile. Nearing timberline, the trail recrosses the stream and returns within a few minutes to the junction in the trees.

169 MOUNT LIPSETT — Map 10

Day hike
Intermediate ski to road's end
Equestrian, bike
Distance 8 km
Height gain 790 m
Maximum elevation 2575 m
Topo map 82 J/10 Mount Rae

Access: Kananaskis Trail (Hwy. 40). Park on the shoulder of the highway 13.2 km south of Highwood Pass and 3.7 km north of Mist Creek crossing. The start of the exploration road on the north side of the highway has been obscured by reconstruction. NOTE: At the time of publication this section of Highway 40 is closed between December 1st and June 15th.

Mount Lipsett, incorrectly shown on some topo maps as being west of Storm Creek, has been gradually misplaced from its correct location in successive map editions. The real Mount Lipsett is the grassy west outlier of Mist Mountain at map ref. 470014.

Follow the old exploration road into the trees. At the first junction you come to, keep left, cross an E-W exploration road (the same one which contours below Eagle Ridge) and climb over a berm onto the Mount Lipsett exploration road. The cloying smell of clover is your lot for the next little while as the reclaimed road winds about the forest of the S.E. ridge gaining altitude at an exasperatingly slow rate. Keep right at the first questionable junction you come to and after that take every uphill option that presents itself. Road cuts disclose coal seams at many points. At treeline, the final half kilometre of road goes winging out across steep west slopes. Don't bother following it; it's quicker to walk up the ridge line or just below it on the east side to a subsidiary top and from there aim for the summit which is now in sight. From its surprisingly rocky top you get a grand view of Highwood Pass whose length and narrow width can only be properly appreciated from the heights. Closer at hand, the west face of the Misty Range exhibits colorful bands of crimson rock strata synonymous with the term "The Rotten Rockies".

170 EAGLE RIDGE — Map 10

Day hike
Distance 4 km to summit
Height gain 655 m
Maximum elevation 2484 m
Topo map 82 J/10 Mount Rae

Access: Kananaskis Trail (Hwy. 40). Park on the shoulder of the highway 16.1 km south of Highwood Pass and 0.8 km north of Mist Creek crossing. NOTE: At the time of publication this section of Highway 40 is closed between December 1st and June 15th.

As you drive south down Highway 40 from Highwood Pass, the high grass ridge to the left just before Mist Creek crossing is bound to attract your attention, particularly if you are an inveterate ridge walker always on the lookout for new ridges to conquer. Although there is no trail to the summit, nor ever likely to be, the approach is simplified by exploration roads through the forest.

Start off on the exploration road which leaves the east side of the highway above a road cut. Arriving at a junction a little way in, turn right and climb uphill to road's end close to treeline. A few metres back from the absolute end look for a game trail which heads uphill. Splinter trails break off to right and left, but it doesn't really matter which one you follow because all trails eventually lead to open ground and once there you can follow any line you fancy to the ridge top; the going is everywhere easy through long and luxuriant grasses requiring little wind to set whole hillsides in rippling motion. A few dead trees standing with limbs outstretched like scarecrows are favorite observation posts for eagles.

The ridge is broad and grassy all the way, offering soft hollows out of the wind in which to lie and appraise the neighbouring ridges of Mist and Odlum should they be on your list of prospective ridge walks. There are two minor tops to negotiate before the final more rocky summit is reached. Mist mountain, which has been sticking up like a giant's thumb over the ridge top for the last kilometre is at last revealed from top to bottom at 3138 m, it is one of the highest peaks in Kananaskis Country.

Either return the same way (easiest) or continue on down broken slopes to the col between Eagle Ridge and the main mass of Mist Mountain at map ref. 498009. A tiresome descent down the creek to the south will return you to the exploration road you started out on — the same road which intersects Mount Lipsett trail 2 km to the west. Turn left and walk back to your starting point, keeping right at one junction.

Looking back down Eagle Ridge towards the Highwood Valley. Mt. Head to left, Odlum Ridge to right in middle ground, Mt. Burke and Plateau Mtn. on skyline at centre.

171 MIST RIDGE — Map 10

Long day hike
Circuit 23 km
Height gain 808 m
Maximum elevation 2515 m
Topo map 82 J/10 Mount Rae

Access: Kananaskis Trail (Hwy. 40) at Mist Creek day-use area. NOTE: At the time of publication, this section of Highway 40 is closed between December 1st and June 15th.

The long grass ridge bounding Mist Creek to the east is one of the most enjoyable ridge walks in Kananaskis Country. It lies in a rain shadow area and is often bathed in sunlight when a mere few kilometres away across the valley the peaks of the Misty Range are shrouded in rain clouds. Hiking the ridge in its entirety to Rickert's Pass and returning down Mist Creek trail is, at minimum, an 8 hour trip. Fortunately, if time is getting short, you can escape into the creek from almost any point along the ridge.

The first 2 km follows Mist Creek trail (# 172). Stay with the exploration road as it climbs into a side valley south of the ridge. After passing a side road to the right (see #173), the road contours around the head of the valley and with a final flourish of switchbacks, ends conveniently close to the most southerly summit.

The ruler-straight ridge between the south and north summits is comfortably broad throughout with rocky outcroppings here and there poking up through short-cropped grass scattered with sheep pellets. A third of the way along, the ridge dips sharply to its lowest point, then rises over a series of false tops to what is perhaps the highest summit. Scramble up a short rock band (probably avoidable) to the northernmost summit which is by far the best viewpoint, for now you can look down into the upper valley of the Sheep River.

Descend in a north-westerly direction to a col. The final summit, guarded from this direction by a difficult rock band, isn't often visited and should be bypassed low down on the left (south) side. Keep traversing and wait for the ridge to come down to your elevation. From where you regain the ridge it is only half a kilometre to Rickert's Pass and the Mist Creek trail which will return you to your starting point.

Looking south along Mist Ridge.

View from Rickert's Pass of the head of Mist Creek. Storm Mtn. above

172 MIST CREEK — Map 10

Day hike, backpack
Easy ski to head of valley
Equestrian
Distance 13 km
Height gain 555 m
Maximum elevation 2332 m
Topo map 82 J/10 Mount Rae

Access: Kananaskis Trail (Hwy. 40) at Mist Creek day-use area. The trail starts from the end of the parking lot. NOTE: At the time of publication this section of Highway 40 is closed between December 1st and June 15th.

The trail up Mist Creek and over a pass into the Sheep River valley follows the line of the old Indian trail "Many Porcupines". Since the coming of the white man, the old route has been overlaid by exploration roads at both ends and by a pack trail in mid section which has recently been improved and realigned in one or two spots by the Alberta Forest Service. The route is signed and marked throughout with red triangles.

Cross Highway 40 and get onto the Mist Ridge exploration road on the east bank of Mist Creek. After about a kilometre, turn left onto the Mist Creek trail proper; if you find yourself climbing into a side valley you've gone too far along the exploration road.

The trail descends to creek level and follows the east bank of the stream with numerous detours to avoid black mucky bogs. From occasional clearings, you can measure your progress up this long valley by the juxtoposition of the Misty Range and its four grassy basins. All of the basins deserve a closer look; you may, for instance, care to search for the hot spring below the S.E. ridge of Mist Mountain. All I will tell you is that it bubbles out of the ground a few hundred metres above treeline and can be recognized from some distance away by brown algae coating on the rocks. It is believed by some that the word Mist (translation of Indian word) derives not from the tendency of the mountain to attract bad weather, but from the clouds of steam arising from the spring whenever the temperature falls below freezing.

When level with the fourth basin under Storm Mountain, the trail winds uphill out of the trees to Rickert's Pass, a rocky defile named after Julius Rickert, a self-styled mining engineer who called himself the Count de Braban, a title later discovered to belong to the Crown Prince of Belgium. Regardless of his doubtful credentials, it was Rickert who first discovered coal in the area in 1902. Notice the black-streaked hillsides falling away from Mist Ridge which a closer inspection reveals as hundreds of little coal heaps below the mouths of ground squirrel holes.

Zigzag down the steep, north slope into fir forest; tree blazes date back to the beginning of the century. The trail emerges from the trees at the top edge of an excavated bank and descends the far side of it onto the top of a slag heap in the heart of Pat Burns Coal Mine. Peeking over the edge, you can see a section of railway line and a log hut which is gradually collapsing into the stream as the bank erodes. Turn left onto the mine road and begin a steep descent intersected twice by the more gentle windings of the railway grade. Near valley bottom, the road fords the side creek and levelling out at last, joins Sheep trail by the side of a stockpile of coal.

173 PICKLEJAR CREEK — Map 10

Day hike
Distance 4 km
Loop 9.5 km
Height gain 625 m
Maximum elevation 2395 m
Topo map 82 J/10 Mount Rae

Access: Kananaskis Trail (Hwy. 40) at Picklejar Creek day-use area. NOTE: At the time of publication, this section of Highway 40 is closed between December 1st and June 15th.

Contrary to what you might expect, the old trail up Picklejar Creek does not lead to Picklejar Lakes, but heads instead towards a pass between two hills where you have the option of climbing further to a viewpoint, or of making a loop with Mist Ridge trail. The trail is unsigned and poorly defined in many areas.

Spend a few minutes searching for the start of the trail at the far end of the picnic area. At first it stays fairly close to the river. As the valley closes in, however, it climbs high over the open shoulder of the hill to the north thereafter settling into a traverse along a forested bench to the forks. All the tributaries from the north have incised deep canyons which is why Picklejar Creek has never been a feasible route to Picklejar Lakes. The trail is forced uphill, and becoming faint climbs the open valley to the west of the first of these tributaries to a pass between two hills at map ref. 544000. Don't stop here. Another 100 m of easy climbing up the grassy hill to the west leads to a tremendous viewpoint.

Either descend the same way, or, if you want to make the loop, go back down to the pass and get onto an exploration road which descends north slopes into a tributary of Mist Creek. At the road junction, turn left onto Mist Ridge exploration road (#171) and follow it back to Mist Creek day-use area which by lucky chance is only 0.5 km north of Picklejar Creek day-use area.

Third Picklejar Lake and cirque.

174 PICKLEJAR LAKES — Map 10

Day hike
4.2 km to first lake
Height gain 380 m
Maximum elevation 2180 m
Topo map 82 J/10 Mount Rae
82 J/7 Mount Head

Access: Kananaskis Trail (Hwy. 40) at Lantern Creek day-use area. The route starts from the east side of the highway a little north of the day-use area. Look for the unsigned trail on the north bank of Lantern Creek. NOTE: At the time of publication, this section of Highway 40 is closed between December 1st and June 15th.

"The fishing is so good it's like catching fish in a picklejar". The rationale behind the name hasn't applied for some years now, not since the lakes were closed to fishing for restocking. Fishing, or no fishing, the lakes are still a very popular destination with hikers wanting quick access into an alpine area.

Oddly enough, you don't follow Picklejar Creek to get to Picklejar Lakes; the valley you are about to start up is Lantern Creek, one valley to the south. After the usual preliminary section through the trees, the trail traverses steep grassy hillsides, wandering up and down and finally dropping to the creek in mid section. A short stint through open forest on the other bank gets you to the forks. Recross the main creek and climb due north up waves of hotter, drier hillsides to a col overlooking Picklejar Creek. On a hot day, what relief to descend into the cool forest! The trail drops 30 m to the gushing stream which is followed up to the first lake.

Picklejar Lakes are paternoster lakes, each one set a little higher in its own saucer of rock and connected one to another by faint trails. First, second and fourth lakes are friendly, shallow bodies of water surrounded by trees and meadows; you can see the trout darting about making shadows on soft brown sand. The third and largest lake is blue, sterile and very, very deep. Circumnavigating the shoreline as one is wont to do with lakes, gives you an uneasy feeling — so clear is the water — of traversing above some precipitous boulder slope.

Third Picklejar Lake.

175 ODLUM POND — Map 10

Long day hike
Easy and intermediate ski
Equestrian, bike
Distance route 1, 9 km
Distance route 2, 13 km
Height gain 305 m
Maximum elevation 1966 m
Topo map 82 J/7 Mount Head

November snow in Odlum Creek. As you can see by the location of Odlum Ridge (top right), the skier is close to Odlum Pond.

Access: 1. Kananaskis Trail (Hwy. 40) at Lantern Creek day-use area.
Access: 2. Kananaskis Trail (Hwy. 40) at Lineham Creek day-use area. NOTE: At the time of publication, this section of Highway 40 is closed between December 1st and June 15th.

Compared to neighbouring valleys west of the Highwood River, Odlum Creek has little to offer except a small pond exquisitely placed in a basin below Mount Loomis and its outliers. Both routes are less than aesthetic, particularly route 2 which is a major logging road best tackled by bicycle. Conversely, they make excellent ski trails. Route 1, though rated intermediate overall, has 2 difficult hills which are usually walked down on the return trip because of insufficient early season snow covering on the rocks.

Route 1. From Lantern Creek day-use area walk north along Highway 40 to a cutline access road whose entrance is partially blocked by a huge boulder painted with a red letter "M". Turn left down the road, keep left at the junction a little way in and descend (1 steep hill) to the Highwood River. Wade across to the west bank and continue along the road which swings around to the right and joins a major E-W cutline. Turn left here and follow the road/cutline up the 2 very steep hills mentioned in the introduction onto a flat bench above Odlum Creek. A gushing side creek below open slopes marks the departure point for Odlum Ridge (see #176).

Soon after, the road descends to Odlum Creek and crosses it twice — awkward fords which are easily avoided by following a game trail along the north bank. A long gradual uphill climb, delightful to ski down, reaches a high point at a junction with a very overgrown road to right which is the return route from Odlum Ridge. Go left here. Disregard both a minor road to the left doubling back and a good road to the right a little farther on. Keep on going downhill and arrive at sawmill site #2 on the main Odlum Creek logging road. Turn left, cross the bridge over Odlum Creek and join route #2 at the junction with the first side road to the right after the creek crossing.

You can follow this side road to within half a kilometre of your destination. Arriving at the ford over Odlum Creek, strike off by the side of waterlogged meadows bordered with tree skeletons to the more cheerful environs of the pond. A waterfall tumbles down the headwall from the cirque above.

Route 2. From Lineham Creek day-use area walk north for 200 m up Highway 40 to the road sign. Turn west onto the main Odlum Creek logging road and follow it across the Highwood River (no bridge) and between masses of raspberry bushes to Loomis Creek crossing at the 3.5 km mark. The next 2 side roads to the left are both branches of route #177 to Loomis Lake and Bishop Creek and should be ignored.

After another 3 km of unmitigated drudgery, the road turns west onto a bench high above Odlum Creek. Pass a sawmill site and a host of minor roads climbing through cutblocks to the ridge above. Just before the road bridges Odlum Creek at the forks and enters a second sawmill site, you join route #1 at the last side road to the left before the creek crossing. See route #1 for a description of the final 2 km to Odlum Pond.

The hiker is descending East Peak to East/Central col. The ridge rises to Central Peak (top right) and to West Peak which is partly seen to the left of Central Peak's summit.

176 ODLUM RIDGE — Map 10

Long day hike
Circuit 18 km
Height gain 1015 m
Maximum elevation 2496 m
Topo map 82 J/7 Mount Head
82 J/10 Mount Rae

Access: Kananaskis Trail at Lantern Creek day-use area. NOTE: At the time of publication, this section of Highway 40 is closed between December 1st and June 15th.

The ridge dividing Odlum and Storm Creeks rises to 3 high summits which were first climbed in 1916 by the Boundary Commission who established camera stations on the east and west peaks. Despite help from logging roads and game trails, a traverse of the 3 summits is a strenuous though technically easy undertaking.

Follow Odlum Pond trail (#175) route #1 for approximately 2.5 km to a gushing side creek below open slopes marking the departure point. Criss-crossing elk trails facilitate the initial climb onto the grassy south ridge of East Peak which lies to your left as you face the hillside. On the ridge proper, the trails consolidate into fewer strands which all head in an up and down direction and eventually converge into one good trail leading to a flat shoulder. Take a well earned rest. Continue climbing past a large distinctively-shaped cairn plainly seen from the highway which marks the point where the ridge turns west, becoming narrower and gravelly as it approaches the summit of East Peak, at 2496 m the highest point on the traverse.

Descend 100 m of steep grass to East/Central Col. Either contour below the gap on the left side or, much more fun, traverse the black pinnacles which are a loose arrangement of big blocks and slabs covered in curly black lichen. Here and there, the urine from resident packrats has built up thick incrustations of a white calcareous material on the rocks. The ridge rising to Central Peak is at first an untidy mixture of the same sort of black-lichened slabs, gravel and krumholz. When the angle eases, it becomes grassy, a seemingly endless green highway leading to the summit and carrying on over and down like a bright ribbon between dark forests into Storm Creek. Probably you have looked at this tantalizing ridge from Highway 40 and been deterred from action by the sight of thick bush between road and ridge.

From the summit cairn, drop 100 m to the gap between Central and West peaks. An easy slope sandwiched between cliffs and spruce trees crouched low to the ground brings you to the summit of West Peak where you'll find the ruins of a cairn. A subsidiary top 400 m to the west was the site of the Boundary Commission's "Storm Creek No. 2" camera station.

The descent to Odlum Creek requires careful navigation and tracking skills. Head south through forest and glades smelling strongly of elk to a creek at map ref. 499956 on topo map 82 J/7. Intermittent game trails on the right bank cross to the left bank at the bend and converge on the dead end of an overgrown logging road lying only a few metres above the stream. This road, truly an obstacle course but probably better than the forest, leads in due course to the cutline you started out on. Turn left and follow it back to your starting point.

177 LOOMIS LAKE — Maps 10 & 11

Day hike, easy ski
Equestrian, bike
Distance 12 km
Height gain 640 m
Maximum elevation 2301 m
Topo map 82 J/7 Mount Head

Loomis Creek logging road west of second sawmill site.

Access: Kananaskis Trail (Hwy. 40) at Lineham Creek day-use area. NOTE: At the time of publication this section of Highway 40 is closed between December 1st and June 15th.

A blue lake nestled close to the British Columbia boundary is the reward of a long walk-in along a logging road. The route is not signed and there is no trail for the final 2 km.

Walk north for 200 m up Highway 40 to the road sign. Turn west here onto the main Odlum Creek logging road and follow it across the Highwood River (no bridge) to Loomis Creek crossing at the 3.5 km mark. Immediately after the crossing, turn left up a stony shortcut leading to Loomis Creek logging road. (Bikers should continue along Odlum Creek logging road for another 0.8 km before turning left onto the logging road proper.) Now head west through the narrows. After 4 river crossings, the first 2 of which can be avoided, the valley broadens out and Bishop Creek exploration road (#178) turns left across the creek. The Loomis Creek logging road, now settled on the north bank, runs in a straight line through one sawmill site half-way up the valley to a second larger site at the forks. Grizzly tracks in the mud tend to cure logging road stupor.

Keep left at the road junction after the second sawmill site. (The right-hand road offers the best route to a small lake due west of Mount Loomis. Take every uphill option until the road peters out, then bushwack.) The road to Loomis Lake dips to Loomis Creek, climbs steeply across a slide slope and ends just short of the stream issuing from the lake. Game trails, starting on the uphill bank, get you across the intervening strip of forest to the creek where the going is much more open. Follow the creek up to a meadow the size of a football field, then climb successive benches to the lake shore. Loomis lake is an excellent example of a lake formed behind an excessively-high wall of terminal moraine.

178 BISHOP CREEK — Map 11

Day hike
Equestrian, bike
Distance 8.5 km to col
Height gain 884 m
Maximum elevation 2545 m
Topo map 82 J/7 Mount Head

Access: Kananaskis Trail (Hwy. 40) at Lineham Creek day-use area. Via Loomis Lake trail (#177). NOTE: At the time of publication this section of Highway 40 is closed between December 1st and June 15th.

The name Bishop Creek is somewhat of a misnomer for a route which takes in a 2500 m summit. But apart from a few kilometres of rough ridge walking at mid section which is optional anyway, the majority of the route is along exploration roads which are suitable for equestrians and all types of hikers undeterred by the distance. Steep, open hillsides — potential avalanche paths — make this route unacceptable to skiers.

Follow Loomis Lake trail (#177) to the 5 km mark. At the unsigned junction turn left onto the Bishop Creek logging road which straightway fords Loomis Creek. Overgrown at first, the road improves as it climbs out of the bush and settles into a traverse of steep, open hillsides above swampy Bishop Creek. Make a mental note that a side road to the right after the obvious gully can be utilized for the return trip. (If you want an easier day, walk up the side road to a grassy col at map ref. 521908. The view isn't as good though.)

In the shadow of Mount Bishop, the road zigs right and ends not too much farther on. Leave it at the zig and walk up 100 vertical metres of easy-angled scree to the col between Mount Bishop and its N.E. outlier which, it should be noted, offers a reasonable route into the head of Loomis Creek. Now climb the broad grassy ridge rising to the summit of the outlier — a dramatic viewpoint, through you are a little too close in to be able to distinguish the succession of cirques and cols which are so characteristic of the Elk Range. Either return the same way (easier) or descend the much steeper N.E. ridge, bypassing pinnacles on the south side, to the lower col mentioned earlier. Pick up the aforementioned side road and follow it downhill to the main exploration road. A more direct route with less backtracking descends the shallow gully using game trails.

Route climbs to the col below Mt. Bishop, then traverses the grassy hill at top right.

179 CAT CREEK INTERPRETIVE TRAIL — Map 11

Half-day hike
Distance 4 km return
Topo map 82 J/7 Mount Head

Access: Kananaskis Trail (Hwy. 40) at Cat Creek day-use area. NOTE: At the time of publication, this section of Highway 40 is closed between December 1st and June 15th.

The gravelled trail crosses Highway 40 and climbs to a seat in a clearing, an unexpected viewpoint less than 30 m above the road. Climb over a forested ridge to gravel flats at Cat Creek, cross the old highway right-of-way and arrive at a second seat near the entrance to Cat Creek gorge. Converging rock walls blackened with coal seams — even the trail is built from coal dust — convey an atmosphere of gloom; you could be entering the gateway to hades. The trail bridges the stream twice, and ends below a step in the creekbed. In late afternoon, the westering sun strikes full into the recess, spotlighting the 6 m waterfall and sending shimmering green glints to the pebbly bottom of the pool below. A much larger waterfall higher up the gorge is only accessible to scramblers willing to take risks.

Lower Cat Creek Falls.

180 FORD MINES — Map 11

Day hike
Distance 4.5 km
Height gain 244 m
Maximum elevation 1798 m
Topo map 82 J/7 Mount Head

Access: Kananaskis Trail (Hwy. 40) at Cat Creek day-use area. NOTE: At the time of publication this section of Highway 40 is closed between December 1st and June 15th.

Although coal in the Highwood had been reported by G.M.Dawson as early as 1882, it wasn't until 1910 that Harry Ford, real estate salesman turned prospector, leased 11,637 acres of government land and developed what came to be known as the Ford Mines. There were apparently 14 seams in all ranging from 5 ft. to 18 ft. in thickness. Although the anthracite coal was of a very high quality, the Ford Mines were doomed to go the same way as the Burns Mine on the Sheep River and for the same reason: high transportation costs. In winter it was a perpetual struggle to keep the coal wagons moving along the Lineham Company road which was the forerunner of today's Kananaskis and Highwood Trails. Plans to build a railway never materialized. This trail, which follows in part the old exploration road, takes you to several coal shafts and the site of Ford's camp. All you are required to bring with you is a little imagination.

Start off along Cat Creek interpretive trail (#179). Arriving at the second seat, ford Cat Creek at the site of an old bridge to an exploration road on the east bank. As you follow the road along, look for a trail climbing the steep bank to the left, not the first straight-up trail you come to, but a reasonably-graded trail marked by a red fleur de lys, souvenir of the World Scout Jamboree in 1983. It rejoins the exploration road which has made a wide sweep to the right at the next right-hand bend. At the cairn a few metres after the bend, turn left onto another shortcut trail which edges along the top of Cat Creek gorge within sound of the waterfalls to the old mine road. Turn left here and descend to a side creek crossing, passing en route the entrance to a coal mine and a side road to the right shortly before the crossing which is route #181. On the far side of the creek you arrive at a junction. Look for the corral in the angle between the two roads.

The right-hand climbs up the north bank of the side valley to a large slag pile and further shafts. The remains of a bridge can be seen in the creekbed below. The road up Cat Creek passes the site of Ford's camp on riverbank meadows, but is of little interest beyond this point unless you're bound for the summits of the Highwood Range; it fords the creek several times then swings up the next side valley to the right and ends in a tangle of bushes.

181 CAT CREEK HILLS — Map 11

Day hike
Distance 3.5 km
Circuit 9 km
Height gain 550 m
Maximum elevation 2130 m
Topo map 82 J/7 Mount Head

Access: Kananaskis Trail (Hwy. 40) at Cat Creek day-use area. Via Ford Mines trail (#180). NOTE: AT the time of publication this section of Highway 40 is closed between December 1st and June 15th.

These grassy outliers of Mount Head rise enticingly to the east of the highway at Cat Creek. There is no formal trail to the summits; the suggested route combines exploration roads and rough off-trail hiking along ridge tops.

Almost as soon as it branches off Ford Mine exploration road, the road commences a stiff 300 m climb onto the ridge top; occasionally you catch a glimpse of the coal mines in the valley below. Arriving at the ridge, follow the road out to a superlative viewpoint above a drop-off where you can at last take a well-earned rest in congenial surroundings.

If you wish to extend the trip, turn 180 degrees and head east through open forest to a minor summit at map ref. 652874. From its grassy top you get a more extensive view of the Highwood Valley and the High Rock Range which becomes the Elk Range north of Weary Creek Gap. From this direction, Mount Head is a mere bump on a long ridge and is definitely not the prominent mountain bestowed with that name by Captain John Palliser. His sketchy map of 1865 places the mountain farther west on the Great Divide in the vicinity of Mount Tyrwhitt; however, due to inaccurate placement of both the Highwood River and the Great Divide, the true Mount Head will always remain an enigma.

Now descend the delectable S.W. ridge. After a rocky knob, which gives a few metres of easy scrambling if tackled direct, the ridge descends in 2 grassy steps to a large flat meadow bisected by the exploration road you started out on. Turn right and keep left at two road junctions. Nearing Cat Creek, you join your outbound route at the cairn.

Looking along the return route from the highest point of the Cat Creek Hills.

182 MCPHAIL CREEK — Map 11

Long day hike, backpack
Easy ski, equestrian, bike
Distance 13 km
Height gain 351 m
Maximum elevation 1890 m
Topo map 82 J/7 Mount Head

Access: Kananaskis Trail (Hwy. 40) at Cat Creek day-use area. NOTE: At the time of publication this section of Highway 40 is closed between December 1st and June 15th.

The old "Elk Trail" from the Elk River over Weary Creek Gap and down McPhail Creek was used by generations of Kootenay Indians hunting elk on open south-facing slopes. Today, large numbers of elk still graze the slopes around McPhail Creek, crossing the Highwood River in late fall to their wintering grounds on the western outliers of the Highwood Range.

For a period of its history, the valley was known locally as Bunk Creek after bunks of logging sleighs were found stacked up against the forge of Mr. Wilson's abandoned winter camp. In his book "The Buffalo Head", Raymond Patterson describes zigzagging back and forth across McPhail Creek (the bridges had all collapsed) as he followed the old logging road to the camp which was sited "on a little flat on the right bank of the creek, tucked up against a low cliff". Even in 1936 the buildings were in bad shape — the logs rotting, the roofs falling in; it's doubtful whether there is anything left to find today. In Patterson's day, this logging road was the key to the inner sanctum. When you reached the camp you found a way up the bank to the Elk Trail on the bench. The subsequent bulldozing of new logging roads and cutlines has changed the line of approach. The present route is along the valley's major logging road which follows the route of the old Indian trail to within half a kilometre of the headwall.

It's possible to hike or ride to trail's end and back in one day, though hardly worthwhile as there would be no time to explore the several interesting side trips starting from the valley head: Weary Creek Gap, Lake of the Horns and the Hill of the Flowers. NOTE: In recent years Fish and Wildlife have been snaring black bears and grizzlies in this valley. For up-to-date information either call in at the Highwood Ranger Station or phone Fish and Wildlife in Calgary before setting out.

McPhail Creek and Carnarvon Lake trails share the same route for the first 2.5 km. Starting from the far end of the parking lot, the old road travels north through buttercup meadows alongside the Highwood River; keep left at the first junction and right at the second one. Three kilometres from the trailhead, the road fords the Highwood River (knee deep at the best of times), and arrives at an important junction on the west bank with the Carnarvon Creek logging road.

Keep right and climb onto the bench above McPhail Creek. When level with the big bend of the river, the road crosses an E-W cutline, then, decending slightly, turns west. The same cutline comes in from the left and leaves on the right 200 m later. The next thing to look out for is a sharp dip in the road which heralds your imminent arrival into a large meadow where Muir Creek logging road turns off to the left across the creek. At the following junction, shortcut left on a corduroy road which eliminates one hill. Rejoin the main road, keep left and start descending towards McPhail Creek. Shortly after repassing the cutline, the road levels off by riverside meadows with beaver ponds and again divides at a lumber camp site which has been reseeded with grasses and clover and now makes an excellent lunch spot or camping area 8 km in from the trailhead.

Follow the right-hand road uphill to an intersection with the cutline. Turn left. For the next 2.5 km, the road/cutline roller coasters between two foothills into the inner basin. Between the first and second rises, it bridges a copious stream identifiable by a log shack on the S.E. bank. The third, final and highest rise climbs over the shoulder of the Hill of the Flowers but unless you're bound for its summit, you should detour around the bottom of the hill to the left.

The inner basin, devastated by the 1936 holocaust, has been extremely slow to rejuvenate. Deadfall and charred stumps litter the valley floor and surrounding ridges; only small patches of original forest remain below the Lake of the Horns and on the Hill of the Flowers. The first trees to have come back are the willows and the aspens, poor stunted specimens which in fall spread their own blaze of orange across the valley.

Cross 2 creeks (the first one is bridged), then watch for a small clearing on your right which is the unobtrusive entrance to Lake of the Horns trail. (You'll find excellent camping spots along the trail 0.5 km in from the road.) Now wade the more copious stream issuing from Lake of the Horns. In another kilometre, cross McPhail Creek and climb to road's end 500 m from the headwall. Carry on in the same direction along a faint game trails which veer right towards McPhail Creek below the waterfall. Lush, bumpy meadows enclosed by walls of willow and aspen thickets make uncomfortable sleeping pads.

A birds-eye view of McPhail Creek from the top of the headwall. The big hill to left is The Hill of the Flowers.

LAKE OF THE HORNS

Backpack
Distance 2 km
Height gain 396 m
Maximum elevation 2210 m

A lake of unusual depth cradled between Mount McPhail and Horned Mountain had its first recorded visit by rancher Raymond Patterson in 1935. He described the headwall below the lake as, "a nasty-looking proposition; it was high smooth and very steep, and there was nothing to hang on to — a couple of small trees widely separated, a patch of grass, a bit of wild rose and a bit of buckbrush, that was all". It's obvious that Patterson didn't take the line of today's trail which is easy and rarely requires the use of hands. Every summer weekend now sees hoards of visitors, particularly fishermen after a cutthroat trout or two, making the pilgrimage to the Lake of the Horns, of McPhail Lake as it's sometimes called erroneously. Don't plan on camping at the lake.

The trail starts from the aforementioned clearing on the McPhail Creek road and for the first half kilometre travels past camping areas in clearings to left and right. Begin climbing up the north bank of the creek issuing from the Lake of the Horns. The going is steep, your progress punctuated by frequent stops to clamber over huge deadfall. By the time the bank levels off, you are too high above the creek and must traverse downhill to the base of the headwall. To your left the creek rushes headlong down between gleaming walls of white limestone. Keeping to less vertiginous right-hand slopes, the trail makes its way up steep grass into a clump of mature spruce trees (rest,shade), then continues up a bit of scree followed by easy white slabs well supplied with ledges to the lake. The grand austerity of the scene is softened by fragile strips of meadow along the north and east shores. Rocks bearing horn coral fossils which littered the shoreline in Patterson's day, seem to have disappeared in the interim.

WEARY CREEK GAP

Backpack
Distance 2.5 km
Height gain 351 m
Maximum elevation 2240 m

Generations of ungulates moving between the Elk Valley and the Highwood River have gouged a staircase up the headwall of McPhail Creek. From below it's not easy to pick out; in 1936, after one failure to climb the headwall by its left-hand side, Raymond Patterson was only alerted to the trail's presence by the movement of sheep.

The trail starts on open slopes to the right of the waterfall as you face it and climbs diagonally from right to left utilizing wide grassy ledges between crags. The going is unexpectedly easy. Twenty minutes walking should see you at the top where you discover that the source of the waterfall is a small lake rimmed with a few live spruce and many dead ones lying on the lakebed. The whole of the uplands between Mount Muir and Mount McPhail is in far worse shape than the inner basin; very few pine and spruce are poking up through the soil in what is still, after nearly 50 years, a graveyard of hollow tree trunks bleached white by the sun of many summers.

The Elk Trail dissipates hereabouts, but picks up again about 100 m beyond the lake, and can be followed without too much trouble up the right-hand side of the valley to the top of the first step. Cross the meadow to the left-hand side of the valley where the trail, gaining strength with every metre, climbs above a second step and veers left into Weary

Creek Gap — a long, narrow pass contained by walls of spruce. A cairn marks the actual watershed. The Weary Creek exploration road starts a half kilometer down the south flank.

A slightly higher pass to the north at map ref. 517846 offers the view lacking at Weary Creek Gap itself. It's best gained by a direct march from the top of the second step; this way your'e sure to pass Patterson's spring, a short-lived stream which feeds tiny islands of firm green meadow, each one big enough to hold a tent. Just over the brow of the hill lies the Great Divide, at this point a wide, windy plain distinguished by a long line of lichen-covered cairns built by the Boundary Survey in 1915. Now you get the view. The low mountains across the Elk Valley are of little interest, but far off to the north rise the stiletto-like peaks of the Italian Group, a tantalizing area at the headwaters of Cadorna Creek which George Pocaterra always referred to by its Stoney name, "Nyahe'-ya-Nibi" which meaning "Go-up-into-the mountains country". Between Mounts Cadorna and Abruzzi lies Walter Wilcox's fabled "Pass in the Clouds" The big, solitary mountain to the S.W. which sorely puzzled Raymond Patterson some 50 years ago and is too far away to be marked on your topo map is Mount Harrison, named after a Cranbrook airman killed during the Second World War and the last of the eleven thousand footers to be climbed.

THE HILL OF FLOWERS

Backpack
Distance 2 km
Height gain 549 m
Maximum elevation 2393 m

Shaped like a large green whale, the Hill of the Flowers stands aloof from the backbone of the Elk Range. Its solitary position makes it an excellent viewpoint; it was while hunting sheep on its upper slopes, that Raymond Patterson and Adolf Baumgart first discovered the Lake of the Horns glinting in the low October sun of 50 years ago.

The normal route up the south ridge starts from the highest point of the McPhail Creek exploration road. Follow a good trail through aspens into a sheltered meadow of long-stemmed asters, bluebells and gaillardias. The trail ends here, so using whatever game trails you can find, push your way through aspen thickets and clamber over huge deadfall reminiscent of the west coast to open hillsides beyond.

Drifts of lupins cover lee slopes like a blue haze. In sunny hollows where the grasses grow tall you'll recognize sticky pink geraniums, bluebeard's tongue, blue flax and many other flowers more commonly associated with prairie meadows. The forest is never more than 100 m below the ridge on the east face of the hill, and it's here at timberline among the lingering snowbanks of early summer that you'll find your acres of golden glacier lilies. Half-way up the hill, larches grow in the shelter of impenetrable spruce hedgerows which cushion the force of battering west winds. On the highest slopes where there is no protection for either man or plant, the delicate flowers of lower altitudes are replaced by hardy alpines lying close to the gravelly ground: forgetmenots, alpine cinqfoils, smelowskias, stonecrops and rose-roots, fleabanes, moss campions, umbrella plants, vetches and pearly everlastings.

View below Weary Creek Gap of Mt. Muir which appears an easy ascent from this direction.

Lake of the Horns headwall. Trail zigzags into the trees, then climbs the rockband above at its narrowest point.

— *Don Hollingshead.*

Headwall below Carnarvon Lake. Route crosses scree slope to the gully below the upper fall, then climbs diagonally right up slabs to a scree slope below the outlet. ►

183 CARNARVON LAKE — Map 11

Long day hike
Intermediate ski
Equestrian, bike
Distance 10 km
Height gain 610 m
Maximum elevation 2149 m
Topo map 82 J/7 Mount Head

Access: Kananaskis Trail (Hwy. 40) at Cat Creek day-use area. NOTE: At the time of publication this section of Highway 40 is closed between December 1st and June 15th.

This exceptionally beautiful lake is guarded by a difficult headwall. Nevertheless, on any summer weekend you'll see fishermen encumbered with tackle box and rod struggling up the "bad step", their lives literally hanging by a thread. Although the headwall is clearly exciting, the rest of the route along logging and exploration roads is extremely tedious, so unless you think you're going to make it to the lake, don't bother setting out along this trail. Non-climbers will appreciate the security of a safety rope; 30 m of 7 mm perlon should be sufficient.

Start as for McPhail Creek (#182). After crossing the Highwood River, follow the road uphill to an important junction. Turn left onto the Carnarvon Creek logging road which is pretty rough for bikers in the vicinity of McPhail Creek crossing, but improves as it winds higher up the hillside onto a bench above Carnarvon Creek. Pass two overgrown roads and one good road to the right at a slight bend. (Skiers! remember this last junction.) The next junction comes a few metres after a side stream crossing on a downhill and is an important one with route #185 at the 5.5. km mark. It can be positively identified by remnants of a logging camp and pieces of wagon lying about in the grass.

You **MUST** turn right here and climb uphill past a grassy road to the left and 2 overgrown roads to the right. A third road to the right can be utilized by skiers looking for a loop. (It switchbacks up the slope, then makes a long traverse north to a T-junction not far below the open ridge line. A right turn here will return you quickly to the Carnarvon Creek logging road at the junction noted earlier.) After this junction, the road descends slightly then climbs in earnest to the bare shoulder of Mount Strachan from where you get a good look at the headwall. Don't descend all the way to valley bottom; about halfway down, a cairn and branches laid across the road guide you onto the Carnarvon Lake trail.

The trail climbs a bit then traverses fans of steep scree between cliff bands to the comfort of a vegetated gully down which flows the infant Carnarvon Creek. From the base of the upper fall, scramble diagonally right up a groove to a ledge. When the ledge merges with the rock face, climb the 10 m slab above with the aid of the knotted rope hanging down between the slab and a corner. (Don't put too much faith in the 5 mm polypropylene rope; although securely placed it would likely snap in the event of a fall There are plans to replace it with a chain in 1985.) Overall, this pitch is easier than the second chain pitch at Ribbon Creek.

Easier ground above still requires vigilance as a slip from here would probably prove fatal. A short scree traverse to the left and suddenly the ground tips back into a horizontal plane again. Youv'e reached the lake. From the outlet a scrambly kind of trail follows the north shore around to good camping spots below the meadows of the Divide. On this side of the lake, shallower waters shade to cobalt blue and pale turquoise under the banks. Looking back towards the lake's outlet you can see why the gap is known as Gunsight Pass.

184 FITZSIMMONS CREEK TO BARIL CREEK — Map 11

Day hike, intermediate ski
Equestrian, bike
Distance 10 km
Alternate start 12.5 km
Height gain 140 m
Maximum elevation 1845 m
Topo map 82 J/7 Mount Head

Access: 1. Kananaskis Trail (Hwy. 40) at Fitzsimmons Creek day- use area. NOTE: At the time of publication this section of Highway 40 is closed between December 1st and June 15th.
Access: 2. Forestry Trunk Road 940. Approximately 1.5 km south of Highwood Junction, a wide track on the west side of the road takes a meandering line through forest to the Fitzsimmons Creek logging road at Fitzsimmons Creek. Use this alternative starting point when Kananaskis Trail is closed or when high water levels discourage hikers from fording the Highwood River at the Fitzsimmons Creek day-use area.

Charlie Fitzsimmons was foreman at No. 1 Lineham logging camp in the years following the First World War. The camp, which was set up in the winter of 1903-04, was sited just a little west of the day-use area and employed about 40 men and a dozen teams. Logs were hauled out and piled up along the banks of the Highwood River to await the spring runoff when they were floated downstream to the sawmill in High River. In 1915, the logging road up Fitzsimmons Creek provided the Boundary Survey with easy access to upper Baril Creek and Fording River Pass. Today, the road can still be used for that purpose, or used as access to the Strawberry Hills or to the fishing ponds east of Coyote Hill. It's an excellent ski trail which must sometimes be shared with snowmobilers.

Straightway, ford the Highwood River. The road can be seen crossing the flats to the mouth of Fitzsimmons Creek where it picks up the alternate start from the left and winds uphill to the bench top. From almost anywhere above the bench, open slopes invite you to climb onto the Strawberry Hills — many hikers do, in fact, make these grassy ridges their day's objective. 4 km from the trailhead, the road dips to cross the north fork, then rises again to an important T-junction with route #185 at the 5 km mark. En route, at the first bend after the stream crossing, a trail doubling back from the left-hand side of the road leads to fishing ponds at map ref. 634813.

Turn left (south). The road rises steadily past secondary logging roads to a pass between Mount Armstrong and Coyote Hill wich is identified by a small pond in a clearing. On the far side of it, the road divides and which way you go depends upon your destination. If you're making for Fording River Pass or Etherington Creek via the Great Divide Trail, keep right on a switchbacking road which joins Baril Creek trail west of the sawmill site. If Baril Creek, Forestry Trunk Road #940 or Etherington Creek via route #188 is your objective, turn left and descend to Baril Creek trail at the junction immediately west of the first creek crossing.

East leg of Strawberry Hills loop looking towards the Great Divide. ➤

185 STRAWBERRY HILLS LOOP — Map 11

Day hike, intermediate ski
Equestrian, bike
6 km between access trails
24 km loop from SR 940
Height gain 440 m
Maximum elevation 1965 m
Topo map 82 J/7 Mount Head

Access: 1. Kananaskis Trail (Hwy. 40) at Fitzsimmons Creek day-use area. Follow Fitzsimmons Creek trail (#184) for 5 km to the T-junction after the north fork crossing.
Access: 2. Kananaskis Trail (Hwy. 40) at Cat Creek day-use area. Follow Carnarvon Lake trail (#183) for 5.5 km to the road junction identified by remnants of a camp. NOTE: At the time of publication this section of Highway 40 is closed between December 1st and June 15th.

The logging road running parallel to the Great Divide west of the Strawberry Hills connects Fitzsimmons Creek trail and Carnarvon Lake trail. In summer, it is strictly a utilitarian link between the two valleys and is of little value to day hikers bound for the Strawberry Hills who have far quicker access from the Fitzsimmons Creek logging road. In winter, the road is worth skiing for its own sake, particularly when joined with another road farther east to make a loop encircling the Strawberry Hills. Remember that after December 1st the Kananaskis Trail is closed and you must start the trip from SR 940. See route #184.

At the 5 km T-junction on Fitzsimmons Creek trail, turn right and recross the north fork. Almost immediately turn left onto a road which climbs over a low forested pass between the highest Strawberry Hill and the Great Divide. Keep right at all questionable junctions until you come to the T-junction close to Carnarvon Creek where you must descend to valley bottom. Ford the creek and wind uphill to the junction with Carnarvon Lake trail on the bench top.

To make the loop, keep right at the last mentioned T-junction and climb back up to a small pass between the Strawberry Hills. On the eastern leg just remember to keep left at all junctions as you follow the major road around the head of Strawberry Creek between grassy hills to the left and the forested hill to the right which is striped with dozens of logging roads. After crossing another small pass (sudden view to the south), the road descends to a junction with the west leg of the loop. Turn left and follow the road back to the T-junction on Fitzsimmons Creek trail.

186 BARIL CREEK TO GREAT DIVIDE TRAIL — Map 11

Day hike, backpack
Intermediate ski
Equestrian, bike
Distance 9 km
Height gain 305 m
Maximum elevation 1814 m
Topo map 82 J/7 Mount Head

Access: Forestry Trunk Road 940. 0.5 km south of Baril Creek, turn west into a parking lot with trail sign.

"Dead Pacer Horse Trail" as the Indians used to call the trail up Baril Creek has for the most part been overlaid by logging roads, exploration roads, and cutlines, and the route is now a tedious one. Nevertheless, because of its relatively short distance, the trail up Baril Creek is the usual way in to Fording River Pass and is consequently well used. Watch for pale blue rectangles painted on trees.

Head west along the cutline/exploration road to riverside meadows where the alternative winter trail from the north bank joins in. A little farther on, a spate of intersecting logging roads pose no route-finding problems now the route is signed; the exploration road twining about the cutline is obvious anyway. Six km in from the trailhead, join route #188 at a major logging road which has come over the ridge from Etherington Creek. Turn right and follow this new road downhill to Baril Creek. Cross, using 2 logs.

On the far bank there is a multiplicity of roads going off in all directions. (The road to the extreme right leads to Fitzsimmons Creek #184.) Make 2 left turns and descend to Baril Creek. Keep right here, following the creek upstream to the mill site where a line of stakes painted blue at the tips guide you across the clearing to the continuation of the road on the far side. Almost immediately keep left at a second junction with Fitzsimmons Creek trail (#184). Cross Baril Creek on 2 logs and climb over a hill — go either way at a split in the road — to another intersection with Baril Creek. Unless you're on skis or a bicycle and bound for Fording River Pass via the exploration road DON'T CROSS. Instead, turn left onto a grassy side road which crosses the creek on logs farther upstream and arrives at the Great Divide Trail about half a kilometre from the crossing.

187 ETHERINGTON CREEK TO GREAT DIVIDE TRAIL — Map 11

Day hike, backpack
Easy ski
Equestrian, bike
Distance 8 km
Height gain 219 m
Maximum elevation 1859 m
Topo map 82 J/7 Mount Head

Access: Forestry Trunk Road 940 at Etherington Creek campground. At the end of the access road between the snowmobile staging area and the group campground, turn right onto a gated logging road.

The Etherington Creek logging road provides easy access to the Great Divide Trail. This is its only attribute, for despite a few meadows in midsection, Etherington Creek is of little interest to the day hiker. In winter, it is the domain of the snowmobiler. NOTE: In recent years, Fish and Wildlife have been snaring black bears and grizzlies in this valley. For up-to-date information, either call in at the Highwood Ranger Station or phone Fish and Wildlife in Calgary before setting out.

The first section of road, which is best tackled by bicycle, crosses Etherington Creek on a good bridge and passes between Raspberry Ridge and a similar unnamed ridge to the north. Two and a half km from the trailhead you arrive at an important junction. The good road crosses Etherington Creek to mill sites near Raspberry Pass; you, however must turn right onto a much rougher road heading up valley towards the mountains. Within half a kilometre you pass 2 roads climbing the hillside which are alternative starts to route #188.

The road winds pleasantly through aspen meadows for another 0.5 km then makes a brief diversion across Etherington Creek to a sawmill site in a large meadow site. On the north bank once more, you pass several overgrown roads to right and left before coming to a questionable junction on the east bank of a side stream at map ref. 643757. Keep left here and cross the stream. (The good logging road to right is part of Baril Loop snowmobile route and joins oute #188 on the ridge top.) Shortly after this junction, the road crosses Etherington Creek twice in quick succession, then climbs uphill to another confusing junction. (The left-hand road is a snowmobile route which joins the Great Divide Trail near the summit of Rye Ridge.) Keep right, following the road around into the narrower, densely forested north fork.

The Great Divide Trail joins the road as the valley begins to open up into meadows. Right now, the Rye Ridge section between Etherington and Cataract Creeks is hard to locate from this direction; the trail tends to grass over in the valley bottom and the red trail markers all face the other way. The addition of blue approach markers as has been done on other approach routes would help enormously. In the meantime, keep looking back over your shoulder.

188 ETHERINGTON CREEK TO BARIL CREEK — Map 11

Day hike, backpack
Intermediate ski
Equestrian, bike
Distance 4 km
Height gain 177m
Height loss 107 m
Maximum elevation 1875 m
Topo map 82 J/7 Mount Head

Access: 1. Via route #187 Etherington Creek to Great Divide Trail. 3 km from the trailhead, turn right (N.W.) up either of two roads climbing the hillside.
Access: 2. Via route #186 Baril Creek to Great Divide Trail. The logging road leaves Baril Creek trail 6 km west of the trailhead.

This uninspiring logging road should never be hiked for its own sake. It does, however, have some value as a connecting trail between Etherington Creek campground and the Baril Creek — Strawberry Hills — Fording River Pass area. In winter, the road makes an excellent ski trail unfortunately shared by snowmobilers. NOTE: In recent years Fish and Wildlife have been snaring black bears and grizzlies on this trail. For up-to-date information either call in at the Highwood Ranger Station or phone Fish and Wildlife in Calgary before setting out.

Both access roads from Etherington Creek join after 0.5 km. Climb past 3 minor roads to the left onto the ridge top where you get a view of sorts through the trees. The road descends a hill, turns sharp left at a T-junction and climbs to a junction with a logging road to left, otherwise known as the Baril Loop snowmobile trail which descends to Etherington Creek at a side stream. (See route #187.) Keep right here. From the highest point on the road 0.25 km farther on, descend in 2 sweeping zigzags to Baril Creek trail.

Lost Creek pine. This view of forest and meadows backdropped by the limestone wall of the Great Divide is typical of all the valleys in the south Highwood.

Eastern escarpment of Raspberry Ridge showing the windings of the fire road.

189 RASPBERRY RIDGE LOOKOUT — Map 12

Day hike, equestrian
Intermediate ski, bike
Distance 7 km
Height gain 649 m
Maximum elevation 2356 m
Topo map 82 J/7 Mount Head

Access: Forestry Trunk Road 940. 6 km south of Etherington Creek campground or 1.5 km north of Cataract Creek bridge, turn west onto the Cataract Creek logging road. Park at the junction with Raspberry Ridge fire road to right, making sure the gate across Cataract Creek logging road is unobstructed; the road still sees occasional use by logging trucks.

Now closed to vehicles, the old fire road to Raspberry Ridge lookout offers an easy walk to a superlative viewpoint. SKIERS NOTE: dangerous avalanche slopes preclude skiing beyond the 3 km mark.

The fire road's gentle windings over a forested ridge are prelude to innumerable zigzags up the steep eastern escarpment of Raspberry Ridge. It's not as bad as it looks from down below; the gradient is always reasonable and there is plenty to look at, from the expanding view of Mount Burke and Plateau Mountain across the valley to the flowers of the meadow under your feet. And if you're there at the right time of year, there's raspberries to eat, but not as many as you would think.

The road gains the south ridge about two thirds of the way along its length. Now turn north and commence the final climb along the ridge line past the helicopter landing pad to the lookout where the full grandeur of the view is at last revealed. I won't even attempt a description; just go armed with a collection of topo maps and binoculars.

Perkinson's cabin.

190 UPPER CATARACT CREEK TO GREAT DIVIDE TRAIL — Map 12

Day hike, backpack
Intermediate ski
Equestrian, bike
Distance 11 km
Height gain 213 m
Maximum elevation 1844
Topo map 82 J/7 Mount Head

Access: Forestry Trunk Road 940. 6 km south of Etherington Creek campground or 1.5 km north of Cataract Creek bridge, turn west onto the Cataract Creek logging road. Park at the junction with Raspberry Ridge fire road to right, making sure the gate across Cataract Creek logging road is unobstructed; the road still sees occasional use by logging trucks.

The logging and exploration roads leading to the Great Divide Trail and beyond to the very foot of the High Rock Range are unexpectedly pleasant. In large measure this is due to the type of country they travel through: the wall-to-wall meadows of the valley, the winding trout stream, the ever-present backcloth of the mountains. In winter all roads in the area become snowmobile trails. NOTE: In recent years Fish and Wildlife have been snaring black bears and grizzlies in this valley. For up-to-date information either call in at the Highwood Ranger Station or phone Fish and Wildlife in Calgary before setting out.

The first 5 km of road to Lost Creek junction is built to forestry trunk road standards, insufferably long to those on foot but a boon to the hiker with a bike. After the initial downhill into the meadows, you cross Cataract Creek twice on good bridges, pass the fish ponds to right and a little later on the Raspberry Pass snowmobile trail which connects with Etherington Creek logging road. Just west of the mill site and on a little knoll between road and river lies the grave of an unknown white man. When dug up several years ago the body was found to be remarkably well-preserved in a coffin made from poles. It's thought he had some connection with the old cabin south of the creek which has a unique waterproof roof made from carved-out poles laid trough up and trough down.

At the junction with route #191 transfer onto the Cataract Creek exploration road straight ahead, a much rougher track signed with pale blue rectangles on trees. It climbs past 2 minor roads to right to a viewpoint on a grassy bank, then drops steeply to valley bottom. Cross the river twice on barely adequate logs. Back on the north bank, disregard the first 2 minor roads to the right. A third road directly after a side stream is a well-used climbers' and hunters' cutline to timberline which bisects the Rye Ridge section of the Great Divide Trail after 2 km — a useful shortcut to know about, but nowhere near as scenic as the official route which continues along the valley bottom.

In another 1.2 km you arrive at Perkinson's Cabin in a meadow. Built and fitted out by range riders (1 bunk which could sleep 2 at a squeeze, table, shelves, chimney), it nowadays sees more use as an emergency shelter by recreationists: chilled snowmobilers, rained-out backpackers, weary trail crews working on the Great Divide Trail, the lone individual out searching for the Lost Lemon Mine, a party of sheep hunters who after a frustrating day on the hills felt impelled to write a poem about it; the registration book and graffiti on the walls reveal a fascinating cross-section of visitors. Pleasant surroundings and a reliable side creek on the west side of the hut make this area an excellent lunch stop or campsite.

You are now very close to the Great Divide Trail. Cross the side creek and continue along the road for another half kilometre or so until 2 blue rectangles on a tree indicate a left turn onto a trail which heads towards Cataract Creek. A flurry of red rectangles marks the T-junction on the bank top.

191 LOST CREEK TO GREAT DIVIDE TRAIL — Map 12

Day hike, backpack
Easy ski
Equestrian, bike
6.5 km from Cataract Creek junction
Height gain 131 m
Maximum elevation 1844 m
Topo map 82 J/7 Mount Head
82 J/2 Fording River

Access: Forestry Trunk Road 940. Follow route #190 for 5 km to the Great Divide Trail.

The logging road up Lost Creek is far from being an aesthetic hiking or equestrian trail, particularly the first 4 km of it to the mill site which still sees occasional use by logging trucks from Spray Lakes Lumber Company. In winter, the whole route and all side roads are designated snowmobile trails. NOTE: In recent years, Fish and Wildlife have been snaring black bears and grizzlies in this valley. For up-to-date information either call in at the Highwood Ranger Station or phone Fish and Wildlife in Calgary before setting out.

Start off along the Upper Cataract Creek logging road. Five km from the trailhead, bear left onto the Lost Creek logging road which straightway bridges Cataract Creek and climbs onto a bench high above Lost Creek. Pass 2 secondary roads to the left, both signed snowmobile routes — thoroughly boring in summer — leading to Cummings Creek and ultimately over a forested ridge to Pasque Mountain trail (#195) in Wilkinson Creek. At the 4 km mark the road bridges Lost Creek to a former mill site on the west bank. From this point on start watching for pale blue rectangles painted on trees.

Turn left at the mill site onto a grassed-over road which winds about pleasant valley meadows and makes 4 unbridged crossings of the creek. A few metres after passing a grassy track to the right, you come to a T-junction with a cutline heading straight for the Divide. (The road carrying on into the south fork of Lost Creek is route #193). Turn right here and follow the cutline for about 100 m to a flurry of red rectangles marking the Great Divide Trail.

192 OLDMAN RIVER TO GREAT DIVIDE TRAIL — Map 12

Day hike, backpack
Equestrian, bike
Distance 5.5 km
Height gain 183 m
Maximum elevation 1996 m
Topo map 82 J/2 Fording River

Access: Forestry Trunk Road 940. 28.8 km south of the junction with Johnson Creek Trail, turn west onto the Oldman River Road which is signposted "Oldman Recreation Area". Drive up the road for 27.3 km, passing the campground at 2.1 km, the group camp and horse corrals at 3.2 km and Arrowhead Drilling Rig access road at 22.9 km. At 27.3 km, keep left at a split in the road and park down in the meadows by the Oldman River. In dry conditions, all-terrain vehicles can reach the unnamed creek west of Oyster Creek.

The Galena Miracle Mine road makes a very fast and easy approach route to the Great Divide Trail. In fall, the route is beseiged by hunters so take all necessary precautions.

The temporary split in the road at the parking area can be taken either way, although the meadow route is considerably wetter thanks to a nearby beaver dam. The next point of interest is the Oyster Creek cutline on the right, followed in a few metres by Oyster Creek itself which is just too wide to jump across. The navigable section of the road ends at the next unnamed creek to the west which coincides with the end of the valley meadows and the entrance of the road, now partly rehabilitated, into the old forest.

When the road turns right up a soggy draw, transfer temporarily onto a pack trail which runs along the bank top for 0.3 km before rejoining the road in a clearing. Turn left here and cross a lively stream with padded moss banks. After 2 km of straight going the road splits into three. Choose the middle course — the right-hand road, although the original mine road, has been partly covered with slash and is not recommended for travel — and arrive shortly afterwards at a 4-way intersection with the Great Divide Trail (red rectangles, cairn).

The Elevators from Oldman River Road.

The Lost Creek scout bridge.

193 OYSTER CREEK TO LOST CREEK — Map 12

Day hike, backpack
Equestrian
Distance 12 km;
Height gain and loss 198 m
Maximum elevation 2027 m
Topo map 82 J/2 Fording River

Access: 1. Via route #192, Oldman River to Great Divide Trail at Oyster Creek.
Access: 2. Via route #191, Lost Creek to Great Divide Trail at the T-junction with the cutline.

A grassed-over cutline offers a totally uninteresting but very fast route between the Oldman River and Lost Creek. If you've time to spare, it may be worthwhile retracing the old pack trail, originally an old Indian Trail used by early explorers including dominion geologist G.W.Dawson. Reportedly, it can be located a little east of the cutline at the Oldman River end; look for blazes low down near the ground. I have been unable to locate it in the south fork of Lost Creek; no doubt the trail has been overlaid in part by the cutline and logging road, or has simply grown over from lack of use.

The cutline starts on the east bank of Oyster Creek at the sign prohibiting motorized vehicles. For most of its length in this valley, it follows riverside meadows which in the lower reaches of the creek are very swampy and require numerous detours. Cross the watershed in mature forest. At the head of the south fork of Lost Creek, you have the option of either continuing on down the cutline or of turning left onto a logging road winding through cutblocks. If you choose the latter course, keep right at all junctions until you reach the west bank of the south fork where the cutline comes in from the right. Ford the river and a few minutes later cross Lost Creek on a log bridge tied together in 1980 by 10 boys from the 153rd scout group. 100 m farther on, a T-junction with a cutline to left marks your arrival at Lost Creek trail.

194 THE GREAT DIVIDE TRAIL

From small beginnings in 1974 when a core group of 6 people undertook a feasibility study under the Federal Opportunities for Youth Program, the Great Divide Trail Association has grown to a number of individuals and supporting organizations "dedicated to the establishment of a protected corridor for the proposed Great Divide Trail and to the initiation of the Trail's construction and maintenance in all sectors outside the National and Provincial Parks".

Trail building began in 1977 with the section described in this book. It took 5 summers to construct the 42.5 km of trail between the Oldman River and Fording River Pass, but it is now complete with the exception of a 2 km stretch over Cataract Plateau. The trail was built to be aesthetically pleasing: it has a narrow tread width and bridges are usually simple constructions of two parallel hewn logs. It is marked throughout by red rectangles painted on trees; two rectangles indicate a junction or sudden change of direction. Approach routes, with the present exception of Etherington Creek and Oldman River trails, are marked with pale blue rectangles. Although it is almost impossible to get lost once you're on the trail, it's always good practice to carry a topo map.

OLDMAN RIVER TO LOST CREEK — Map 12

Backpack, equestrian
Distance 17 km
Height gain 555 m
Height loss 661 m
Maximum elevation 2240 m
Topo map 82 J/2 Fording River

Access: 1. Via terminus of route #192, Oldman River to Great Divide Trail.
Access: 2. Via terminus of route #191, Lost Creek to Great Divide Trail.

From the 4-way junction with cairn at the terminus of route # 192, turn right (north) past Memory Lake — possible camping spot — to the Galena Miracle Mine road. Turn left and start climbing. Just after the first left-hand bend, watch for red rectangles on the uphill slope indicating a shortcut which delivers you to the left-hander one zig higher up. At the corner of this bend (also the jumping-off point for Galena Miracle Mine), the Great Divide Trail leaves the road and heads north under scree slopes strewn with an ore cart, pinion gears and other paraphernalia fallen down from the mine above.

The trail follows the larch belt in and out of the cirque, rounds a dividing ridge and travels in much the same sort of way around another cirque at the head of the west fork of Oyster Creek. A high knobbly ridge jutting out to the N.E. from the Divide puts an end to this pleasurable form of progress and you must climb steeply to gain a col at map ref. 633595. Turning your back on the mountains now, wind around the south slopes of knobs #2 and #3 to the col west of knob #4 which on the topo map is marked as a triangulation point of 7446 feet. A young forest and many open slopes allow excellent views from all along this section of trail.

From the col, the trail turns north and climbs over the top of knob #5 (cairn) and down the other side through fir forest to a 4-way junction with a logging road at the edge of a cutblock. Go straight along a new trail which intersects another road at the northern edge of the cutblock then descends to Lost Creek. Cross the bridge. The trail continues through meadows suitable for camping and emerges within a few minutes onto a cutline which is the terminus of route #191.

Wind-blown environs of Galena Miracle Mine looking south to Beehive Mtn. (left) and Mt. Lyall (right).

GALENA MIRACLE MINE (2377 m) Backpackers should allow at least 2 hours for this diversion. The mine and its environs is also accessible to the day hiker from the Oldman River Road; the total distance is 20 km with a height gain of 564 m.

From the junction of road and Great Divide Trail at the second left-hand bend it's quicker to forgo the mine road which is a long drawn-out affair and climb instead up the obvious ridge through the larches. The faint trail peters out on grassy slopes rolling up against the bulwark of the Divide. Alrady there is a good view of Mount Lyall and Beehive Mountain which from this direction has a decided lean to the east as if shaped by the winds which blow with such ferocity in this part of the country.

The mine is much higher up than you think and situated not on the windswept ridge but 30 m down the precipice to the right. The first things you notice as you look cautiously over the edge are iron stanchions scattered about the face and then a faint trail in the scree leading down to the mouth of a shaft. Closer investigation reveals 2 tunnels 100 m long, one of which is shaped like the letter T with arms extending 50 m in opposite directions. An ore cart and section of rail still remain. Opened in 1920, the mine closed in 1938 after only fifty dollars worth of lead, silver and zinc had been removed — hardly enough to pay for the building of the road.

LOST CREEK TO UPPER CATARACT CREEK VIA CATARACT PLATEAU — Map 12

Backpack, equestrian
Distance 8 km
Height gain 427 m
Height loss 427 m
Maximum elevation 2271 m
Topo map 82 J/2 Fording River
82 J/7 Mount Head

Access: 1. Via terminus of route #191, Lost Creek to Great Divide Trail.
Access: 2. Via terminus of route #190, Upper Cataract Creek to Great Divide Trail.

Follow the cutline towards the mountains. In about 100 m, at a kink in the cutline, turn right onto a hunters' pack trail which climbs 1100 m up a forested ridge issuing from Cataract Plateau which is not really a plateau at all but a spreading out of the east ridge of Mount Farquar. The trail ends in a deep coulee almost separating the 2 distinct halves of the plateau.

There is no trail, markers, cairns or flagging for the next 2 km. Pending further talks with Fish and Wildlife, the Great Divide Trail Association has not yet decided on the line the trail will take through what Fish and Wildlife claim is prime elk habitat. What I suggest you do in the meantime is the obvious; that is, head N.W. up a short open slope to the ridge top at map ref. 623663 topo map 82 J/2, then continue walking in a north- westerly direction along the open crest of the ridge which allows spectacular views in all directions and is not to be missed. When the ridge dips below treeline watch for flagging and the reappearance of the trail winding down right-hand (N.E.) slopes to Cataract Creek. Cross the bridge and climb the north bank to a junction with Upper Cataract Creek trail and the next section of the Great Divide Trail over Rye Ridge.

View from the slopes of knob #5 towards next section of trail over Cataract Plateau. The sharp peak in the centre of the photo is unnamed and unclimbed.

View from Rye Ridge of Mts. Farquhar (left), unnamed, Holcroft and Scrimger.

UPPER CATARACT CREEK TO ETHERINGTON CREEK VIA RYE RIDGE — Map 12

Backpack, equestrian
Distance 7.5 km
Height gain 259 m
Height loss 244 m
Maximum elevation 2103 m
Topo map 82 J/7 Mount Head

Access: **1. Via terminus of route #190, Upper Cataract Creek to Great Divide Trail.**
Access: **2. Via terminus of route #187, Etherington Creek to Great Divide Trail.**

The trail initially heads towards the mountains through cinquefoil bushes massed along the river bank. Close to the north fork, it turns north and climbs quite steeply to an exploration road which in turn is followed uphill to a T-junction with the climbers' and hunters' access cutline starting from route #190. Walk right along the cutline for a few minutes. Opposite another exploration road coming in from the right, red rectangles and a snowmobile sign on the left-hand side of the cutline indicate the start of the trail over Rye Ridge.

The trail, which takes more or less the same line as the snowmobile route gains height exceedingly slowly through fir forest and the only way you have of knowing when you've reached the ridge top is the sighing of the wind through the treetops. Higher up, you emerge onto wind-blasted meadows dotted with spruce and pine thickets, islands of calm if you can fight your way through to the hollow centres. To your left screes dribble down the western escarpment above Etherington Creek. The route follows cairns around the edge of the escarpment over the highest point of Rye Ridge (really an outlier of Mosquito Hill to the east) and down the far side into the main fork of Etherington Creek. Meanwhile, the snowmobile route has turned off to the right, aiming for a cutblock. Bridge Etherington Creek and cross the triangular piece of forest in the angle of the 2 creeks to the north fork. Join Etherington Creek logging road on the east bank.

ETHERINGTON CREEK TO BARIL CREEK — Maps 11 & 12

Backpack, equestrian
Distance 5 km
Height gain 274 m
Height loss 320 m
Maximum elevation 2134 m
Topo map 82 J/7 Mount Head

Access: **1. Via terminus of route #187, Etherington Creek to Great Divide Trail.**
Access: **2. Via terminus of route #186, Baril Creek to Great Divide Trail.**

Follow the logging road up the north fork of Etherington Creek into meadows suitable for camping. It intersects a grassy road, then at the next junction turns left across the creek. At the second bend after the crossing, transfer onto a marked trail which shortly recrosses the creek on a single log, an exercise in tightrope walking you can avoid by using the equestrian trail to the right. For a long time, the trail gains height slowly through the old forest and when you think you must surely be arriving at the watershed ridge, it changes direction and climbs straight up towards the N.E. outlier of Baril Peak. The reason for this deviation is "Lunch Stop Meadow" — acknowledgedly a fine viewpoint and resting spot.

From here it's all downhill into Baril Creek. In an area of intersecting logging roads low down, keep a close watch on the red rectangles; keep left at the first road you come to, turn right onto a second road but follow it for only a few metres before resuming your downward course on the trail. At valley bottom cross Baril Creek on a wide log to a logging road on the north bank, turn right and arrive within a few minutes at the junction with Baril Creek trail straight ahead and the Fording River Pass section of the Great Divide Trail to left.

FORDING RIVER PASS — Map 11

Backpack, equestrian
Difficult ski, bike
Distance 5 km
Height gain 555 m
Maximum elevation 2368 m
Topo map 82 J/7 Mount Head

Access: **Via terminus of route #186, Baril Creek to Great Divide Trail.**

Fording River Pass which is renowned for the magnificence of its cirques, is at the time of publication the northern boundary of the Great Divide Trail. In recent years the Great Divide Trail Association has uncovered the old Indian trail and this is now the normal route for hikers and equestrians. Skiers (and bikers) coming in from Baril Creek should keep to the exploration road throughout and be prepared for long, steep hills requiring not only herringboning but traversing with kick turns as well.

From the junction in Baril Creek, climb the hill to a T-junction above James Lake. (The right-hand trail leads past camp sites at the lake's outlet to the Baril Creek exploration road.) Walk left a few metres to the registration box, then continue up a small side creek to the road. A short stint through the trees north of the road is followed by a longer section south of the road close to the west fork of Baril Creek. Although the trail cuts out

Mt. Cornwall cirque from Fording River Pass.

2 horrendous hills on the exploration road as it climbs around the south ridge of Mount Armstrong, it only postpones the inevitable and later rather than sooner you are climbing uphill onto the stony spur above the right-angled bend in the creek. Follow cairns. The trail recrosses the road, and running parallel with it, descends to valley bottom where sheltered camping spots can be found on scraps of meadow between willow bushes. Upstream of the creek crossing at map ref. 587773 the creek divides. A little way up the lively left-hand fork which issues from the dip between Mounts Boulton and Armstrong you'll find a log hut dating back to the turn of the century. At a pinch, for there isn't much space between floor and roof, it could be used as an emergency shelter.

You get no idea from looking at the topo map that the valley at this point is enclosed by a ring of cliffs. The road takes the line of least resistance through the headwall — another steep hill. The trail winds between road and the lively left-hand fork to meadows above the headwall where it joins the road for the final stretch across a wasteland of polished bedrock littered with rocks dropped by melting glaciers. Half a kilometre to the south a glint of water marks the true location of Fording River Pass at a pond in a rocky defile.

The road carries on into British Columbia, zigzagging down the west slope past the south shore of a lake to a road junction. Backpackers have the choice of either turning left onto Fording River road or of going straight down the Aldridge Creek road, though what you do when you reach the Elk Valley is uncertain since there is no ongoing trail at the moment. However, there is plenty to occupy you around the pass area for at least 2 days. You could, for instance, spend a day visiting the celebrated cirques enclosed by Mounts Shankland, Maclaren and Armstrong which are easily reached by a side road branching off from the Aldridge Creek road 0.5 km west of the aforementioned junction. A quicker, more interesting route into that valley starts from the dip between Mount Bolton and Mount Armstrong, but don't try this route in winter; the steep slope on the B.C. side is a lee slope and potentially hazardous.

Boundary Survey cairn on north summit.

195 PASQUE MOUNTAIN — Map 12

Day hike
Equestrian, bike
Distance 8.5 km
Height gain 729 m
Maximum elevation 2543 m
Topo map 82 J/2 Fording River

Access: Forestry Trunk Road 940. 8.5 km south of Cataract Creek bridge, park on the west side of the road at the entrance to a logging road signed "No Motorized Vehicles".

Pasque Mountain in the S.W. corner of Kananaskis Country has a beautiful north ridge which deserves to be better known by connoisseurs of ridge walks. Access is made easy by a progression of logging and exploration roads between Highway 940 and the open slopes.

Start off by walking along the logging road. Just after crossing Wilkinson Creek, turn right onto a major road which in turn crosses a smaller creek issuing from the north side of Pasque Mountain. Round the next bend, 3 lesser roads converge on the road, the second one to the right being the Cummings Creek snowmobile trail which offers a route of sorts to Lost Creek (see route #191). Stay on the major road for another kilometre, then turn left onto a narrower, rougher road which recrosses the small creek and ends in a large clearing stacked with logs. So far, height gain has been minimal, but now your imminent entry onto an exploration road heralds the start of a steep climb onto the summit ridge. Mountain bikers should consider taking to their feet.

The road leaves the top left-hand corner of the clearing, crosses another small stream and begins climbing up a ridge at the demarcation line of pines and steep, grass slopes falling away to the valley bottom. A flat meadow on a saddle at map ref. 716621 allows a brief respite before you tackle even steeper windings of the road through a lovely larch forest extending all the way round the cirque N.E. of the mountain. The windings sharpen into definite zigzags during the final climb up open slopes onto the north end of the ridge which is gained at map ref. 710613. Take a well-earned rest.

Now walk south along the broad grassy ridge to a slight dip where you can pick up a game trail traversing east-side meadows below a little rocky crest. The trail peters out on flat ground below the north summit which is unmarked on the topo map but which lies at map ref. 713594, a rocky knobbin topped by a cairn built by the Boundary Survey in 1915 and easily climbed.

Strong hikers should continue on to the south summit which is actually 1.5 m higher and connected for the most part by a narrow ridge of blocks covered in black lichen. The only bit where you need to use your hands occurs during the descent to the gap. The first of two small rock steps — the projecting ends of vertical rock strata — is best taken direct; the second one is turned more easily on the left-hand side. As you walk up the final red shale slope to the summit, search the ground for cushions of skunkweed, an unfortunate name for a most beautiful plant which is related to the sky pilots of the Sierra Nevada. It's usually found growing much farther south on the high ridges of Waterton National Park, and can be distinguished from Jacobs ladder — a less brighter and more spindlier species which is common in meadows and on grassy ridges throughout Kananaskis Country — by its compact form, crested-shaped leaves and larger flowers of an intense royal blue.

From the summit cairn (the Boundaray Survey's No. 1 camera station on Pasque Mountain), look west across hectares of forest bisected by cutlines. Snowmobile trails wind in and out of valleys close in; farther out, the Great Divide Trail traverses the skirts of the mountains and can be seen in part where it follows the windings of the Galena Miracle Mine road. To the left of easily-identifiable Beehive Mountain rise twin rock towers known to residents of the Nanton area as The Elevators for obvious reasons. Despite numerous attempts by Glen Boles and Don Forest, the left-hand tower remains unclimbed. Of more interest to hikers perhaps is the view to the south which is a powerful inducement to keep on walking along a chain of high grassy ridges lying in the angle between the Oldman and the Livingstone Rivers. With help from exploration roads criss-crossing the area, the ridges could be joined up to make a high-level walk lasting several days.

Ridge between north and south summits.

196 PLATEAU MOUNTAIN — Map 13

Day hike
Equestrian, bike
Distance 9.5 km
Circuit 14.5 km
Height gain 527 m
Maximum elevation 2524 m
Topo map 82 J/2 Fording River

Access: 1. Forestry Trunk Road 940 at Wilkinson Summit. The gated access road on the north side of the highway is Plateau Mountain Road which until a few years ago was open to public vehicles.
Access: 2. Forestry Trunk Road 940 at Dry Creek. Park at the gated access road 0.7 km east of Wilkinson Summit.

Plateau Mountain is unique in the Canadian Rockies. Once a nunatuk rising above the glaciers of the last ice age, a refuge for animal and plant life of that period, it is today a steep- sided tableland with over 14 square kilometres rising above the 2,300 m level. There are no trails to the top, only roads leading to lonely gas wells. Both the routes described make use of the roads — one can hardly do otherwise — and for this reason neither route is completely satisfactory to those on foot. A bike is the recommended mode of travel.

Plateau Mountain Road, which in its early stages is usually in better shape than the Forestry Trunk Road itself, gains height exceedingly slowly, following an unnamed valley for 4 tedious kilometres. The route begins to improve after the first hairpin bend; you have climbed up out of the trees, and by the time the next bend is reached on the rim of a lower plateau, a glorious view has opened up behind you. The peaks of the Divide, nearly all pyramidical in form, are strung out along the horizon like a paper cutout.

Plateau Mtn. Road.

After you've crossed the lower plateau and climbed onto the plateau proper you arrive at a junction. The forever road to the left does eventually end at a gas well. By an unhappy coincidence, Plateau Mountain ice cave is close by. Because large numbers of people could in the past drive almost to the cave's mouth, the inevitable damage occurred to such delicate features as ice flowers and corkscrew stalagtites. I am not talking specifically about vandalism, although I daresay there was some of that too, but the more subtle damage caused by heat radiating from bodies. Nowadays, a locked gate bars entry.

If you go right at the aforementioned junction, you walk past a gas well to the highest point of Plateau Mountain appropriately marked by a gas valve and an underground pipeline. The road divides hereabouts, the right-hand branch leading to a radio tower on the edge of the southern escarpment and the left-hand branch winding down to further gas wells and access roads which all converge on Hailstone Butte fire road.

Notice how the southern half of the plateau is decorated by a latticework of black-lichened rocks. Differential sorting caused by continual freezing and thawing during a colder epoch has forced the larger rocks upwards and outwards from areas of finer material into a self perpetuating pattern of circles and polygons known as "patterned ground". On steeper ground at the edge of the plateau the stones are aligned in stripes.

Either return the same way or make a circuit with Dry Creek. From the gas valve on the summit, walk west along the buried pipeline to the edge of the escarpment where an access trail shaped like the letter M on its side zigzags slowly down the hillside into Dry Creek. Pick up the valley road at the valves and follow it out to Highway 940. Plateau Mountain Road lies less than a kilometre away to the west.

197 WINDY PEAK HILLS — Map 13

Day hikes
Equestrian
Maximum elevation 2249 m
Topo map 82 J/1 Langford Creek

Access: 1. Johnson Creek Trail (SR 532) at the Summit parking lot.
Access: 2. Forestry Trunk Road 940 at South Twin Creek, 1 km south of the junction with Johnson Creek Trail. Park just south of the texas gate.
Access: 3. Johnson Creek Trail (SR 532) at the southern terminus of Timber Creek trail 1.5 km west of the Summit. Via North Twin Creek (#201).

The name refers to a compact group of grassy ridges, of which Windy Peak is the highest summit, lying in the angle between Johnson Creek Trail (Hwy.) and Forestry Trunk Road 940. Due to some configuration of the mountains to the west, the Windy Peak Hills, true to their name, lie in an incredibly windswept region of the Livingstone Range. Lenticular clouds are a familiar formation above the ridge tops; on the ground, notice the dense sprawling mats of spruce thickets and the clear-cut demarcation line between leeward and windward slopes.

For a few months in 1931 the area around North and South Twin Creeks was the site of much hullabaloo when gold was purportedly discovered. The year before, King Bearspaw (grandson of Jacob Bearspaw of Lost Lemon Mine fame) had been prospecting in the area and was being followed around by two white prospectors who thought he was on to something big. The Lost Lemon Mine perhaps? When he gave them the slip for two weeks and later turned up at the King George Hotel in High River with some gold in his hand, the two prospectors immediately staked claims on the spot as did dozens of other aspirants in the weeks following. Needless to say, all that was ever found were a few iron pyrites.

The most popular route onto the hills starts from the parking lot at Johnson Creek Trail Summit; the open slope rising to the northernmost ridge top is irresistible. The old roads up North and South Twin Creeks provide other ways in. The North Twin Creek road passes between the northern and central ridges and carries on down into Timber Creek (see route #201). The road up South Twin Creek ends at a col between the central and southern ridges. Half-way along, a cutblock on the north side can be used as a a shortcut to North Twin Creek and Highway 532. Opposite the cutblock, the beautiful north ridge of Windy Peak rises to a well-defined summit. From the cairn look across at Lake-at-the-end-of-the- ridge, a tantalizing eye of blue easily reached via a subsidiary ridge jutting east from the central ridge.

By using the 2 roads up the Twin Creeks and by following in- between ridges which are faintly marked by game trails, you can concoct circuit walks varying in length from a few hours to a full day. And if you have several days to spare you can continue in this fashion over saddle-shaped Shaddle Mountain, Horseshoe Ridge and Chaffer Ridge — all the way south to where the Oldman River cuts through the mountains onto the prairies.

198 HAILSTONE BUTTE LOOKOUT — Map 13

Day hike
Equestrian, bike via fire road
Distance 3.5 km
Distance via fire road 10 km
Height gain 336 m
Maximum elevation 2363 m
Topo map 82 J/1 Langford Creek

Access: 1. Johnson Creek Trail (SR 532) at the Summit parking lot.
Access: 2. Forestry Trunk Road 940. Park at the entrance to the fire road a few metres west of the junction with Johnson Creek Trail.
Also accessible from the southern terminus of Sentinal Pass trail (#210) and the western terminus of Iron Creek trail (#203).

Generally a fire road offers the best route to a fire lookout. Not in this case, though. Over half of it has been incorporated into the Savanna Gasfield road system and a more thoroughly boring route would be hard to imagine although Plateau Mountain Road comes close. It's best tackled by bicycle. Keep right at every road junction.

The best route for hikers starts from Johnson Creek Trail Summit. Walk south down the road for a few metres, then turn west up an open valley on a beginning trail which is largely superfluous. Arriving at the valley head at map ref. 817645 you have a choice of 2 routes. The easier route follows a sketchy trail across a concave scree slope poised above colorful Skene canyon. On reaching the security of the terrace on the other side, traverse across to the fire road and follow its gentle windings up the escarpment — now bereft of the rockband — onto the summit ridge. Backtrack along the ridge for 1 km to the lookout.

Hailstone Butte. The alternative hiking route climbs the steep slopes below the lookout.

View from the slopes of Hailstone Butte of Johnson Creek Trail (Hwy.) and the Windy Peak Hills. Windy Peak (centre middleground) is located between saddle-shaped Shaddle Mtn. (centre top) and Mt. Livingstone (right top).

The alternate route is steep and direct; incredibly, the graduating grade 6 class from Nanton Elementary School comes up this way every year, bearing poems and drawings for the lookout. From the valley head you turn left and climb ever steepening and very slippery grass slopes rolling up to the rockband below the lookout. Scramble easily up the bottom tier of rock then head diagonally right up loose ground to a sloping ledge below the top tier. Traverse right above the steepest part of the cliff — this is the only potentially dangerous part — until an easy line through the band presents itself. You should emerge by the helicopter pad, only a few steps away from the lookout. Take care when topping-out not to let the strong west winds catch you off balance.

The lookout is the second one on Hailstone Butte. In 1979 it replaced a one-room box erected in 1952 which was removed in the summer of 1982 after it appeared to be in danger of falling over the eroding cliff edge. Wind permitting, plan on spending another hour walking south along the broad grassy ridge to a summit of equal height.

199 BEAR LAKE — Map 13

Half-day hike
Distance 1 km
Height gain 61 m
Topo map 82 J/1 Langford Creek

Bear Lake with Windy Peak Hills as backdrop.

Access: Johnson Creek Trail (SR 532). The all-terrain vehicle road signed "No motorized vehicles" leaves the north side of the highway approximately 10.5 km west of Kananaskis Country boundary or 2.8 km east of the Summit.

If you look towards the prairies from Johnson Creek Trail Summit, your eye is held by the blue circle of a lake sitting astride the long ridge running east from Hailstone Butte. This is Bear Lake, less than half an hour's walk from the highway up a grassed-over road, later a well-used trail which climbs fairly steeply through meadow and mixed forest to the lakeshore. The trail crosses a small earth dam and continues along the east shore, finally dissipating at the northern end in a web of diverging trails leading nowhere.

200 NORTH FORK OF JOHNSON CREEK — Map 13

Half-day, day hike
Equestrian
Distance 3 km
Height gain 98 m to meadow
Maximum elevation 1874 m at end of trail
Topo map 82 J/1 Langford Creek

Access: **Johnson Creek Trail (SR 532). Approximately 7.8 km west of Kananaskis Country boundary or 5.5 km east of the Summit, park at an informal camping area on the east side of the highway.**

This short, easy trail leads to the long meadow below the eastern escarpment of Hailstone Butte — a delightful spot in which to idle away a hot summer afternoon. Restless hikers have the option of going farther, all the way to Hailstone Butte lookout if they want to though the route is not one I'd reccommend.

Cross the highway to an old road which travels along the south bank of the north fork. Initially, the road stays close to the rushing stream (keeping low at a temporary division), then, narrowing to single cow width, moves away to cross a side creek in a small luxuriant meadow. It returns to the north fork on a forested bench high above the stream which is now closeted in a deep trough; in this way, both trail and stream turn west and enter the long meadow between outposts of straggly willow trees. At this end of the meadow the grass grows waist-high and is resplendent with red and white sticky geraniums, cow parsleys and yellow buttercups.

If you want more exercise, follow the trail down the centre of the meadow into trees at the far left-hand corner — a distance of about 1 km. Cross a muddy streamlet of no consequence, then head up a small side valley to the south of the main creek. Be sure to stay on the north bank of this side valley; don't cross the creek or follow what appears to be a larger trail branching right near the beginning. When the ground levels, the trail turns right onto a bench below a steep grass escarpment carpeted with thousands of blue lupins. A dead tree trunk propped into an upright position marks the end of the trail. Walk a bit farther until you can look across at the north fork of Johnson Creek falling in cascades down a rocky gully. Both the gully and the escarpment are vulnerable to a determined attack by the hiker aiming for Hailstone Butte lookout, but be warned: the going is relentlessly steep.

201 TIMBER CREEK — Map 13

Day hike
Equestrian, bike
Distance 18 km
Height gain 640 m
Maximum elevation 2057 m
Topo map 82 J/1 Langford Creek

Access: 1. Johnson Creek Trail (SR 532). 3.8 km west of Kananaskis Country boundary, turn S.E. onto the Willow Creek Road. (This is not the road nearest Willow Creek bridge which dead-ends.) Since the road is outside of Kananaskis Country, you can drive as far as conditions permit, certainly to the first gate at the half kilometre mark and maybe another 3.5 km to the beaver pond which floods the road at a side creek at map ref. 915669.
Access: 2. Johnson Creek Trail (SR 532). Park on the east side of the highway 1.5 km west of the Summit.

A grassed-over exploration road — snowmobile route in winter — runs the length of this lovely aspen-clad valley, crossing the Windy Peak hills at its head into the Livingstone River drainage where it joins Highway. 532. En route, various side roads offer all kinds of possibilities for further exploration.

From Highway 532 the Willow Creek Road travels through riverside meadows to a junction. Ford the river and continue on past the side creek with beaver pond to the mouth of Timber Creek where you arrive at a second gate at the point where another road joins in from the left. Keep right. It takes about 5 minutes to walk through private land to the boundary gate by the side of a pond. Shortly afterwards you ford Timber Creek, keep left at a junction on the riverbank and climb a hill to a complicated convergence of 2 roads and an E-W cutline. Go right, following the road which winds about the cutline. In 2 km, it cuts loose and fords the creek to north-bank meadows. The crossing of a N-S cutline signals the crossing and recrossing of the creek below the forks. Disregard a side road to the left before the second crossing. Similarly, after the forks, walk on by another road to left which also heads up the south fork of Timber Creek to the base of Windy Peak.

Begin climbing to the pass up shaley ground supporting pines and not much ground cover. Take a breather on a col overlooking Johnson Creek, then continue in much the same sort of fashion as before to a high point level with the pass. Traverse intervening grass slopes, stopping often to admire the tremendous view of Timber Creek spread out below. Bits of blue color in the distance are the Chain Lakes Reservoirs. From the gate at the pass the view to the west is cut off by a nearby ridge, so without further ado, for the west wind batters ceaselessly at these slopes, descend into North Twin Creek through a remnant of the old forest. In just over 2 km from the pass the road emerges onto meadows adjoining Johnson Creek Trail.

202 WILLOW CREEK — Maps 13 & 14

Day hike, backpack, easy ski
Equestrian, bike
Distance 12 km
Height gain 192 m
Maximum elevation 1640 m
Topo map 82 J/1 Langford Creek
82 J/8 Stimson Creek

Access: **Johnson Creek Trail (SR 532). 3.9 km west of Kananaskis Country boundary, park in a dead-end road S.E. of the highway. (Thisis the road nearest Willow Creek bridge.)**
Also accessible from Pekisko Creek trail (#209), the eastern terminus of Iron Creek trail (#203) and the western terminus of Stimson and Hay Creek trail (#207).

This former all-terrain vehicle road is an important link between Secondary Road 532 and Pekisko Creek trail where you can pick up ongoing connections to Forestry Trunk Road 940 and the Highwood Trail (Hwy.). It also serves as an artery for trails peeling off to east and west: Indian Graves Ridge (#205), Iron Creek (#203), Willow Creek Hills (#206), Corral Creek (#204), Stimson & Hay Creeks (#207), all of which can be utilized in a variety of loops incorporating the mother trail. The route is well-marked with snowmobile signs throughout.

Cross the highway to Willow Creek trail opposite. Known to the Indians as Stiapiskan, meaning Ghost Hound, Willow Creek exhibits none of its sinister connotations. On the contrary, it is a bright, sunny valley with wall to wall meadows bound by low, friendly hills to the east and the familiar profiles of Hailstone Butte and Sentinel Peak to the west. 2 km along the road, just past a side creek, route #206 to Willow Creek Hills turns off to the right, followed a few metres on by a cutline access road and then the E.W. cutline itself. Cross another small side stream. The first road to the left — very much grassed over — is Iron Creek trail (#203). Next to intersect the road is a major N-S cutline, followed in 1.3 km by a road on the right from Willow Creek Hills (#206) and 2 cutlines in quick succession. Ford Willow Creek. Corral Creek trail (#204) turns left in the big meadow just before the road recrosses to the east bank. In 1 km ford Willow Creek for the third time. Watch for Stimson & Hay Creeks trail (#207) heading upstream on the west bank.

At this point the road turns away from the main valley, following instead the north bank of a side creek for a short distance, then crossing over a low forested pass into the west fork of Willow Creek. Cross the creek and pass through a gap in the hills to the north out of the Willow Creek drainage into that of Pekisko Creek. Enter a large meadow holding two dark ponds. 1.5 km downstream of the ponds, keep left at a junction and cross the creek to the west bank. Disregard a cutline and arrive shortly afterwards at a 4-way road junction with Pekisko Creek trail (left, straight) and the road to Devil's Bite (right).

203 IRON CREEK — Map 13

Day hike
Equestrian
Distance 9 km
Height gain 570 m
Maximum elevation 2057 m
Topo map 82 J/1 Langford Creek

Access: Via Willow Creek trail (# 202), 2.75 km from the trailhead. Also accessible from Hailstone Butte fire road (#198).

Iron Creek offers the best route to Hailstone Butte lookout and the Sentinel Pass area from Willow Creek. The pack trail is heavily used by local range riders so is good and clear for most of the way; only the final 2.5 km climb out of the valley is indistinct and may not at this time be reasonable for equestrians.

The trail, which is an all-terrain vehicle road initially, fords Willow Creek then swings left across a meadow to join a N- S cutline. Keep left and a few minutes later, on the north bank of Iron Creek, turn right onto a continuation of road which shortly refashions itself into 2 diverging E-W cutlines. The left- hand cutline is the one you want, but because the start is overgrown, follow a cow trail along river meadows until a trail returning to the cutline up a grass slope presents itself. About a kilometre farther on, turn left at a 4-way intersection onto the valley pack trail proper.

The trail leads back to the creek, crosses it and passes through a gate in the drift fence. In only 0.2 km, recross to the north bank and begin a steady climb through pine forest to sunny aspen woodlands in mid valley where the trail becomes temporarily lost in a large meadow. The general line of travel is obvious, however, and you should have no trouble getting back on track.

The head of Iron Creek.

Six km from Willow Creek the valley narrows; steep rocky slopes press in from either side. The trail is much less distinct here, especially in the area of a drift fence stretched across the valley floor; you must watch carefully for where the trail makes a detour to the south bank. At the big bend, rock steps laced with falls which dry up in the heat of summer are avoided by a zigzagging trail up scree onto the bank top. As is the way of all cattle trails, this one is making for succulent meadows below the ridge of white cliffs which of course is not in the direction you wish to go, so head left soon after the trail flattens out and follow bits of trail between dense thickets of engelmann spruce back into the creek bed above all difficulties. At last trees, pick up a trail on the east bank. Higher up, the trail switches to the west bank and is quite plainly seen climbing out of the grassy valley head onto the terrace below Hailstone Butte.

The terrace is really an uptilted bowl with a spongy heart of sedges and tiny beer-colored ponds. Rather than squelch through the middle of it, contour under the white rock ridge until you can pick up the trail again on drier ground lower down. In 5 minutes, Hailstone Butte fire road is reached at the point where threads of water trickling out of the fen are gathered into a culvert under the road and emerge on the far side as the infant Livingstone River. If you are making for Hailstone Butte lookout, turn left and ascend the fire road for 3 km. For Sentinel Pass, walk down the fire road for 1.2 km to where another branch of the Livingstone River comes in from the north, then follow route #210.

204 CORRAL CREEK — Map 13

Day hike, equestrian
Intermediate ski to end of road
Distance 6 km
Height gain 290 m
Maximum elevation 1798 m
Topo map 82 J/8 Stimson Creek
82 J/1 Langford Creek

Access: Via Willow Creek trail (#202), 5 km from the trailhead.

Although the Corral Creek exploration road doesn't lead anywhere – it dead-ends in forest below the unassailable face of the eastern escarpment – it does open up some really fine foothills country for people wanting to get off the beaten track.

Right at the start don't be misled by a white sign luring you across the creek into cut-blocks on the north bank. The Corral Creek exploration road heads up south bank meadows, in 0.5 crossing to the north bank briefly, then recrossing to the south bank for a much longer stretch to the forks. So far the valley has been flat and open; the tinkle of water spilling over beaver dams has been a constant background noise. Now, with another creek crossing just below the forks and a crossing of the north fork 5 minutes later, the scenery changes dramatically. Begin a steep climb through dry pine forest, stopping often to admire the bristly hill behind you at map ref. 830707 (a possible objective). At the top of the hill intersect a N.W.-S.E. cutline offering a route of sorts into the pastoral headwaters of the north fork and onwards to the 6-way junction on Pekisko Creek trail, then descend and for the fourth time cross the main fork of Corral Creek. A few minutes later, cross a much smaller stream which arises from the rock escarpment in front of you. It's probably more worthwhile following the game trail by the stream than continuing on up the road which dead-ends in another kilometre. Deadfall discourages further progress in any direction.

Looking towards the cliffs enclosing the head of Corral Creek.

A typical view along Indian Graves Ridge.

205 "INDIAN GRAVES RIDGE" — Map 13

Half-day, day hike
Distance to well site 4 km
Height gain 168 m
Maximum elevation 1631 m
Topo map 82 J/1 Langford Creek
82 J/8 Stimson Creek

Access: Johnson Creek Trail (SR 532). 3.9 km west of Kananaskis Country boundary, park in a dead-end road S.E. of the highway. (This is the road nearest Willow Creek bridge.)

The open ridge on the north side of the highway above Willow Creek bridge is a big attraction to campers from nearby Indian Graves recreation area who can be seen on any summer weekend huffing and puffing their way up the craggy west face. An easier route onto the ridge top is described below.

Start off by crossing the highway to Willow Creek trail opposite. Almost immediately, turn right up the buried pipeline right-of-way, then cut left through a belt of aspens to open slopes beyond. As the slope steepens make for the barbed-wire fence where a trail of sorts leads to the ridge top — an unexpectedly fine viewpoint for so modest an altitude gain. Notice how the white rocks of the west face below you have been folded into tight arches.

You can easily extend the walk by following the fence trail north along the open ridge top. In 2 km the trail drops down the west slope to a gap, then, still following the fence, climbs up to Dome Petroleum's well site on the Willow Creek Hills. If you've got this far you may as well utilize either the ascent or descent trails, for route #206 — depending on how far you want to walk — and make a loop with Willow Creek trail (#202) back to your starting point.

Limber pine.

206 WILLOW CREEK HILLS — Map 13

Day hike,equestrian
Easy ski to well site
Distance 5.5 km
Height gain 274 m
Maximum elevation 1737 m
Topo map 82 J/1 Langford Creek
82 J/8 Stimson Creek

Access: Via Willow Creek trail (#202), 2 km and 4.2 km from the trailhead.

This little loop uses a combination of exploration road, cutline access road and trail to take you to a viewpoint on the Willow Creek Hills.

Start off along Willow Creek trail. Two hundred metres from the trailhead, turn right onto a rehabilitated exploration road signed "No Motorized Vehicles". Do not confuse the road with a cutline access road a few metres farther on. The bright green swath of the reclaimed exploration road sweeps north, then west of a small creek dividing the Willow Creek Hills from Indian Graves Ridge and ends at a gap in the hills near a fenced-in meadow which was the site of a Dome Petroleum oil rig during the 1970's. Pick up a trail which climbs half a kilometre up the ridge to the south. Spring comes early to these hills and although the snow banks linger on Hailstone Butte and Sentinel Peak to the west, here on the open hilltop, the silky shimmer of new grass is already resplendent with drifts of magenta shooting stars.

Retrace your steps a few metres and look for a steep trail down the west side of the hill, a rather nebulous route between widely-spaced pines for the first little while. It soon develops into a good trail and then into a road. Intersect 2 minor cutlines, pass a cutline access road to the right, and a few minutes later, keep straight at a 4-way junction with a major N.W.-S.E. cutline. Disregard a steep cutline to the left a few metres farther on and a cutline to the right near the bottom of the hill where the road emerges onto the Willow Creek trail. If you walk the route in reverse direction, this road can be identified from neighbouring cutlines by its easier angle and by bands of red and blue paint encircling the occasional tree on the uphill side of the road.

207 STIMSON & HAY CREEKS TRAIL — Map 13

Day hike
Equestrian
Distance 13 km
Height gain 421 m
Maximum elevation 1734 m
Topo map 82 J/8 Stimson Creek

Access: Johnson Creek Trail (SR 532). Park at Stimson Creek 1.5 km west of Kananaskis Country boundary or 2.4 km east of Willow Creek bridge. The trail is the former all-terrain vehicle road signed "No motorized vehicles" at the trailhead. Also accessible from Willow Creek trail (#202) at the 6 km mark.

This trail follows the headwaters of Stimson and Hay Creeks over the Willow Creek Hills to Willow Creek. It can be used as part of a multi-day trip or incorporated with Willow Creek trail (#202) to make a 21.5 km loop which involves a bit of road bashing to get back to your starting point. The trail is also excellent for strolling, especially on warm fall days at the height of the color change when you should try to get as far as the viewpoint on Hay Creek where the photographer is rewarded by a dazzling landscape of variegated aspen forests blending orange, yellow and rich green-gold colors depending on aspect.

Gaining little height at first, the road wanders along the east bank of Stimson Creek through meadows rutted by cow trails. Circular beaver ponds alternate with dams of various ages making lines across the valley floor. At the forks, follow the N.E. branch through a pass marked by a drift fence into a south branch of Hay Creek. Watch for turkeys in this area. No, your eyes are not deceiving you; it's believed that the Hay Creek birds are

Hay Creek meadows in fall.

an offshoot of turkeys released as an experiment on the Porcupine Hills some 15 years ago. In another 2 km, the road crosses in quick succession the south fork of Hay Creek, then Hay Creek itself in lush aspen meadows dappled in shade and sunlight. The long ridge bounding the valley to the east is crowned with limber pines which from a distance resemble an unrestrained bonsai garden.

Now turn left, following the road which climbs up the north bank of Hay Creek towards the Willow Creek Hills. Cross a N-S cutline and wade through waist-high grasses mixed with flowers to a high point on a side slope — a satisfying viewpoint and perfect for a snooze. Here and there contented cattle have flattened out deep depressions within the grass. Shortly after the road descends to creek level it turns south and makes a beeline across the damp mouth of a tributary to a big meadow where it peters. Pick it up again at the point where it turns west into the spruce forest of the upper valley. After a straight half kilometre, it switchbacks up dry open slopes onto the backbone of the Willow Creek Hills, an excellent vantage point for Hailstone Butte and Sentinel Peak too if you walk south a bit along the ridge top.

The road continues through a gate in the drift fence, then descends forested west slopes to Willow Creek where it emerges just north of the tiny side creek it has followed downhill. Turn left onto a trail. Shortly after it crosses to the west bank, you arrive at Willow Creek exploration road (#202) which is obvious. If Pekisko Creek is your objective, there is no need to make this dogleg to the south; in Willow Creek simply turn right and follow cow trails — keep left at the forks — until you intersect route #202 at ford #4.

Bear Creek.

208 BEAR CREEK — Map 14

Day hike
Equestrian
Distance 9.5 km
Height gain 564 m
Maximum elevation 1966 m
Topo map 82 J/8 Stimson Creek
82 J/7 Mount Head

Access: From Hwy. 922 south of Longview, drive west along the Pekisko Creek Road (SR 540) to a junction with the E.P. Ranch road on the left. Keep right, entering the Cartwright Ranch. John and Lynn Cartwright are agreeable to visitors passing through their land en route to Kananaskis Country as long as they ask permission. This applies particularly to equestrians who must register. Be aware that the gate across the road at the ranch buildings is kept locked during times of high fire hazard and when the road beyond is in poor driving condition. About 2 km past the ranch buildings, you arrive at the Miller Creek Road junction. Park here. The trail starts between 2 posts in the angle of land between the 2 roads. Also accessible from the southern terminus of Zephyr Creek trail (#214).

The pack trail up Bear Creek connects with Zephyr Creek trail at Zephyr/Bear Col and up to now has been used mainly by hunters after sheep and bear. Providing you take precautions and remembering that no hunting is permitted on Sundays, don't let this fact deter you from visiting Bear Creek in the fall when the valley is at its most beautiful.

In its early stages the route is an old road which winds through ranch land to the gate in the boundary fence. Keep left here and head S.W. across the skirts of the Miller Creek hills towards Bear Creek. Shortly after the second side creek crossing, the road intersects a N.W.-S.E. cutline and then a major N.E.-S.W. cutline at right angles. Descend to Bear Creek and cross another small side creek and a second N.W.-S.E. cutline.

At the valley narrows, the road reverts to pack trail. Apart from one 5 minute section along the south bank half-way to the col, the trail winds in and out of the folds of the hills high on the north bank, traversing dry, open hillsides luxuriating in the warmth from the midday sun, even in late fall when ice is curdling on the stream below you and there is a dusting of snow on the shaded facets of Grassy Mountain to the left.

As you climb higher, the number of cattle dwindles to twos and threes, the hillsides become stonier and patches of dark spruce appear — survivors of the Phillip's fire. At the head of the valley, the trail climbs to the right of a round, forested hill, aiming for the lowest gap between Bear and Zephyr Creeks. The view from the col is cut off by hillsides and ridges in all directions so I suggest you either climb up the grassy slope to the north, or, if you have an hour to spare, get onto the north ridge of Mount Burke which is vulnerable to a determined party from several locations near the pass.

209 PEKISKO CREEK — Maps 13 & 14

Day hike, backpack
Equestrian, bike
14.5 km from Miller Creek Road junction
9.5 km from Kananaskis Country boundary
Height gain from forest boundary 396 m
Maximum elevation 1935 m
Topo map 82 J/8 Stimson Creek
82 J/7 Mount Head

Access: From Hwy. 922 south of Longview drive west along the Pekisko Creek Road (SR 540) to a junction with the E.P. Ranch road on the left. Keep right, entering the Cartwright Ranch. John and Lynn Cartwright are agreeable to visitors passing through their land en route to Kananaskis Country as long as they ask permission. This applies particularly to equestrians who must register. Be aware that the gate across the road at the ranch buildings is kept locked during times of high fire hazard and when the road beyond is in poor driving condition. About 2 km past the ranch buildings, you arrive at the Miller Creek Road junction, a possible parking spot if Pekisko Creek Road to left is in too bad a shape. In order to drive a further 5 km to the Kananaskis Country boundary you need dry conditions and a vehicle with good clearance. If both of these conditions are met turn left onto the Pekisko Creek Road which fords Pekisko Creek at a picnic area and bumps along fairly uneventfully until it reaches McConnell Flats, site of the first weather station in Alberta which was run by a rancher named Cameron in 1890. To your right a side road descends to a picnic area above McConnell falls. Shortly after this junction you pass through a second gate level with Major Burke's house, ford Pekisko Creek a second time and pass through a third gate, ensuring as you go that both gates are closed behind you. The road recrosses the creek near its confluence with Greenfeed Creek at a picnic area then climbs uphill to a parking area at the Kananaskis Country boundary fence. This trail is also accessible from the northern terminus of Willow Creek trail (#202), the northern terminus of Sentinel Pass trail (#210) and the eastern terminus of Salter Creek trail (#211).

The old Pekisko Creek drovers' road to Cataract Creek, formerly the domain of the range rider and hunter, will no doubt prove popular with the recreationist who has the option of using this trail in conjunction with other trails such as Willow Creek, Iron Creek, Sentinel Pass, Salter Creek, Lower Cataract Creek, Zephyr Creek and Bear Creek trails in their various permutations to make loops of varying lengths.

It's really an extension of the Pekisko Creek Motor road which carries on from the boundary fence across the long meadow to the site of Pekisko Ranger station which was removed to the Cartwright Ranch in the 1950's. 1.2 km farther on you arrive at an important 4-way junction with Willow Creek road straight ahead and a road to left which crosses Devil's Bite into Sheppard Creek and so passes out of Kananaskis Country. Turn right (west) here and descend to riverside meadows. A notable feature of this route, and one which people who like to get off the beaten track can take advantage of, is that every side valley has its own road or cutline leading to meadows and viewpoints around the 2000 m level. The first of these is the Salt Creek cutline which leaves the right-hand side of the road a few metres after the confluence in the meadows. From this junction you climb onto an open bench and in 2 km arrive at a star-shaped 5-way meeting of cutlines. The road, which is obvious, passes straight through the middle and descends to Pekisko Creek. (En route a side road to the right a few metres after the aforementioned junction heads up an unnamed creek to the west.) After 0.5 km along the riverbank you ford Pekisko Creek and a side creek in quick succession. (As before, a road travels up the south bank of the side creek to an open ridge.)

Now begin a gradual climb along the west flank of the inner valley towards Salter Pass. Up ahead, Sentinel Peak is an arresting sight framed between steep valley walls; it's hard to realize this mountain's an easy walk up from Sentinel Pass. Level with the forks, the easterly approach to Sentinel Pass trail — a cutline — plummets down the hillside from the left- hand side of the road. This junction signals 2 switchbacks and an overall steepening of the road for the next half kilometre. After the road settles back into its former easy gradient, it intersects the westerly approach to Sentinel Pass in a clump of trees, traverses a steep grass slope above a snow fence and climbs a little more through trees to its highest point. Descend, using either road at the junction, to a large damp meadow which is Salter Pass and also the source of Salter Creek. See Salter Creek trail (#211) for a description of the ongoing road to Cataract Creek campground.

View from upper Pekisko Creek of Sentinel Peak and Sentinel Pass (right).

Plateau Mtn. from Sentinel Pass trail above headwall in Pekisko Creek.

210 SENTINEL PASS — Maps 13 & 14

Long day hike, backpack
Equestrian
Distance 6 km
Height gain 350 m
Maximum elevation 2118 m
Topo map 82 J/8 Stimson Creek
82 J/1 Langford Creek

Access: **1. Via Pekisko Creek trail (#209) 0.75 km and 1.4 km east of Salter Pass.**
Access: **2. Via Hailstone Butte fire road (#198) 6 km from the trailhead at Forestry Trunk Road 940.**

Long before there were roads in this part of the country, the old pack trail between the upper Oldman and Highwood Rivers took an easy line up Livingstone Creek to a pass between Plateau Mountain and Sentinel Peak, then descended into Pekisko Creek which was followed out to the plains. The pass has been neglected for decades, no doubt due to the plethora of gas well roads effectively discouraging access from the Livingstone Creek end since the 1930's. Similarly, the approach from the north side has been overlaid with exploration roads and cutlines so that nowadays, only a small section of that historic trail remains.

From the Pekisko Creek trail end you must first descend into the west fork of Pekisko Creek. There are 2 ways of doing this depending on whether you are approaching from the east or the west.

Route #1. from the east 1.4 km east of Salter Pass descend a steep cutline to your left into the west fork. As is the way of cutlines, you must ascend an equally steep hill out of the valley onto a bench above the south fork. Route #2 which is an overgrown exploration road comes in from the right a little way beyond the top of the hill.

Route #2 from the west 0.75 km east of Salter Pass watch for a crossroad of overgrown roads in the clump of trees coming immediately after the open hillside with snow fence. Turn right down steepish slopes into meadows just above the west fork. When the road swings left keep right on another road which crosses the dry boulder bed of the creek and climbs to a T-junction with a cutline which is route #1. Turn right.

Walk south along the cutline and when it ends transfer onto a narrow trail which carries on in the same line as before and crosses the creek after a short half kilometre. It can be traced along the east bank for a few more metres, then peters out in a tangled meadow watered by a muddy side creek. It's best to follow a game trail up the left bank of the side creek until you are above a snag of fallen trees, then cross and wade thigh-deep through yellow meadow parsnips into the trees on the far side where you can pick up the old pack trail. It's quite obvious despite deadfall lying across it in one or two places. As you follow it uphill, the trail's pleasant forest windings change into tight well-constructed zigzags up a talus slope marking the eastern boundary of a rock band encircling the head of the valley. A long traverse to the right leads to a grassy bench above the cliffs. From the cairn, **descend** slightly, aiming to cross the headwaters of Pekisko Creek on flat ground between 2 gorges. More zigzags, through trees this time, gets you to the top of a second bench. Shortly afterwards, the trail fades out in low brush, not that it matters really for the final 0.75 km to the pass is a simple walk up open slopes. However, if you're hiking this route in reverse direction you might well have problems locating the trail and it is absolutely essential that you do so if you want to get through the rockbands without hassle.

The pass is wide and flat, one vast meadow scattered with spruce trees and bounded by Sentinel Peak and Plateau Mountain whose sprawling bulks severely limit views in all directions. If you carry on walking in the same direction, you'll start to descend into the Livingstone drainage. Here you have the choice of either continuing on down the draw (dry meadows, cow trails), or of following a truncated cutline through trees to its right. Either way, you arrive at Hailstone Butte fire road 6 km from Forestry Trunk Road 940.

SENTINEL PEAK (2373 m) This impressive-looking mountain has a friendly back side which any reasonably fit person can walk up in an hour or less from the pass. It's probably easiest to make for the shallow cirque at the head of Pekisko Creek, from where it's a simple walk up orange-colored rocks to the dip in the ridge just south of the summit. Whichever route you choose, take care not to venture too close to the northern and eastern precipices for the rock is unusually friable. Wedged in the summit cairn lying in the angle between the two faces is a bronze plaque dedicated to a father and son who died within 2 years of each other. A more fitting memorial would be hard to imagine, for this mountain which is such a landmark from the east is, conversely, a magnificent viewpoint for these same foothills and prairies.

211 SALTER CREEK — Map 14

Day hike, easy ski
Equestrian, bike
Distance 7 km to pass
Height gain 283 m
Maximum elevation 1935 m
Topo map 82 J/7 Mount Head

Access: Forestry Trunk Road 940 at Cataract Creek campground. A few metres before the campground gate turn right into a small parking lot. Backtrack to an old road marked by a snowmobile sign which starts near Salter Creek bridge. Also accessible from the western terminus of Pekisko Creek trail (#209).

The route up Salter Creek follows the old Cataract Creek- Pekisko Creek drovers road to a low point between Plateau Mountain and Mount Burke. Fill water bottles before you go; by mid summer, Salter Creek and all its tributaries are usually dry.

Almost straightway the road crosses Salter Creek to the south bank, then winds pleasantly for the next 1.5 km or so through meadows and aspen groves to Plateau Creek. So far, the valley has been wide open, but now the forested walls close in and the road is forced back and forth across the dry stony creek bed several times. 2.5 km from the trailhead, the trail to Mount Burke turns off to the left. After this junction, the scenery becomes very much more dramatic with forested slopes on both sides breaking down into slabs, screes, and later on, thrusting rock buttresses pockmarked with black cave openings. A box canyon cut into the side of Plateau Mountain invites a closer inspection. The final 2 km of route follows a long, thin meadow to Salter Pass which is properly located at the east end of the meadow above a drop-off. The top half of Sentinel Peak sticks up above the gap. If you have time, it pays to wander up the green and flowery slopes of Mount Burke for a more comprehensive view.

Looking back down Salter Creek from the meadow near the pass.

212 MOUNT BURKE — Map 14

Day hike
Equestrian
8 km to summit
Height gain 845 m
Maximum elevation 2450 m
Topo map 82 J/7 Mount Head

The narrow ridge preceding the final slopes of Mt. Burke.

Access: Forestry Trunk Road 940 at Cataract Creek campground. A few metres before the campground gate turn right into a small parking lot. The trail, initially an old road, starts near Salter Creek bridge and is marked by a snowmobile sign.

The old pack trail to Cameron Lookout on the summit of Mount Burke is one of those trails where you can enjoy the feeling of mild exposure from a place of perfect safety. Bring along a 1:250000 Kananaskis Lakes map for identification of major peaks and valleys.

Start off on Salter Creek trail (ffl211). In 2.5 km, an old wooden sign tacked to a tree points to the start of the Mount Burke trail to your left. Well-graded and soft underfoot, it zigzags back and forth up the tapering ridge to treeline. A short, grass slope is prelude to an unimaginably wild landscape of yellow talus slopes and cliff bands which will surely frighten the faint-hearted novice hiker. Remind yourself that this is a horse trail you are following. Nevertheless, the trail is not in such good condition as it used to be and equestrians may elect to take to their own two feet from this point on.

Cross the crest of a short rocky ridge so badly exposed to gusty cross-winds pack horses carrying supplies to the lookout were always led one at a time across this narrow section to more comfortable slopes beyond. On the final approach to the lookout, you can either stick to the trail which traverses scree slopes above a rockband or follow the ridge above, being careful if you choose the latter course not to trip over the old telephone wire.

The lookout occupies the entire summit. Built in 1929, it was superseded in 1953 by Raspberry lookout to the west. Although it lacks a door and is generally in a dilapidated condition inside, it serves well enough as a refuge from the winds. The original cooking stove complete with kettle is still in the corner, but the old-fashioned oil heater was removed when the lookout was abandoned and now resides in the museum at Hinton. You will probably wonder where the lookouts got their water from in the days before the helicopter. It seems it was a chancy, even risky business that involved suspending a bucket over the northern precipice to catch drips percolating down through the summit boulderfield.

213 LOWER CATARACT CREEK — Map 14

Day hike
Distance 13.5 km
Height loss 198 m
Topo map 82 J/7 Mount Head

Access: 1. Forestry Trunk Road 940 at Cataract Creek campground. The trail, initially an old road, starts behind campsite #27.
Access: 2. Highwood Trail (SR 541) at Sentinel day-use area. The logging road starts from the south bank of the Highwood River opposite the first parking area along the right-hand access road.

True to its name, lower Cataract Creek is a delightful composite of waterfalls higher and more impressive than either Sheep River or Elbow Falls, deep green pools, rapids and quiet stretches where the water moves lazily over shallow pebble beds. Most people venture a kilometre or two from the parking lots at either end; adventurous hikers should consider going right through utilizing the old pack trail, unlikely to be upgraded, which crosses the creek 5 times. Be aware that the Highwood River at the Highwood Trail end is impassible during runoff and over knee-deep the rest of the year.

From Cataract Creek campsite #27, follow the road out into dry meadows decorated with locoweeds and vetches. After 2.5 km of flat going, the road fords the creek. On the west bank, leave the road which ends soon anyway, and climb to a trail higher up the grassy slope. Turn right. In 0.5 km the trail skirts the top of a cliff overlooking Upper Falls, then descends to creek level. Keep left at a junction and contour round an inverted S- bend past smaller falls to trail's end at some fire circles.

A ruddy-hued weeping wall prohibits further progress down this side of the valley, so cross to the east bank via 2 precariously- placed logs. Walk uphill for 0.1 km (faint trail) and intersect the old pack trail. This is a very difficult junction to locate if you're coming from the other direction; a pointed tree stump in the angle of the two trails is your only guide. (Unfortunately, the pack trail to right which seems to offer the best route to the campground fades out in half a kilometre above cliffs.)

Turn left and follow the trail across a stony side ridge to grassy headlands overlooking Middle Falls. The trail descends gradually to stream level, then follows the odd cairn around the first half of an S-bend to an easy ford marked by blazes on the east bank and a large cairn on west bank. The stream is relatively subdued for the next 1.5 km, which is just as well since the trail fords it twice more before finally settling on the west bank for the rest of its duration. Shortly after the final crossing, a deepening gorge of long chutes and deep pools forces the trail high onto a bench where it joins a logging road. This junction occurs after a side creek crossing and is easily missed by hikers walking the trail in reverse direction; don't rely on the red flagging always being there.

Turn right. In 1 km, the road emerges from the forest and the stream from the gorge into lovely meadows. Keep left at an indistinct junction with the road to Zephyr Creek. For the last time the stream funnels into a canyon and drops unseen over a final step in the bedrock. It is at this point that the road moves away from the creek and descends to flats bordering the Highwood River. Ford the river to the parking lot on the north bank.

TO ZEPHYR CREEK The connecting road leaves the logging road in the meadows 1.4 km south of the Highwood River. Very much grassed over in the area of the junction, it can be positively identified by a large square rock a little way in. In 200 m it fords Cataract Creek and, much improved, rises slowly through pine forest to a large meadow between a bluff and Mount Burke's north ridge. Contour right and intersect the Zephyr Creek exploration road at the edge of the trees. In the height of summer, both roads are almost obscured by long grasses.

214 ZEPHYR CREEK PICTOGRAPHS — Map 14

Day hike, easy ski
Equestrian
4.5 km to pictographs
8.5 km to Zephyr/Bear col
Height gain to col 520 m
Maximum elevation 1966 m
Topo map 82 J/7 Mount Head

Access: Highwood Trail (SR 541) at Sentinel day-use area.
Also accessible from the western terminus of Bear Creek trail (#208).

Access to this trail is even more difficult than when the first edition of this book was published; the problem of the river crossing has been compounded by the plowing up of the access road during reconstruction of Highwood Trail and the dumping of boulders and dirt across the entrance. This has necessitated a new starting place from Sentinel day-use area 0.4 km to the west. As before, the whole trip hinges on the crossing of the Highwood River; at runoff it may be impassible even for horses.

Head east along the river bank until you hit the old road. Ford the Highwood River and wend left to a T-junction with a road in slightly better repair which has come in along the south bank of the Highwood River all the way from the forest boundary. Turn right here and follow this new road into the large meadow below the north ridge of Mount Burke. At an ill-defined junction with route #213 at the meadow entrance, keep left and wind around the perimeter of the trees into the confines of Zephyr Creek.

The road travels uneventfully up the flat valley floor to the first side creek on the east. Leave the road at this point and make your way along a faint trail into Painted Canyon. Just before the canyon opens up, look for rock paintings about 1 m up from the ground on an overhanging wall on the north side. In 1975 part of the wall collapsed, destroying 6 of the 8 paintings which lie in fragments beneath your feet — a jigsaw which can never be put together again. All that remains is a stick figure of a man closely pursued by an unindentifiable large animal with erect ears and a long tail, and half of a bird trailing feathers which lies half a metre to the right. Archeologists believe that the artists were either Kootenai or Salishan Indians who lived on the fringe of the prairies some 300 years ago, and that the paintings were the successful conclusion of a Vision Quest ceremony. This would explain the isolated location of the site which is well away from known campsites and the major trail along the Highwood River.

ZEPHYR/BEAR COL From Painted Canyon junction, carry on climbing up the road into upper Zephyr Creek. The road soon gives way to a hunters' pack trail which follows east bank meadows to springs at the head of the valley, then cuts left up a steeper slope to the col at map ref. 747785. There join Bear Creek trail (#208).

215 GRASS PASS — Map 14

Day hike
Equestrian
3.2 km to pass
Height gain 430 m
Maximum elevation 1875 m
Topo map 82 J/7 Mount Head

Access: Highwood Trail (SR 541) at Sentinel day-use area. Also accessible from Wileman Creek trail (#221).

Raked by warm chinook winds, Grass Pass and its environs is an excellent choice for the short days of early spring and late fall. In mid summer with longer daylight hours you should consider extending the walk, either onto the Bull Creek Hills (#216), or down Wileman Creek to Flat Creek in which case you'll need a car at both ends. (See also routes #220 & #221.)

Start off by walking east along Highwood Trail for 0.2 km. Choose any one of numerous trails radiating from the north side of the highway into Pack Trail Coulee; all merge into one valley road within 0.5 km. The stony track farthest to the right is probably the most direct. As you climb, mixed forest and fire- ravaged douglas firs in the lower reaches of the valley give way to extensive bunch grass meadows imprinted with tire tracks around the pass. At the 4-way junction on the pass itself, the road continues on into Wileman Creek. The all-terrain vehicle road to the east is the start of route #216 up the Bull Creek Hills.

Because views from the pass itself are somewhat limited by the V-shape of the valley, I suggest you either walk out onto Fir Creek point to the S.E., or climb another 100 m up an all-terrain vehicle road onto the ridge to the west.

Looking down on Grass Pass from the Bull Creek Hills.

Zephyr/Bear col.

216 BULL CREEK HILLS — Maps 14 & 15

Day hike
Distance from Grass Pass 3 km
Height gain from highway 716 m
Maximum elevation 2165 m
Topo map 82 J/7 Mount Head

The highest summit of the Bull Creek Hills has a rocky east ridge.

Access: Via Grass Pass (#215) from Highwood Trail (SR 541).

This large group of hills lying between the Highwood River and Flat Creek are ideal for off-trail hiking in almost any month of the year. The open slopes above the highway offer the usual routes of ascent, be it either the deep valleys and sharp ridges to the west or the more billowy hillsides freckled with limber pines further east. By far the easiest route is to ascend Pack Trail Coulee to the 4-way junction at Grass Pass, then turn east up an old all-terrain vehicle road leading to a prominence overlooking Fir Creek. Already there is an excellent view of Holy Cross Mountain across Wileman Creek. In early summer, lingering snow in the gullies and ledges of the east face conform to the shape of a cross which can be seen from as far away as the town of High River.

There is no trail beyond this point, but the going is straightforward around the head of Fir Creek to 2 lower summits. So far, trees have obscured the views to north and east and it is only on reaching the highest summit that the vista of prairies and foothills is fully revealed.

217 FIR CREEK — Map 14

Half-day hike
4 km one way
Height gain 335 m
Topo map 82 J/7 Mount Head

Access: Highwood Trail (SR 541) at Fir Creek day-use area.

Walk east along the highway for 0.5 km to Fir Creek. Unfortunately, many of the douglas firs which have identified the creek to travellers since the turn of the century were removed during reconstruction of the highway in 1982/83. At the same time, the old road leading into the valley was left high and dry above a road cut and now starts farther east of the creek crossing than previously. It takes you beyond the first belt of trees into glades massed with poisonous purple larkspurs where a trail takes over. Reentering forest, the trail splinters into several cow trails all converging above a small gorge with waterfall into one good trail which heads up valley. Follow cow patties to meadows boxed in on 3 sides by the Bull Creek Hills.

218 MARSTON CREEK — Map 14

Half-day, day hike
Equestrian
Distance to creek 1.7 km
Circuit 9 km
Height gain to creek 122 m
Maximum elevation 1570 m
Topo map 82 J/7 Mount Head

Access: **Highwood Trail (SR 541). The trail (an overgrown exploration road) starts from the north side of the highway about 0.3 km west of the Kananaskis Country boundary. It's also easily accessible on foot from the Highwood River group camp.**

The old road follows a fold in the grassy hillside, winding past small clumps of aspens and droopy limber pines to the ridge top. Descend alongside the boundary fence into Marston Creek named after Ed Marston who homesteaded in the valley just outside the forest boundary in 1902. He was a colorful character, remembered chiefly for his set of false teeth made from cowhide!

Shortly after crossing the creek to the north bank, you arrive at a junction with a road to right which climbs about 100 m up the south ridge of the most easterly summit of the Bull Creek Hills. Straight ahead, the valley road soon degenerates into a cow trail which takes you to the forks at map ref. 740874. After a brief sortie through trees in the angle between the two branches, the trail dissipates on open hillsides within easy reach of the highest summit — a steepish climb broken up by shallow steps where the bulls like to lie in long grasses. A circuit incorporating the 2 summits and the 2 roads makes a logical extension to this otherwise short, easy trail.

Typical Bull Creek Hills terrain with Holy Cross Mtn. (left) and Mt. Head in the background.

219 SOUTH SULLIVAN CREEK — Map 15

Half-day hike, backpack
Equestrian, bike
2.5 km to beaver ponds
11 km to Sullivan Creek road
Height gain 152 m
Maximum elevation 1661 m
Topo map 82 J/7 Mount Head
82 J/10 Mount Rae

Access: Highwood Trail (541). 21.4 km west of Longview, turn west onto the Flat Creek Road (unsigned). The trail, very indistinct at first, leaves the north side of the road about 0.3 km after entering Kananaskis Country.
Also accessible from Sullivan Pass trail (#224).

The South Sullivan Creek all-terrain vehicle road can be utilized in 3 ways: as a half-day stroll to the beaver ponds, as a long-distance, bad-weather trail to the Sheep River or as a section of equestrian/bike loops incorporating Flat Creek, High Rock Ridge and Sullivan Pass trails. Take your choice.

After a brief passage through spruce forest during which the trail upgrades to all-terrain vehicle road, you cross a lovely meadow knee-deep in summer flowers and arrive at the beaver ponds. Generations of beavers have done a thorough job in this little tributary; even the road has been dammed in one place, necessitating a detour around the new pond.

From the bridge, the road travels north along the fringe of meadows to South Sullivan Creek. Cross to the north bank and follow the creek upstream into the lodgepole pine zone at the foot of High Rock Ridge. Disregard an intersecting cutline half- way. At map ref. 727975, the road leaves the creek and heads north for 5 km across the grain of the country to Sullivan Creek. Nearing the creek, other roads join in from left and right, but the major road is generally obvious as it turns N.E. paralleling the stream a way before crossing it to the N.W. bank. Join Sullivan Creek exploration road approximately half a kilometre west of the cutline to Coal Creek. See trail #224 for ongoing routes.

220 FLAT CREEK — Map 15

Day hike, backpack
Equestrian, bike
Distance 13 km
Height gain 600 m
Maximum elevation 2124 m
Topo map 82 J/7 Mount Head

Access: Highwood Trail (SR 541). 21.4 km west of Longview, turn west onto the Flat Creek Road (unsigned). Park 0.6 km west of Kananaskis Country boundary at a locked gate.
Also accessible from the northern terminus of Wileman Creek trail (#221), the southern terminus of High Rock Ridge trail (#223), and the western terminus of Sullivan Pass trail (#224).

Since the first edition of this book was published, there have been two important changes to this valley; first, the valley's name has reverted to Flat Creek from Trap Creek (it's official), and second, the valley has been closed to all motorized vehicles. This means that all the routes radiating out from the main valley road — Wileman Creek, Head Creek, Sullivan Pass and High Rock Ridge — are no longer easily accessible in one day unless you have a horse or a bicycle. Nowadays, it's best to reserve Flat Creek for weekend and backpacking trips.

From the parking area continue along the road, traversing steep hillsides above Flat Creek to a high point on a bend overlooking the confluence with Wileman Creek. The contorted shapes of the aspens hereabouts testify to the strength of the Highwood winds which blast over Grass Pass and funnel down Wileman Creek, finally expending their energy against this corner, one of many "windy points" in Alberta's foothills. Turning N.W. now, the road descends to riverside meadows and passes Wileman Creek exploration road on the left, and in another half kilometre, the road to High Rock Ridge on the right. There are excellent campsites all through this section. If you have time to spare, search the riverbank for coal shafts dating back to the first decade of this century and known collectively as the Walker Mine after owner Wellington Phillips Walker of High River.

Approximately 7.2 km from the trailhead, the road fords Flat Creek for the first time. Keep right at the following road junction with Head Creek exploration road, then recross to the N.E. bank. (You can avoid both crossings by keeping to a narrow trail along the N.E. bank.) 2 km farther on you arrive at Spruce Bluff range rider's cabin which somehow escaped the 1936 holocaust — the jumping-off point for Sullivan Pass.

Keep left on the Flat Creek road which shortly fords the creek and after another 1.7 km of easy going along gravel flats ends near the forks under the Dogtooth Mountains. A rough trail carries on up the V-shaped west fork, crossing and recrossing the stream innumerable times. When the creek turns south, the trail is on the east bank and can be traced a way through a remnant of old spruce forest towards the lake at the valley head. Shallow and inclined to dry up in fall, it is not the lake which draws the eyes, but rather the flower meadows around it which are the last sub-alpine meadows left in Flat Creek until the forest grows old again.

◄ *Flat Creek near Spruce Bluff cabin, looking towards the Dogtooth Mtns.*

Wileman Creek in November.

221 WILEMAN CREEK — Map 15

Day hike, backpack
Equestrian, bike
Distance 8 km
Height gain 320 m
Maximum elevation 1875 m
Topo map 82 J/7 Mount Head

Access: Via Flat Creek trail (#220).
Also accessible from route #215 at Grass Pass.

The lovely south fork of Flat Creek was named after Harvey Wileman, ranger at the Sentinel Ranger Station during the Phillip's fire of 1936. Although the fire devastated most of the Highwood Valley, spreading to Flat Creek and east to Sullivan Creek, somehow this valley remained largely unscathed. The spruce trees still grow tall here.

If you are approaching from the east via Highway 541, leave Flat Creek road at "windy point", a few metres after the second texas gate. Drop down steep grass to Flat Creek just west of the confluence with Wileman Creek and wade across to an old road on the south bank. A short walk brings you to the Wileman Creek exploration road proper where you should turn left. When approaching from the west, having entered Flat Creek via Sullivan Pass or High Rock Ridge trails, you can follow the Wileman Creek exploration road right from its starting point in the big meadow 0.5 km east of High Rock Ridge trail junction.

Shortly after both routes merge, the road enters a narrow draw and passes through the drift fence effectively sealing off the lower valley. Jump across Wileman Creek. Suddenly the valley opens out into meadows with small beaver ponds. The grey bulwarks of Holy Cross Mountain and Mount Head provide a satisfying backdrop to the scene and are probably seen to their best advantage from this distant spot; higher up the trail, foreshortening reduces their shapely outlines to formless slopes of rubble, cliffs and gullies.

After a long straight stretch the road wends right and crosses a shallow bed of white stones masquerading as Wileman Creek. Pass a cutline to right heading into the cirque between a large forested hill shaped like a trapezium and Mount Head. Three more similar creek crossings follow. Now on the east bank, the road begins climbing resolutely towards Grass Pass. At the half-way point, a large, level meadow resplendent with magenta shooting stars in spring allows unrestricted views in all directions. This is your nearest approach to Holy Cross Mountain and from close in you can make out the large horizontal ledge which, together with the central gully, molds lingering snow patches into the shape of a cross. The pass is in sight and another 20 minutes of uphill work below the open slopes of the Bull Creek hills should see you there. See Grass Pass (#215) for a description of the ongoing route to Highwood Trail (SR 541).

222 HEAD CREEK — Map 15

Long day hike, backpack
Equestrian, bike
8.5 km to ridge
Height gain 885 m
Maximum elevation 2515 m
Topo map 82 J/7 Mount Head

Access: Via Flat Creek trail (#220).

The exploration road up Head Creek dates back to the early 1960's when gypsum was discovered on a high ridge near Mount Head. To reach the claim an incredible road was constructed consisting of 29 zigzags up a 300 m scree slope. Although the upper part of the road is gradually filling in, it still offers an easy hike to a fine viewpoint.

7.2 km from the trailhead, Flat Creek road fords the river for the first time. At the road junction immediately following, turn left onto an exploration road heading into the confines of Head Creek. It's a good idea to wear runners for the first part of the route; the first 6 stream crossings are unavoidable, and you can waste a lot of time searching for crossing places.

In mid valley, slow regrowth after the 1936 fire allows excellent views of surrounding ridges bristling with cockscombs of wafer-thin rock. Higher up, after the valley opens out into meadows, 2 minor roads heading up a stony ridge to the right should not be mistaken for the main trail. The Head Creek exploration road crosses 2 side streams before switchbacking up scree below a diagonal rock band. If you want, the first 7 switchbacks can be avoided by an obvious short cut up the side of the second stream. Arriving on a ridge top, the road turns right and traverses below outcroppings of pure white gypsum to a small summit — the apex of three ridges. Fine orange shale supports clumps of yellow draba and the thick-rooted spring beauty.

223 HIGH ROCK RIDGE — Map 15

Day hike, backpack
Equestrian
Distance 11 km
Height gain 631 m
Height loss 433 m
Maximum elevation 2170 m
Topo map 82 J/7 Mount Head
82 J/10 Mount Rae

Access: 1. Via Flat Creek trail (#220).
Access: 2. Via Sullivan Pass trail (#224).

Between Flat Creek and the prairies is a long ridge some 6 km in length which Raymond Patterson in his book "Buffalo Head" referred to as The High Rock Ridge, although it is neither high nor particularly rocky. It is traversed by an old exploration road connecting Flat Creek to Sullivan Creek, an interesting high-level route with superb views which takes you to within 100 vertical metres of the highest summit.

4.5 km west of the trailhead in Flat Creek, turn north onto an exploration road. For the first 2 km the road backtracks through open limber pine forest to the extreme S.E. tip of the ridge then, zigzaging, climbs to the ridge top through a curious checkered region of impenetrable matchstick pines and boulder slopes. Follow the edge of the eastern escarpment around to flat open areas from where you can look down onto the South Sullivan Creek beaver ponds. As you approach the highest tops, the road sets N.W., beginning a long traverse across the east face towards Sullivan Creek. From its high point at map ref. 704964, take time to scramble onto the summit knob — it's your last chance to view the Highwood Range which is nowhere seen to better advantage than from the highest point of High Rock Ridge. Experienced hikers have the option of continuing along the ridge tops to Sullivan Pass (the second gap), then returning to Flat Creek trail via route #224.

The road now drops steadily downward across across the 2 heads of South Sullivan Creek and 2 side ridges. Keep left at a junction on the first ridge. Arriving at a square-shaped well site, head to the bottom left-hand corner and pick up the Sullivan Creek exploration road. 1 km and 2 stream crossings later, at the point where the road makes a sharp turn to the N.E. beginning its descent of Sullivan Creek, Sullivan Pass trail (#224) comes in from your left.

Mount Head massif from Sullivan Pass. ➤

224 SULLIVAN PASS — Map 15

Long day hike, backpack
Equestrian, bike
3.25 km from Flat Creek to pass
12.5 km to Coal Creek
Height gain 365 m
Maximum elevation 1996 m
Topo map 82 J/7 Mount Head
82 J/10 Mount Rae

Access: **1. Via Flat Creek trail (#220) at Spruce Bluff Cabin.**
Access: **2. Via the northern terminus of High Rock Ridge (#223).**
Access: **3. Via the northern terminus of South Sullivan Creek trail (#219).**
Access: **4. Via Junction Mountain trail south.**

Sullivan Pass and its environs is an excellent choice for a day trip, be it either a long day hike from the highway or a short visit from a campsite in Flat Creek. More importantly, the pass is the usual route taken by long-distance backpackers and equestrians passing between Flat Creek and The Sheep, (other routes being High Rock Ridge and South Sullivan Creek), and as such will be described right through to Junction Mountain trail south in Coal Creek.

The Sullivan Pass all-terrain vehicle road starts behind Spruce Bluff cabin on Flat Creek trail. In 1 km keep left at Black Creek (true to its name a stinking morass of oily black soils), and head up steepening grass slopes to the pass which is the **second** lowest gap in the ridge. On a fine summer's afternoon when the usual westerly blast has softened to a light breeze, these south-facing meadows — a superlative viewpoint for the Highwood Range opposite — are ideal for idling away a few hours before you start on your return trip. Hikers with energy to spare can wander over High Rock Ridge to the east or traverse westward to the friendly S.E. ridge of Junction Mountain.

If you are going through to The Sheep, carry on down the north side of the pass into the infant Sullivan Creek. Just above the forks you join the Sullivan Creek exploration road which has entered the valley from an abandoned well site below High Rock Ridge (see route #223). Follow this well-graded road downstream for nearly 5 km until you're well out of the hills. Suddenly, there are several things to look out for: South Sullivan Creek exploration road coming in from the right across the creek, a thin meadow with small stream to the left followed almost immediately by a cutline and then a side road which joins the cutline a little way in.

Leave Sullivan Creek exploration road at the side road and head left (north) across the barely discernable watershed to Coal Creek. From the point of view of routefinding, it's easiest if you keep a straight, straight line along the cutline, disregarding all roads to left and right. In a clearing on the Coal Creek side cross 2 cutlines a short distance apart and arrive at a road on the riverbank which is Junction Mountain trail south and can be identified by red markers. Turn left for Junction Mountain lookout and right for the Junction Mountain south/Phone Line/Wolf Creek trail junction 0.5 km to the east.

SANDY MCNABB SKI TRAILS — Map 16

25 km of trails
Topo map 82 J/10 Mount Rae

Access: Sheep River Trail (SR 546). There are 2 starting points: Long Prairie parking lot 3.3 km west of Kananaskis Country boundary and Sandy McNabb recreation area equestrian parking lot 1.6 km farther to the west.

Twenty five km of groomed trails winding through predominantly aspen woodlands can be combined in numerous ways to give trips lasting anything from an hour to all day. Most of the trails are easy; intermediate and difficult sections are found mainly on trails north of the highway. This is not a high snowfall area and in years of frequent chinooks skiing conditions can be marginal. Trail maps are available from both trailheads.

225 LONG PRAIRIE LOOP

Intermediate
Distance 5.5 km

The trail starts off up the meadows of Long Prairie Creek. Half-way up the valley, the trail climbs onto a forested ridge to the turnaround point — keep left at a junction with Death Valley loop — then descends a good fast hill to a second junction with Death Valley loop in a clearing. The easy return leg follows various roads and trails below open hillsides often denuded of snow during chinooks.

226 CURTAINS

Difficult
Distance 0.25 km

Connects the west and east legs of Long Prairie loop along a cutline. The steep drop on the east side has a long run-out.

227 EASY-OUT

Intermediate
Distance 0.3 km

Offers an easier descent from the high point of Curtains to the east leg of Long Prairie loop.

228 DEATH VALLEY LINK

Easy
Distance 1 km

A gently-winding trail which connects Sandy McNabb parking lot and trails south of the highway to northern trails at Long Prairie loop.

229 DEATH VALLEY LOOP

Intermediate
Distance 3.5 km

This trail takes you over the watershed into the head of Death Valley at an E-W cutline. Be prepared for steep hills, wide and step-like on the west leg which utilizes part of the Death Valley exploration road, and narrow and twisting on the east leg which follows the summer trail down from the ridge top junction with Long Prairie loop. In icy conditions these hills upgrade to difficult.

230 ARCTIC HILL

Intermediate
Distance 1.2 km

This interesting link trail climbs aspen hillsides to a viewpoint overlooking the Front Ranges. Best skied in a W-E direction to take advantage of a long,thoroughly enjoyable run down the cold, east slope. Be ready for a right-angled bend to the left near the bottom of the hill.

Alder trail viewpoint above the Sheep River.

231 MACABEE LOOP

Easy
Distance 3.9 km

A pleasant circuit best skied in a clockwise direction if you wish to take advantage of gentle downhills with good snow in the east fork of Macabee Creek. Conversely, the western leg which travels along the base of open hillsides in Macabee Creek tends to suffer from Chinook winds.

232 WHITETAIL

Easy
Distance 0.3 km

Offers the shortest and easiest access from Long Prairie loop to Macabee loop.

233 WOLFTREE LINK

Easy
Distance 0.9 km

The trail follows an aspen draw to a junction with Pine Ridge trail in 0.8 km, then continues on for another 0.1 km (one short downhill) into the Macabee Creek drainage and arrives at a second junction with Pine Ridge and Macabee loop trails.

234 PINE RIDGE

Intermediate
Distance 3.5 km

This loop trail climbs to 2 viewpoints on a ridge top which at 1640 m is the highest point on the trail system. Steep hills are encountered between Wolftree and Balsam Link and between Macabee loop and the summit. Best skied in a clockwise direction to take advantage of better snow conditions during the descent.

235 BALSAM LINK

Intermediate
Distance 1.6 km

Initially, the trail follows the west bank of Long Prairie Creek through open woods of aspens and balsam poplars extensively gnawed by elk and moose. Half-way along its length, it crosses the creek and climbs much more steeply into pine forest on the ridge top where it joins Pine Ridge trail.

236 LOGGER'S LOOP

Easy
Distance 6 km

Starting from Long Prairie parking lot, the trail crosses the highway and basically follows flat logging roads past 2 clearings that were logged in the late 1960's and early 1970's for fence posts. The 2 arms of the logging road are connected by a narrow trail winding about the base of 2 wooded hills.

237 CHAIN-UP

Easy
Distance 0.5 km

A wide, flat trail which bisects Logger's loop.

Skiing between the aspens on Sandy McNabb loop.

238 MEADOW TRAIL

Easy
Distance 1.4 km

This trail connects the two parking lots via meadows on the south side of the highway.

239 SINK HOLE

Easy
Distance 0.2 km

The large sink hole, likely formed by a melting glacial ice block, is located half-way along the trail.

240 ALDER

Easy
Distance 0.6 km

This useful trail connects Logger's loop with Sandy McNabb loop. After crossing Tussock Pond, the trail descends to a viewpoint overlooking the Sheep River.

241 SANDY MCNABB LOOP

Easy
Distance 5.7 km

The trail starts behind the signboard at Sandy McNabb equestrian parking lot and heads left, following an old river terrace to Alder trail. Immediately after this junction comes a rather awkward downhill section to a viewpoint with seat. Novice skiers can avoid this hill, which upgrades to intermediate in icy conditions, by skiing the trail in an anti-clockwise direction. The trail doubles back across the day-use area access road and visits another viewpoint overlooking the Sheep River before returning to the starting point via the campground road.

242 WIDE OPEN

Easy
Distance 0.4 km

This trail, which uses a section of the Sandy McNabb day-use area access road, bisects Sandy McNabb loop to the east of Campers Link. It offers a good downhill run when skied in the N- S direction.

243 CAMPERS LINK

Easy
Distance 0.4 km

A wide flat campground road which bisects Sandy McNabb loop and can be used as a shortcut.

244 SANDY MCNABB INTERPRETIVE TRAIL — Map 16

Half-day hike
Distance 1.75 km
Topo map 82 J/10 Mount Rae

Access: Sheep River Trail (SR 546) at Sandy McNabb recreation area. Drive down the access road to the third road on the left which widens into a parking lot with trail sign. Brochures are available at the trailhead.

Walk along the signed trail running parallel to a grassed-over road. Just after passing the spring and a beautifully-landscaped water tap, the trail makes a loop which is best hiked in a clockwise direction, so head left through open forest with an understorey of foxtail grasses and palely gleaming campions to the edge of the terrace overlooking the Sheep River. Seats facing the view and a spate of trail stops encourage a rest break — it's a good place to read through the brochure which talks mainly about zoning regulations in the foothills. Down below you in the recreation zone on the riverbank is Sandy McNabb day-use area which is very close to where Turner Valley pioneer Sandy McNabb had his favorite fishing spot. The trail reenters forest and meanders on past a pumphouse and across small streamlets to the end of the loop at the aforementioned water tap.

245 DEATH VALLEY — Map 16

Day hike, backpack
Equestrian
Distance 12.5 km
Height gain 222 m
Maximum elevation 1539 m
Topo map 82 J/10 Mount Rae

Access: Sheep River Trail (SR 546) at Sandy McNabb recreation area. Turn first left off the access road into the equestrian parking lot.
Also accessible from the northern terminus of Windy Point trail (#246), the eastern terminus of Ware Creek trail (#274), and the southern terminus of 9999 trail (#277).

The name is intriguing; the beautiful meadows and aspen woodlands are hardly an epitome of a death valley as you imagine it. It's rumored that a band of horses died in this valley in the eighteen hundreds. What **is** known is that the creek used to be called Sinnot Creek after Harry Sinnot who homesteaded near the confluence with Ware Creek and that he died in mysterious circumstances during a Christmas Eve fire, not in Death Valley unfortunately for our story, but in a little shack on Whiskey Row north of Turner Valley. The most likely explanation for the name arises from the finding by range riders of a skeleton believed to be that of a trapper who had gone into the valley some years earlier and disappeared. The body was respectfully buried where it was found and the skull taken back to the Fisher Ranch where it was placed on a fence post and on occasions used as a football.

The trail down the valley to Ware Creek has many uses. It's ideal for early and late season conditioning walks to the beaver ponds, is an important link between the Sheep River trails and the trails of the North Fork (Threepoint Creek), and (most popular) can be combined with Windy Point and Sheep trails to make very pleasant 10.5 and 18 km loops. The trail is signed and marked with red rectangles throughout.

It starts behind the signboard in the parking lot. Turn right, cross Sandy McNabb recreation area access road and in less than 200 m turn right at a junction, cross the highway and wind up Death Valley Link ski trail to Long Prairie loop ski trail. Turn left here. At the next junction go right up the hill, still following Long Prairie loop ski trail to a viewpoint between aspens on the ridge top (2 hitching rails). Now turn left and descend Death Valley loop ski trail into the Death Valley drainage. After crossing an E-W cutline and a stream which is the infant Death Creek, watch for where Death Valley trail turns off to the right uphill.

For the next 3 km the trail traverses dry, aspen hillsides, then descends to beaver ponds in the valley bottom — a good lunch spot. As you walk downstream note the old beaver dams, upraised and cut in two by the flowing stream. Shortly after intersecting the valley exploration road (very wet, not recommended for travel), the trail crosses Death Valley Creek to a signed junction with Windy Point trail on the west bank. Turn right here and cross the side stream. The route follows a cutline upstream a short way then heads right through a belt of trees to another side creek where red markers guide you across the driest part of the valley floor which, it should be noted, lies downstream of the obvious track. Meadows in both side creeks are spotted with huge piles of droppings from feral stallions who, having once established a home range with a band of mares, will leave droppings at the same spot repeatedly.

The trail now moves away from Death Valley and cuts across 2 low ridges towards Ware Creek. Intersect an E-W cutline and pass through a gate on the apex of the first ridge. Follow the next E-W cutline to the right for a few metres, then turn left and, back on course, cross a side creek. Intersect a third E-W cutline on the second ridge top. A few minutes later, the crossing of a S.W.-N.E. cutline signals the trail's final descent down the east bank of a side creek — forded low down — to a signed junction with Ware Creek and 9999 trails in Ware Creek meadows.

Death Valley, showing a typical view of meadows and aspen forest.

246 WINDY POINT TRAIL — Map 16

Day hike, equestrian
Distance 6.5 km
Height gain 198 m
Maximum elevation 1600 m
Topo map 82 J/10 Mount Rae

Access: Sheep River Trail (SR 546). 8.2 km west of Kananaskis Country boundary, turn left into a parking lot.
Also accessible from Sheep trail (#255) and Death Valley trail (#245).

The Windy Point exploration road offers an alternative way into or out of Death Valley and is most often used by day hikers and equestrians in conjunction with Sheep and Death Valley trails to make loops of 10.5 and 18 km starting from Sandy McNabb recreation area. Follow the red markers.

A trail sign a few metres down slope of the parking lot at a T- junction with Sheep trail's alternate start indicates the proper start of the Windy Point trail. It crosses the highway and climbs fairly steeply for 1.5 km through meadows and aspens to a pass between Windy Point Ridge and Foreign Grade Ridge. At the highest point Sheep trail turns off to the right.

Carry on down the east bank of the unnamed creek to the north. In 1.2 km you cross the stream and pass through a gate out of the Sheep River Wildlife Sanctuary; you're now moving away from the creek and heading across a lightly-timbered ridge to a more northerly tributary of Death Valley. Entering a heart-shaped meadow, make for a raised island of aspens in the centre of the meadow (red triangle) where you are very close to Death Valley beaver ponds; you could, in fact, easily walk across to the main valley trail which lies only 0.2 km to the east at map ref. 73517. The Windy Point trail, however, turns north at the island and follows a forested rib of high ground between Death Valley Creek and willowy meadows to another tributary where it joins Death Valley trail at a sign on the south bank (map ref. 731181).

Windy Point Ridge near first top.

247 WINDY POINT RIDGE — Map 16

Half-day hike
1.5 km one way
Height gain 275 m
Topo map 82 J/10 Mount Rae

Access: **Sheep River Trail (SR 546), 9.4 km west of Kananaskis Country boundary.**

The south buttress of the ridge separating Death Valley from Canyon Creek rises steeply from the highway. Snow free for much of the year, it makes a good conditioning hike in early spring.

The section of road immediately below the ridge is known as Windy Point. Prior to a widening of the road in the 1930's, motoring around the point in Model T Fords used to be a hairy business, particularly during chinooks in winter when seepages below the ridge spread ice all over the road. Ruts would be cut in the ice to prevent cars sliding over the cliff edge into the Sheep River. Even so, many passengers still elected to get out and walk around Windy Point.

To avoid climbing over the barbed-wire fence, start west of the texas gate. The route follows the grassy ridge all the way to the first top; in places the going is quite steep and sometimes narrow. From the apex of east face cliffs, descend slightly to a col, then climb up through trees to a summit which has a cairn. Considering the lowly altitude of 1740 m, the view over forested foothills towards the Front Ranges is unusually fine.

248 WOLF CREEK — Maps 15 & 16

Day hike, backpack
Easy ski to pass
Equestrian
Distance 11 km
Height gain 305 m
Maximum elevation 1661 m
Topo map 82 J/10 Mount Rae

Access: **Sheep River Trail (SR 546) at Sandy McNabb recreation area. Equestrians and skiers should turn first left into the equestrian parking lot. Hikers may drive farther down the access road to the fourth road on the left which opens out into a parking lot.**
Also accessible from the northern terminus of Mount McNabb trail (#253), the southern terminus of Phone Line trail (#249), and the eastern terminus of Junction Mountain trail south (#251).

This signed, marked route follows exploration roads and cutlines up Wolf Creek and over a low pass to Coal Creek and Wolf Creek back-country campground. Its wide tread and gentle grades make it an ideal ski trail to the pass, after which the route is severely affected by chinook winds. NOTE: during runoff this trail is inaccessible to hikers because of dangerously high water levels in the Sheep River.

From the back of the signboard in the equestrian parking lot, turn left, then almost immediately right onto a descending trail which crosses the group camp access road, the interpretive trail parking lot, the hikers' parking lot (use right-hand trail), and the day-use area access road en route to the Sheep River. Wade across to a trail sign and road on the south bank. For the next 2 km you climb gently through mixed forest to a very large meadow above Wolf Creek. A view of Blue Ridge ahead — a perfect pleat in the forest floor — gives you some idea of how far you have to go to the pass which is located another 2 km beyond the ridge line. The road gradually reverts to faint trail as it winds around the perimeter of the meadow. Cross a small creek issuing from its boggy heartland, and then a more copious stream arising from the west flank of Mount Dyson. A little farther on, you join a wide N.W.-S.E. cutline. If you're returning the same way or hiking the trail in reverse direction, take special note of this junction; at no point does the route cross Wolf Creek!

At the junction then, turn right and follow the cutline through the drift fence into the inner fastness of Wolf Creek between Blue Ridge and Mount Dyson. After passing through a second gate you arrive at the forks. The cutline turns right up the north fork, then heads straight up a steep slope to the watershed ridge. Rather than follow the cutline's impractical line, the trail swings farther west and climbs more moderate slopes to a pass.

Open south slopes allow a comprehensive view of the headwaters of Coal and Sullivan Creeks including Junction Fire Lookout. In my opinion the best view is discovered by walking a few metres to your right. In this country of shallow valleys and low hills, it comes as quite a surprise when the ground suddenly drops away below your feet into a savage, black shale gorge. Although of short duration, the Coal Creek Gorge is just as impressive as its better-known counterparts elsewhere in the Sheep.

The route continues down an open draw marked by red triangles on posts, crosses the aforementioned cutline, picks up the cutline access road at the same time and follows it downhill to Coal Creek at the sharp bend upstream of the gorge. A delightful stretch through riverside meadows brings you to Wolf Creek back- country campground (toilets, firepits, hitching rails). Very faint now, the road crosses to the north bank, intersects the same N.W.-S.E. cutline, then recrosses the creek to a signed junction in a meadow with Phone Line trail and Junction Mountain trail south.

Coal Creek gorge.

249 PHONE LINE — Maps 15 & 16

Backpack, equestrian
Distance 7 km
Height gain 180 m
Maximum elevation 1673 m
Topo map 82 J/10 Mount Rae

Access: 1. Junction of Wolf Creek trail (#248) and Junction Mountain trail south (#250) in Coal Creek.
Access: 2. Junction of Green Mountain trail (#252) and Mount McNabb trail (#253) in North Coal Creek.

Linking trails in Coal and North Coal Creeks, Phone Line follows the line of the old telephone wire between Sentinel Ranger Station in The Highwood and Bighorn Ranger Station in The Sheep. Built in the 1920's, the telephone remained the main means of communication between stations until replaced by radios 30 years later. The wire was strung on high wooden tripods, some of which are still standing today.

From the trail junction in Coal Creek, Phone Line crosses the creek to north bank meadows. Walk upstream a short distance then turn right up a side valley to a wooded pass at map ref. 706053 where the trail joins a cutline access road which has come in from a N-S cutline to your left. The road dips into a tributary of Coal Creek, then swings left across a broad ridge of lodgepole pines separating Coal and North Coal Creek drainages. Watch for tripods in this section. Just over the height of land, a new trail circumvents the old road's foray into a swampy meadow, birthplace of a small stream; so when you see the road suddenly turning left into the meadow, keep straight on following red markers to the same N-S cutline mentioned earlier.

At this point, Hidden lake is only five minutes walk away and well worth a visit. Just walk north along the cutline to the first drainage bump, then turn right onto a game trail leading through the first few metres of forest to a grassy draw which in turn leads to the lakeshore.

Phone Line crosses the N-S cutline at right-angles, then swings right along the bank of the embryo stream, finally crossing it and doubling back to meet the road again on the far bank top. Turn right here and follow the road over 2 low ridges well- endowed with tripods into North Coal Creek proper. Walk downstream for about 0.4 km and ford the creek to a 4-way junction with an E-W cutline on the north bank. Don't make the mistake of thinking the road opposite is Green Mountain trail. You must turn right and walk another 0.25 km downstream to a signed T-junction in a large meadow under Green Mountain.

250 JUNCTION MOUNTAIN TRAIL SOUTH — Map 15

Backpack, equestrian
Distance 8.5 km
Height gain 658 m
Maximum elevation 2240 m
Topo map 82 J/10 Mount Rae

Access: 1. At junction of Wolf Creek trail (#248) and Phone Line trail (#249) in Coal Creek.
Access: 2. Via Junction Mountain trail north (#251) at the lookout.

This trail follows the headwaters of Coal Creek and is a much pleasanter route to Junction Fire Lookout than the fire road. Usually combined with routes #251, 252, 253, 249, 248, and 255 in their various permutations as part of a circuit.

From the 3-way trail junction in Coal Creek meadow, the trail edges along the river bank and joins a cutline access road which has come in from the other side of the river. Pass an unsigned, unmarked road to the left which is the northern terminus of route #224 to Sullivan Creek. A few minutes later cross a N.E.-S.W. cutline. In a clearing, half-way between this cutline and another one, turn off the road onto a trail heading right (west) into the confines of the upper valley. Ford Coal Creek 7 times during the next 4 km. From the meadows of the inner sanctum the lookout is a conspicuous landmark sitting astride a high grassy ridge in line with the trail and as you can see, nearly all the route's height gain occurs in this last kilometre as the trail makes its way via short, steep switchbacks up the side of a supporting rib to the ridge top. On outside bends the trail disappears in long grasses which are treacherously slippery when wet; take special care on the descent. The rib is gained at a prominent red marker which should be watched for carefully by descending parties since the last section of the route up grassy slopes is without a trail. Top out at the lookout where, in the shelter of a wall and with a certain smug satisfaction, you can look down on other backpackers toiling up the switchbacks below.

251 JUNCTION MOUNTAIN TRAIL NORTH — Maps 15 & 16

Long day hike, backpack
Intermediate ski, equestrian, bike
Distance from Sheep trail 9 km
Distance from parking lot 13.5 km
Height gain 792 m
Maximum elevation 2240 m
Topo map 82 J/10 Mount Rae

Access: **Sheep River Trail (SR 546) at Indian Oils parking lot 19.5 km west of Kananaskis Country boundary.**
Also accessible from Sheep trail (#255) at Dyson Creek, Green Mountain trail (#252) at Dyson Creek, and Junction Mountain trail south (#250) at the lookout.

Standing on a high grassy ridge N.E. of Junction Mountain, Junction Fire Lookout attracts hundred of visitors each season. Theoretically, the trail to the lookout — Junction Mountain trail south — starts from Sheep trail in Dyson Creek. In reality, the fire road starts from Indian Oils parking lot which is the usual point of departure for the day visitor. Distance and height gain are given from the parking lot. It's an excellent trail for mountain bikers and skiers alike, but skiers please note that at the present time, Sheep River Trail (SR 546) is closed at Sandy McNabb recreation area 14.6 km to the east during winter months.

Cross the bridge over the Sheep River at Tiger Jaws fall. Equestrians must use the ford 200 m to the west, then double back on Sheep trail to the fire road. For the next 4.5 km you follow the fire road which is also Sheep trail over the shoulder of Mount Hoffman into Dyson Creek. At the T-junction above Dyson falls, turn right (east) onto Junction Mountain trail south. It's a good idea to fill up your waterbottles at Dyson Creek crossing as streams higher up the road can't be relied upon. In 0.2 km bear right at the junction with Green Mountain trail.

The fire road parallels Dyson Creek a way, then, as if a steep hill was the signal, settles into an ascending traverse, winding in and out of all the headwaters of North Coal Creek on the heavily-forested east slopes of a ridge. At map ref. 656046 emerge from the trees onto a col. Either follow the winding fire road or make a direct assault up the broad stony ridge flagged on the east side by a line of wind-battered spruce trees to the lookout, the third to be sited at this location.

The fire road near the lookout.

252 GREEN MOUNTAIN TRAIL — Map 16

Day hike, backpack
Intermediate ski
Equestrian, bike
Distance 3.5 km
Height gain to Green Mountain 259 m
Maximum elevation at Green Mountain 1844 m
Topo map 82 J/10 Mount Rae

Access: **1. Via Junction Mountain trail south (#250) in Dyson Creek.**
Access: **2. At junction of Mount McNabb and Phone Line trails (# 253, #249) in North Coal Creek.**

This trail is an important connector between Dyson and North Coal creeks. It's also the jumping-off point for the ascent of Green Mountain (no trail) which is feasible in one day from Indian Oils trailhead even if you don't have a bike. Most likely named after Nigger Green, a "comical little fellow" who worked as a cook during early ranching days in the Sheep, Green Mountin looks insignificent from the highway, but concealed behind that facade of lodge pole pines lies open slopes and a fascinating sandstone escarpment. Standing as it does in comparative isolation, Green Mountain is an exceptional viewpoint.

0.2 km after Junction Mountain trail south fords Dyson Creek, at a right-hand bend above the first hill to be precise, turn left onto a narrower more vegetated road. Simply follow this road up the north bank of an unnamed creek to a pass, then down the north bank of another unnamed tributary into North Coal Creek where you join the northern terminus of Phone Line trail and the southern terminus of Mount McNabb trail at a T-junction. Its easy gradient and exquisite blending of meadows and aspen woodlands makes this a very pleasant trail to follow.

GREEN MOUNTAIN Just past the highest point of the road, you'll see a largish clearing to your left. From its top edge push your way through a belt of trees to the bottom of the open slopes then, veering slightly left, climb a steep grass rib leading to a transverse valley hidden from down below and filled with pinnacles and sandstone "mushrooms" clearly showing the swirls of the original sand dunes. A shallow gully leads up through the escarpment to the summit plateau which is open.

Sandstone "mushrooms" on the west face of Green Mtn.

Aspen meadows near North Coal Creek.

253 MOUNT MCNABB TRAIL — Map 16

Day hike, backpack
Equestrian
Distance 10 km
Height gain 311 m
Height loss 213 m
Maximum elevation 1570 m
Topo map 82 J/10 Mount Rae

Access: **Sheep River Trail (SR 546) at Sandy McNabb recreation area. Equestrians should turn first left into the equestrian parking lot. Hikers may drive farther down the access road to the fourth road on the left which opens out into a parking lot. Also accessible from the northern terminus of Phone Line trail (# 249), the eastern terminus of Green Mountain trail (#252), the northern terminus of Wolf Creek trail (#248) and the eastern terminus of Price Camp trail (#254).**

A mixture of old exploration roads and cow trails takes you through the beautiful meadows and aspen forests of North Coal Creek and it tributaries to a 3-way trail junction under Green Mountain. Early in the season, be prepared for a difficult river crossing right at the beginning. Skiing isn't recommended beyond the junction with Price Camp trail.

From the back of the signboard at the equestrian parking lot, turn left, then almost immediately right onto a descending trail which crosses the group camp access road, the interpretive trail parking lot, the hikers' trailhead and parking lot (use right- hand trail) and the access road to the day-use area. Ford the Sheep River, aiming not for the trail sign but for the old road upstream of North Coal Creek. Follow this road which soon narrows to trail width onto a higher terrace level and through a gate to the junction with Price Camp trail at the 3 km mark. Turn left here and climb steeply at times over a wooded pass 1.5 km west of Mount McNabb into a side valley. Cross a low ridge into another side valley parallel to the first one, a smooth trough of close-cropped grass which is followed downstream almost to North Coal Creek; at the last moment, however, the trail turns right and traverses yet another ridge and side valley before finally reaching the grassy banks of North Coal Creek itself. Far off to the west, the pointed peaks of the Highwood Range are sticking up above low, forested foothills.

The next objective is the side creek to the north at map ref. 708096 where the trail crosses to the S.E. bank. From this point on you can either follow the valley trail with its numerous creek crossings, or at the first opportunity get onto a trail high on the grassy N.W. bank. It doesn't matter which route you choose for both trails join about 0.3 km east of the T-junction with Phone Line and Green Mountain trails.

254 PRICE CAMP TRAIL — Map 16

Day hike, intermediate ski
Equestrian
Distance 2.5 km
Height gain 46 m
Maximum elevation 1509 m
Topo map 82 J/10 Mount Rae

Access: 1. Via Mount McNabb trail (#253)
Access: 2. Via Sheep trail (#255)

Together with Mount McNabb trail, this short connector gives equestrians an alterative start (or finish) to Sheep trail. Its width and easy grade make it a surprisingly good ski trail; when you tire of the nearby groomed trails, try combining it with Mount McNabb and Sheep trails to make an 11 km loop starting from Sandy McNabb ski parking lot. The trail is signed and marked throughout.

From the junction with Mount McNabb trail, Price Camp trail moves away from the Sheep River and enters pine forest. Cross a N.E.-S.W. cutline and a little later on, March Creek whose north bank is followed upstream to a large meadow where you'll happen upon the ruins of 2 log buildings — all that's left of Mr. Price's Logging Camp of nearly 80 years ago. At this spot, the trail makes a right-angled turn to the right (north) and descends a steep hill to an intersection with a major N.E.-S.W. cutline. A few metres on, you arrive at the T-junction with Sheep trail.

Tiger Jaws Fall, Sheep River. Bridge is start of Junction Lookout fire road.

255 SHEEP TRAIL

Total distance 46 km

Access: 1. Sheep River Trail (SR 546) at Sandy McNabb recreation area. Turn first left into the equestrian parking lot.
Access: 2. Sheep River Trail (SR 546) at small parking lot 1.6 km west of Sandy McNabb recreation area.
Access: 3. Sheep River Trail (SR 546) at Windy Point parking lot 3.3 km west of Sandy McNabb recreation area.
Access: 4. Sheep River Trail (SR 546) at Indian Oils day-use area.
Access: 5. Sheep River Trail (SR 546) at Bluerock campground and Bluerock equestrian campground.
Access: 6. Sheep River Trail (SR 546) at terminus of highway at Junction Creek day-use area.
Also accessible from Windy Point trail (#246), Price Camp trail (#254), Junction Mountain trail north (#251), Indian Oils trail (#261), Bluerock trail (#260), Mist Creek trail (#172), and Big Elbow trail (#306).

From its beginning at Sandy McNabb recreation area, Sheep trail runs west up the Sheep River Valley to Big Elbow trail. There is no one trail to follow; rather the route is made up of a multitude of disused roads, cutlines, logging roads, fire roads and newly-cut trails all signed and marked with red rectangles. Numerous crossings of the Sheep River make this a difficult, even dangerous route for foot travellers early in the season.

View west from Foreign Grade Ridge of Windy Point Ridge (right) and the Sheep River valley. Next section of Sheep trail follows, with some diversions, the cutline at the left of the photo.

SANDY MCNABB TO WINDY POINT VIA FOREIGN GRADE RIDGE — Map 16

Day hike, equestrian
Distance 6 km
Height gain 253 m
Height loss 238 m
Maximum elevation 1685 m
Topo map 82 J/10 Mount Rae

Start behind the sign board at Sandy McNabb equestrian parking lot. The trail heads west across the access road and in a few minutes passes Death Valley trail to right. At the next junction with the alternate route, turn right and cross the highway to a small parking area which is the usual starting point for day hikers wanting access to Foreign Grade Ridge.

The trail continues from the north side of the highway, angling left all the while (disregard a cutline to right near the road) and climbing gently through aspens and pines onto Foreign Grade Ridge where clearings at mid point allow exceptional views of the Sheep River Valley and the mountains to the west. From the highest point the trail descends to meadows about the pass between Foreign Grade and Windy Point Ridges and it's here that you join Windy Point trail at the trail sign. Turn left and make a quick return to the highway and parking lot.

Alternate route: The old route, which is 2 km shorter and has no height gain, is still in use despite encroachment by highway construction. It starts from the second trail junction and simply parallels the highway to a junction with Sheep trail below Windy Point parking lot. Keep a close watch on small children at the point where the trail traverses high above the Sheep River gorge.

WINDY POINT TO INDIAN OILS DAY-USE AREA — Maps 16 & 17

Day hike, intermediate ski
Equestrian
Distance 13.6 km
Height gain 320 m
Height loss 244 m
Maximum elevation 1646 m
Topo map 82 J/10 Mount Rae

Wind downhill to the Sheep River and ford it at the one spot where the black shale walls of the canyon break up into trees and meadow. On the south bank the trail climbs to a terrace, then bears right and crosses a cutline. Follow the next N.E.-S.W. cutline you come to up a hill, but before starting up a second, steeper hill, turn right onto a newly-cut trail which parallels the cutline to the junction with Price Camp trail.

The trail continues running parallel with the cutline, sometimes using the cutline itself. After 4 km of uninspiring going the trail fords Dyson Creek and, rejoining the cutline, climbs uphill for 1.5 km to a 4-way intersection with the old telephone road coming in from the Sheep River opposite Gorge Creek. (Although not part of the official trail system, the telephone road offers by far the fastest access from the highway onto this part of Sheep Trail.) Turn left here and follow the telephone road through mostly open country to the

T-junction with Junction Mountain fire road above Dyson Creek. Meadows plus Dyson Falls make this an extremely attractive spot to linger over. Be aware, though, that there is a much larger than usual concentration of black bears around Dyson Creek; anyone camping in the valley should take stringent precautions.

Keep right and pass through the gap between Mount Hoffman and an unnamed hill to the north. Indian Oils coal mine comes into view as you descend the steeper west slope to the Sheep River. At the last bend in the fire road, pass the next section of Sheep trail to the left and arrive at the log bridge over Tiger Jaws Fall which is the only bridged crossing of the Sheep River and the only certain access for hikers during runoff to trails south of the river. Indian Oils day-use area lies a few minutes walk away on the north bank. Equestrians should use the access trail which fords the river a little farther along the next section of Sheep trail.

Dyson Falls in Dyson Creek meadows.

INDIAN OILS DAY-USE AREA TO BLUEROCK CAMPGROUNDS — Map 17

Day hike, easy ski
Equestrian
Distance 4 km
Height gain 61 m
Topo map 82 J/10 Mount Rae

From the last bend in the fire road above the bridge, turn left and pass through a gate onto a narrow trail running along the south bank of the Sheep River. Almost straightway the equestrian route to Indian Oils day-use area turns off to the right. Between this junction and Indian Oils west junction another kilometre upstream, the river looses height in a series of picturesque falls, the most notable of which is Sheep River Falls. Unfortunately, after the initial stretch the trail wanders away from the river, making bushwacking forays necessary to viewpoints. For the next 2 km the trail follows a grassy terrace offering occasional views of Mount Gibralter up ahead.

Shortly after re-descending to the riverbank, the trail fords the Sheep River at a quiet spot just west of Bluerock Creek highway bridge and climbs up to Secondary Road 546. A little way up the north bank the next section of Sheep **hiking** trail turns off to the left. Arriving at the highway, hikers should turn right, cross the bridge over Bluerock Creek, then almost immediately climb the stepped trail by the side of Bluerock Creek to the campground loop road. Equestrians should follow the trail which crosses the highway, climbs the bank, intersects the old highway and arrives via the mouth of the equestrian campground loop road at the corral which is the jumping-off point for the next section Sheep **equestrian** trail.

BLUEROCK CAMPGROUNDS TO BIG ELBOW TRAIL — Maps 17 & 18

Day hike, backpack
Easy ski, equestrian, bike
Distance 23 km
Height gain 518 m
Height loss 131 m
Maximum elevation 2118 m
Topo map 82 J/10 Mount Rae

For the first 2.2 km, hiking and equestrian trails follow different routes.

Hiking trail: From Bluerock campground follow route #258 along the river bank to the terminus of the highway. Slip through the gate onto the old road which, with every twist and turn, offers increasingly dramatic views of Gibralter Rock up ahead. 1 km from the gate, the equestrian trail comes in from the right.

Equestrian trail: The logging road leaves the corral in the equestrian campground and climbs uphill past a side road to the right and Bluerock hiking trail to the left. After crossing a small side stream and climbing some more past 2 overgrown side roads to the right, you arrive at a 4-way junction. Turn left onto a narrower trail marked by red rectangles which leads to a meadow holding a fair-sized pond. Rimmed with snails feeding on a scum of pale green algae and backdropped by a mountain known as Shunga-la-she, which translates to "mountain white man shit on", the pond and its environs is, nevertheless, a very pleasant spot in which to linger awhile before continuing on around the north shore into the trees. Here you join a grassed- over logging road which is followed downhill (keep right at one junction low down) to the old Sheep River road. Turn right.

Now merged, the hiking and equestrian trails follow the road for only a short distance before swinging left into the forest for a stint. Then it's back to the road again where you pass close to noisy rapids inviting a closer look. A major ford for equestrians and bikers occurs at the 4 km mark. Although the old road bridge is becoming more skeletal with each passing season, it is at the time of publication still navigable by careful hikers. A little farther on, the road crosses Cliff Creek and passes beneath the vertical, sometimes overhanging north face of Gibralter Rock — scene of an incredible 9-day climb in 1971 which had the distinction of being the first extended aid climb in the Canadian Rockies.

The river is forded twice more before you reach the junction with Mist Creek trail at a corral and a stockpile of coal. For the last 3 km you have been travelling through private land still owned by the Burns family. It was in 1911 that Pat Burns bought the mining and surface rights from Julius Rickert and 2 years later established the P. Burns Coal Mine Company. A charter was obtained to build a railroad — the Calgary and South-western — along the Sheep River valley on the site of today's road, and it was during the clearing of the right-of-way that the terrible fire of 1919 was ignited, one of 3 major fires on the eastern slopes which, fanned by strong west winds, burned right through to the forest boundary. The railway came to naught when the mine ceased operations a few years later, a cessation brought about by the post-war slump and not by the quantity or quality of the coal which was stockpiled waiting for a railroad that never came.

The meadows close to Mist Creek trail junction were the site of the mine "town" consisting of bunkhouses, a cookhouse, hospital, storage cabins, bathhouse, barns and corral. Gibralter Mountain, or "Sheer Cliff" as it was known in those days and which overlooked the townsite, was the scene of a tragic accident in 1918 when a young mine worker, who with 3 companions had climbed to the summit by the easy way, slipped and fell down the eastern precipice. His body was never found, no doubt caught up on some ledge or swallowed by a gully. In 1960 when the Forest Service burned down the remaining buildings, they discovered a trunk containing all of his belongings still lying in the corner of a room in the hospital.

The old road follows private land for another 4 km, passing out of fire succession lodepole pine forest into the old spruce forest of the upper valley. All this section of road between the mine and the forks at map ref. 467130 is bisected by many fords which though shallow enough are all too wide to be jumped across. Shortly after passing Harry Denning's cabin, you wade Burns Creek and in another 0.7 km arrive at Burns Creek exploration road (unsigned and unmarked) which turns off to the left. Another 3.5 km of easy going brings you to the forks at a point where the left-hand fork of the Sheep River, named Rae Creek on the topo map, swings south below the east glacier of Mont Rae into the heart of the Misty Range. The road follows this creek a bit, then climbs up an open rib between the two forks onto a ridge top. Look back one last time into the headwaters of Rae Creek and the tantalizing grassy ridges enclosing it to the east. What fine country there is here for further exploration!

Traverse gentle, open sideslopes to the T-junction with Big Elbow trail — another old exploration road. En route, you cross the effluence from Rae Lake, an irregular-shaped body of water backed by tremendous cliffs which is worth a visit if you have an hour or two to spare. Just to the south of the effluence a side road to right points you in the direction of 3 shallow ponds sitting astride the Elbow/Sheep watershed. Equestrians eastbound along Big Elbow trail can save a kilometre by picking up a pack trail on the east bank of the creek arising from the northernmost pond and following it downstream to Big Elbow equestrian trail in the Elbow River valley bottom.

Gibralter Rock from the slope above the bridge.

256 BURNS CREEK — Map 10

Backpack, equestrian
Bike to falls
5.5 km to falls
Height gain to lake 380 m
Maximum elevation at lake 2255 m
Topo map 82 J/10 Mount Rae

Access: Via Sheep trail (#255). An exploration road leaves the west side of the road 14.3 km north of Bluerock Creek bridge or 8.8 km south of Big Elbow trail junction.

A side trip to Burns Creek waterfall, candidate for the highest fall in Kananaskis Country, is a must. Lovers of high alpine lakes should carry on into the cirque behind, but be aware that a penance must first be exacted in the shape of a stiff climb. The route is unsigned.

Good time can be made along the road in the forested valley bottom. Keep left near the start. In mid valley, where the road crosses Burns Creek twice in quick succession, look for a by-pass trail to the right. Arriving at valley head, turn left at a junction and descend to meadows below a 400 metre-high waterfall which you discover is not a single fall but a picturesque arrangement of stepped cascades.

Anyone who wants to go farther must climb up the headwall using whatever game trails they can find to the right of the waterfall. Aim for the top of a rocky bluff overlooking the lake. The lake is pie-shaped, wedged between a boulder slope and a rock wall which makes shoreline navigation very difficult. From the top of the bluff, though, it's an easy descent to flat meadows bordering the wide north shore — an idyllic camping spot. White rivulets issuing from upper cirques and fed by melting snowbanks rush furiously down mixed slopes of grass, larch and spruce. If you have time, explore the left-hand cirque which reaches far back under Mount Rae and supports a small tarn.

257 JUNCTION CREEK — Maps 10 & 17

Day hike, backpack
Equestrian
Bike to mill site
8.5 km to lake
Height gain 440 m
Maximum elevation 2040 m
Topo map 82 J/10 Mount Rae

Access: Sheep River Trail (SR 546) at Junction Creek day-use area.

Junction Creek is built on the grand scale with numerous side valleys branching off to east and west. Most hikers seem drawn towards the first valley to the west which holds a fair-sized lake. The route to the lake, and indeed up all the other side valleys, is very rough and best avoided by inexperienced hikers. All of the Junction Creek trails including the main artery are unofficial and therefore unsigned.

Between the first woodpile and the second parking lot a trail descends to within a few metres of the Sheep River where it is immediately apparent that attaining the Junction Creek logging road on the south bank is dependent on low water levels. The next 2.5 km to the sawmill site are tedious but fast. If you're not in a hurry, I suggest you follow the west bank of Junction Creek looking for traces of log dams built to ease the passage of logs through the rapids between the mill and the Sheep River.

Beyond the mill site, a good pack trail carries on past the Junction Lake turnoff to a hunters' campsite two-thirds of the way up the valley. Hikers will be most interested in the side creek S.W. of Junction Mountain (meadows), and in the second valley to the west (waterfalls) which can be followed to a col overlooking Picklejar Lakes. There have been reports of competent parties finding a route down to the lakes (steep scree and slabs).

JUNCTION LAKE Turn right up the first sizable side stream flowing out of the west. A faint trail running along the north bank above a little canyon is easy to follow but much less fun than crab-crawling round deep pools and solving problematical rock steps in the creekbed. Sooner or later, though, you have to descend to creek level and start boulder hopping. This frustratingly slow kind of progress ends at the point where the creek turns S.W. Here, a deeper rift not apparent from the topo map forces you to climb to a high bench on the north side of the valley. Once you've gained the height, it's easy walking for many kilometres through lush green meadows.

The lake is beautifully situated in a glacial basin at the head of the valley. At runoff, waters spill over the lip of the cirque to tumble down a rocky creekbed. By late summer, when the snowbanks have melted, underground drainage reduces the lake to 2 shallow puddles.

258 BLUEROCK CAMPGROUND TO JUNCTION CREEK DAY-USE AREA — Map 17

Half-day hike
Distance 1.2 km
Topo map 82 J/10 Mount Rae

Access: **1. Sheep River Trail (SR 546) at Bluerock campground. The trail starts from the far end of the campground loop at the trail sign.**
Access: **2. Sheep River Trail (SR 546) at Junction Creek day-use area.**

This useful snippet of trail built in 1984 is a boon to hikers camped at Bluerock campground who no longer have to get in their cars and drive for 3 km along the highway to the start of the Junction Creek and Bluerock trails. Looked at logically, it is part of the backpackers' long-distance trail up the Sheep River. In reality, less ambitious campers and picnickers at Junction day-use area are using this little bit of trail as access to a very beautiful stretch of river between the two points.

From the trail sign at Bluerock campground, turn left and walk down steps to the highway. Cross the bridge over Bluerock Creek. In a few metres turn left onto Sheep trail (which intersects the road), then, as soon as you reach the trees, turn right and climb the bank with the help of more steps, to the narrow strip of forest between the highway and the Sheep River now closeted in a gorge. Rapids and deep pools follow one another without variance. Close to Junction Creek day-use area, the gorge breaks down and the river calms — temporarily. Cross a meadow and arrive among the picnic tables. The first trail to right which intersects both the Junction Creek day-use area access road and the highway is Bluerock east access hiking trail. In the middle of the picnic area cross the trail between the parking lot and Junction Creek trail on the other side of the river.

Keep following the gravelled trail out of the picnic area to a viewpoint above a ciff, only then turning away from the river and climbing to the terminus of Sheep River Trail (Hwy.) which is also the start of Bluerock west access hiking trail and the continuation of Sheep hiking trail (both signed). NOTE: A few metres beyond the viewpoint, an old trail carrying on along the cliff top is very popular with picnickers. It leads to an inside bend of the river above the cataract seen from the viewpoint.

259 BLUEROCK CREEK INTERPRETIVE TRAIL — Map 17

Half-day hike
Distance 2 km
Topo map 82 J/10 Mount Rae

Access: Sheep River Trail (SR 546) at Bluerock campground. The trail starts from the far end of the campground loop road at a trail sign. Brochures are available at the trailhead.

Turn right and climb to a junction where the trail loops. Trail stops are arranged in an anticlockwise direction so switchback up the hill to your right and cross a moderately-steep gravel slope giving good views of nameless peaks at the head of Bluerock creek. At the turnaround point, the trail descends to a seat in a cutblock close to the river. Look around you. Saw dust, boards, rusty nails and bolts hidden in the long grass tell you this was the site of Napp Lefavre's sawmill which operated on this spot in 1947. The lumber was trucked out across a bridge below the camp onto what is now Bluerock equestrian trail. Homeward bound now, follow the trail across the gravel slope crossed earlier, but now traversed low down above the gorge, and arrive back at the start of the loop in the trees.

260 BLUEROCK TRAIL — Map 17

Day hike
Equestrian
Distance 11.5 km
Height gain 625 m
Height loss 472 m
Maximum elevation 2134 m
Topo map 82 J/10 Mount Rae

Access: 1. Sheep River Trail (SR 546) at Junction Creek day- use area.
Access: 2. Sheep River Trail (SR 546) at terminus of highway.
Access: 3. Sheep River Trail (SR 546) at Bluerock equestrian campground.
Also accessible from Gorge Creek trail (#265).

This fairly strenuous trail connects the Sheep River valley to the middle section of Gorge Creek. It makes an excellent day trip and is most often used as such by hikers and equestrians aiming for timberline meadows below Bluerock Mountain. Note that equestrians and hikers take different routes for the first 0.7 km.

Equestrian trail: The trail (also Sheep trail) starts from the corral at Bluerock equestrian campground and follows the logging road uphill. Keep left at a road junction and watch for where the hiking trail comes in from the left.

Hiking trail: There are 2 starts to complicate matters further. The first one begins from the parking lot at the terminus of the highway. It climbs the bank to the north, gradually moving away from the highway and cutting across country to a T-junction with a logging road which is the equestrian trail. Turn left. You can also join start #1 from Junction Creek day-use area parking lot. The trail branches off route # 258, but it's probably easiest to walk back along the access road and pick up the trail where it crosses both the access road and the highway in quick succession. Now climb the bank and join the first trail close to the edge of the forest.

Equestrians and hikers together follow the logging road in a westerly direction across a side stream and up a hill past overgrown secondary logging roads to right. At a signed junction, leave Sheep trail which turns off to the left and carry on climbing up the major logging road for another 2 km. At the mill site at road's end transfer onto a trail which soon turns right and switchbacks downhill through mossy spruce forest to Bluerock Creek. How galling it is to loose 100 m of hard-won altitude and backtrack at the same time! Hopefully the trail builders will forge a trail along the riverbank one day.

Cross the bridge and climb a steep rib leading to the S.E. ridge of Bluerock Mountain which is in turn followed in a north- westerly direction to the rocky foot of the mountain; it's a lovely stretch of trail alterating between forest and meadows where the route is marked by large cairns. Look down into the headwaters of Bluerock Creek. At the highest point gained, the trail swings over to the east side of the ridge and reveals an aerial view of Gorge Creek and all its tributaries. The meadows hereabouts are the highlight of the trip, but unless you're a climber there is little scope for further exploration, so without further delay (for there is still a long way to go), continue along the trail which soon starts a descending traverse across the north face of Bluerock Mountain to Gorge Creek gained at map ref. 578149. En route, be careful not to lose the trail in long grasses at tributary crossings.

The tributary crossed at map ref. 573141 offers a tantalizing shortcut to Indian Oils trail at map ref. 597133. The terrain is mostly open rangeland imprinted with cow trails and a section of road in the middle which once led from Gorge Creek to a range riders' cabin, now demolished.

261 INDIAN OILS TRAIL — Map 17

Half-day, day hike
Equestrian
Distance 8.5 km
Height gain 396 m
Height loss 131 m
Maximum elevation 1829 m
Topo map 82 J/10 Mount Rae

Access: 1. Sheep River Trail (SR 546) at Indian Oils day-use area.
Access: 2. Sheep River Trail (SR 546) at Sheep River Falls day- use area. Walk west along the highway for 0.1 km to the intersection of the trail.
Also accessible from Sheep trail (#255) 0.1 and 1 km west of the fire road bridge over the Sheep River, from Gorge Creek trail (#265), and from the western terminus of South Gorge Creek trail (#262).

This signed trail, which crosses the group of low hills between the Sheep River and Gorge Creek, meanders through a typical foothills mix of meadows and forest, and is carefully routed to include several fine viewpoints. The coal mine at the half-kilometre mark makes a good half-day trip.

There are 2 ways of starting this trail. I prefer to begin the trip from Indian Oils day-use area where a trail leaves the far end of the equestrian parking lot and arrives in a few metres at a T-junction. (The left-hand trail is an equestrian link trail to Sheep trail on the S.E. bank of the Sheep River.) Indian Oils trail turns right, crosses the highway and begins a gradual climb along the old mine access road to a strip mine which is

At the highest point of Bluerock trail, you travel through meadows overlooking the headwaters of Bluerock Creek.

Indian Oils trail, looking west from the saddle towards Bluerock Mtn.

immediately identifiable by slag heaps barely disguised by new tree growth. Take time to explore the area up-slope which for a few years at the beginning of the century was occupied by Indian Oils oilwell. After the great fire of 1910, the area was strip- mined, but like most other ventures of the this kind in the upper Sheep, was doomed to failure by the high costs of transporting the coal over long, difficult distances to the nearest market.

Continue along the trail to a side creek and there join the trail from access #2 which has come in from across the Sheep River 100 m west of Sheep Falls day-use area, the alternate starting point. The trail now travels along the north bank of the side creek to the 1.5 km mark, then cuts over the open ridge to the north into the headwaters of a creek issuing from a small lake — scenario of the grizzly scare in 1980. Traverse into the headwaters of another creek and pass through a gap between 2 grassy hills into a sizable tributary of Gorge Creek known as South Gorge Creek. Near valley bottom, make a left turn onto an old exploration road which climbs past the junction with South Gorge Creek trail to right to a saddle — good views of Bluerock Mountain — then continues steeply down the west flank to the Gorge Creek drainage. Cross 2 small side streams, branches of the same creek which at runoff affords hikers with some amusement. Your trail turns north at the next side creek you come to and passes between 2 conical hills into the main fork of Gorge Creek. Wade Gorge Creek to the north bank where you can pick up the Gorge Creek trail. Disregarding 2 side creeks which are of little consequence, west-bound hikers can save themselves 2, possibly 3 major fords of Gorge Creek by a bushwack along the south bank.

262 SOUTH GORGE CREEK TRAIL — Map 17

Day hike
Equestrian
Distance 5 km
Height gain 213 m
Maximum elevation 1783 m
Topo map 82 J/10 Mount Rae

Access: 1. Via Gorge Creek trail (#265), 0.2 km west of the north fork crossing.
Access: 2. Via Indian Oils trail (#261) at head of South Gorge Creek.

This signed trail, which is chiefly of interest to equestrians on account of a river crossing at the 200 m mark, enables the day tripper to make a loop with Gorge Creek and Indian Oils trails. You ford Gorge Creek to the south bank a few minutes after leaving Gorge Creek trail. Now head in a south-westerly direction to a T-junction with a N.W.-S.E. cutline and turn left. Follow the cutline, with one diversion around boggy ground, into South Gorge Creek, then turn west onto a new trail which travels for 2.5 km through typical foothills country of mixed forest and meadow to the valley head. Bridge the stream and join Indian Oils trail just east of a saddle in the watershed ridge at map ref. 613124.

263 SHEEP RIVER FALLS — Map 17

Half-day hike
Distance 0.5 km
Topo map 82 J/10 Mount Rae

Access: Sheep River Trail (SR 546) at Sheep River Falls day- use area.

Until there is an official trail to the falls, it's easiest to follow a well-used unofficial trail downstream along the river bank from the picnic area. Rocky bluffs beyond the 8 metre-high falls make the ideal viewpoint.

264 BIGHORN LOOKOUT — Map 16

Half-day hike
Distance 0.5 km
Topo map 82 J/10 Mount Rae

Access: Sheep River Trail (SR 546) at Bighorn day-use area.

This ten-minute trail crosses a meadow of tall foxtail grasses to a hide where, with luck, you'll be able to spy on the area's large flock of bighorn sheep who divide their time between the craggy slopes of Missinglink Mountain to your right and the meadows in front of you. Bring binoculars.

It is probably the ancestors of this particular flock that give the river and the area its name; the Sheep River was called "itou-kai-you" on David Thompson's map of 1814, and "itukaiup" on the Arrowsmith map of 1859, both words refering to "the sheep at the head of the river". Thanks mainly to the efforts of ranger Joe Macovic, the sheep all along the Sheep River from Windy Point to Sheep Falls day-use area are protected from hunters by the establishment of the Sheep River Wildlife Sanctuary.

265 GORGE CREEK — Map 17

Day hike, backpack
Equestrian
Distance 11 km
Height gain 411 m
Maximum elevation 1951 m
Topo map 82 J/10 Mount Rae

Access: Gorge Creek Trail (Hwy.) at Gorge Creek day-use area. Also accessible from the southern terminus of Gorge Link trail (#272), the northern terminus of South Gorge Creek trail (#262), the northern terminus of Indian Oils trail (#261), the northern terminus of Bluerock trail (#260), the western terminus of Volcano Creek trail (#267) and the southern terminus of Threepoint Mountain trail (#266).

Gorge Creek is a long, winding valley of alternating gorges and meadows reaching far back into the Front Range between Mount Rose and Bluerock Mountain. It is traversed by a marked trail, heavily travelled on weekends by hikers and equestrians alike who can choose from a large number of ongoing long distance trails and circuits.

The new start to this trail begins from the far end of Gorge Creek day-use area behind the toilets. A little way in you join the original route (exploration road) coming in from the left and make a descending traverse into the meadows of Gorge Creek. Listen for the cascade below the trail near the confluence of Gorge Creek with its north fork; it makes a worthwhile diversion at runoff. Ford North Gorge Creek above the fall and arrive at the junction with Gorge Link trail to right at the 1.5 km mark. Keep left on the road which returns to Gorge Creek. Pass the northern terminus of South Gorge Creek trail to left a few minutes after leaving the junction, then begin climbing along the bank top to a high point at a cutline. Losing all the height gained previously, descend to valley bottom where a section of trail along the north bank omits 2 river crossings by the road. When the road turns steeply uphill, transfer to the new valley trail which takes you safely through the narrows, climbing high at one point in order to circumvent the troublesome little gorge criss-crossed by the old trail. Go through a gate in the drift fence and descend once more to valley bottom, now broadened out into meadows tinged pink with Old man's whiskers. 4.5 km from the trailhead, Indian Oils trail turns off to the left. A little further on, a lone pine landmark signals the start of 3 creek crossings none of which can be easily avoided. The meadow between the second and third crossing is the best place for energetic day-hikers to strike off towards the summit of Mount Ware (2040 m), the shapely hill to the north whose name has been omitted from the 3rd edition of the topo map. It has a narrow summit ridge, much too good to miss, which should be traversed from west to east for full enjoyment.

Now on the S.W. bank, walk another 2 km through cow meadows to the junction with Bluerock trail on the left. The valley is narrowing quickly now and you must climb up and down a forested side ridge to get around the next bend. Cross the creek for the fourth time and begin climbing steeply up the bank in anticipation of the black shale gorge ahead. The labor of the ascent is well-worthwhile for a far-reaching view suddenly unfolds of the upper valley between Mount Rose and Bluerock Mountain, the splendor of the scene further enhanced by the dramatic situation of the trail as it follows the lip of the gorge to the big bend where the valley turns west. Here the trail parts company with Gorge Creek and continues in a northerly direction over the height of land into Volcano Creek. En route you pass the Volcano Creek shortcut trail to right about 0.3 km before the trail terminates at a T-junction with Threepoint Mountain trail (straight) and Volcano Creek trail proper (right).

GORGE/COUGAR GAP (2149 m) At the big bend, turn west onto a well-used hunters' trail which follows the edge of the gorge through alternate forest and small, well-watered allotments of wild onions. In 1.7 km, the trail peters out on open hillsides below Mount Rose and you must make your own route to the obvious gap between Mount Rose and Bluerock Mountain at map ref. 543168. The going is easy and delightful as you wade through great drifts of larkspurs, valerians, fleabanes, long-stemmed forgetmenots and multi-stemmed shooting stars growing on the damper facets of the hillside. Looking back, the eye is caught by the sparkle of water on a distant ridge, one of numerous small ponds unmarked on the topo maps. A few metres of steeper, rockier ground leads to the gap — a flat meadow — which could be considered the gateway to the middle reaches of Cougar Creek (no ongoing trail) and also the jumping-off point for Bluerock Mountain which from this side is a steep but non-techical ascent within the ability of any strong, experienced hiker. Simply traverse back into Gorge Creek above all difficulties and follow sheep trails to its source under the talus slopes of the north face. Gain the easy N.W. ridge half a kilometre from the summit cairn.

Route leaves the gorge at the bend and makes for the forested notch on the skyline above the figures.

266 THREEPOINT MOUNTAIN TRAIL — Map 17

Long-day hike
Backpack, equestrian
Distance 10.5 km
Height gain 152 m
Height loss 457 m
Maximum elevation 2027 m
Topo map 82 J/10 Mount Rae
82 J/15 Bragg Creek

Access: **1. Junction of Gorge Creek (#265) and Volcano Creek (#267) trails.**
Access: **2. Via Big Elbow trail (#306) 5 km south of Little Elbow recreation area.**
Access: **3. Via Upper Threepoint Creek trail (#270).**

A mixture of new and old trails, Threepoint Mountain trail is an important link between the trails of The Sheep and The Elbow. Expect a difficult river crossing early in the season.

From the head of Volcano Creek, the trail travels north through a mosaic of meadow and forest below the eastern precipices of Mount Rose and Threepoint Mountain. It dips into Rock Creek wherin lies Threepoint Mountain back-country campground (firepits, toilets and hitching posts), then rises gently over the height of land into Threepoint Creek which is entered not by the obvious south fork but by a much smaller creek farther west. A hunters' campsite is located in trees to the left of the trail just before you merge with the main valley which at this point is a shallow, heathy basin; oil oozing out of the ground runs in rainbow-hued rivulets among the sedges of the north bank.

At the unsigned T-junction with Upper Threepoint Creek trail on the riverbank, turn right and follow the exploration road across the creek to another junction. The exploration road heads downstream. You, however, must double back up the north bank until opposite your entrance into the valley, then leave Threepoint Creek by a marshy draw holding a small, sedge-enclosed pond. Enter forest at the watershed and traverse the head of an unnamed creek. Numerous false trails on the north side of the creek crossing are confusing; the real trail is blazed. Arriving in meadows allowing a superlative view of the Elbow valley and the mountains to the west (the Cornwall Creek waterfall is plainly visible), follow large cairns to the start of the pack trail in the trees. Now wind slowly down a forested ridge to the Elbow River — the crossing point is marked by cairns between braids and a large cairn on the west bank. After about 100 m you intersect Big Elbow equestrian trail (red markers on trees) and the valley exploration road which is the hikers' route (sign).

Rest break at upper Threepoint Creek river crossing.

Volcano Creek and Bluerock Mtn.

267 VOLCANO CREEK — Map 17

Backpack, equestrian
Distance 4 km
Height gain 122 m
Maximum elevation 1951 m
Topo map 82 J/10 Mount Rae

Access: 1. Via Volcano Ridge trail (#268) at Volcano Creek.
Access: 2. Junction of Threepoint Mountain (#266) and Gorge Creek (#265) trails.

An improved cow trail offers an easy link between Volcano Ridge trail and Threepoint Mountain and Gorge Creek trails farther to the west. It leaves Volcano Ridge trail on the north bank of Volcano Creek and travels along the north side of the valley the whole way, keeping to dry pasture above a soggy valley bottom choked with willow brush. About half-way along, Bluerock Mountain — framed by the forested side slope — comes into view.

The trail splits at the head of the valley. The right-hand trail, still following the north bank of the stream, reaches the Gorge Creek/Threepoint Mountain trail junction in 1 km. If you're making for Gorge Creek its shorter to follow the left-hand trail across the creek and through an open draw left of the low forested hill to a 4-way junction with Gorge Creek trail. (The trail to the west, which is more or less a continuation of the one you are on, isn't part of the trail system and should be ignored.)

268 VOLCANO RIDGE TRAIL — Map 17

Day hike, backpack
Equestrian, bike
Distance 13 km
Height gain 290 m
Height loss 268 m
Maximum elevation 1935 m
Topo map 82 J/10 Mount Rae
82 J/15 Bragg Creek

Access: 1. Via Gorge Link trail (#272).
Access: 2. Via the junction of Wildhorse (#304) and Threepoint Creek (#276) trails in Quirk Creek.
Also accessible from the eastern terminus of Volcano Creek trail (#267), the eastern terminus of Forgetmenot Mountain trail (# 269) and the western terminus of Link trail (#271).

This signed, marked trail which runs from south to north between Gorge Creek and Threepoint Creek via the south fork of Volcano Creek is usually travelled in combination with other trails to make big loops. The smallest possible loop — a 13 km circuit incorporating Gorge Creek, Volcano Ridge, Link and Gorge Link trails in their various permutations — takes in the pass between drainages, a very fine viewpoint indeed which is popular with day trippers.

The trail leaves Gorge Link trail in the north fork of Gorge Creek at map ref. 627161 and straightaway heads up a narrow forested valley which could be called the N.N.W. fork. Half-way along, you cross a bridge over the creek and climb, steeply at times, up slopes of orange shale under the pines to an old exploration road on the watershed. Turn right, then almost immediately left onto another road running parallel to the first one, the junction of the two roads being the western terminus of Link trail. Your new road climbs to the top of a sandy knoll where an extraordinary scene unfolds of foothills stretching away to the Front Ranges on the horizon.

The view from Volcano Ridge trail at the watershed. Mountain in middle foreground to right is Mount Ware.

Half-way down the hill on the other side, turn right onto an exploration road doubling as a cutline which descends the south fork of Volcano Creek. Keep left near the top and straight at intersections with cutlines lower down; the road is obvious. The first side stream you come to is the main fork of Volcano Creek as marked on the topo map and is followed almost immediately by Volcano Creek trail to left. Snippets of old roads before and after Rock Creek should similarly be ignored. The next side road to the left just after a third and anonymous creek crossing leads to the top of a 2270 m grassy hill and is a worthwhile trip in itself if you want to get off the beaten track.

Momentarily, the route approaches the top of the fledgling Volcano Creek gorge, then, shortly after passing a semi-circular road to the right, turns off the cutline onto a pack trail to the east of it. In 1.5 km you join a cutline access road at a T-junction, turn right and follow this new road across Threepoint Creek, here a shallow trough, to the old Forgetmenot Mountain lookout fire road on the north bank. Turn right. Suddenly, around a corner of the fire road, the hitherto unremarkable creek plunges into a vertiginous black shale gorge which joins forces with Volcano Creek gorge to become the most celebrated of all the black shale gorges in the Sheep. The road allows a few startling glimpses into the depths then turns away a bit, passes through a drift fence and crosses muddied streamlets signalling your arrival onto the Quirk Creek cow meadows from where it is only a short distance to the junction with Wildhorse and Threepoint Creek trails.

269 FORGETMENOT MOUNTAIN — Map 17

Backpack, equestrian
Bike to end of fire road
Distance 7 km
Height gain 610 m
Maximum elevation 2320 m
Topo map 82 J/10 Mount Rae
82 J/15 Bragg Creek

Access: **1. Via Volcano Ridge trail (#268) 2.5 km west of Quirk Creek.**
Access: **2. Via the eastern terminus of Upper Threepoint Creek trail (#270).**

What may be the highest point and is certainly the sharpest summit of Forgetmenot Ridge has been distinguished by the name of Forgetmenot Mountain. Between 1952 and 1975 it was topped by a fire lookout served by a 25 kilometre-long road from the forest boundary. Today, sections of the fire road have been utilized in Threepoint Creek and Volcano Ridge trails whilst other sections have been reclaimed, most recently the stretch between Quirk Creek and Muskeg Creek. On the mountain itself, a partial restoration has left an adequate hiking and equestrian trail which to date is unofficial and therefore unsigned.

Leave Volcano Ridge trail at the point where it turns south to cross Threepoint Creek. Carry on along the fire road past intersecting cutlines to the big bend where the road reverts to trail and starts the long haul across the steep eastern escarpment onto the east ridge. Now the gradient eases off and you wind from one side of the broad ridge to the other through meadows and remnants of old spruce forest. Shortly after passing ruinous rock castles on your right, the trail steepens again and switchbacks up a tapering ridge to the summit. On the highest point a concrete base and scattered red-painted rocks are all that remains of Forgetmenot Lookout. The trail crosses over all the summit bumps to gently sloping meadows beyond, then turns downhill, aiming for a spring at treeline.

270 UPPER THREEPOINT CREEK — Map 17

Backpack, equestrian
Distance 10 km
Height gain 290 m
Height loss 268 m
Maximum elevation 2027 m
Topo map 82 J/10 Mount Rae

From the high point on the trail, looking across the Elbow River valley to unnamed valleys and mountains. Note the descent trail at lower right.

Access: 1. Via Forgetmenot Mountain trail (#269).
Access: 2. Via Big Elbow trail (#306) at 2 locations.
Also accessible from Threepoint Mountain trail (#266) at Threepoint Creek.

This is an unofficial, unmarked trail which is very useful to know about, offering as it does an alternative route to the Elbow River from the north fork of the Sheep River which is Threepoint Creek.

The trail branches off Forgetmenot fire road at its most westerly point in Threepoint Creek. The start is not at all obvious; just before the big bend, an overgrown road to left looking more like a clearing doubles back to a cutline. Turn right here and follow the cutline until it's possible to descend to valley bottom on a good pack trail. For the next 6 km the trail (later on, an overgrown exploration road) follows the north bank of Upper Threepoint Creek between the intimidating south slope of Forgetmenot Mountain, all crags and twisted gorges, and the equally steep-sided 2270 m hill to the south which is best approached by an exploration road from the other side — see route #268.

At map ref. 548218, Threepoint Mountain trail comes in from the right just a few metres before the road fords the creek to the south bank. At this point the valley opens out suddenly into a wide heathy basin, a soggy catchment area for innumerable small streams seeping off Threepoint Mountain. Banded Peak and its outliers beyond the Elbow River are sticking up above the basin's western rim. When Threepoint Mountain trail turns left up a side valley, keep following the old road farther up the basin to a faint junction where you should turn right across the stream and climb through a wooded notch on the basin's rim to a well-defined road junction on the Elbow side of the watershed. The road to the right descends to the Elbow River at map ref. 524233 and is of little use these days, so keep left and climb onto a grassy ridge top fully justifying a half-hour's rest to absorb the tremendous view which has opened up to the west. When ready to tear yourself away from this delectable spot, carry on along the road which at a faint junction turns right downhill and describes a semi-circle to a junction with a cutline in the trees. Follow the cutline downhill to the Elbow River at map ref. 513215, a displeasing section of route which is redeemed solely by its directness. Join Big Elbow trail on the west bank close to Big Elbow backcountry campground.

North Gorge Creek below the junction of Gorge Creek and Gorge Link trails.

271 LINK TRAIL

Total distance 11.5 km

Access: 1. Gorge Creek Trail (Hwy.) at Ware Creek parking lot 14.8 km north of Sheep River Trail (SR 546) and 7.1 km south of McLean Creek Trail (Hwy.).
Access: 2. Gorge Creek Trail (Hwy.) at Volcano Ridge parking lot 7.9 km north of Sheep River Trail (SR 546) and 14.0 km south of McLean Creek Trail (Hwy.). Also accessible from the northern terminus of Missing Link trail (#273), Volcano Ridge trail (#268) at the pass, and the northern terminus of Gorge Link trail (#272).

Named after Link Creek which is followed by the first section of trail, Link trail is also a link trail in the sense that is connects trails in the east Sheep to those lying in the shadow of the Front Ranges to the west. The trail is signed at junctions and marked throughout with red triangles.

WARE CREEK PARKING LOT TO VOLCANO RIDGE PARKING VIA LINK CREEK — Map 16

Day hike, equestrian
Distance 6.5 km
Height gain 198 m
Height loss 60 m
Maximum elevation 1600 m
Topo map 82 J/10 Mount Rae

From Ware Creek parking lot, the trail passes through a gate and heads upstream along the west bank of Link Creek. After about a kilometre, ford Link Creek — it can be jumped across easily — and travel along the east bank within sight and sound of highway traffic for another 1.75 km to the forks. Recross the stream and arrive at the junction with Missinglink trail near a bend on the highway.

Keep right, following the west fork of Link Creek through meadows usually thronged with cattle. Near the end of the meadows, on soggy ground, transfer from the improved cow trail you have been following onto an old road which climbs uphill in a straight line through pine forest and arrives at a pass (map ref. 657184) below the craggy north face of Missinglink Mountain. The road swings south here. Just a little way along this new change of direction, turn sharp right onto a narrow trail which descends to Ware Creek. Jump across and climb up the west bank onto the highway, then slip through a narrow belt of trees into Volcano Ridge parking lot.

Volcano Ridge from near the western terminus of Link trail. ►

VOLCANO RIDGE PARKING LOT TO VOLCANO RIDGE TRAIL — Maps 16 & 17

Day hike, equestrian
Distance 5 km
Height gain 375 m
Maximum elevation 1914 m
Topo map 82 J/10 Mount Rae

At the trail sign, descend the bank and cross another fork of Ware Creek. The trail — an overgrown exploration road throughout — veers left, travelling through alternate pine forest and glades on the lower skirts of Volcano Ridge. Watch for where Gorge Link trail turns off to the left. A little farther on, cross a side creek and climb more steeply up an open ridge giving fine views across frost-shattered boulder slopes which comprise the east face of Volcano Ridge. The subsidiary ridge you are following leads to the main N-S ridge of the mountain where Volcano Ridge summit trail turns off to the right. Keep straight and descend slightly onto the watershed separating Gorge Creek and Volcano Creek drainages. A splintering of the road identifies the junction with Volcano Ridge trail.

VOLCANO RIDGE SUMMIT TRAIL (2118 m) Distance 2.5 km. The unsigned, unmarked exploration road heads north following the ridge top some 50 m above an expanse of spongy meadow as flat and as green as a billiard table. A steep grass slope is tackled direct, after which the road resumes its former easy gradient as it contours around the west side of the ridge to its end conveniently close to the highest point. If you have half a day to spare, plan on traversing the bumpy summit ridge to its northernmost summit which has been blessed with the name Allsmoke Mountain and is worth visiting for the aerial view into Threepoint Creek gorge. The Alberta Forest Service has plans to make this trail official and further, to extend it north to Allsmoke Mountain then east to Ware Creek parking lot, thus opening up a new 26 km loop.

272 GORGE LINK TRAIL — Map 17

Day hike, equestrian
Distance 4.5 km
Height gain 85 m
Height loss 61 m
Maximum elevation 1661 m
Topo map 82 J/10 Mount Rae

Access: 1. Via Gorge Creek trail (#265) 1.5 km from the trailhead at the north fork.
Access: 2. Via Link trail (#271) 1.5 km west of Volcano Ridge day-use area.
Also accessible from the southern terminus of Volcano Ridge trail (#268).

At the trail junction on the west bank of North Gorge Creek, turn north and cross to the east bank in about 100 m. (Obviously, if you're coming from Gorge Creek day-use area, both crossings of the north fork can be avoided by a traverse along the east bank.) The third crossing can't be avoided, but since it occurs above the confluence with the more effluent N.W. fork, there is never enough water in the stream to worry about. At the end of a large meadow beloved by cattle, recross to the east bank and arrive shortly aftewards at a T-junction with Volcano Ridge trail to left. Keep right and cnter a side creek. The trail runs along the west bank and crosses the watershed into a tributary of Ware Creek almost imperceptably; watch for a change in vegetation from aspen meadows to mixed forest. Cross a side creek and join Link trail 1.5 km west of Volcano Ridge day-use area.

273 MISSINGLINK TRAIL — Map 16

Day hike, intermediate ski
Equestrian, bike
Distance 8 km
Height gain 137 m
Height loss 183 m
Maximum elevation 1615 m
Topo map 82 J/10 Mount Rae

Access: Sheep River Trail (SR 546) at Missinglink day-use area.
Also accessible from Link trail (#271) 3 km west of Ware Creek parking lot.

Missinglink is primarily an equestrian trail, forested throughout, which follows a chain of cutlines and cutline access roads between Canyon Creek and Link Creek. Watch for red trail markers on trees.

Pick up the trail (which actually starts from the north side of the highway) from behind the signboard and cross the height of land into a tributary known for a half century as Canyon Creek on account of the small canyon bridged by the highway. Ford a side creek and then the main fork of Canyon Creek itself. Now begin climbing up a cutline access road to the watershed, keeping right low down and straight at another intersecting cutline/access road half-way up the hill. Intersect a major N.E.-S.W. cutline on the watershed and descend to the true pass in a small meadow. (Arriving at the N.E.-S.W. cutline it's easier for mountain bikers to make a dogleg i.e. to turn right (east) at the cutline and descend to the head of Canyon Creek's north fork where you can pick up an access road heading left (north) to the meadow and the junction with the official route.) NOTE: If travelling in reverse direction, it's very tempting to slip through the pass into the meadows of Canyon Creek's north fork. You won't encounter a trail until you reach the forks where an intersecting exploration road can be followed in a southerly direction across the combined creeks to the highway which is gained approximately 1.5 km east of Missinglink day-use area.

From the pass at the meadow follow the access road cum cutline down the east bank of Link Creek. After a flat stretch along the west bank, the road recrosses to the east bank of the creek for its duration and, I'm sorry to say, takes on some very unpleasant cutline characteristics. A steep uphill and downhill brings you to a T-junction with a N.E.-S.W. cutline. Turn right, then almost immediately left onto a continuation of the road (still making waves) which gradually flattens out as it nears the forks in the big meadow. Cross Link Creek and join Link trail close to Gorge Creek Trail (Hwy.).

274 WARE CREEK — Map 16

Half-day hike, day hike
Equestrian
Distance 3.5 km
Height loss 50 m
Topo map 82 J/10 Mount Rae

Access: **1. Gorge Creek Trail at Ware Creek parking lot, 14.8 km north of Sheep River Trail (SR 546) and 7.1 km south of McLean Creek Trail. Within the next few years, an equestrian centre and campground will be built approximately 1 km N.E. of the bridge and will, no doubt become the new starting point for this trail. Also accessible from from the northern terminus of Death Valley trail (#245) and the southern terminus of 9999 trail (#277).**

A ford at the 1 km mark deters casual strollers from going farther along this little trail which has an importance out of all proportion to its length. It makes possible the popular 18.5 km loop incorporating North Fork, Threepoint Creek and 9999 trails, and, more importantly, provides access to Death Valley trail which in turn connects with ongoing trails south and west of the Sheep River. Watch for red markers on trees.

Start off by crossing the highway bridge east of the parking lot. The trail follows the strip of meadow adjoining the road for 0.5 km, then at the second clearing heads down to Ware Creek. Cross to the south bank. For the next little while the trail stays fairly close to the stream, alternating between willowy meadows and aspen groves. Pine forest heralds the start of a more hilly section to a side creek where a signpost, lonely in a big meadow, pinpoints the 3-way junction with Death Valley trail to right and 9999 trail to left.

Ware Creek meadows

275 NORTH FORK TRAIL — Map 16

Day hike, intermediate ski
Equestrian
Distance 5 km
Height gain 177 m
Maximum elevation 1579 m
Topo map 82 J/10 Mount Rae
82 J/15 Bragg Creek

Access: 1. Gorge Creek Trail (Hwy.) at Ware Creek parkig lot, 14.8 km north of Sheep River Trail (SR 546) and 7.1 km south of McLean Creek Trail (Hwy.). Within the next few years, an equestrian centre and campground will be built approximately 1 km N.E. of the bridge and will no doubt become the new starting point for this trail.
Also accessible from Threepoint Creek trail (#276) 4 km west of the trailhead.

North Fork trail follows a small section of the old telephone trail between Bighorn Ranger Station in The Sheep and the North Fork Cabin which was located just east of the present-day North Fork campground in Threepoint Creek. Nowadays the section between Ware Creek and Threepoint Creek is used mainly by equestrians travelling the 18.5 km loop incorporating Ware Creek, 9999 and Threepoint Creek trails. The route is signed and marked throughout with red triangles on trees.

From Ware Creek parking lot either cross the highway bridge east of the lot or use the ford alongside to reach a reclaimed exploration road heading west along the north bank of Ware Creek. After about 100 m, turn off to the right (north); the trail is barely evident in the meadow so aim for a gap in the aspens signifying the start of the old telephone road. As it slowly climbs to a pass in the low hills to the north, the road intersects a cutline, the valley creek which feeds a chain of beaver ponds downstream, and a second cutline close to the pass. Cross over the watershed onto the steeper north slope where the sunny aspen woodland of the ascent route is replaced by a dim, damp spruce forest with a mossy understory. Not long after the trail levels, you arrive at a T-junction with Threepoint Creek trail positively identified by an old wood sign tacked to a tree.

276 THREEPOINT CREEK TRAIL — Maps 16 & 17

Day hike, backpack
Easy ski to Muskeg Creek
Equestrian
Bike via access # 3
Distance 12 km
Height gain 320 m
Maximum elevation 1707 m
Topo map 82 J/15 Bragg Creek

Access: **1. McLean Creek Trail (Hwy.) at Mesa Butte equestrian campground.**

Access: **2. McLean Creek Trail (Hwy.). A few metres north of Mesa Butte equestrian campground, turn west onto an exploration road. Cross the bridge and drive to a road junction. Turn left. Park at the end of the road, being careful not to block the entrance to the wellsite. Now walk along the fence trail towards the river until you intersect Threepoint Creek trail at the N.E. corner of the fence.**

Access: **3. McLean Creek Trail (Hwy.) A few metres north of Mesa Butte equestrian campground, turn west onto an exploration road. Cross the bridge and drive to a road junction. Keep right. Not long after crossing a second bridge, park at the entrance to Forgetmenot Mountain fire road to left below a steepening of the exploration road. Walk, ski, or bike along the fire road for approximately 2 km until red markers on trees indicate the official route coming in from your left across the river. Also accessible from the northern terminus of North Fork trail (#275), the northern terminus of Volcano Ridge trail (#268), and the southern terminus of Wildhorse trail (#304).**

This trail, which is a mixture of old telephone trail, fire road, pack trail and newly-cut trail, follows Threepoint Creek from McLean Creek Trail (Hwy.) to the junction with Wildhorse and Volcano Ridge trails at Quirk Creek. Although the trail officially starts at Mesa Butte equestrian campground, it can also be picked up by those on foot from access #2 which cuts out the first 1.5 km — something to consider if you're aiming for Quirk Creek and back in one day. If the river's high, hikers can omit the first 1.9 km and the ford by starting from access #3 on the fire road. Skiers and bikers should also use this alternative start, but be aware that the first section of trail lies on the southern fringe of the McLean Creek all-terrain vehicle area.

From Mesa Butte equestrian campground head north through a gate onto an exploration road. Turn left, cross the bridge over Threepoint Creek, then, transfering to trail, climb up the left- hand bank onto a powerline right-of-way. Turn right here, but before arriving back on the exploration road look for a red trail marker in trees to the left of the right-of-way which diverts you onto a newly-cut portion of trail which parallels the exploration road a way, then crosses the road for a similar stint between road and river. Cross the right-hand branch of the exploration road. A little farther on, the spur trail from access #2 comes in at the N.E. corner of the fence enclosing the wellsite. Now follow the line of the old telephone trail to the junction with North Fork trail at the 3 km mark. Keep straight along an old pack trail which in less than 0.5 km fords Threepoint Creek and joins Forgetmenot Mountain fire road (access #3) on the north bank. Turn left and travel along the fire road for 2.5 km, a rather boring stretch without a bike though enlivened somewhat at runoff by 2 side stream crossings. Shortly after passing a cutline to right, the official route leaves the fire road in a spate of red trail markers. Two possible routes to Quirk Creek present themselves at this junction.

Route 1. Skiers and bikers are advised to keep to the fire road which in less than half a kilometre moves away from Threepoint Creek and heads up Muskeg Creek instead with its many fords. A stiff 200 m climb over a high forested ridge brings you into Quirk Creek meadows at the terminus of Wildhorse and Volcano Ridge trails. En route watch for where route #2 trail comes in from the left near the bottom of the hill. Note that since the first edition of this book was published the section of road between the ridge top and Quirk Creek has been rehabilitated and is now very rough indeed for mountain bikers who will feel cheated of a good downhill run.

Route 2. Hikers and equestrians should turn left onto the marked trail which wanders along the riverbank, at one point traversing a slope of good quality coal! Two major crossings of Threepoint Creek give access to the narrow isthmus of land separating Threepoint Creek from Muskeg Creek up which a steep trail climbs unerringly to the top of a high, grassy hill sliced cleanly down the middle by the eroding action of the river, the shale slope plunging to the riverbed being the first indication of the gorge to come. Now follows a long, undulating passage through pine forest with no views until, suddenly, you emerge onto airy meadows above the fully-fledged Threepoint Creek Gorge — both literally and figuratively the high point of the whole trail. Look for sheep on the black shale slopes. Close to Quirk Creek the trail turns its back on the gorge and descends to the fire road. Make a left turn here and descend some more to Quirk Creek meadows at the junction of Volcano Ridge and Wildhorse trails. Because this area is an important bighorn sheep habitat, Fish and Wildlife request no camping within a 2 km radius of this junction.

Rain and mist soften the dramatic scene of Threepoint Creek's confluence with Volcano Creek gorge.

277 9999 (FOUR NINES) TRAIL — Map 16

Day hike, intermediate ski
Equestrian, bike
Distance 7 km
Height gain 90 m
Maximum elevation 1448 m
Topo map 82 J/15 Bragg Creek
82 J/10 Mount Rae

Access: 1. McLean Creek Trail (Hwy.) at Mesa Butte equestrian campground.
Access: 2. McLean Creek Trail (Hwy.) at North Fork campground. Via Curly Sand trail (#278).
Access: 3. Gorge Creek Trail (Hwy.). The trail intersects the road 0.8 km west of McLean Creek Trail (Hwy.). Hikers can use this access when Threepoint Creek is in spate after heavy rain or during runoff.
Also accessible from the northern terminus of Death Valley trail (# 245), and the eastern terminus of Ware Creek trail (# 274).

If you had been around this area between 1885 and 1902 you would have discovered that cattle grazing in the upper reaches of Ware Creek and the north fork of the Sheep River all bore the brand "9999". This was the registered brand of John Ware, celebrated negro cowboy renowned for his strength and horsemanship who homesteaded just east of here at the fork of the 2 rivers. The signed trail between the 2 valleys — mostly a conglomeration of old roads suitable for the biker — is usually travelled in conjunction with Curly Sand, Threepoint Creek, Ware Creek and North Fork trails in order to make loops.

It leaves the south end of Mesa Butte equestrian campground and straightway crosses Threepoint Creek. In about 0.25 km, you join an old road which has arisen out of the creek bed and follow it uphill to Gorge Creek Trail (Hwy.) which is access #3. At the junction a large sign reads "No Motorized Vehicles". Cross the highway onto the powerline right-of-way and turn left. Leave the right-of-way at a small hut where the powerline changes direction and, keeping to the same line as previously, follow a new trail into the trees. At the far end of a rectangular meadow it joins an old road, the junction of trail and road marking the eastern terminus of Curly Sand trail (access #2) which has come in from across the river near North Fork campground.

Turn right here and climb waves of uphills to a pass in the hills to the south. On the down slope, tall, graceful aspens arching overhead make a tunnel through which the road descends to Ware Creek in one long sweep. Near the bottom of the hill turn left onto a cutline which, thanks to beavers, joins the Ware Creek exploration road under a metre of water, so shortcut to the right along the the bank top and join the road farther to the west. Now follows a delightful section of road which travels upstream for 1.5 km through meadows sweeping up whole hillsides to the ridge tops. Opposite the next side valley south of the creek, the route leaves the road, fords Ware Creek and arrives at the signed junction with Ware Creek and Death Valley trails in a large meadow.

Looking south from Curly Sand viewpoint towards Threepoint Creek, North Fork campground and John Ware ridge.

278 CURLY SAND TRAIL — Map 16

Half-day hike
Equestrian
Distance 4 km
Height gain 137 m
Height loss 174 m
Maximum elevation 1509 m
Topo map 82 J/15 Bragg Creek
82 J/10 Mount Rae

Access: 1. McLean Creek Trail (Hwy.) at Mesa Butte equestrian campground.
Access: 2. McLean Creek Trail (Hwy.) at North Fork campground. Park in the day-use area.
Also accessible from 9999 (Four Nines) trail (#277).

This little trail connects Mesa Butte equestrian campground with 9999 (Four Nines) trail near Kananaskis Country boundary. It can be used as an alternative start (or finish) to 9999 trail or used in conjunction with it to make a small equestrian loop. It also offers the nicest half-day hike in the area for hikers based at North Fork Campground. Signed and marked throughout.

The trail starts from the opposite side of the highway to Mesa Butte equestrian campground entrance and begins by climbing quite steeply through mixed forest towards a gap in the hills to the east, but before quite reaching it turns right and climbs instead onto a hilltop crowned with aspens. Walk south along the ridge between east slope aspens and west slope meadows where prairie sage and pasture sage give a silvery-blue cast to long, waving grasses. The viewpoint at the end of the ridge where the meadows sweep down to the highway is the trail's piece de resistance and you'll want to linger here awhile and look out across valley flats towards John Ware ridge.

So as not to disturb the lovely meadows, the trail descends by the edge of the trees, swings left and crosses an exploration road a few metres in from the highway. (North Fork campers and day equestrians parked at the day-use area can easily join the trail at this spot since the exploraton road just happens to lie opposite the campground access road.) The trail now crosses the highway, runs alongside it for a bit to an old corral marking the site of North Fork ranger cabin, then turns toward Threepoint Creek. Pass through a gate to the ford and join an old road which has come in from the highway at the forest boundary. Follow the road up the far bank to where 9999 (Four Nines) trail joins the road at the east end of a large rectangular meadow.

279 MCLEAN CREEK INTERPRETIVE TRAIL — Map 20

Half-day hike
1.7 km from parking lot
Topo map 82 J/15 Bragg Creek

Access: **McLean Creek Trail (Hwy.) at McLean Creek recreation area. Turn first right off the access road into the campground entrance. At the next junction turn left, then almost immediately right into a parking lot. The trail leaves the far end of the lot at the trail sign.**

Surrounded by a network of all-terrain vehicle roads and cutlines, the McLean Creek interpretive trail is hardly your typical quiet forest stroll; on weekends and holidays the drone of trail bikes is a constant background noise. You start off by following the cutline past 2 trails to the right (playground and Loop "A" of the campground) and 1 trail to the left (amphitheatre). At a 4-way junction turn right onto another cutline, then almost immediately left onto the interpretive trail itself which can be distinguished from all kinds of bisecting trails by its gravelled surface.

A little way in, the trail makes a loop which the brochure suggests you walk around in a clockwise direction. Two lush meadows relieve the monotony of a matchstick forest with little understory apart from blackened stumps and deadfall, evidence of the disasterous 1910 fire which swept the entire eastern slopes from the headwaters of the Sheep and Elbow Rivers to the forest boundary.

Old picnic shelter, now removed.

280 BRAGG CREEK PROVINCIAL PARK TRAILS

Half-day hikes
1.8 km of trails
Topo map 82 J/15 Bragg Creek

Access: 1. Bragg Creek Provincial Park at the campground. The trail starts close to campsite #13 and is signed.
Access: 2. A parking lot on the east side of the access highway 0.1 km south of the Provincial Park entrance.

From the campground (access #1), the trail climbs uphill to the highway then continues from the other side of the road to a 4-way trail junction whre you can either turn left or keep straight to get onto a loop trail which is also accessible from the highway parking lot (access #2). As you stroll through the forest you may care to reflect on some of the history of Bragg Creek Provincial Park. In 1914, the picnic area close to where you started from was the site of the Mowbray-Berkeley oil well which operated exclusively from coal hauled in summer months by team and wagon from Dr. Ing's coal mine at Canyon Creek and in winter by sleigh from Joe Wooling's mine in the south fork of Fish Creek. When British capital ran out during the third year of the First World War, the well was dismantled and parts thrown into the Elbow River.

That same year, most of what is the Provincial Park became the property of John McIntosh who built a cabin close to where the parking lot for access #2 is now. For a living "Old Mac", as he was known to neighbours, cut firewood and hauled it to Calgary. Now I come to the part of the story that will make you quicken your step, perhaps make you look back over your shoulder, particularly if you are alone at dusk and it's the dreary tail-end of the year, for it was a winter day when Old Mac set out for the last time to Calgary. Afterwards, there were rumors that his wagon and team, driverless, had been seen travelling along the road near Twin Bridges. What **is** known is that the team and wagon, still with its load of wood, returned to the cabin later that day without Old Mac. Despite a thorough police search no trace of him was ever found. His land was leased to the Fullerton family who professed an uneasy feeling whenever they were in the vicinity of the empty cabin.

A few years passed by, then in 1932, the year the big flood swept away the 3rd bridge over the Elbow River, David Bearspaw who was out mending fences for the Fullertons discovered a grave in the creek bank. Some of the skeleton had washed away in the flood and what was left crumbled to the touch. Not long after this gruesome discovery, another body, buried in quicklime, was unearthed during grading of a summer cottage access road. Subsequent finds begged more questions than answers. Were these Indian graves as some people have suggested or was one of them the last resting place of John McIntosh, victim of foul play?

WEST BRAGG CREEK SKI TRAILS — Map 20

Approximately 45 km of trails
Topo map 82 J/15 Bragg Creek

Access: Bragg Creek Road. 1.3 km west of Kananaskis Country boundary, turn right into a large parking lot.

The Bragg Creek cross-country ski trails, signed, packed and trackset by Alberta Recreation and Parks, have something to offer every class of skier from novice to racer. The longest loops are located north of the road and take you into diverse rolling countryside of open valleys and forested hillsides. South of the road, the trails – logging roads, cutlines, some new trails – are compacted into a small area of patchwork forest and cutblocks. In addition to the named trails, there are innumerable connectors and variations which enable the racer to make loops of 5, 7.5, and 10 km.

Unfortunately, the area is subject to chinook winds which, having deposited all the snow on the mountains to the west, roar through the treetops under blue skies and denude snow from open areas in a matter of hours; most snowfall at Bragg Creek occurs when the wind is blowing out of the north and east.

Pick up trail maps from the signboard in the parking lot. Advice on trails and trail conditions is available from the Canadian Ski Patrol who also patrol the trails (Telephone trail excepted) at weekends and holidays between the hours of 8:30 a.m. and 4:30 p.m. If you wish, you can register your trip at the ski patrol hut located in the parking lot.

281 SUNDOG

Intermediate
Distance 4.7 km

Sundog loop has many variations and detours, 2 of which are rated difficult for the average skier. The east leg is very scenic with views across a reclaimed mill site towards Moose Mountain. In chinook conditions, I'd advise skiing the loop in a clockwise direction so as to reserve good snow for the descent. In any case, a descent of the winding west leg is a lot of fun; as you hurtle out onto the Crystal Line watch out for passing skiers.

282 ELBOW TRAIL

Intermediate
8 km to Allen Bill Pond

The trail starts from the far end of Sundog loop and follows the summer route (#289) with all its ups and downs to Allen Bill Pond day-use area on Elbow Falls Trail (Hwy. 66). Snow conditions are usually very good except in the area of Elbow River meadows which catch the wind.

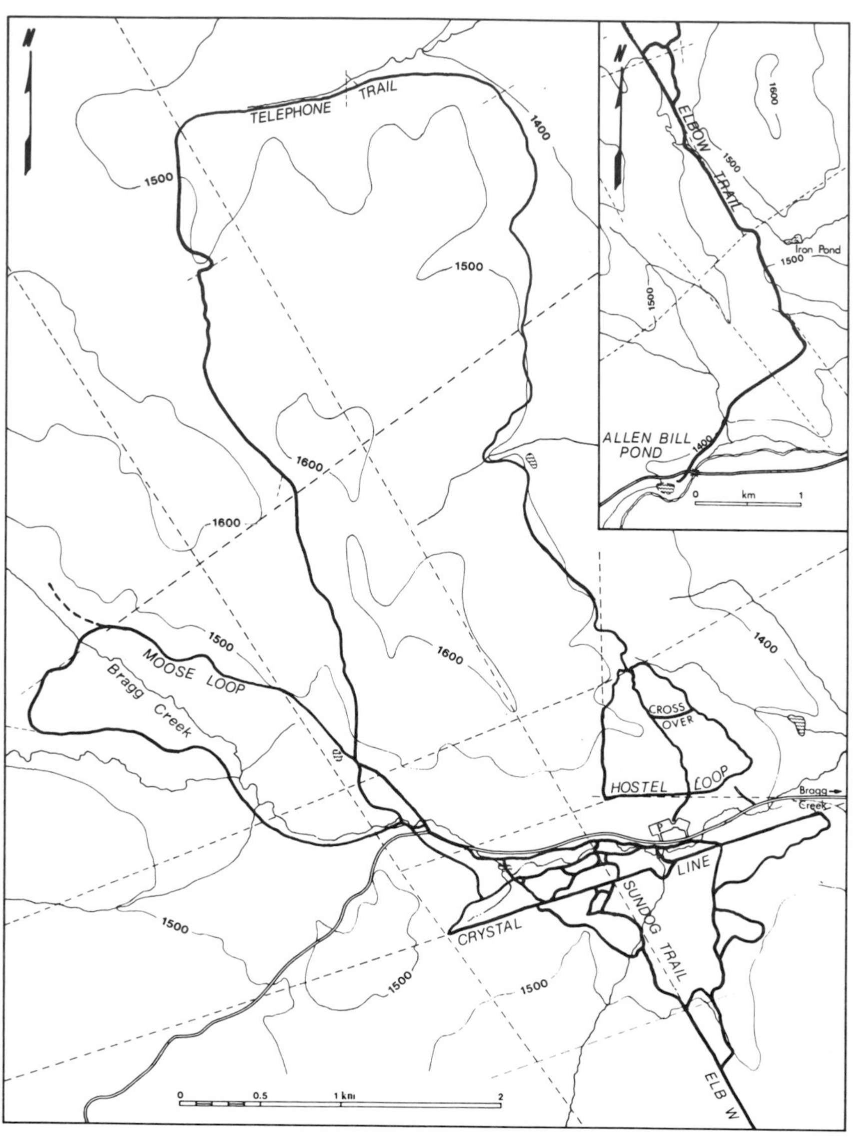
TELEPHONE TRAIL
1400
1500
1500
1600
1600
1500
MOOSE LOOP
Bragg Creek
1600
1400
CROSS OVER
HOSTEL LOOP
Bragg Creek
LINE
SUNDOG TRAIL
CRYSTAL
1500
1500
1500
ELB W
0
0.5
1 km
2
ELBOW TRAIL
1600
1500
Iron Pond
1500
1500
ALLEN BILL POND
1400
0
km
1

283 CRYSTAL LINE

Easy
Distance 3.4 km

This cutline is the main thoroughfare among the trails south of the road. It's a good trail for beginners with the possible exception of 2 hills which in fast icy snow conditions upgrade to intermediate.

284 MOOSE LOOP

Intermediate
Distance 5.5 km

The east leg follows a belt of meadows between aspen hillsides and riverside willow bushes glowing wine-red in the low winter sunlight. It makes for delightful, easy skiing which, unfortunately for the beginner, is sandwiched between 2 intermediate sections of trail. The hilly section shared with Telephone trail can be avoided by an unofficial but well-used route up the truncated exploration road — see sketchmap. Because of 2 steep hills, the one shared with Telephone trail (which can be avoided) and one in the middle of the loop above Bragg Creek, it's easier for beginners to ski the loop in an anticlockwise direction. In warm weather, watch out for ice- flows at numerous creek crossings.

Moose Loop (east leg) in West Bragg Creek meadows.

285 TELEPHONE

Intermediate
Distance 16.5 km

The largest loop in the trail system utilizes in part the old telephone trail built in the 1920's between the Elbow and Jumpingpound ranger stations. The gentle south leg and its alternate route along flat meadows bordering Bragg Creek Road are excellent for beginners, but the rest of it is for strong tourers only who can handle its intermediate hills and its remoteness from the road. Remember, this is the only trail not patrolled. Most of the hills occur along the east leg as it dips in and out of little side valleys. On the portion of trail shared with Moose loop, a steep hill — snowplowed into a hard, dished shape — has a fast, tricky runout across the barely concealed rocks of Bragg Creek, so be cautious. If you would rather ski up the steep hills, ski the loop in a clockwise direction.

286 HOSTEL LOOP

Intermediate
Distance 3.8 km

Sheltered to some extent from chinook winds by the hill to the west, this little loop circling about telephone trail holds the snow well. Midway along the eastern leg, Cross Over trail connects Hostel loop with Telephone trail, thus further enlarging the possibilities from simple loops into more complicated figures of 8 and letters p and b.

287 MOOSE MOUNTAIN FROM BRAGG CREEK — Map 20

Day hike
3 km to fire road
9 km to lookout
Height gain to fire road 285 m
Elevation at fire road 1915 m
Topo map 82 J/15 Bragg Creek

Access: Bragg Creek Road. From the Kananaskis Country boundary, drive for 7.4 km to the end of the road near an old well site. NOTE: At the time of publication, an oil rig is in the area and the Bragg Creek Road is closed to vehicles beyond the ski trails parking lot. This is a temporary situation. To find out the status of the road, I would advise phoning Gooseberry Travel Information Centre before leaving home.

This useful little trail, undeveloped and unsigned, connects the Bragg Creek area to the normal route up Moose Mountain via the fire road.

From road's end at the posts, walk across the reclaimed well site into the forested conclaves of upper West Ranger Creek. The trail switchbacks onto the open ridge to the north and there joins a cutline which has arisen from Ranger Creek. Turn left and follow this cutline, soon to deteriorate into a narrow, muddy trail, as it contours below a minor top to a low point in the S.E. ridge of Moose Mountain at map ref. 562436. On reaching the fire road, turn right and follow #295 to the summit.

288 FULLERTON LOOP — Map 20

Half-day hike
Circuit 5 km
Height gain 213 m
Maximum elevation 1600 m
Topo map 82 J/15 Bragg Creek

Your starting point at Allen Bill Pond.

Access: Elbow Falls Trail (Hwy. 66) at Allen Bill Pond day-use area. Use the left-hand parking lot. The trail starts at a signboard among the picnic tables.

Fullerton Loop trail, named after the Fullerton family who have ranched in the Bragg Creek area since the beginning of the century, is a very popular trail which takes you to a viewpoint on Ranger Ridge. You start off by following the gravelled trail underneath the highway bridge and across Ranger Creek (bridge) to an overgrown cutline access road running alongside the Elbow River. Be careful not to miss the left turn onto a narrow shortcut trail. Squeeze through a gap between fences and arrive back on the road where you should turn left, climbing uphill past 2 roads branching right — in each case keep left — onto a narrower trail which enters the confines of a small valley. Cross 2 streams and arrive at the junction with the return loop.

If hiked in the recommended clockwise direction, seats facilitate the climb onto Ranger Ridge. From the edge of steep grassy slopes falling away into Ranger Creek, look out across the residences of the Elbow Ranger Station towards Station Flats and the mountains of the upper Elbow poking up above the treetops. The ridge levels at the highest seat and turns N.W. Join a cutline access road which has arisen from Ranger Creek and follow it across an E-W cutline to a notch below a step in the ridge where the road makes a steep descent to the valley met with earlier in the walk. The road winging its way up the far hillside is an unwelcome sight; fortunately, you need only follow the first few metres of it before transferring onto a narrow trail which wanders downstream through a chequerboard of aspens and fields guilded by goldenrods. Recross the E-W cutline. A bridged crossing of the creek at the confluence with another creek coming in from the north heralds your return to the outgoing loop. Unless you feel like doing the whole thing again, turn left and head for the parking lot.

289 ELBOW TRAIL TO WEST BRAGG CREEK — Map 20

Half-day hike, day hike
Intermediate ski
Equestrian, bike
Distance 8 km
Height gain 120 m
Maximum elevation 1508 m
Topo map 82 J/15 Bragg Creek

Access: 1. Elbow Falls Trail (Hwy. 66) at Allen Bill Pond day- use area. Use the left-hand parking lot. The trail starts at the signboard among the picnic tables and is signed "Fullerton Loop".
Access: 2. Bragg Creek Road at Bragg Creek ski trails parking lot.

Before the Bragg Creek Hostel burnt down in the spring of 1984, this amalgamation of logging roads, cutlines and cutline access roads was a popular access route with hostellers travelling between Bragg Creek Road and Elbow Falls Trail (Hwy. 66). Since the raison d'etre is no longer there — the hostel is unlikely to be rebuilt on the same spot — it's probably best these days to use this route for short strolls from both trailheads, Iron Pond at mid point being the logical destination. SKIERS: See also Elbow trail, West Bragg Creek Ski Trails (#282).

From Allen-Bill Pond day-use area follow the gravelled trail underneath the highway bridge and across Ranger Creek (bridge) to an overgrown cutline access road running alongside the Elbow River. Be careful not to miss the left turn onto a narrow shortcut trail. Depending on your mode of transportation and girth, either squeeze through a gap between fences or use the gate to the left and arrive back on the exploration road. Turn left up the hill, still following Fullerton Loop past a snowmobile road to right to a second junction where you **must turn right** onto the road you will be following for the next 4 km. Ski signs at questionable junctions make routefinding easy, which is just as well since there is a plethora of turnoffs. You start off by intersecting the aforementioned snowmobile road, and then a N.W.-S.E. cutline; keep right at a cutline access road doubling back to the left, and left at a cutline access road heading right towards the Elbow River. Arriving at a T-junction with a major N.W.-S.E. cutline, turn left (N.W.) and pass between 2 low hills into the Iron Creek drainage. En route, disregard a cutline access road climbing up the left-hand hill. A side trip to Iron Pond, the result of a long-abandoned beaver dam lying half a kilometre downstream below high grassy banks, is best undertaken from the obvious dip in the road after the last mentioned junction (no sign or trail).

Now climbing, the road makes a dogleg to the left along a N.E.- S.W. cutline, then resumes its north-westerly direction up a hill to what is probably the highest point on the route. This signals the start of a short roller-coaster section through shabby pines with bark peeling off in great strips. Pass through a fence and travel alongside the meadows of the upper creek to a dark pond marking the watershed. Skiers have the option of turning right here onto a shortcut; since there is no discernable summer trail however, everyone else must carry on along the road which drops off steeply to a road junction. Unless you're cutting across country to Tom Snow trail via the West Bragg Creek ski trail system and the Bragg Creek Road, turn right onto a logging road signed "Sundog trail" which is followed steadily downhill — keep left at all junctions — to a sawmill site in a large clearing. It's good to get out of the trees again and get a view, albeit a distant one, of Moose Mountain. The final stretch of road down the bank to Bragg Creek Road has been rehabilitated, so as soon as you've intersected the cutline signed "Crystal Line", turn left onto another ski trail which fords Bragg Creek to the Bragg Creek Road opposite the ski trails parking lot.

290 DIAMOND T LOOP — Map 20

Half-day hike, equestrian
Circuit 3.5 km
Height gain 122 m
Maximum elevation 1539 m
Topo map 82 J/15 Bragg Creek

Access: Elbow Falls Trail (Hwy. 66) at Station Flats day-use area.

Diamond T, the cattle brand of pioneer rancher Len Mickle, is the name given to a short loop trail — chiefly of interest to equestrians — which climbs onto the knoll west of Station Flats. The first kilometre is shared with Elbow Valley trail; that is, you turn left at the T-junction a few metres beyond the trailhead and carry on to another junction at the mouth of a side valley. Turn right here, following the winding trail which doubles back to a point above the short-cut (not recommended from either direction), then continues climbing up forested south slopes to an E-W cutline where the trail makes a brief jog to the left before continuing on in the same line as before to the crest of the knoll. A spur trail to right leads past a hitching post to "Windy Point Viewpoint" where wider spaces between pines allow glimpses of Ranger Ridge and Station Flats.

Back on the loop, descend the west slope to a N-S cutline at a fence. Turn right and follow this cutline all the way down the hill and over an unnamed creek to an intersection of cutlines on the creek's north bank. (En route, disregard a cutline access road to left immediately after the stream crossing.) The route carries on for a metre or two beyond the intersection, then turns right across a small side creek coming in from the N.W., crosses over the E.W. cutline and running parallel to it, travels down the sunny side of the unnamed valley to the junction with Tom Snow trail. Cross the bridge and arrive back at the T-junction close to Station Flats day-use area within 0.75 km.

The big meadow west of Wildhorse Creek backdropped by the familiar profile of Mt. Glasgow.

291 ELBOW VALLEY TRAIL

Total distance 16.5 km

Access: 1. Elbow Falls Trail (Hwy. 66) at Station Flats day- use area.
Access: 2. Elbow Falls trail (Hwy. 66) at Paddy's Flat campground via River View trail (#294).
Access: 3. Elbow Falls trail (Hwy. 66) at Powderface Creek south parking lot.
Access: 4. Elbow Falls trail (Hwy. 66) at Cobble Flats day-use area. From the right-hand picnic area access road.
Access: 5. Elbow Falls Trail (Hwy. 66) at Little Elbow recreation area via Big Elbow trail (#306) and at Forgetmenot Pond day-use area.
Also accessible from the southern terminus of Tom Snow trail (#324), Diamond T Loop trail (#290), Sulphur Springs trail at 2 locations (#292), Moose Mountain Road (no parking lot), the northern terminus of Wildhorse trail (#304), the junction of Elbow Falls Trail (Hwy. 66) and Powderface Trail (Hwy.), and the eastern terminus of Little Elbow equestrian trail (#308).

The Elbow Valley trail was planned as a long-distance trail between Station Flats just west of Elbow Ranger Station and Little Elbow recreation area at the confluence of the Elbow and Little Elbow Rivers. However, at the time of publication, there is a gap in the system between Powderface Creek and Cobble Flats with the result that trail sections are most often used as access to other trails or used in conjunction with them to make loops.

STATION FLATS TO PADDY'S FLAT — Map 20

Half-day hike, equestrian
Distance 2.5 km
Height gain 91 m
Maximum elevation 1478 m
Topo map 82 J/15 Bragg Creek

At the T-junction a little way beyond the trailhead, turn left along a short section of trail shared with Diamond T Loop. Keep left at the next junction, cross the mouth of a side valley and climb up, then down a wooded hillside to a T-junction on the north bank of Sulphur Springs Creek. This is your first meeting with Sulphur Springs trail to right. Cross the bridge and climb onto a low, forested ridge which is followed for 0.6 km to the eastern terminus of River View trail to left which descends to Highway 66 opposite Paddy's Flat campground access road. Keep right.

PADDY'S FLAT TO POWDERFACE CREEK — Map 20

Day hike, equestrian
Distance 8 km
Height gain 274 m
Maximum elevation 1631 m
Topo map 82 J/15 Bragg Creek

The drone of traffic which has never been quite absent finally fades away as the trail turns its back on the highway and climbs 152 vertical metres to the top of a hill at map ref. 592389. On grassy hillsides the route is marked with cairns. From the top, descend open south slopes to a creek where the cattle like to congregate, then climb up to Moose Mountain Road which is crossed approximately 1 km in from Highway 66. Continue climbing below the end buttress of Moose Mountain's S.E. ridge and arrive at a 4-way junction with Sulphur Springs trail to right and the western terminus of River View trail to left. Keep straight on and begin the descent to Canyon Creek; it's a lovely way down through meadows and aspens, and finally, above an oblique cliff band, via the coal dust trail which debouches onto the stony creekbed. Three tall posts bearing red triangles guide you across gravel bars to the west bank where you must head down creek a little way before crossing Canyon Creek Road 0.3 km north of the junction with Highway 66.

The final stretch is a soft forest trail with a surprising number of ups and downs. Gradually you edge closer and closer to the highway, finally dropping down the cutbank to the road at Prairie Creek. The 0.2 km of trail between Prairie Creek and Powderface Creek has been obliterated by road construction, so walk down the shoulder to Powderface Creek south parking lot which is the terminus.

Anyone wishing to reach Cobble Flats can do so quite easily by following the highway up Rainy Creek to Rainy Pass from where the disused highway — partly restored near the pass — winds down forested south slopes to the day-use area. More adventurous hikers could consider a bushwack along the west bank of the Elbow River from Beaver Flats campground.

COBBLE FLATS TO LITTLE ELBOW RECREATION AREA — Maps 18 & 19

Day hike, equestrian
Distance 6 km
Height gain 55 m
Maximum elevation 1631 m
Topo map 82 J/15 Bragg Creek

With pant legs rolled up as high as they will go and socks stuffed in a pocket, head down the right-hand picnic road (actually the Quirk Creek exploration road) towards the Elbow River. Straightway, a quiet forest stream anesthetizes the feet in preparation for faster, deeper channels to come. Arriving at the first gravel bar, wade the Elbow River to a point slightly upstream of where you are standing; you are aiming for the continuation of the road on the far bank.

Now on the S.E. bank, leave the road at the first snowmobile route you come to, turn right and follow snowmobile signs back to the gravel bars. The trail wanders downstream a bit, bridging what is probably Wildhorse Creek twice, then climbs up the bank to a junction with Wildhorse trail at the top of the hill. Keep right here, recross Wildhorse Creek and enter a long meadow liberally sprinkled with cow patties and big heaps of droppings from feral horses. Well-manured, white spruce trees stand in magnificent isolation down the meadow's centreline. 0.5 km after leaving the meadow, the trail arrives at a T-junction in the shadow of Forgetmenot Ridge, a parting of the ways for equestrians and hikers, though backpackers can of course use the equestrian route if going on through to Big Elbow trail.

Equestrian route: Keep left, following red trail markers around the base of Forgetmenot Ridge. The trail crosses a dry creekbed — starting point for the route up Forgetmenot Ridge — then swings away to the Elbow River and crosses it to the west bank. Intersect a N-S cutline and arrive shortly afterwards at an important 4-way junction with Big Elbow and Little Elbow equestrian trails (left, right and straight respectively). Turn right here and follow Big Elbow trail across the Little Elbow River to Little Elbow recreation area parking lot from where you can pick up ongoing trails to the equestrian campground.

Hiking route: This unofficial trail which follows the winter snowmobile route has a big advantage over the equestrian route: bridged river crossings. Following snowmobile signs then, turn right and walk down the old road to the Elbow River where a bridge spans the widest, deepest channel. Except at runoff, you can usually navigate all other channels dryshod by means of large rocks and logs. A few metres on, cross a second bridge over Ford Creek and wend left to a small meadow below Elbow Falls Trail (Hwy. 66) opposite Powderface Trail (Hwy.) junction. From here on it's easiest to walk up the highway for 0.5 km to Forgetmenot Pond day-use area where campers can transfer to the interpretive trail (#313). See sketchmap for a plan of Little Elbow recreation area trails.

Prairie Mtn. from S.E. ridge of Moose Mtn. Pasture sage in foreground.

292 SULPHUR SPRINGS TRAIL — Map 20

Day hike, equestrian
Distance 4.5 km
Height gain 213 m
Maximum elevation 1661 m
Topo map 82 J/15 Bragg Creek

Access: **1. Via Elbow Valley trail (#291) at 1.9 km and 6.4 km west of Station Flats day-use area.**
Access: **2. Via the western terminus of River View trail (# 294).**
Access: **3. Moose Mountain Road, 2.3 km from Elbow Falls Trail (Hwy. 66). Park at a well site on the left-hand side of the road.**

This is an excellent trail for the Sunday tourist who with very little effort can reach a superb viewpoint less than half a kilometre from Moose Mountain Road. Most often though, this trail is and should be combined with either Elbow Valley trail or River View trail to make loops of varying lengths depending on your starting point. Watch for red markers on trees.

From Sulphur Springs Creek on Elbow Valley trail (access #1), head N.W. up the east bank of the creek to a T-junction with an E-W cutline. Travel due west (left) along the cutline for about 100 m before branching off to the right by the side of a small tributary fed by sulphurous springs pouring out of a 1930's well casing. The trail now climbs out of the valley, levelling off temporarily at an intersection with the same E-W cutline met with earlier, then crosses the head of the creek and climbs some more to a cairn at an intersecting N.W.-S.E. cutline. A brief flat section brings you to Moose Mountain Road.

Cross the road to a well site which is access #3. From here the trail climbs to an open ridge top, the southernmost buttress of Moose Mountain's S.E. ridge which is not of any great height, but a fine viewpoint nevertheless encompassing all of the McLean Creek all-terrain vehicle lands and, of more interest to hikers perhaps, the waves of ridges — Prairie, Powderface, Forgetmenot and Nihahi (how easily the names roll off the tongue) — off to the west. Leave this delightful spot among the flowers with reluctance and wind down dry south slopes redolent with sage to a bench and a 4-way junction with Elbow Valley trail (left, right), and River View trail (straight on).

293 PADDY'S FLAT INTERPRETIVE TRAIL — Map 20

Half-day hike
Distance 2.2 km
Topo map 82 J/15 Bragg Creek

Access: Elbow Falls Trail (Hwy.66) at Paddy's Flat campground. Start from the far end of loop ''B''. Campers can also pick up the trail from loop ''A'' (down the bank), loop ''C'' (behind the water pump), loop ''D'' (by site #13), loop ''E'' (between site #36 and the garbage bin), and from behind the amphitheatre.

This is the ideal trail for a hot sticky summer afternoon when paddling and sunbathing are the order of the day.

From loop "B" descend the bank to a signed junction. Turn right here and traverse a terrace, actually an old river bed, below the various campground loops. En-route, pick up access trails from "C" loop, the amphitheatre, "D" loop and "E" loop. (The trail to left between "C" loop and a side creek crossing is a shortcut to the river). Shortly after the turnaround point close to "E" loop, the trail keeps left at a junction with River View trail and descends to the Elbow River. Walk downstream, detouring often to admire the river which flows over successive ledges of resistant sandstone exposed at low water levels. In between shelving slabs are sandy bays each one likely occupied by a young family from the campground and strewn with beach towels, buckets and spades and all the paraphernalia of the beach. After a side creek crossing (watch out for the shortcut trail to left), the river quietens and you are likely to be alone for the last half kilometre along the river bank before the trail climbs the bank and brings you back to your starting point. Keep right at a junction near "B" loop.

294 RIVER VIEW TRAIL — Map 20

Day hike, equestrian
Distance 4.5 km
Height gain 107 m
Maximum elevation 1539 m
Topo map 82 J/15 Bragg Creek

Access: Elbow Falls Trail (Hwy. 66) at Paddy's Flat campground. Also accessible from Elbow Valley trail (#291) at two locations.

This trail was built with the express purpose of providing campers and day visitors to Paddy's Flat campground with a loop longer than the interpretive trail. In fact, two loops are possible: an 8.5 km loop with Elbow Valley trail, and a longer 9.5 km loop with Sulphur Springs trail.

This route really starts from Elbow Valley trail 0.6 km west of Sulphur Springs Creek. It descends to Elbow Falls Trail (Hwy. 66), and crosses the highway to Paddy's Flat campground access road. Walk down the road and turn first right into "E" loop where you can pick up the trail again beside campsite #36 at the trail sign. Keep right at the first junction, then turn next right off Paddy's Flat interpretive trail which you have been sharing for the last 0.1 km onto River View trail proper.

The trail heads west along a forested river terrace within earshot of rapids. Shortly after intersecting a N.W.-S.E. cutline, you pass numerous unofficial trails to left descending to a lively section of the Elbow River at the confluence of Silvester Creek which issues from a dark little canyon. The bank is rising up now in anticipation of the gorge and rapids just east of Canyon Creek and by the time you've crossed another N.W.- S.E. cutline, you're a long way up indeed, travelling along the edge of the bank top — a delectable stretch of trail which all too soon turns inland, crosses an old grassed-over road and arrives at Hwy. 66. The trail continues from the far side of the highway, climbing up aspen hillsides to a 4-way junction with Elbow Valley and Sulphur Springs trails in a meadow.

Elbow River gorge a little west of River View trail.

295 MOOSE MOUNTAIN FIRE ROAD — Maps 20 & 21

Day hike, intermediate ski
Equestrian, bike
Distance 7 km
Height gain 470 m
Maximum elevation 2437 m
Topo map 82 J/15 Bragg Creek

Access: Elbow Falls Trail (Hwy. 66). 0.7 km west of Paddy's Flat campground access road turn north up Moose Mountain Road and drive for 7.3 km to a small parking area on the left-hand side of the road opposite the gated fire road.

Although of comparatively low altitude, Moose Mountain has all the characteristics of a high alpine peak: sharp ridges, cirques and talus slopes. Geologically, it is the apex of a major structural feature called the Moose Mountain Dome. Water eating into the hard limestone of the dome has carved out deep valleys of which Moose Dome Creek and Canyon Creek are the most spectacular examples.

The summit has been topped with a fire lookout since 1929. The normal route follows the fire road which was built in 1950 along the S.E. ridge onto a subsidiary summit east of the highest point. In 1974 the road was improved to facilitate the building of the third and latest lookout and again widened in the late 1970's and early 1980's when drilling rigs moved into the area. Since the first edition of this book was published, the road has been opened to public vehicles to the 7.3 km mark — 2.9 km farther than previously. However, be aware that this is not a permanent arrangement and that as rigs move in, temporary closures are to be expected. Although this is the second most popular trail in The Elbow (Canyon Creek ice cave is the first), because of uncertainty of access this route remains unofficial and therefore unsigned.

The fire road follows the undulating S.E. ridge below minor tops barely rising out of the trees. Watch for where route #287 comes in from the right. At the 4 km mark, the road turns west, switchbacking up stony slopes to its end a litle beyond a gently-rounded 2330 m summit. From here on, the character of the mountain changes dramatically. Novice hikers tend to be fearful of the exciting prospect ahead, for who can dispute that the final ridge of naked rock rearing upwards to the summit is not a little intimidating at first glance? On closer acquaintance, you discover that the trail is wide enough for a string of pack horses; indeed, it was built for this very purpose. So stride out confidently, following a line of old telephone poles into the gap between the 2 summits, then climb first on the north side and then on the south side of the ridge above deepening scree slopes falling away into Moose Dome Creek. Five minutes from the lookout, the trail regains the ridge which is comfortably wide again and composed of large, shattered blocks, home to innumerable marmots. The summit is surprisingly small and occupied entirely by the lookout which, being located midway between the prairies and the First Range of the Rocky Mountains, commands an unequalled view for 120 km in all directions. In early summer, thirsty hikers may locate a source of ice-cold water about 15 m down the north flank.

Moose Mtn.; the final ridge.

296 CANYON CREEK ICE CAVE — Maps 20 & 21

Half-day hike
Distance 1.5 km
Height gain 140 m
Topo map 82 J/15 Bragg Creek

Access: From Elbow Falls Trail (Hwy. 66), turn north onto Canyon Creek Road and drive to a parking lot near the mouth of Moose Dome Creek.

Beer bottles in the bush and candy wrappers glued to the ice of the cave floor testify to the popularity of this hike. Every weekend, hordes of people seem willing to risk rocks being kicked down from above as they tackle the steep climb from the valley floor to look at the most celebrated cave in the area. Discovered in 1905 by Stan Fullerton of Bragg Creek, it was only in the 1970's that a thorough exploration was carried out; so far, 494 m of passages have been discovered. It is advised that only experienced cavers, properly equipped, venture beyond the first cavern.

From the parking lot, walk farther along the road to Moose Dome Creek. Descend a trail by the side of the creek to a T-junction with the valley exploration road, then turn right and follow the road across the creek bed (usually dry) and on down to Canyon Creek flats. At the point where the road sallies into the creek bed at a bend, use the bypass trail to right which climbs to the bank top and there splits into two. You can either return to the road or, more suitable for your purpose, follow the right-hand trail which travels along the north bank for about 0.3 km to the base of scree slopes. Looking up, you can see the black slit of the cave mouth at the base of the cliff and the numerous trails gouged out of scree and gravel leading up to it. It is far, far better to reserve these trails for the descent (if at all) and climb up slopes farther left which are more vegetated and offer firmer footing.

In the 5 years since the first edition of this book was published, the steep ramp beyond the first cavern has changed considerably. Former bare rock and boulders now glisten with thick layers of ice which threaten to plug the passageway at the top of the slope.

297 CANYON CREEK — Maps 20 & 21

Day hike, equestrian
Distance 10 km
Height gain 150 m
Topo map 82 J/15 Bragg Creek

Access: **1. From Elbow Falls Trail (Hwy. 66), turn north onto Canyon Creek Road and drive to a parking lot near the mouth of Moose Dome Creek.**
Access: **2. Powderface Trail (Hwy.) at Canyon Creek recreation area due to be built during reconstruction of the highway. Right now, park at the junction of the highway with Canyon Creek exploration road 0.4 km north of the creek crossing.**

To most people, the words Canyon Creek are synonymous with Canyon Creek ice cave; relatively few hikers bother to go farther up this magnificent valley despite a beckoning trail which goes right through to Powderface Trail (Hwy.). The trail is due for upgrading within the next few years and will then be signed at both ends. Be prepared for 19 creek crossings!

From the parking lot on Canyon Creek Road (access #1), walk farther along the road to Moose Dome Creek. Descend a trail by the side of the creek to a T-junction with the valley exploration road, then turn right and follow the road across the creek bed(usually dry) and on down to Canyon Creek flats. One kilometre from the trailhead the road crosses Canyon Creek for the first time and passes beneath the ice cave (much hollering and the clatter of falling rocks). An old camping spot in a clearing provides an excellent view of aspiring cavers whose antics on the scree slope are painful to watch.

Canyon Creek exploration road near the ice cave (dark slit in cliff face above the figures).

During the next 2 km the narrow width of the valley floor forces the road to and fro across the stream 11 times. In the dry midsummer, when the heat is reflected tenfold off canyon walls and the water, if any, trickles lazily between mounds of riverbed stones, getting through this section isn't a problem. At runoff, or after days of heavy rain, though, it's another story. Remember, this stream originates below the highest peaks of the Fisher Range. Then, muddy waters raging from bank to bank make it almost impossible to get through the canyon dryshod, especially in the area of Dr. Ing's coal mine which is just around the next bend. The mine, which supplied coal to Bragg Creek's "Mowbray-Berkeley" oil well during the First World War, is not easy to spot. Look for remnants on both banks: the ruins of the mine shaft, a small earth hut which probably stored explosives, the inevitable piles of rusted cans, plus the usual mishmash of bricks, buckets, cables, planks and concrete blocks.

The road ends just before the canyon walls converge for the last time. Climb over the drift fence strung across the narrowest part and get onto a five-star cow trail on the north bank. There are still numerous creek crossings ahead, some of which can be circumnavigated, though the effort of doing so is hardly worthwhile at this stage in the game as your feet are undoubtably wet from paddling through the drift fence narrows from which there was no escape. The valley floor is widening out all the time now and there is a great temptation to linger overlong in sunny meadows and plot routes up the intriguing south slopes of Moose Mountain. At a beaver pond at map ref. 508413, the exploration road reappears and carries on in much the same sort of fashion as before, crossing and recrossing the creek another 4 times. Half a kilometre to the west of Moose Mountain Creek (passed on the south bank) the road fords Canyon Creek for the last time and arrives at a T-junction on the north bank with a more modern exploration road. Turn left and follow this new road out to Powderface Trail (Hwy.). En route, Ford Creek trail comes in from the left opposite the next side creek to the south and Jumpingpound South Ridge trail leaves the right-hand side of the road at the last side creek to the right.

298 ELBOW FALLS — Map 20

Half-day hike
Distance 1 km
Topo map 82 J/15 Bragg Creek

Access: Elbow Falls Trail (Hwy. 66) at Elbow Falls parking lot.

Since the first edition of this book was published, the old trail has been tamed. Stone and concrete steps, wooden balustrades and safe viewing platforms have made the trail fit for a whole spectrum of visitors from toddlers to octegenarians in wheelchairs. The attraction is not just the waterfall thundering into the deep pool, but the exquisite blending of rock, water and forest along this stretch of river as a whole. Upstream of Elbow Falls, a riverside trail enclosing the picnic area extends the walk another half kilometre.

Hiker is avoiding 2 crossings of Canyon Creek by a detour along the north bank near Moose Mtn. Creek. S.W. peak of Moose Mtn. in the background.

Elbow Falls before the viewing platform was built.

299 PRAIRIE MOUNTAIN — Map 20

Day hike
Distance 4 km
Height gain 716 m
Maximum elevation 2210 m
Topo map 82 J/15 Bragg Creek

Access: Elbow Falls Trail (Hwy. 66) at Powderface Creek south parking lot located half-way between Powderface and Prairie Creeks.

There is no trail to the top of Prairie Mountain, although traces of one low down and a few cairns here and there indicate that many people do at least set out with the intention of climbing to the summit which is a superlative viewpoint and well worth the extra effort involved.

Start off by walking east along the highway for 0.2 km. A few metres east of Prairie Creek, an indistinct trail, blazed and flagged in a few spots, climbs up the left-hand edge of a steep open slope overlooking the highway. At the top, it veers slightly left, making a beeline along the flat ridge top above Prairie Creek to a cairn in a meadow — an unexpectedly good viewpoint — where it peters out. Probably this is as far as most people go.

Fit and enthusiastic hikers should climb another 450 vertical metres of intervening pine forest to the summit ridge; lack of understory makes the going quite reasonable. Wend left when the ground steepens half-way up the slope, aiming to top out onto wind-buffeted meadows at map ref. 545388. Follow the edge of the eastern escarpment around to the small summit cairn. The view is an extensive one, particularly to the south and west where the welter of peaks rising towards the horizon require a topo map for identification. Nearer at hand, Moose Mountain effectively dominates the view to the east. Look down into Moose Dome Creek which is closed to the public because of dangerous levels of hydrogen sulphide gas emanating from natural seepages along the creekbed. The black cleft to the left of it in Canyon Creek is the celebrated Canyon Creek ice cave.

Resist the temptation to descend any of the ridges falling away into Canyon Creek unless you have a parachute. It's best to descend the same way but even the ordinary route has its hazard; you must make sure when leaving the summit ridge that you veer to the left, otherwise you'll find yourself pussy-footing around steep broken, ground above Prairie Creek gorge.

Moose Mtn. from the summit of Prairie Mtn. "S. W. Peak" at left.

Prairie Creek near Prairie Link junction.

300 PRAIRIE CREEK — Map 20

Day hike, equestrian
Distance 8.5 km
Height gain 180 m
Topo map 82 J/15 Bragg Creek

Access: 1. Elbow Falls Trail (Hwy. 66) at Powderface Creek south parking lot located half-way between Powderface and Prairie Creeks.
Access: 2. Powderface Trail (Hwy.). Until a new trailhead is built in conjunction with road reconstruction, park off the road a few metres north of Prairie Creek crossing.

Relatively few people follow this trail from highway to highway. The vast majority start from the Elbow Falls Trail (Hwy.) end, and either make a loop with Prairie Link and Powderface Creek trails or take a stroll to the 2.5 km mark where the creek is closeted in a most unprairie-like gorge. The trail is signed and marked with red triangles on trees throughout.

Walk east along the highway for 0.1 km to Prairie Creek where a trail on the west bank leads into the valley confines. The next kilometre of trail has been completely rerouted, the fording of the creek and the slightly hairy traverse above the rockband are gone, replaced by a log bridge and a safe trail through the aspens below the cliff. Back on the original line, the new trail traverses around the big bend, climbing all the while to get onto a rocky rib protruding from the south flank of Prairie Mountain whose screes and rock crevices are an oasis for tiny alpine plants more often seen at higher altitudes. It's a beautiful spot, which serves as a destination for half-day trippers.

Losing all the height gained previously, the trail now drops to creek level and passes through the drift fence. For the next 2.5 km, the trail alternates between the bank top and valley bottom cow trails. Be very careful not to cross the river on a good cow trail which was the former route to Powderface Creek trail; the official Prairie Link trail turns left across the creek at a sign half a kilometre farther on. Stay on the north bank. The valley floor is widening all the time, the low hills on either side framing a spectacular view of Compression Ridge up ahead. 0.25 km short of Powderface Trail (Hwy.), leave the "obvious" trail which bends right, and follow instead a line of red triangles on posts across marshy ground to the highway.

301 POWDERFACE CREEK — Map 20

Day hike
Intermediate ski
Equestrian, bike
Distance 9 km
Height gain 509 m
Height loss to Trail Creek trailhead 289 m
Maximum elevation 2027 m
Topo map 82 J/15 Bragg Creek

Access: 1. Elbow Falls Trail (Hwy. 66) at Powderface Creek north parking lot.
Access: 2. Powderface Trail (Hwy.) at Trail Creek trailhead, 7.3 km north of Elbow Falls Trail (Hwy 66).
Access: 3. (Unofficial) Powderface Trail (Hwy.) at pass (map ref. 492346) 6 km north of Elbow Falls Trail (Hwy 66).

The name Powderface Creek commemorates a Stoney Indian family who lived near the Elbow Ranger Station during the 1920's. Prior to this, the creek was known as Rainy Creek, a name recently resurrected and transposed to the neighbouring valley carrying the highway. It is traversed by a signed and marked exploration road and higher up by a trail which carries you over a pass at the head of the valley into Trail Creek on Powderface Trail (Hwy.). The road section is widely regarded as the best ski trail outside of groomed trails in The Elbow.

The climbing starts as soon as you leave Powderface Creek north parking lot; waves of uphills are followed by a long, gentle runout to a bridged creek crossing. Now on the north bank, the road levels and travels through occasional meadows allowing views of Powderface Ridge up ahead. At the 3 km mark, Prairie Link trail turns off to the right.

The flat middle section of Powderface Creek.

A creek crossing at 4 km signals the start of a steep, winding climb through spruce forest festooned with lichen into the head of the valley. One final switchback to the north across the infant Powderface Creek and the road ends, abutting against a grassy hillside which is the usual springboard for the unnamed hills to the north. A trail carries on up valley through more open forest to Powderface Pass (cairn) at the demarcation line of forest and meadow. This is a windy spot; the prevailing west wind is heard from far away as it comes sighing among the long grasses of the west flank, bringing with it the sounds of traffic on the highway only 1 km distant as the crows flies. To your left, route #317 climbs steeper, more buffeted hillsides of close-cropped grass and dark green islands of krummholz to the top of Powderface Ridge.

Follow red markers on solitary trees down into the sheltering forest where a trail materializes on the north bank of a stream. Low down on the south bank the unmarked trail to access #3 turns off to the left, a very nebulous trail indeed for the first few metres until it merges with an exploration road which is followed downhill (right) to the Sacramento rain gauge and from there out to Powderface Trail (Hwy.) at a pass. (When hiked in the opposite direction, branches laid across the exploration road signal the cutoff point.) The official trail to access #2 recrosses the creek below the junction and, heading north now, loses another 122 m in elevation as it drops to Trail Creek parking lot on Powderface Trail (Hwy.).

302 PRAIRIE LINK TRAIL — Maps 20 & 21

Day hike, intermediate ski
Equestrian
Distance 3 km
Height gain 85 m
Maximum elevation 1762 m
Topo map 82 J/15 Bragg Creek

Access: **1. Via Powderface Creek trail (#301) 3 km from Elbow Falls Trail (Hwy. 66).**
Access: **2. Via Prairie Creek trail (#300) 5 km from Elbow Falls Trail (Hwy. 66).**

Because the trailheads for Powderface and Prairie Creek trails are only 0.2 km apart, a circuit using this trail as the connector makes a logical 11 km trip.

After Powderface Creek trail crosses to the north bank, start counting gaps in the timbered hills to your right. The third gap is the one you want. In any case the trail is well signed and starting from a meadow climbs up the east bank of a side creek and joins what is probably a fire break at the height of land. Contrary to expectation, the trail does not take the most direct line to Prairie Creek, but meanders instead in a north-westerly direction through a thick lodgepole forest strewn with deadfall before descending to Prairie Creek meadows opposite a similar break in the hills to the north.

303 BEAVER FLATS TRAIL — Map 20

Half-day hike
1.5 km of trails
Topo map 82 J/15 Bragg Creek

Access: 1. Elbow Falls Trail (Hwy. 66) at Beaver Flats Campground.
Access: 2. Elbow Falls Trail (Hwy. 66) at Powderface South parking lot located half-way between Prairie and Powderface Creeks.

This trail was built with two purposes in mind: to enable campers at Beaver Flats to reach Prairie Creek and Powderface Creek trailheads without resorting to road walking or driving, and to serve as the campground trail. It's popularity as the latter is very much is evidence as you start off down the trail from Beaver Flats campground no doubt in the company of aspiring fishermen off to the beaverponds. Cross a bridge and walk down the length of a creek augmented by springs bubbling out of mossy mounds to the first beaver pond where dead trees sticking up out of the water wear white socks. After a bridged crossing of Powderface Creek, the trail divides. Hikers bound for Powderface or Prairie Creeks should keep left and reach Powderface South parking lot within a few minutes. The trail to right heads down to the Elbow River and makes a loop past picnic tables to a series of beaver ponds evidentally still in use.

304 WILDHORSE TRAIL — Maps 17 & 20

Day hike, backpack
Equestrian
Distance 11.5 km
Height gain 357 m
Maximum elevation 1844 m
Topo map 82 J/15 Bragg Creek

Access: 1. Via Elbow Valley trail 1.25 km west of Cobble Flats.
Access: 2. At the western terminus of Threepoint Creek trail and the northern terminus of Volcano Ridge trail in Quirk Creek.

Lying just outside the McLean Creek all-terrain vehicle land use area, this signed trail offers a quieter route through unspoilt country between the Elbow River and the Sheep River drainages. It runs parallel to Quirk Creek exploration road (alternative route for mountain bikers), threading a winding route over pine-covered ridges and crossing numerous creeks issuing from the precipitous eastern escarpment of Forgetmenot Ridge. If you go softly, there's a good chance of spotting the feral horses.

From Elbow Valley trail, Wildhorse trail — an old exploration road at this point marked with a "No snowmobiles" sign — switchbacks uphill a bit, then settles into a rising traverse across open slopes above Wildhorse creek. After the creek has swung away to the west, the road enters damp spruce forest on the north side of the first and highest ridge you cross over and,winding about a great deal,passes a large cairn prior to its arrival at the highest point on the route. A clearing allows a superb view of Forgetmenot Ridge whose stony east face is a constant backdrop to the trail throughout.

Now descend a grassy draw into the north fork of Mac Creek (water). The valley is crossed at right angles. Watch for red markers on trees signifying the resumption of the road over a low ridge into Mac Creek proper (often dry). Then it's back into the pine forest again to face a longer, higher climb over ridge #3 into the Howard Creek drainage which is erroneously marked on the present topo map as Quirk Creek. Here the road circles round a duck pond at the edge of a very large meadow whose northern rim is followed in an easterly direction to a T-junction with a S.W.- N.E. cutline which in turn is followed downstream. At the point where the cutline starts to ascend, turn right across Howard Creek bridge and climb over ridge #4 into Duke Creek.

All ridge crossing at an end, head downstream past Wildhorse back-country campground (20 sites, firepits, hitching posts) to Quirk Creek which is crossed by a log bridge. Arriving at a T- junction on the east bank with the Quirk Creek exploration road (by this point it's passed the well site and is pleasantly overgrown), turn right and travel the final, flat 2 km to the junction with Threepoint Creek and Volcano Ridge trails on the brink of Threepoint Creek gorge. Notice how the cattle congregate in great numbers in "The Muskeg" as the meadows of upper Quirk Creek and adjoining Muskeg Creek used to be called. Only 30 years ago it was also a favourite spot with grizzlies; Curly Sand, called in by the North Fork Stockman's Association to protect yearlings, is reported to have killed 11 grizzlies and numerous black bear in the area within a two year period. Another interesting fact concerning the valley is the recent finding of dinasaur bones in banks of exposed shale.

The Howard Creek duck pond.

305 FORGETMENOT RIDGE — Maps 17 & 18

Day hike
8 km to highest point
Height gain 740 m
Maximum elevation 2340 m
Topo map 82 J/15 Bragg Creek

Access: Elbow Falls Trail (Hwy. 66) at Little Elbow recreation area. Park at Forgetmenot Pond day-use area.

There are no trails leading onto Forgetmenot Ridge; the following description merely indicates the quickest route from a highway. Despite the ridge's pastoral appearance, the route is very rough and steep in its lower reaches and should be shunned by anyone unused to off-trail hiking.

Walk east along Highway 66 to the junction with Powderface Trail. Get onto Elbow Valley hiking trail (see #291) and follow it across Ford Creek and the Elbow River to the T-junction at the base of Forgetmenot Ridge where you should turn right onto Elbow Valley equestrian trail. In half a kilometre a stony side creek signals your jumping-off point up the mountain.

Climb the ridge to the left (north) of the creek. Whichever route you take, be it either the rocky ridge crest or the trees and meadows farther to the right, be prepared for 450 m of unrelieved drudgery before a saddle of white rocks two thirds of the way up the ridge and in plain view from Little Elbow recreation area is gained. More moderate slopes of short-cropped grass follow to the most northerly summit (cairn).

Having done all the hard work, you may as well reap the reward by walking south for 3.5 km along the broad, grassy ridge to the highest point at map ref. 549261. It's particularly satisfying in late spring when the grass is newly green yet the triad of Mounts Glasgow, Cornwall and Banded Peak across the Elbow River is still clothed in snow, the very epitome of Anthony Henday's "Shining Mountains". Very noticable from Calgary is one obstinate snow patch on the N.E. face of Mount Cornwall which lingers well into mid summer. About half-way along, the ridge jogs to the west and tapers to a rocky knob. Where the ridge resumes its broad width and southward direction, you pass upheavals of frost-shattered rocks and areas of patterned ground where the rocks are aligned in stripes down the west slope. The ground is rising up now towards the highest summit. As you approach the summit cairn, the sharper outline of Forgetmenot Mountain to the south comes into sight — a worthwhile extension to the hike for fit and enthusiastic hikers who can hack another 3 km each way.

306 BIG ELBOW TRAIL

Total distance 26.5 km

Access: 1. Elbow Falls Trail (Hwy. 66) at Little Elbow recreation area. Start from the equestrian parking lot on the south side of the campground access road. Also accessible from the western terminus of Elbow Valley trail (#291), the northern terminus of Sheep trail (#255), the western terminus of Little Elbow trail (#308), the northern terminus of Elbow Lake trail (#163), and the northern terminus of Threepoint Mountain trail (#266).

The old exploration road which follows the Elbow River from its confluence with Little Elbow River to its source at Elbow Lake forms the basis of this trip. Although it would appear easy to follow a road, the route is complicated by numerous detours and by further division between hiking and equestrian trails; fortunately, all deviations are well signed with red markers and cairns. The final section is most often travelled in reverse direction by people wanting quick access from Kananaskis Provincial Park into the headwaters of The Elbow and The Sheep.

LITTLE ELBOW RECREATION AREA TO THREEPOINT MOUNTAIN TRAIL — Maps 17 & 18

Day hike, easy ski
Equestrian, bike
Distance 4.5 km
Height gain 46 m
Maximum elevation 1670 m
Topo map 82 J/15 Bragg Creek

Hikers and equestrians follow different routes throughout this section. The hard road surface of the hikers' route is ideal for mountain bikers who will encounter just one steep hill.

Equestrian route: From the mid point of the parking lot, a trail leads down the bank to the Little Elbow River. Cross to the south bank, being careful not to confuse the more "obvious" cutline opposite for Big Elbow trail which lies farther upstream. 0.25 km into the trees, keep straight at the 4-way intersection with Elbow Valley and Little Elbow equestrian trails. On reaching the Elbow River, the trail (remnant of old road) climbs up and down the bank twice, describing 2 semi- circles, then heads back to the flats again, fords numerous thin channels and one side creek too wide to be jumped which probably issues from a spring. Reenter forest and in a little while arrive at South Glasgow Creek where large cairns and a flurry of red triangles mark the crossing point only 100 m downstream of the hiking trail. From here on to the junction with Threepoint Mountain trail, the trail makes few marks on a tough carpet of creeping juniper and kinninick so follow the red markers carefully.

Hiking route: From the parking lot follow Little Elbow interpretive trail upstream to the red suspension bridge. Cross and backtrack downhill to the old valley road (arisn from the river) which you will be following all the way to Threepoint Mountain trail junction. Keep straight at a junction with Little Elbow equestrian trail, and a little farther on squeeze around a locked gate preceding the climb over a ridge of higher land into South Glasgow Creek whose wide shallow creek bed heaped with white stones is unmistakable. At this point, the equestrian trail lies only 100 m downstream and you could if you wanted to join it for the final 1.5 km to the junction with Threepoint Mountain trail, rather than keep to the road alongside which is flat, straight and rather boring; best left to the bikers, perhaps.

Big Elbow trail near Big Elbow campground. Threepoint Mtn. in background.

THREEPOINT MOUNTAIN TRAIL TO TOMBSTONE CREEK — Maps 9, 17 & 18

Backpack, intermediate ski
Equestrian, bike
Distance 16 km
Height gain 305 m
Maximum elevation 1981 m
Topo map 82 J/15 Bragg Creek
82 J/10 Mount Rae

Hiking and equestrian routes join at the next bend in the road after the signpost. After 100 m, turn left onto a trail which rejoins the road at a road junction on stony Cornwall Creek. (If you have time to spare, it's worth walking up the creekbed to the waterfall.) Bikers must keep right at this junction; hikers and equestrians should follow the secondary left-hand road towards the river, at the last moment turning right onto a flagged trail which returns you to the major road at a large cairn. At your side, the Elbow River is rushing noisily over a pebble bed. When road and river are closest, Upper Threepoint Creek trail — unofficial and unsigned — turns left across the creek. A few metres farther on, Big Elbow hiking and equestrian trail makes another detour, this time to Big Elbow back-country campground which is sited on a wedge of alluvial flat below the curious west peak of Threepoint Mountain. Back on the road again, travel past the confluence with Cougar Creek to a junction at a bridge over the Elbow River. The river upstream is closeted between high rock walls and the valley sides are closing in rather ominously. Cross the bridge and wind up, then down the shady side of Cougar Mountain to a ford upstream of the impasse. This is the last reasonable place to cycle to.

Now on the north bank, the disintegrating road — littered with rocks — roller coasters across the bright, stony slopes of Banded Peak. On a downhill stretch which ends in the river, watch for a new trail to right (just passable for bikers) which bypasses a particularly onerous section of road which not only zigzags back and forth across the Elbow River but shares the riverbed as well in some places. Road and trail come together at a camping area used by scouts during the World Jamboree in 1983. In another 0.5 km, at the top of a long, steep hill, road and trail again part company. Keep left. The junction is a good place to catch your breath and look around. The gorge is nearly behind you, perhaps submerged in the deep shade of late afternoon, and not too far ahead are the meadows of the upper valley, still open to the sunshine. Already, pockets of grass are appearing on both sides of the trail which traverses soft, friendly hillside to a division of hiking and equestrian trails.

Hiking trail: Keep right. Pick up the road again at the next T-junction, turn left and follow it to an important junction with Little Elbow trail to right which is also a road at this point. Head downhill on the former Little Elbow motor road to Tombstone Creek and arrive at Tombstone Creek back-country campground which is located on the left-hand (south) side of the road a few metres after the creek crossing.

Equestrian trail: The equestrian trail to left descends to the Elbow River and crosses it. On the east bank of the following side creek you pass an old pack trail heading south to 3 shallow lakes sitting astride the Elbow-Sheep watershed — a worthwhile 6 km diversion, but probably better left for another day; the lateness of the hour and the proximity of Tombstone Creek back-country campground promising rest and a good meal urge you onwards. So without further ado recross the Elbow River and join the former Little Elbow motor road a little west of the campground.

TOMBSTONE CREEK TO ELBOW LAKE — Maps 9 & 18

Day hike, backpack,easy ski
Equestrian, bike
Distance 6 km
Height gain 128 m
Maximum elevation 2100 m
Topo map 82 J/10 Mount Rae
82 J/11 Kananaskis Lakes

Follow the former Little Elbow motor road westwards across a bridge over the Elbow River and up a hill to the signed junction with Sheep trail at the 0.8 km mark. Turn right here onto a much rougher road. Winding through a wide, open valley periodically scoured by chinook winds (notice how the willow bushes and spruce trees huddle together in sheltered hollows), the road passes between Tombstone Mountain, named in 1844 by geologist George Dawson, and the complex mass of Mount Rae whose diminutive north glacier — the true source of the Elbow River — catches your eye as it shines in the morning sun. As you draw nearer to Elbow Pass, the denuding effect of the wind lessens, and the trees close in again obscuring views.

A Kananaskis Provincial Park boundary sign pinpoints the pass at the north end of Elbow Lake. Jump the infant Elbow River near the outlet and follow the road around the rocky, west shoreline where the sun's heat is reflected tenfold off white talus fanning out below the cliffs of Elpoca Mountain. Stop often to admire the translucent blue waters of the lake and to nibble on blackcurrent and raspberry bushes poking up between rocks. Arriving at the shady, south shore, either head for the campground which is located at the S.E. corner of the lake or a continue down the road to Highway 40. (See #163, Elbow Lake trail.)

307 "PIPER" CREEK — Maps 9 & 18

Long day hike
Backpack
Distance 5 km
Height gain 442 m
Maximum elevation 2438 m
Topo map 82 J/10 Mount Rae
82 J/11 Kananaskis Lakes

Access: Via Big Elbow trail (#306) 3 km east of Elbow Pass.

The valley between Tombstone Mountain and Mount Elpoca is a candidate for the most beautiful alpine valley in the Eastern Slopes. Known for years to alpinists as Elpoca Creek, it has been left nameless by the recent assignment of that name to a creek on the west side of Elpoca Mountain. The Kananaskis Country naming committee is presently considering the name "Piper Creek", after Norma Piper, wife of George Pocaterra and a personage in her own right (a world class opera singer and after her retirement, a music teacher in Calgary until her death in 1983). However, this name is by no means a fait accompli and you may well find this lovely valley again nameless by the time the next edition of this guide goes to press.

Fleabane meadows in "Piper Creek".

Near its source, the infant Elbow River travels through windswept meadows.

The first part of the old pack trail up the valley is too diffuse to be followed. It is first seen rising out of willow brush at a ford over "Piper Creek" and is definitely discernable a few metres on where it traverses a grassy hillside below the south ridge of Tombstone Mountain at map ref. 413147, right at the edge of the 2 topo maps. From Big Elbow trail then, it's easiest to aim for the bottom of this ridge from a point directly opposite or slightly downstream. You must, of course, cross both the Elbow River and "Piper Creek".

The trail, which is quite clear from this point on, gains height slowly up the east bank of the creek. In mid valley, the creek, meshed in willow brush thus far, breaks free and falls in cataracts between the icy north face of Mount Elpoca and the sunbaked slabs of Tombstone Mountain which are arranged in rows and tiers like vertical tombstones. Pockets of flower meadows increase until at treeline you are wading through great avenues of purple fleabanes, trying not to lose the trail which leads you out of the trees onto the short turf of the upper valley before petering out. Here is the home of the alpines — the saxifrages, the forgetmenots, the campions, the alpine willow herbs and the mountain sorrels. Rivulets interlace across the surface of the grass, sometimes sinking into trenches a metre deep and a few centimetres across.

The main fork of the creek, tumbling and leaping over rock steps, issues from a tarn tucked under the highest summit of Tombstone Mountain. Across the valley, hidden in a fold of moraine, lies another tarn. Fed by a perpetual snow bank, it lies in the deep shadow of a 2850 m peak known to climbers as "Mount Schlee" after Gerry Schlee, a well-known Calgary climber who forfeited his own life trying to save 2 canoeists caught in the Bow River weir in Calgary.

Experienced backpackers used to steep, scree slopes can cross the ridge at the head of the valley into the west fork of the Little Elbow River. There are actually 2 passes separated by a hump of red screes. A white boulder as big as a two storied house marks the start of a sheep trail which climbs to the right- hand pass (cairn) at 2576 m. If you're carrying on, I would advise climbing over the hump in the middle to the left-hand pass where the angle of descent is less intimidating.

Upper "Piper Creek" looking towards glaciated Mt. Rae (left) and spectacular Elpoca Mt. (right).

308 LITTLE ELBOW TRAIL

Total distance 23 km

Access: Elbow Falls Trail (Hwy. 66) at Little Elbow recreation area. Accessible from the equestrian parking lot via Little Elbow interpretive trail, loop "A" and "B" of the equestrian campground, and loop "E" of the campground.
Also accessible from Big Elbow trail at Tombstone Creek (#306), and the southern terminus of the North Fork of the Little Elbow River (#310).

This long-distance trail follows with some diversions the old motor road along the Little Elbow River. At the forks it turns into the south fork and climbs over a low pass to the Elbow River where it joins route #306 with which it is often combined to make a loop. It provides access for 4 trails: Nihahi Ridge (# 312), Nihahi Creek (#311), West Fork of the Little Elbow River (#309), and the North Fork of the Little Elbow River (#310); and for a host of other untracked valleys and ridges which invite exploration.

LITTLE ELBOW RECREATION AREA TO THE FORKS — Maps 18 & 19

Backpack, easy ski
Equestrian, bike
Distance 12 km
Height gain 189 m
Maximum elevation 1798 m
Topo map 82 J/15 Bragg Creek

For the first little while, the hiking and equestrian trails go their separate ways.
Hiking trail Unless you are dropping off packs or passengers, vehicles are not allowed past the campground check-in station to the trailhead at the far end of campground loop "E". This regulation may change in future years with the building of a small parking lot at the trailhead. Right now, though, hikers must start from the equestrian parking lot nearly 2 km to the east and follow Little Elbow interpretive trail to its terminus on campground loop "E", then turn left and walk a few metres up the road to the trailhead at a gate. Keep heading west along what is a continuation of the campground access road. One kilometre from the gate, Nihahi Ridge trail turns off to the right and is followed in quick succession by both equestrian routes joining in from right and left respectively.

Equestrian trails To confuse matters further, there are 2 possible routes depending on whether you are starting from the equestrian parking lot or the equestrians campground.
1. The shortest trail leaves the equestrian campground between sites #4 and #5 of loop "B", but can be picked up from almost anywhere within the campground including "A" and "B" corrals. Keep left at a junction and contour round the base of Nihahi Ridge, intersecting Nihahi Ridge trail after 1 km and exiting shortly afterwards onto Little Elbow motor road.
2. The second equestrian route leaves the equestrian parking lot via Big Elbow trail which fords Little Elbow River right off the bat. At the 4-way junction turn right, cross Big Elbow exploration road and for the next 2 km follow a pleasant, forest trail which gradually wends its way back to the river and crosses it just west of North Glasgow Creek. Join Little Elbow motor road a little west of route #1.

Hikers and equestrians together follow the road winding into the heart of the First Range. The gentle, grass ridges of Powderface and Forgetmenot fall behind and are replaced by a much more dramatic scenario of steep, forested slopes rising to scree and rock. Half seen, half heard when the wind's right, waterfalls tumble down parallel gullies from Mount Glasgow's outliers. 3.5 km from the hiker's trailhead, Nihahi Creek trail turns up the hillside just east of Nihahi Creek crossing. In another kilometre, the crossing of the old blue bridge over the Little Elbow River leads you into a long stretch along the south bank which would be tedious were it not for the grandeur of the scenery. Watch carefully for where the hiking and equestrian trails again part company.

Equestrians should turn right onto a brand new trail which links together patches of riverside meadows below the rosy-hued cliffs of Mounts Romulus and Remus. Knowing in advance that there are 4 major river crossings will dissuade most hikers from following what appears to be the more attractive route. Shortly after the 4th crossing you arrive at Mount Romulus back-country campground which is located on the south bank at the forks. The trail continues up the east bank of the south fork, crosses the west fork exploration road and rejoins road at a bend.

Hikers and bikers are strongly advised to keep to the road which has no insuperable problems (2 side creeks are easily forded). If you are breaking your journey at the forks or switching to the west fork or north fork trails, turn right onto the unsigned west fork exploration road 0.5 km before reaching the south fork of the Little Elbow River. This brings you to a 4-way junction with the equestrian trail on the east bank of the south fork just slightly upstream of Mount Romulus back-country campground.

Tombstone Mountain above Little Elbow (Larch) Pass.

THE FORKS TO TOMBSTONE LAKES — Map 18

Backpack, intermediate ski
Equestrian, bike
Distance 9.4 km
Height gain 482 m
Height loss 122 m
Maximum elevation 2280 m
Topo map 82 J/15 Bragg Creek
82 J/10 Mount Rae

At the junction of equestrian and hiking routes, the road turns south and begins the long haul up the south fork of the Little Elbow River to a pass. Bikers bound for Big Elbow trail must stick to the road throughout. Seven kilometres from the forks, just after the second creek crossing, hikers and equestrians have the option of turning right onto a dirt track which leads within a few minutes to a meteorological station. You have arrived at the most rewarding part of the whole route, the tradeoff for many tedious kilometres of road bashing. Now every step is a joy as you follow a narrow trail, soft underfoot, which departs from the right-hand side of the building and mounts steadily through meadows alongside a small, bubbly stream towards the watershed. One or two larches multiply into a forest by the time you reach the ridge top which is, without doubt, one of the premier larch locations in Kananaskis Country. Above their feathery fronds tower the grey walls of Tombstone Mountain.

Leave this fairy-tale forest with regret and plunge downhill into the dim spruce forest of Tombstone Creek. Low down, at a small opening in the trees big enough to let the sun pour in, the trail loses itself in long grasses. (The trail at 2 o'clock leads to upper Tombstone Lake.) The main trail makes a right- angled turn to the left and arrives shortly after at an equestrian campground equipped with firepits and hitching posts. To get to lower Tombstone Lake and the water supply, turn right at a 4-way junction in the middle of the camping area and descend to Tombstone Creek at the outlet. The silky, dark-green waters of the lake are most easily fished from the rocky west shoreline where a trail has developed. The trail continues to the upper lake which despite its even grander location below the cliffs of Tombstone Mountain can be a bit of a disappointment when the plug's not in, its picturesque little island — really a huge boulder sprouting spruce trees — left high and dry on the mud flat.

TOMBSTONE LAKES TO BIG ELBOW TRAIL — Map 18

Backpack, equestrian
Distance 1.6 km
Height loss 177 m
Maximum elevation 2158 m
Topo map 82 J/10 Mount Rae

At the 4-way junction in the middle of the camping area, turn left. The trail passes through a few small meadows, then descends the east bank of Tombstone Creek to the Little Elbow motor road at a bend. Walk down the road to a second bend where you join Big Elbow hiking trail to left and right. The road to right, really a continuation of the Little Elbow motor road, leads past Tombstone Creek back-country campground which is located on the left-hand side of the road just after the creek crossing. Because of the campground's proximity to the lakes, it's not unusual for fishermen to make the pre-breakfast hike up the trail to try their luck.

Upper Tombstone Lake below Tombstone Mtn.

309 WEST FORK OF LITTLE ELBOW RIVER — Map 18

Backpack, equestrian
Easy ski, bike
Distance to end of road 7 km
Height gain 107 m
Maximum elevation 1905 m
Topo map 82 J/11 Kananaskis Lakes
82 J/14 Spray Lakes Reservoir
82 J/15 Bragg Creek

Access: Via Little Elbow trail at the forks (#308).

The west fork of the Little Elbow River, boxed in by the most spectacular peaks of the Opal Range, is an easy side trip from Little Elbow trail and should on no account be missed. Although generally regarded as a cul-de-sac, it is possible for experienced backpackers to leave the valley by steep passes to the north and south.

The trail, which is an exploration road, actually starts from Little Elbow hiking trail (road) 0.5 km east of the south fork but can also be picked up from Little Elbow equestrian trail a little south of Mount Romulus back-country campground. Don't expect signposts or red trail markers; this is an unofficial route which straightway fords the south fork of the Little Elbow River, then heads due west up the west fork, passing between an outlier of Tombstone Mountain and a most impressive saw-toothed mountain of 3008 m lying in the angle between the north and west forks. The road fords the river a few times (easy crossings) and ends on the west bank close to the large tributary coming in from the N.W. (see route #310). Small clearings hereabouts make good campsites.

The inner valley is not a pretty place, there being very little in the way of meadows; rather the vegetation is a rough mix of heaths and willow brush through which game trails thread a tortuous route. It is the wild grandeur of the setting amongst the most spectacular peaks of the Opal Range which make this valley special. Named by Dominion geologist George Dawson after the finding of quartz crystals covered in a film of opal the Opals are arrayed along the western skyline for your inspection. Farthest to the north and, like most of the other peaks in the range, named after a British admiral engaged in the Battle of Jutland lies Mount Evan-Thomas, then follows Mounts Packenham, Hood, Brock and Blane, a curious gendarme called "The Blade" which is not to be confused with the next peak which is unnamed; Burney, Jerram, and an unnamed summit which is sometimes referred to as the S.E. peak of Mount Jerram. The pass between the latter mountain and Tombstone Mountain off to the east is susceptible to a determined attack. From the heart-shaped tarn below the final scree slope, it's easier to make for the right-hand of the two gaps, then cross over the intervening hump to the lower gap where you can pick up a really good game trail descending into "Piper Creek". (See route #307.)

310 NORTH FORK OF LITTLE ELBOW RIVER — Maps 6, 18 & 19

Backpack, equestrian
Distance 8 km
Height gain 503 m
Maximum elevation at pass 2179 m
Topo map 82 J/14 Spray Lakes Reservoir
82 J/15 Bragg Creek

Access: 1. Via Little Elbow trail (#308) at the forks.
Access: 2. Via Evan-Thomas Creek trail (#80) at pass.

Although this appears to be a major connecting trail between Little Elbow River and Evan-Thomas Creek on the topo map, the trail remains undeveloped with no signs or markers. It has some very rough sections low down which require route-finding ability and may not in its present state be suitable for the inexperienced hiker or equestrian.

Start off by wading Little Elbow River opposite Mount Romulus back-country campground. On the north bank, search for a beaten-down track in grass which winds upstream through open forest to a large alluvial fan where the trail can be positively identified. After a small stream crossing the trail climbs steeply, entering the north fork of the Little Elbow River almost at timberline. Traverse steep, forested slopes high above the gorge, the occasional rocky side creek and open hillside causing no problems until you reach the 3.5 km mark where care must be exercised in crossing a slabby slope where the trail is breaking away. Equestrians should dismount here and find an alternative way down through the trees to the riverbed. In the scree gully immediately following the impasse, it's easiest to leave the trail and walk down the far side of the gully to valley bottom and there pick up the Evan-Thomas exploration road which has arisen phoenix-like from the river. The trail joins the road 100 m farther on.

The rest of the route is easy: a simple road walk across predominantly open hillsides to Evan Thomas Pass. The road takes a much higher line than that shown on the topo map, gradually moving away from the creek, which now moves lazily through broad, wet meadows below its source at a lake, and crossing the watershed 30 m above and to the east of the lowest gap at Map ref. 373283, topo map 82J/14. See route #80 for a description of the ongoing road down Evan-Thomas Creek to Highway 40.

CIRCUIT FROM MOUNT ROMULUS BACK-COUNTRY CAMPGROUND. An option the experienced hiker may wish to consider is a 21 km circuit around a 3008 m mountain which takes in both the north and west forks of the Little Elbow River. There is no trail in the difficult middle section. The best plan is to leave the north fork road below the final rise to Evan-Thomas Pass and, keeping as high a line as possible, squelch along the valley floor to a small lake below "Mount Potts" — a good lunch spot. Thus fortified, climb over a steep grass and shale pass at map ref. 360253 into the N.W. tributary of the west fork where the going is a lot easier. Low down the tributary, pick up the west fork road on the north bank and return to your starting point via route #309.

311 NIHAHI CREEK — Map 18

Day hike, equestrian
4.5 km to forks
Height gain 238 m
Maximum elevation 1914 m
Topo map 82 J/15 Bragg Creek

The canyon.

Access: Via Little Elbow trail (#308) 3.5 km west of Little Elbow campground.

Nihahi, meaning "rocky" in Stoney Indian, aptly describes this desolate valley reaching far back into the Fisher Range. A signed, marked trail takes you to alluvial flats in mid valley from where you can wander at will for many kilometres. Carry water with you.

The lower 2 km of trail bypasses the gorge by a wide detour over a forested side ridge jutting out from the side of Nihahi Ridge. Once over the ridge the trail levels, even descends a little, at one point skirting the edge of a narrow rift in the forest floor which deserves a closer look from the bottom side up. It's quite easy getting down to the start of the canyon, but a lot more difficult (though lots of fun) trying to work your way up and out of the top end without sliding off polished walls into potholes filled with stagnant water. Allow about an hour for this little divertissement.

On entering the creek bed above the gorge, follow it up to a large cairn marking the spot where the trail makes a detour into the trees. All it does is cut off a corner; you can if you want stay in the creek bed. The trail ends at a second cairn. From this point on, the valley floor widens to its maximum width of 200 m, a wall to wall carpet of gravel, bereft of any stream, which extends to narrow belts of forest below the cliffs of Nihahi Ridge on the right and Mount Fuller on the left. Travel is easy.

At the forks, the creek splits into 2 pincer-like branches converging on Mount Howard. The left-hand branch, which appears to be the major valley, carries on in much the same way as before. The right-hand branch starts off with a short gorge — quite easy to get through — before opening out into similar gravel flats. Both valley heads are enclosed by slopes of scree offering relatively easy ascents to ridges overlooking upper Canyon Creek.

312 NIHAHI RIDGE — Map 18

Day hike
Distance 3 km
Height gain 350 m
Maximum elevation 2012 m
Topo map 82 J/15 Bragg Creek

Access: Via Little Elbow hiking trail (#308) 1 km west of the hikers' trailhead at Little Elbow campground.

This signed, marked trail which supercedes the trail described in the first edition of this guide takes you to a superb viewpoint on the south ridge of Nihahi Ridge.

After the usual preliminary stretch through trees during which you intersect Little Elbow equestrian trail, the trail zigzags to the top of a grassy ridge billowing out of the hillside. Now traverse towards Nihahi Ridge across easy-angled slopes which steepen suddenly below the ridge top. Even with the aid of a handrail, the last few metres to the top is an undignified scramble up rock and dirt. Take a breather, then continue more easily up the ridge to a saddle. Beyond this point the ridge steepens and narrows, becoming more the realm of the mountaineer.

From where you first gained the ridge, the view was channelled by a foreground ridge towards Shoulder Creek and Fisher Peak at the valley head. What a difference another 50 m of height gain makes. Now you get a birds-eye view of the Little Elbow River and its west fork; against the late afternoon sun, a silvery, shining snake winding out of the shadowy recesses of the Opal Range and flanked by some of the most spectacular peaks of the Front Ranges.

The Little Elbow River from Nihahi Ridge showing the route of trail #308 to the forks. Mts. Romulus and Remus to right; the Blade, Mt. Blane and Mt. Brock (Opal Range) on the skyline at the head of the west fork.

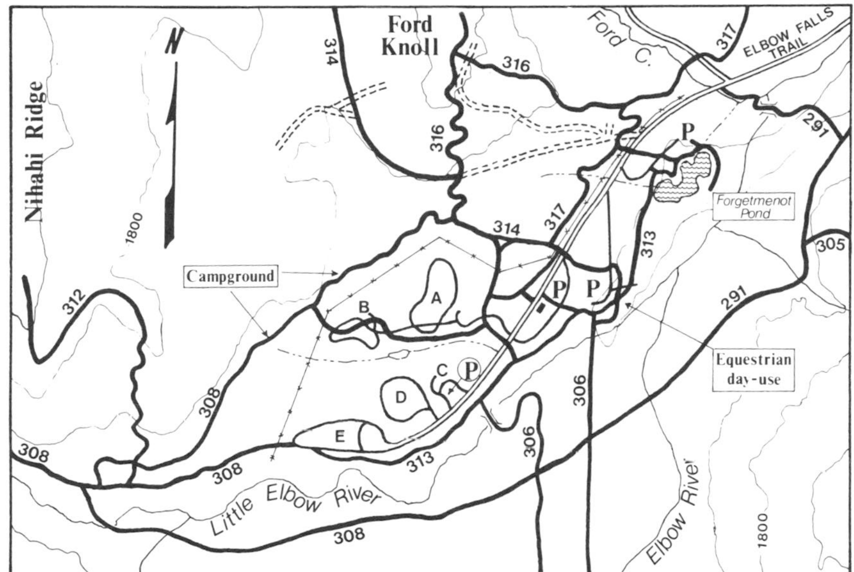

313 LITTLE ELBOW INTERPRETIVE TRAIL — Map 18

Half-day hike
Distance 2.5 km
Topo map 82 J/15 Bragg Creek

Access: Elbow Falls Trail (Hwy. 66) at Little Elbow recreation area. Accessible from Forgetmenot Pond day-use area, the equestrian day-use area, the checking station parking lot, the equestrian campground trail, and the campground access road at loop ''E''.

Despite its title, this trail is strictly utilitarian in character: its main purpose is to connect the various sectors of the recreation area and to provide access to outgoing trails.

Leaving the environs of the parking lot at the trail sign, the trail travels past gravel piles to the equestrian day-use area then swings around the south side of it and intersects Big Elbow equestrian trail en route to the river crossing. Shortly after, a trail to right leads to the parking lot at the checking station. Pass the pumphouse. The next trail to look out for is the equestrian campground trail which comes in from your right adjacent to a dried-up creek bed. The bank is rising up now and the land between river and road is narrowing to a strip. Almost opposite "C" campground loop, the red suspension bridge — gateway to Big Elbow trail for hikers and bikers —spans the Elbow River. From this point on, the trail stays close to the campground access road on the bank top, eventually merging with the road close to its turnaround point in "E" campground loop. The trailhead for Little Elbow hiking and biking trail lies a few metres farther to the west.

314 FORD CREEK TRAIL

Total distance 20 km

Access: 1. Elbow Falls Trail (Hwy. 66) at Little Elbow recreation area. Accessible from the equestrian parking lot and the equestrian campground.
Access: 2. Powderface Trail (Hwy.) at Prairie Creek.
Also accessible from the western terminus of Trail Creek connector (#315), and Canyon Creek trail (#297) 2 km east of Powderface Trail (Hwy.).

This signed, marked trail with decided schizophrenic tendencies (it's not the easy valley trail you think it is) connects Little Elbow recreation area with trailheads along Powderface Trail (Hwy.). Be aware that the first section of trail as far as Trail Creek takes an illogical line across the east face of Nihahi Ridge, a much higher line than one would expect with the result that while connecting trails in the area are all clear of snow by the end of May, Ford Creek trail is still choked up with avalanche debris in the gullies and may be impassable.

LITTLE ELBOW RECREATION AREA TO TRAIL CREEK — Maps 18 & 20

Day hike, equestrian
Distance 12 km
Height gain 591 m
Maximum elevation 2040 m
Topo map 82 J/15 Bragg Creek

The trail can be approached from several locations within the recreation area, but the usual route starts from the equestrian parking lot south of the campground access road. After you've crossed the access road, keep right, pass through a gate in the cattle fence, keep left and climb a short uphill to a triangular- shaped junction with the equestrian campground access trail from loop "A". Keep right. There is hardly time to admire the expanding view of the Elbow Valley before you arrive at a second junction with the equestrian campground access trail from loop "B". Again, keep right and climb to a 4-way intersection with an exploration road (left, right) and Ford Knoll trail (straight). Turn left. You should now be following the old exploration road around the west slope of Ford Knoll to a boggy meadow where the road changes course towards Nahahi Ridge. Do not cross the meadow. Ignore, too, a steep track marching up the knoll from the right-hand side of the trail a few metres on. Instead, the Ford Creek trail is making for the wooded gap at map ref. 504304 between Ford Knoll on the right and a minor elevation on the left which is marked as hill #2 on map 18. Once through the gap, the trail descends and crosses a side stream, then veers towards a second gap, but at the last minute doubles back and climbs over a wooded ridge to the west of hill #3.

Thus far the trail has been very pleasant and undemanding, but at the next side stream you come to at map ref. 488321 the trail changes character dramatically and you'd better be fit for the gruelling climb up the side stream out of the trees, and on up the ensuing avalanche gully nearly to the rocks of Nihahi Ridge. Just when you've become convinced the summit is the trail's objective, the trail happily makes a right-angled turn to the right into the trees and, still climbing, reaches the top of a forested spur.

The so-called traverse which follows is rarely level; you are either climbing up or climbing down many more of these forested spurs jutting out from the east face of Nihahi Ridge. Numerous avalanche gullies crossed high in the runout zone provide the only points of interest. Watch for saplings leaning downhill, trees with scarred trunks and broken branches broken on the uphill side, and mature trees with their crowns lopped off as if with a giant saw. A longer, steeper descent than usual by the side of Trail Creek signals the end of the traverse. Cross the creek in its middle reaches and climb uphill (the trail hasn't quite done with you yet) to the junction with Trail Creek connector (#315) on an open hillside. If you want to make a circuit with Powderface Ridge trail, this is where you turn off to the right.

Route follows avalanche gully almost to rockline, then traverses to the right.

TRAIL CREEK TO PRAIRIE CREEK — Map 20

Half-day hike, equestrian
Distance 3.5 km
Height loss 198 m
Maximum elevation 1890 m
Topo map 82 J/15 Bragg Creek

Keep left at the junction. The trail gradually drops towards Prairie Creek, and crosses it just west of forested hill #8. Turn right onto a narrow trail (indistinguishable from the many cow trails in that green, open valley) which climbs to the bank top and joins a former all-terrain vehicle road that once led to a favourite camping spot. Follow the road downstream to Powderface Trail (Hwy.).

PRAIRIE CREEK TO CANYON CREEK — Maps 20 & 21

Half-day hike, equestrian
Distance 4.5 km
Height gain 122 m
Maximum elevation 1814 m
Topo map 82 J/15 Bragg Creek

Walk north along the highway to the next left-hand bend where the trail is seen continuing up the east bank of a small N-S valley. After 2 km of uneventful going, you cross over a wooded pass at map ref. 479401 into a tributary of Canyon Creek which, it should be noted, lies only half a kilometre from the highway; you can if you wish bail out at this point. The trail, heading off in the opposite direction to the highway, crosses the creek, then follows it below high grassy banks to Canyon Creek. It fords the creek west of the confluence and joins Canyon Creek exploration road on the north bank.

315 TRAIL CREEK CONNECTOR — Map 20

Half-day or long-day hike
Backpack, equestrian
Distance 2 km
Height gain 152 m
Maximum elevation 198 m
Topo map 82 J/15 Bragg Creek

Access: Powderface Trail (Hwy.) at Trail Creek trailhead 7.3 km north of Elbow Falls Trail (Hwy. 66).

This short, connecting trail between the highway and Ford Creek trail starts from the west side of the highway a little upstream of the parking lot. It crosses Trail Creek within a few minutes then slips through the gap between 2 forested hills (#6 and #7 on map 20) into a meadow. A side creek crossing signals the start of a moderately steep climb all the way up the north bank of Trail Creek to the junction with Ford Creek trail on an open hillside.

316 FORD KNOLL LOOP — Map 18

Half-day hike
Equestrian
Distance 2.5 km
Height gain 235 m
Maximum elevation 1835 m
Topo map 82 J/15 Bragg Creek

Nihahi Ridge from summit clearing.

Access: Elbow Falls Trail (Hwy. 66) at Little Elbow recreation area. Hikers start from Forgetmenot Pond day-use area parking lot. Equestrians must start from Powderface Ridge trail (#317) which is accessible from either the equestrian day-use area or the equestrian campground. See sketchmap.
Also accessible from Ford Creek trail (#314).

This steep little trail leads to several viewpoints on the hill north of Little Elbow recreation area and is best tackled in an anti-clockwise direction in order to take advantage of an easier ascent route. Follow red trail markers.

From Forgetmenot Pond day-use area parking lot, follow the trail heading north across the highway and through a gate in the cattle fence to a T-junction with Powderface Ridge trail. Turn right, intersect an old exploration road and climb through trees to a junction where you should turn left off Powderface Ridge trail and begin climbing up the S.E. ridge of Ford knoll to an intersection with an old exploration road on the apex of the hill. Arriving shortly afterwards at a junction with your return route, turn right and walk up to the stony summit on the brink of the eastern escarpment where a clearing in the trees directs your gaze torwards majestic Nihahi Ridge and its entourage of 8 pine- covered hills.

Retrace your steps to the junction; this time, keep right. The trail touches the aforementioned exploration road twice briefly then winds down south slopes sufficiently open to allow a tremendous view of the Elbow Valley and the mountains to either side. Join Ford Creek trail at a 4-way intersection with another exploration road. Equestrians can return to the equestrian day- use area or the campground via Ford Creek trail opposite. The return to Forgetmenot Pond day-use area may be made along the unofficial exploration road to left which descends past a junction with the exploration road met with earlier on the hilltop to Powderface Ridge trail at the 4-way intersection near the cattle fence. Follow the route of the outward journey back to Forgetmenot Pond where a picnic on the grassy shore of this erstwhile gravel pit would make a perfect ending to the day.

Looking south from Powderface Ridge towards the mountains of the Elbow River. Banded Peak, Mt. Cornwall and Mt. Glasgow to right.

317 POWDERFACE RIDGE — Maps 18 & 20

Day hike, equestrian
Distance 8.5 km
Height gain 640 m
Height loss 183 m
Maximum elevation 2210 m
Topo map 82 J/15 Bragg Creek

Access: Elbow Falls Trail (Hwy.66) at Little Elbow recreation area. Accessible from Forgetmenot Pond day-use area (hikers) or from the equestrian day-use area (equestrians).
Also accessible from the junction of Elbow Falls Trail (Hwy. 66) and Powderface Creek Trail (Hwy.), and from Powderface trail (#301) at Powderface Pass.

This is a fairly strenuous hike up a marked trail to an open ridge. The trail connects with Powderface Creek trail which in turn connects with a great variety of other trails heading off to all areas of The Elbow and The Jumpingpound. Be warned that the obvious loop with Ford Creek trail touted by the Alberta Forest Service on their trail map of Elbow River Valley hiking and horseback trails is an arduous undertaking with a height gain of over 1,000 m whichever way round you tackle it.

From the equestrian day-use area parking lot, get onto Ford Creek trail which heads north across the highway. Immediately after passing through the gate in the cattle fence, turn right onto the official start of the Powderface Ridge trail and follow it alongside the fence for 0.7 km to the junction with the hiking trail which comes in from the right from Forgetmenot Pond parking lot. Next cross an old exploration road. The trail now climbs over the tail end of Ford Knoll's S.E. ridge (keep right at junction with Ford Knoll trail), crosses Ford Creek and Powderface Trail (Hwy.), and in another 100 m comes very close to the junction of Powderface Trail (Hwy.) with Elbow Falls Trail (Hwy. 66); many hikers do, in fact, make this junction their starting point.

Nearly all the height gain occurs in the next 2 km as the trail climbs relentlessly upwards to a col between the ridge and a grassy outlier to the S.E. which is a worthwhile objective in itself. In order to avoid rocky ground at the south end of the ridge which in the past has precluded equestrians from going further, a new trail has been built which traverses in a northerly direction to a high neck of grass at a cairn, then continues in the same line as before across the eastern escarpment, now steep and densely forested. At a junction where the ongoing trail starts to descend (it dead ends later), turn left and wind up to the ridge top which is gained at a break in the cliff band at map ref. 517339. Now turn north and follow cairns embedded in clumps of rocks along the gently-rising grass ridge to the summit. If you're lucky, the day will be calm and you'll be able to enjoy the 360 degree panorama to the full. Usually though, the wind is blasting from the west and after reaching the highest point your only thought will be to hurry down the trail which slips down the northern flank of the ridge's western outlier to Powderface Pass. There join route #301.

318 UPPER CANYON CREEK — Map 19

Day hike, backpack
Equestrian
6.5 km to end of trail
Height gain to forks 222 m
Height gain to pass 805 m
Maximum elevation at pass 2527 m
Topo map 82 J/14 Spray Lakes Reservoir
82 J/15 Bragg Creek

Access: Powderface Trail (Hwy.) at Canyon Creek. Park south of the bridge at the point where an overgrown exploration road signed "No motorized vehicles" heads west up upper Canyon Creek. When built, the Canyon Creek recreation area will be the logical starting place.

Because it lies in the rain shadow of the Fisher Range, upper Canyon Creek and all its tributaries is an arid wilderness of screes, cliffs and intermittent streams; forest is minimal and wildlife almost non-existent. Water can be a problem; on occasions, backpackers will have to travel all the way to the tributary heads before finding a reliable source by which to pitch their tents. Right now there is no official trail and no trails at all beyond the forks.

The exploration road, lightly imprinted on gravel flats, takes you almost to the forks at map ref. 412382 topo map 82 J/15. Travelling is easy and you'll want to stop often to admire the big, red cliffs of Mount Bryant and the scarcely less impressive cliffs of Compression Ridge on the shady side of the valley. 6.5 km from the trailhead and 1 km after the gravel flats end, you arrive at the forks which is the usual turning-back point for day hikers and equestrians.

SOUTH FORK The creek bed provides the easiest path through the initial narrows. After the vally opens out patches of meadow appear on damp west slopes, while across the valley white-flowering avens form stripes down runnels on gravelly hillsides. Water is nearly always running in the vicinity of a prominent rocky knoll which protrudes into the head of the valley and it is here, on a flat meadow below the knoll, where you'll find the best camping spots.

WEST FORK The west fork which is undoubtedly the main fork of Canyon Creek narrows quickly to a V. It's probably easiest to walk up the creek bed, the one vertical rock step/sometime waterfall at the head of a small canyon being easily turned on the left-hand side. The valley opens out temporarily in the area of two side creeks which enter the creek diametrically opposite each other. Keep your eyes skinned for pieces of metal, perhps from a crashed plane, which appear to have been washed down the creek bed during runoff. Because the main creek later becomes enclosed in walls of steep shale which are difficult to escape from, walk up the side creek to the north and at treeline simply traverse left along a bench into the cirque. At first glance the cirque is completely barren, a moon landscape covered in flat rocks tinted a delicate salmon-pink color which is repeated ad nauseam on surrounding ridges. But if you look more closely at the ground, you'll notice tiny cushion plants growing in the lee of larger rocks, and bright flourishes of orange jewel lichen adhering to rocks wetted with urine from pikas.

UPPER CANYON CREEK TO EVAN-THOMAS CREEK This cross-country route has been known and utilized by experienced backpackers for many years. The idea is to gain the watershed ridge at map ref. 398360 topo map 82 J/14. Although this can be achieved from several points in the west and south forks, the climb is much lcss tiresome if you start from the knoll at the head of the south fork. So without further ado head up a shallow grassy recess to the right of the knoll, angling right all the while to get onto steeper slopes above an island of trees. Keep moving right and slightly upwards across a slope furrowed with shallow gullies; you are aiming for the lowest shelf of scree below the ridge line. Once you gain the shelf, don't climb directly up the slope above which is beginning to rear up like a breaking wave. Instead, walk along the shelf to a broad scree ridge delineating the northern limit of the slope and follow it up to the ridge top. A cornice which forms during winter months along the eastern side of the ridge adds interest early in the season.

Descend 240 m of scree and boulders into the head of an unnamed creek where you are at once confronted by nasty, greasy waterfall steps. Traverse left through trees and and as soon as you reach the avalanche chute return to the creek bed which can now be followed for 3 obstacle-free kilometres to a major artery of Evan-Thomas Creek. Turn right. About 10 minutes before you reach Evan-Thomas Creek itself and the exploration road, the hitherto placid stream erupts in a short chain of falls and deep pools.

Falls in tributary of Evan-Thomas Creek.

319 "BRYANT" LAKE — Map 19

Day hike
Distance 7 km
Height gain 381 m
Maximum elevation 2103 m
Topo map 82 J/14 Spray Lakes Reservoir
82 J/15 Bragg Creek

Access: Powderface Trail (Hwy.), at Canyon Creek. Park south of the bridge at the point where an overgrown exploration road signed "No motorized vehicles" heads west up upper Canyon Creek. When built, the Canyon Creek recreation area will be the logical starting place.

"Bryant Lake" below Mount Bryant, has the distinction of being the only sizable body of water in the Fisher Range. Although there is no trail to the lake at present, a trail following the same route as that described below is due to be built within the next few years during reconstruction of the highway.

Start off by following upper Canyon Creek exploration road. In 2 km, turn right (north) up a sizable tributary to the east of Mount Bryant which, like most other creeks in the Fisher Range, is a dry stony creekbed offering easy travelling. Careful route finding is necessary at the 5.5 km mark where a side creek unmarked on the topo map masquerades as the main creek. You must turn left here and follow a much narrower creekbed overhung by a canopy of trees which passes between steep, rocky slopes en route to meadows at the height of land. Now descend a grassy draw and push your way through a tangle of spruce trees and willow bush to the lakeshore. The lake occupies a deep hole at the bottom of plunging scree slopes. If you are lucky, the tub will be filled to vegetation line.

"Bryant Lake"

From the summit of "S. W. Peak" looking towards "West Peak" (extreme left), North Peak and Moose Mtn. main summit. "South Peak" is just off the photo to the right. This photo shows the final approaches of trails 320, #295 and #327.

320 MOOSE MOUNTAIN FROM CANYON CREEK — Maps 20 & 21

Day hike
Distance 8.5 km
Height gain 745 m
Maximum elevation 2437 m
Topo map 82 J/15 Bragg Creek

Access: Powderface Trail (Hwy.) at Canyon Creek recreation area due to be built during reconstruction of the highway. Right now, park at the junction of the highway with Canyon Creek exploration road, 0.4 km north of Canyon Creek crossing.

This is a route for adventurous hikers who like to get off the beaten track, away from the usual weekend pilgrimage of the tourist route on the other side of the mountain. There is no trail other than the exploration road and game trails low down which get you pointed in the right direction.

Follow Canyon Creek trail (#297) for 4.5 km. At the unsigned junction in the meadow, stay left with the exploration road as it climbs over a forested rib into Moose Mountain Creek. Cross to the east bank. There is little point in following the road farther, so strike up Moose Mountain Creek for five minutes or so, then, using a conglomeration of moose and cattle trails, turn up the first side creek to the right. In mid valley, an excellent game trail on the right-hand bank climbs to a dip in the ridge enclosing the valley to the S.E. (map ref. 505432).

Now climb the ridge to the north. Although there is no trail, the going is easy enough through forest with little understory and it isn't long before you emerge onto meadows laced with shale. Stop often to look at the view unfolding behind your back as you climb to the summit of what I call "West Peak" (2332 m, map ref. 516442). From its narrow ridge, the sight of the final pyramid, all scree and slab, is a real downer to the tired hiker and worse, before you can even set foot on the slope, you must first descend 122 m of steep grass and rock to the broad saddle between the 2 summits. Be assured that on closer inspection the slope falls back and the footing is firm; nevertheless, this is still a laborious climb with not even a remnant of trail to help you until, nearing the summit you can pick up a trail leading the last few metres from the marmot colony to the lookout.

"South Peak" 2323 m If the final slope of Moose Mountain is too overfacing, or if you want to try somewhere new and interesting, I suggest you head out in a south-easterly direction from the saddle towards "South Peak" at map ref. 527437. The going is everywhere easy on short-cropped grass which is a pleasure to walk upon. The summit, topped by a cairn and 2 branches tied together in the shape of a cross, is the apex of 2 ridges offering further delights as well as opportunities for alternative descent routes into Canyon Creek.

The inadequacy of topo maps is nowhere better illustrated than in this area, for the narrow ridge rising to "S.W. Peak" (2310 m, map ref. 523428) is neither exposed nor difficult, the one rock step two-thirds of the way along being easily managed on the east side. From its long summit ridge you can descend almost anywhere into Canyon Creek without fear of running into obstacles. Conversely, the apparently broad and easy S.E. ridge has a difficult 7 metre-high rock step below "South Peak" which just as surely brings the non-climber to a halt as if it were a 70 m precipice. It's a pity really, for the walk over "S.E. Peak" (2262 m, map ref. 537435) is delightful and when you reach ridge's end, a break in the cliffbands on the west side allows a safe descent to be made into the side valley which debouches into Canyon Creek. This "forever" creek between the two ridges offers a third route of descent. A steep upper section (keep east of the waterfalls), a stony creek bed smothered in willow brush and avalanche debris, a 30 m rock step (keep east on bypass trail) all conspire to make it twice as long to navigate as the more technical S.E. ridge above.

Impending storm on summit of "West Peak". "South Peak" to left.

A fine view of Nihahi Ridge (right) and its 8 foothills. Farther to the left is Powderface Trail (Hwy.) and Powderface Ridge. In the distance are the mountains bordering the Elbow River.

321 JUMPINGPOUND SOUTH RIDGE TRAIL — Map 21

Day hike, equestrian
Distance 7 km
Height gain 549 m
Maximum elevation 2240 m
Topo map 82 J/15 Bragg Creek

Access: Powderface Trail (Hwy.) at Canyon Creek recreation area due to be built during reconstruction of the highway. Right now, park at the junction of the highway with Canyon Creek exploration road 0.4 km north of the creek crossing.
Also acessible from the southern terminus of Jumpingpound North Ridge trail (#323), the eastern terminus of Jumpingpound Summit trail (#322), and the western terminus of East Ridge trail (#326).

Together with Jumpingpound North Ridge trail and East Ridge trail, this trail is an important link in the trail system connecting The Jumpingpound to The Elbow. Most people, though, will use the trail for day trips to the summit of Jumpingpound Mountain.

Head east along Canyon Creek exploration road (#297) for 1 km. Immediately after the first side creek crossing (last reliable water), turn left or north onto Jumpingpound South Ridge trail which almost straightway gains entrance onto steep, forested slopes between 2 gate-like cliffs. The trail levels temporarily at a bridge over a small creek, then continues zigzagging, first to the right and then to the left of the creek all the way up the slope to the south ridge. Emerge from the pines onto a grassy hogback pimpled with rock outcrops. Even if you get no farther, it's worth coming this far for the view of Moose Mountain and 12 kilometre-long Nihahi Ridge which has opened up behind your back as you climbed through the trees.

At a gap, the trail slips over to the west side of the ridge, and in order to avoid the bristly ridge, line traverses well below it in enclosed forest to the junction with route #322 at a cairn. Keep right here and climb back onto the ridge, now smooth and grassy. A line of cairns signals the trail's traverse 60 m below the summit of Jumpingpound Mountain to a merger with North Ridge trail on the west flank, so if you want to take the opportunity of climbing to the summit, this is the point where you should strike off uphill; the way is marked with small cairns and ends with a few metres of rock clambering below the summit cairn.

322 JUMPINGPOUND (MOUNTAIN) SUMMIT TRAIL — Map 21

Day hike
Distance 4 km to summit
Height gain 411 m
Maximum elevation 2240 m
Topo map 82 J/15 Bragg Creek

Access: **Powderface Trail (Hwy.) at the Jumpingpound Mountain parking lot due to be built during road reconstruction. Right now, the trail starts from the east side of the highway 0.4 km south of the pass between Jumpingpound Creek and Canyon Creek drainages.**
Also accessible from Jumpingpound South Ridge trail (#321).

This is by far the shortest route to the summit of Jumpingpound Mountain. Just a few metres after it leaves the highway, the trail bridges a small creek, follows it upstream a bit, then gradually turns away and climbs onto a subsidiary ridge falling away from the south ridge of Jumpingpound Mountain. A well engineered section of trail switchbacks to a clearing with bench at the mid-way point, then continues in tighter switchback formation through more open forest to a junction with Jumpingpound South Ridge trail at a cairn. Turn left and follow route #321 onto the summit of Jumpingpound Mountain, now only 0.5 km distant.

323 JUMPINGPOUND NORTH RIDGE TRAIL — Map 21

Day hike, equestrian
Distance 8.5 km
Height gain 610 m
Maximum elevation 2240 m
Topo map 82 J/15 Bragg Creek

Access: **Powderface Trail (Hwy.) at Cox Hill parking lot approximately 10 km south of the junction with Sibbald Creek Trail (Hwy. 68).**
Also accessible from the northern terminus of Jumpingpound South Ridge trail (#321), the southern terminus of Cox Hill trail (#328), and the western terminus of East Ridge trail (#326).

Noted for its chain of immaculately-constructed cairns, this new (1983) trail to the summit of Jumpingpound Mountain opens up some really fine country above treeline which is often in condition right through to December 1st when the highway closes. Together with its southern counterpart, route #321, it links routes to the north like Lusk Pass and Cox Hill trails to Canyon Creek and ongoing trails leading to the Elbow River.

As soon as you've crossed the bridge over Jumpingpound Creek, the trail makes big switchbacks up a densely-forested ridge with little in the way of views until, at the second levelling, a side trail to right descends to a glade with a spring (last water). The trail continues more or less up the ridge line, passing the southern terminus of Cox Hill trail on the left shortly before it climbs out of the trees onto the north ridge proper where you are still over 3 km distant from the summit of Jumpingpound Mountain. You'll find no pretty meadows here, only the windswept slopes of the alpine tundra and rocky outcroppings which act as shelter for trees creeping up lee slopes onto the ridge top.

Head south along the broad ridge with the unnamed peaks of the Fisher Range for company on your right-hand side. Bits of trail are joined by long trailless sections marked by cairns nearly 2 m high; in this way you pass 60 m below the summit of Jumpingpound Mountain on the west flank and merge with South Ridge route. Barring a thunderstorm or a whiteout (this is when the cairns really come in useful), a trip to the summit is a worthwhile digression, so at the obvious place cut left and climb past small cairns to the summit rocks where the view to the south — ridge on ridge and range on range receding into the noonday sun — is suddenly disclosed.

Cox Hill from Jumpingpound Mtn's. north ridge. Connecting route #328 follows open ridge shown face on.

324 TOM SNOW TRAIL

Total distance 29 km

Access: 1. Powderface Trail (Hwy.) at Dawson day-use area.
Access: 2. Bragg Creek Road at 4.9 and 6.4 km west of Kananaskis Country boundary.
Access: 3. Elbow Falls Trail (Hwy. 66) at Station Flats day-use area.
Also accessible from route #334 Sibbald Viewpoint to Tom Snow trail, route #335 Thomas Road to Tom Snow trail, and the eastern terminus of East Ridge trail (#324).

This long distance trail, named after Chief Tom Snow of the Wesley Band of Stoney Indians, connects The Jumpingpound to The Elbow via West Bragg Creek. You follow a maze of old exploration roads, logging roads and new trails through the meadows and forests of the valley bottoms; the intricacies of the route are, fortunately, well signed and marked with red triangles throughout. With sufficient snow, all sections make excellent ski trails.

DAWSON DAY-USE AREA TO THOMAS ROAD — Map 21

Day hike, easy ski
Equestrian, bike
Distance 5.5. km
Height loss 100 m
Maximum elevation 1497 m
Topo map 82 O/2 Jumpingpound Creek

A few metres beyond the trailhead at Dawson day-use area the trail divides at the N.W.-S.E. cutline. Keep left and follow the west bank of Jumpingpound Creek for 0.5 km to another trail junction where you should keep straight past a future campground site and cross Jumpingpound Creek. At the top end of the meadow the trail joins an exploration road at a T-junction. (The road to right connects with Cox Hill trail in 1 km.) Turn left and follow the road past Sawmill trail west access road on the right (no sign) to another T-junction. (The road to left is route # 334 to Sibbald Viewpoint day-use area.) Turn right up the hill, intersect a N.W.-S.E. cutline and get onto a newly-cut trail which heads across a longer stretch of unbroken forest to a T- junction with a third N.W.-S.E. cutline. (Route #334 from Sibbald Viewpoint day-use are comes in from the left.) Turn right. Shortly after the cutline upgrades to road, Sawmill trail east access road turns off to the right across the west fork of Coxhill Creek.

Now follows a very pleasant stretch through young pine plantations and sandy meadows allowing views in all directions of mountains rimming the horizon; you can probably recognize Ole Buck Mountain, Deer Ridge, Cox Hill and Moose Mountain. The road parallels the windings of the creek on the bank top, eventually descending to creek bottom and joining Thomas Road at a road junction near the bottom of the hill. (Thomas road to right crosses the west fork of Coxhill Creek and climbs to a pond on the open ridge.) Keep left and after a few more metres of travelling arrive at the junction with Moose Creek exploration road (right) and route #335 (straight) in riverside meadows.

Cutblocks above west fork of Coxhill Creek. Ole Buck Mtn. on skyline.

THOMAS ROAD TO EAST RIDGE TRAIL VIA MOOSE CREEK — Maps 20 & 21

Day hike, easy ski
Equestrian, bike
Distance 7 km
Height gain 149 m
Maximum elevation 1545 m
Topo map 82 O/2 Jumpingpound Creek
82 J/15 Bragg Creek

Turn right onto Moose Creek exploration road which immediately fords Coxhill Creek. Shortly after passing through a large reclaimed meadow of dandelions and clover, hikers and equestrians should turn right onto a new 2 kilometre-long trail which bypasses a frustrating section of road winding about Moose Creek. Rejoin the road a little north of a major E-W cutline. Now follows a delightful section through meadows with many crossings of small tributaries. Shortly after intersecting a N.E.-S.W. cutline, you come to a road division which is not at all clear from this direction. (The better defined right-hand road eventually peters out in wet, moose meadows harboring delicious arctic raspberries which make a squelch through the muskeg worth your while come August). The Tom Snow trail follows flagging and red triangles leftwards across what appears to be a grassy clearing into the trees where the road becomes immediately obvious. In less than 100 m from this junction it crosses Moose Creek to the east bank and climbs up to a T-junction festooned with snowmobile and trail signs. East Ridge trail turns off to the right.

EAST RIDGE TRAIL TO BRAGG CREEK ROAD — Maps 20 & 21

Day hike, intermediate ski
Equestrian, bike
Distance 8.5 km
Height gain 107 m
Height loss 146 m
Maximum elevation 1548 m
Topo map 82 J/15 Bragg Creek

Turn left. In just a short distance the road swings around to the direction it should be going in and becomes trail. After the boggy watershed meadow is behind you, join up with an overgrown exploration road and follow it downstream for 3.5 km through the lovely meadows and aspen forests of upper Bragg Creek,. Arriving at a broad, green swath of the reclaimed Shell Oil exploration road, turn right onto a newly-built portion of trail which crosses the creek (a jump) and follows the line of the exploration road uphill to a junction with Moose Loop ski trail at a N.E.-S.W. cutline. Keep straight. In about 0.2 km, leave the reclaimed strip which is about to make a hairpin bend to right and transfer to an older exploration road marked with ski signs to left which eventually leads back down to the valley bottom.

Cross 2 side creeks. Just after the second crossing, turn right off Moose Loop ski trail onto a trail which climbs corkscrew-fashion up the bank into a young pine tree plantation. Now follow the plantation road along the banktop of the side creek and through the centre of a 6-way junction; the way is obvious and well-marked in any case. At the top of a hill, the road swings around to the S.E. away from the side creek into sunny cutblocks and natural meadows allowing good views of West Bragg Creek. Intersect 2 N.E.-S.W. cutlines, keep left at a road junction — your road is always obvious — and arrive at Bragg Creek Road after less than half a kilometre of pleasant, easy going.

BRAGG CREEK ROAD TO STATION FLATS VIA WEST RANGER CREEK — Map 20

Day hike, intermediate ski
Equestrian
Distance 8 km
Height gain 110 m
Height loss 201 m
Maximum elevation 1570 m
Topo map 82 J/15 Bragg Creek

Turn right (west) and walk for 1.5 km up Bragg Creek Road. After Ranger Creek crossing, turn first left onto a logging road which traverses a very large cutblock overlooking Ranger Creek swamp to the east. Entering trees, the road reverts to trail briefly and descends to West Ranger Creek through aspens stripped of bark by wintering moose. Now follow the sluggish creek downstream to the confluence with Ranger Creek in a meadow with salt lick. Cross West Ranger Creek. Although you are very close to Elbow Ranger Station at this point, you must turn right after a few metres walking onto a cutline access road which joins a N.E.-S.W. cutline. Climb up the cutline a short distance, then head left over the summit of a small hill — fun to traverse on skis — into an unnamed creek to the south where you join Diamond T trail. Turn left over the bridge and reach Station Flats day-use area on Elbow Falls Trail (Hwy. 66) after 0.75 km of flat, easy going.

325 SAWMILL LOOP — Map 21

Day hike, equestrian
Distance 5.5 km
Height gain 174 m
Maximum elevation 1637 m
Topo map 82 O/2 Jumpingpound Creek

Access: **Via Tom Snow trail (#324) 2 km and 4 km east of Dawson day-use area.**

This route will probably be upgraded to official trail status by the Alberta Forest Service within the next few years. Meant primarily for equestrians, it is not very interesting as a hiking trail and probably shouldn't be used as such unless you're just out for exercise. Right now, the route is marked with snowmobile signs.

From the most easterly junction with Tom Snow trail, the old mill road bridges the west fork of Coxhill Creek and begins a gradual climb along the east bank of the creek through enclosed spruce forest. En route you pass a cutline and 2 cutline access roads on the left, and a major intersecting N.W.-S.E. cutline. Higher up, the road splits into a dry road braiding about a soggy cutline. After the first braid, leave the road, which carries on into the sawmill site, and walk along the cutline to a junction with a grassed-over road to right marked by a snowmobile sign.

The new road crosses the west fork of Coxhill Creek and becomes so indistinct in wet meadows, it's easiest to navigate from one snowmobile sign to another, watching carefully all the while for where the road resumes on dry ground at the base of a forested hill. Now well defined, it climbs steeply over the shoulder of the hill and descends in 2 steep waves to Tom Snow trail which is joined 2 km east of Dawson day-use area.

326 EAST RIDGE TRAIL — Maps 20 & 21

Long-day hike, backpack
Equestrian, bike
Distance 15 km
Height gain 1128 m
Height loss 417 m
Maximum elevation 2240 m
Topo map 82 J/15 Brgg Creek

Access: **1. Via Tom Snow trail (#324) in Moose Creek.**
Access: **2. Via terminus of Jumpingpound North and South Ridge trails (#323 and 321) and Jumpingpound Summit trail (#322) on the summit of Jumpingpound Mountain.**

East Ridge trail connects Tom Snow trail in Moose Creek to routes #321, 322 and 323 on the summit of Jumpingpound Mountain. It should be thought of as much more than just a useful connector, for the trail takes a magnificent high line along the north ridge of Moose Mountain and the east ridge of Jumpingpound Mountain, reaching a height of 2240 m at the apex of an unnamed summit. **Important note** : At the time of publication the trail is incomplete; there are no signs, cairns or red markers anywhere along its length, nor is there any trail on sections above treeline. I'm told that trail building will

North ridge of Moose Mtn. Looking back from lowest (and widest) point towards North Peak.

East Ridge trail. Hikers are descending from "First Summit" towards saddle at left centre. From here the trail heads diagonally right up scree slopes to the east ridge of Jumpingpound Mtn. (background).

recommence in the summer of 1985. Until then, any hiker who can map read will have no difficulty in following the proposed route. Equestrians, however, may run into technical difficulties on the ridges and before planning their trip should contact Alberta Forest Service to find out the status of the trail.

From the junction with Tom Snow trail in Moose Creek, follow the exploration road heading in a south-easterly direction which may or may not be signed "East Ridge trail". Arriving at another junction marked with a snowmobile sign, turn right, ford Moose Creek to the N.W. bank and follow a very straight and tedious section of road cum cutline showing recent signs of seismic activity past a cutline and cutline access road to right. Just after crossing a side creek issuing from a large beaver pond, you come to a road junction on the bank of Moose Creek. Keep right. (The road to left, which crosses the creek and winds a laborious route across a series of ridges to the reclaimed Shell Oil access road in West Bragg Creek, is sometimes used as an alternative access route.)

A little farther on, the Moose Creek exploration road crosses and recrosses Moose Creek in quick succession. Fill up water bottles; this stretch of river is the last reliable source of water on the trail. Back on the N.W. bank again, the road swings away through good camping meadows to a rendezvous with a N.W.- S.E. cutline to right (possible route to upper Coxhill Creek), then returns to the creek which is usually dry at this point. Again the road crosses back and forth across the creek bed, then settles into a gradual climb along the N.W. bank where exciting views begin to open up of the precipitous north face of Moose Mountain.

Road and cutline, having shared an uneasy alliance thus far, part company at the bottom of a steep hill just after a side creek crossing. Follow the road around to the right. East Ridge trail leaves the right-hand side of the road at the second left- hand bend where the road, having achieved the necessary height gain, is returning to the cutline. Though not quite as simple as it sounds, you push your way through a belt of trees into a small side valley known as Lucky Valley which is the key to the north ridge of Moose Mountain. In the first meadow you come to, a good trail materializes on the N.E. bank and can be followed upstream through aspen groves and lush meadows of an amazing bright green color which belie the sluggish creek; with luck campers may be able to deepen mud holes sufficiently to fill a billy can or two. The trail climbs out of the valley head into the pines and arrives at a small pass between Moose and Coxhill Creeks. Still following the trail, traverse left onto the north ridge of Moose Mountain which is gained at map ref. 513488.

The route bears south, and after a short, flat stretch through trees, mounts a broad slope of grass, shale and scree in that order to a large cairn. Near the top, watch for geodes scattered about the rocks like little brown cannonballs. Now follow a runner of grass, wide enough and long enough to land a small plane, to a rocky knob — easily scrambled up — which at 2240 m is the highest point on the trail. I will call it the First Summit. Descend the sometimes narrow and slabby ridge on the far side to the col between First Summit and the North Peak of Moose Mountain at map ref. 509465 which is the jumping-off point for route #327 to the summit of Moose Mountain.

East Ridge trail strikes off downhill to the saddle between the south fork of Coxhill Creek and Moose Mountain Creek, then, regaining all height lost, angles right up talus slope below the intermittent rock band onto the most easterly point of Jumpingpound Mountain's east ridge. Now head east along a lovely ridge comprised of 4 tops connected one to the other by cols of roughly the same height. The resultant up-and-down trail alternates between open forest at the cols and windswept hilltops where magenta shooting stars grow thick on the ground. The fifth hilltop, a little taller than the rest and topped by a cairn, is Jumpingpound Mountain.

North Ridge of Moose Mtn. as seen from Jumpingpound Mtn. North Peak to left; main summit with lookout to right. Route #320 follows right-hand skyline.

327 MOOSE MOUNTAIN NORTH RIDGE — Map 21

Long day hike, backpack
Distance 2 km
Height gain 340 m
Maximum elevation 2437 m
Topo map 82 J/15 Bragg Creek

Access: Via East Ridge trail (#326).
Also accessible from Moose Mountain Fire Road (#295) and #320 Moose Mountain from Canyon Creek on the summit of Moose Mountain.

Because the delectable north ridge of Moose Mountain is several ridges removed from any highway, this route – surely the most satisfying of all the routes to the summit – has in the past been largely ignored. The building of East Ridge trail in 1985 will facilitate access, reducing the time needed to one long day if you start from the Jumpingpound Mountain end and make a 23 km- long circuit with route #320. This is bound to become a classic ridge walk with strong hikers who can hack 1,470 m of ascent. Unfortunately, the suggested loop misses out the first half of the ridge, so if you wish to hike the ridge in its entirety, you have to start from the Moose Creek end which necessitates a 2 or 3 day trip. There is no trail; nor is one needed; only the final climb to summit of Moose Mountain requires careful route finding and a steady foot.

From the col at map ref. 509465, leave East Ridge trail and climb broad, comfortable slopes spotted with clumps of red saxifidge to the summit of North Peak. The final few metres narrow to a runner of grass whose highest point, truly an island in the sky, is crowned with a cairn and a well-gnawed moose antler. The appearance of the connecting ridge to the highest summit of Moose Mountain is at first sight a little intimidating. A few tentative steps along the ridge should convince you that it's nowhere near as narrow as it looks and certainly not exposed; you can just about cross the whole thing with your hands in your pockets. It's the final steep climb, where the ridge abuts against the north face, that's a bit tricky from the route finding point of view. Tackle the first easy rock band direct, then climb diagonally right to where talus spills through a gap in a second higher rockband. Above this, move delicately leftwards to the skyline ridge and scramble up 2 metres of rock to boulder slopes lying back at a more comfortable angle. The route emerges at the outhouse below the lookout.

From Cox Hill looking west towards Mt. Kidd, Mt. Sparrowhawk, 3 summits of Mt. Lougheed, and Wind Mtn. Baldy Pass is notch in middle distance above figure's head.

328 COX HILL — Map 21

Day hike
Equestrian
7 km to summit
10 km to Jumpingpound North Ridge trail
Height gain 872 m
Height loss 314 m
Maximum elevation 2219 m
Topo map 82 O/2 Jumpingpound Creek
82 J/15 Bragg Creek

Access: Powderface Trail (Hwy.) at Dawson day-use area. Also accessible from Jumpingpound North Ridge trail (#323).

This lowly foothill barely rising above the pines is a superlative viewpoint superior, in my opinion, to Moose Mountain since that massif, looking very unfamiliar from this direction, is also included in the view. Hikers with 2 vehicles should seriously consider hiking the "Jumpingpound Highline" — an amalgamation of Cox Hill trail and Jumpingpound North and South Ridge trails which offers 20.5 km of delightful ridge wandering, most of it above treeline.

At the trail junction a few minutes from the trailhead, turn right and cross Jumpingpound Creek on a bridge. The trail is not the N.W.-S.E. cutline but the road to the left which takes a longer more circuitous line. Arriving at a T-junction, turn right and in a few minutes join the cutline above the steep hill. Turn left, then almost immediately right onto a trail which winds qite steeply at times up the N.E. ridge of Cox Hill. Low down, the pine forest is choked with alder bushes and deadfall making you feel glad you have a trail to follow. At map ref. 487526, a spur trail to right leads to a viewpoint on the ridge top. The summit still looks an awful long way off, so head on back down to the main trail for another spell through forest now bereft of all understorey; the angle has eased and the ground is alternately sandy and stoney. At 5.25 km pass grassy bluffs allowing a birds-eye view of Coxhill Creek.

Below the final steeping, the trail makes a big zig to the right and emerges onto meadows. Switchback up a steep grass slope red-finged in fall from the preponderance of alpine fireweeds and snow willows to the lower summit (small cairn) from where it is merely a short walk along a connecting ridge (large cairn half-way) to the main summit. Purposely it seems, the trail takes you through a spruce thicket on the brow of the hill so that the view to the west bursts upon you suddenly. Flat- topped rocks above little escarpments on the east and west sides make good ringside seats.

The trail continues on down the grassy south ridge, after the initial drop settling into a descending traverse on the west side. In the trees the trail turns more westerly and descends a supporting ridge to the gap between Cox Hill and Jumpingpound Mountain. Make one big switchback up Jumpingpound Mountain's N. ridge then contour right below the apex of the N. and N.W. ridges to join Jumpingpound North Ridge trail at map ref. 456388 (topo map 82 J/15 Bragg Creek).

329 EAGLE HILL — Map 21

Day hike, equestrian
10.5 km from Dawson day-use area
7 km from Sibbald Lake
Height gain 332 m
Maximum elevation 1722 m
Topo map 82 J/O2 Jumpingpound Creek

Access: 1. (Equestrian) Powderface Trail (Hwy.) at Dawson day- use area.
Access: 2. (Hiking) Sibbald Creek Trail (Hwy. 68) at Sibbald Lake day-use area parking lot.

This marked trail and all its variants takes you through typical foothills country of meadows and aspen forests to a viewpoint on the northern boundary of Kananaskis Country. Note that there are 2 widely-separated starts to this trail and that equestrians **MUST** start from Dawson day-use area.

Equestrian Route A few metres beyond the trailhead at Dawson day-use area the trail divides at the N.W.-S.E. cutline. Keep left and follow the west bank of Jumpingpound Creek for 0.5 km to another trail junction where you should turn left, intersect the highway and running parallel to it, cross Sibbald Flat. At the meadow's northern rim, you intersect the highway (again), Sibbald Creek and Sibbald Creek Trail (Hwy. 68) in quick succession. NOTE: when Powderface Trail (Hwy.) is rebuilt during the next few years, the trail will lie on the EAST side of the highway throughout. Now climb over the low ridge to the north. Pass Deer Ridge trail to left on the ridge top then descend to Moose Pond whose eastern shoreline, lined with balsam poplars, is followed around to the lake's N.E. corner where you can pick up the unofficial hiking trail from Sibbald Lake parking lot. Turn left and follow an overgrown exploration road along the north bank of a valley characterized by muskeg and willow brush. A few metres after the road intersects a N.W.-S.E. cutline, it makes a lengthy detour round the soggy head of a side creek where, at the zenith of the curve, it joins forces with the official hiking trail.

Hiking Route From Sibbald Lake day-use area parking lot, you can choose from 2 alternative routes. The unofficial route — a faint trail — slips around the south end of the interpretive trail ridge beside the parking lot and joins the equestrian route at Moose Pond in half a kilometre. The official route, signed and marked, leads off in the opposite direction towards the Boys and Girls Clubs of Calgary Camp. Turn first left off the access road onto a cutline access road, then in 0.3 km make another left turn onto a road which climbs to a ridge top where it joins a N.E.-S.W. cutline. Walk left along the cutline for a few metres, watching carefully for where a newly-cut trail turns left down through the trees, losing all height gained previously, to the junction with the equestrian route at an old exploration road in a valley bottom. After so many left turns when it seems you must surely be walking in a circle, it's nice to turn right.

Equestrian and hiking routes combined, the route progresses along the exploration road up valley. Repass both the N.W.-S.E. cutline and the N.E.-S.W. cutline. Shortly after passing the northern access to Deer Ridge on the left, the road fades away in a low pass between 2 wooded hills and is replaced by a new trail which, ignoring an old pack trail descending towards Crane Creek, keeps a high line, even climbs to a higher elevation than the pass as it traverses aspen hillsides to a gap at map ref. 465600. Cross marshy ground on a 3 metre-long bridge. Now begin winding up the lower slopes of Eagle Hill which lies to the N.W. of the gap. In a clearing you join a cutline access road at a bend and follow it uphill to the cutline it serves at the boundary fence between Kananaskis Country and Stoney Indian Reserve. You don't quite make the summit, but it doesn't matter, for the summit is closeted in trees and here, on open S.W. slopes prickly with wild rose and gooseberry shoots, you can look out across the Bow Valley to the familiar outlines of the mountains about Canmore.

Bow Valley from Eagle Hill

330 DEER RIDGE — Map 21

Day hike, equestrian
Distance 3 km
Height gain 183 m
Maximum elevation 1698 m
Topo map 82 O/2 Jumpingpound Creek

Access: **Via Eagle Hill trail (#329) at 2 locations.**

Deer Ridge is the double-headed hill overlooking Sibbald Creek Trail (Hwy. 68) west of Powderface Trail junction. It is traversed by a signed trail which can be used as an alternative to Eagle Hill trail, but is more usually climbed for its own sake to a viewpoint on the most easterly summit.

Leave Eagle Hill trail on the low ridge south of Moose Pond at map ref. 490564. The trail heads west and switchbacks up a steepening aspen hillside into the pines of the summit ridge where the angle lessens somewhat. Level with the east summit, a spur trail to left brings you to an overlook above a cliff where open areas of shale and rocks blanketed with juniper and kinnikinnick allow an excellent view of Sibbald Creek gorge, Moose Mountain and the lonely hills south of the highway which no one ever visits. According to a weathered sign tacked to a tree, this little summit is really "Weaver Mountain", a name presumably bestowed by the Boys and Girls Club of Calgary (who have a cabin nearby) after the species of bird "ploceidae" of which the sparrow is the best known member.

A slightly higher summit of Deer Ridge or "Weaver Mountain" — call it what you will — lies 0.3 km to the west, but since the view is obscured by trees, there is no incentive to linger and you may as well continue on down the N.W. ridge to an intersecting cutline. Turn right here and keep right until you reach valley bottom, then turn left onto a grassy road which heads upstream for 0.4 km before crossing the creek and rejoining Eagle Hill trail on the N.E. bank at map ref. 480578.

331 SIBBALD FLAT INTERPRETIVE TRAIL — Map 21

Half-day hike
Distance 0.75 km one way
Height gain 82 m
Maximum elevation 1570 m
Topo map 82 O/2 Jumpingpound Creek

Access: **Sibbald Creek Trail (Hwy. 68) at Sibbald Lake day-use area parking lot.**

The trail switchbacks up the ridge above the lake, eventually levelling off in aspen forest and arriving at a viewpoint overlooking Moose Pond meadow. There are 3 seats from which to look at the view and read the trail brochure which discusses the multiple land uses to which the country roundabout has been subject, from cattle grazing in the early days to logging, oil and gas exploration, and now, recreation.

332 OLE BUCK LOOP — Map 21

Day hike
Distance 3.5 km
Height gain 168 m
Maximum elevation 1640 m
Topo map 82 O/2 Jumpingpound Creek

Sibbald Flat interpretive trail in fall. ➤

Access: Sibbald Creek Trail (Hwy. 68). Via route #333 Sibbald Viewpoint to Sibbald Lake. The shortest route to Ole Buck Loop starts from the far end of loop "C" of Sibbald Lake campground where a short access trail by the side of the toilets leads to route #333 just west of the trailhead.

This steep loop trail culminates at a viewpoint on the west ridge of Ole Buck Mountain. If it sounds a little to strenuous for your tastes, an easy stroll up Bateman Creek to the beaver ponds is worth your while especially in fall when the soft colors of summer are replaced by garish tones of reds and yellows. The preponderence of willow bushes and aspens turn Bateman Creek into a photographer's dream at this time of year, so don't forget to bring your camera.

After crossing Bateman Creek by a log bridge the trail divides. The right-hand trail starts gently enough up a side valley, then, as if a side creek crossing were the signal, climbs very much more steeply through old forest onto Ole Buck's west ridge. At the trail's highest point, a spur trail lined with stones leads to a viewpoint with seat. Back on the main trail again, descend a little to a second viewpoint with seats in a meadow, the inclusion of Sibbald Lake in the scene making this much the superior viewpoint. Dropping steeply now, the trail zigzags back down to Bateman Creek opposite the beaver ponds and returns you to your starting point at the bridge 0.7 km downstream.

333 SIBBALD VIEWPOINT TO SIBBALD LAKE — Map 21

Half-day hike
Equestrian
Distance 2.7 km
Topo map 82 O/2 Jumpingpound Creek

Access: 1. Sibbald Creek Trail (Hwy. 68) at Sibbald Viewpoint day-use area.
Access: 2. Sibbald Creek Trail (Hwy. 68) at Sibbald Lake day-use area.
Also accessible from loop "C" and loop "A" of Sibbald Lake campground.

This trail connects visitors to Sibbald Viewpoint day-use area with the plethora of trails accessible from Sibbald Lake recreation area, including Ole Buck loop, Sibbald Flat interpretive trail, Eagle Hill and Deer Ridge trails. Try this walk on a quiet day in the off season or in the evening when the hordes of visitors have all packed up and driven home to Calgary or else retired to their campsite for the night. Then, if you tread quietly, you might just see the Bateman Creek beavers who, following their secret ways through the willow bushes to the lake, come to claim their territory.

At the trail sign, follow the trail out to the bank top and turn right. Two strategically-placed seats allow contemplation of the big meadow to the west which is that cows' paradise Sibbald Flat. Named after Frank Sibbald who introduced cattle grazing to the area in 1890, the meadow was once the favorite gathering place of the buffalo and other ungulates whose presence in large numbers has attracted hunters to the area since prehistoric times.

Their campsites, located on the terrace above the meadow between Sibbald Lake access road and Powderface Trail (Hwy.), were thoroughly investigated and all artifacts removed before reconstruction of the present highway in 1981. The prehistoric site turned out to be particularly important, apparently the only site in Canada found to contain fluted point tradition artifacts in good stratigraphic context.

Three hundred metres from the trailhead the trail crosses the highway. Edge around the perimeter of the cutblock — a dismal scene of charred stumps and log piles — then bear right into pine forest by the side of Bateman Creek. This is also the boundary of Sibbald Lake campground. Pass Ole Buck Loop trail to right and 4 four trails to left connecting with "C" loop and "A" loop. After a gap of perhaps 0.25 km, 3 trails to left connect with the tenting area, the last one being the major access route between the tenting area and Sibbald Lake which lies just a few steps away beyond a strip of meadow. You can either walk clockwise round the lakeshore and mount the steps leading to Sibbald Lake day-use area parking lot, or, just before you reach the picnic area loop road, turn left onto a trail leading to "B" loop eventually. Follow it for just a few metres, then turn right onto a trail which crosses both loops of the picnic road and a stretch of meadow en route to the day-use area parking lot.

Sibbald Lake on a quiet day.

334 SIBBALD VIEWPOINT TO TOM SNOW TRAIL — Map 21

Half-day hike
Equestrian
3 km to west access
4 km to east access
Height loss 30 m
Topo map 82 O/2 Jumpingpound Creek

Access: Sibbald Creek Trail (Hwy. 68) at Sibbald Viewpoint day-use area. Also accessible from Tom Snow trail (#324) at 2 locations, and the eastern terminus of #333 Sibbald Viewpoint to Sibbald Lake.

This is an unofficial but extremely useful link which makes use of existing cutlines, logging roads and exploration roads.

It starts by following route #333 out to the edge of the high bank. Turn left, then almost immediately right onto a wide sandy track lined with wind-tattered aspens which descends to valley bottom. Thanks to beavers damming Sibbald Creek upstream, the east end of Sibbald Flat is cut off from the main body of it by a chain of ponds, puddles and swamps and you'll be lucky to escape with dry feet. On the far side of this impasse, the road, lightly imprinted on grass, follows the edge of trees lining Jumpingpound Creek to the fringe of the reclaimed campground where you should turn first left onto another old road which fords Jumpingpound Creek. The road passes beneath a cutline climbing the steep bank and joins it on the bank top. Where you go next depends on your destination.

TO DAWSON DAY-USE AREA Walk up the cutline and turn down the next road to the right. Just after the right-angled bend to the left, a road to right — difficult to spot at the junction because of slash piled across it — descends the bank to Sibbald Flat and could, if you wished, be used as an alternative way out of the meadow. A few metres beyond this junction you arrive at a second junction identified by red markers as Tom Snow trail (straight, right). Turn right for Dawson day-use area.

TO THOMAS ROAD Walk up the cutline for a few metres, then turn left onto a road which intersects another cutline and describes a semi-circle past a pond in a meadow back onto the second cutline. Turn left. Follow the straight line of the cutline for 1 km to where red markers on trees signal the meeting with Tom Snow trail (cutline straight ahead, trail to right). Keep straight if Thomas Road or Moose Creek is your objective.

Deer Ridge (right) from Sibbald Flat.

Thomas Road bridge over the Jumpingpound River.

335 THOMAS ROAD TO TOM SNOW TRAIL — Map 21

Half-day hike, backpack
Easy ski, equestrian, bike
Distance 2.5 km
Height loss 43 m
Topo map 82 0/2 Jumpingpound Creek

Access: Sibbald Creek Trail (Hwy. 68) at Thomas Road, 7 km west of Kananaskis Country boundary.
Also accessible from route #336, Pinegrove Group Campground to Thomas Road, and from Tom Snow trail (#324) at Moose Creek.

This unofficial, unsigned road offers the shortest route from any highway onto the Moose Creek section of the Tom Snow trail. When Thomas Road is open for wood cutting or Christmas tree cutting, you can drive a farther 1.5 km to the road junction with route #336 on the bank top. Usually though, the road is barricaded and you must use non-mechanized forms of travel to arrive at the same place.

Turn right at the junction and descend a steep hill to the bridge over Jumpingpound Creek which, it should be noted, is unsafe for motor vehicles. The road mimics the windings of Jumpingpound Creek downstream to the confluence with Coxhill Creek, then turns up Coxhill Creek where the sudden appearance of red markers marks the merger with Tom Snow trail in the meadows. If going through to Dawson day-use area, keep right on Thomas Road. For Moose Creek, turn left onto the overgrown Moose Creek exploration road which fords the creek.

336 PINEGROVE GROUP CAMPGROUND TO THOMAS ROAD — Map 21

Day hike
Equestrian, bike
Distance 5 km
Height gain 46 m
Topo map 82 0/2 Jumpingpound Creek

Access: **1. Sibbald Creek Trail (Hwy. 68) at Pinegrove group campground.**
Access: **2. Homestead Road at Jumpingpound Creek.**

This unoffical, unmarked trail could be considered part of a hypothetical long-distance trail along Jumpingpound Creek between Pinetop day-use area and Dawson day-use area. Sections between roads make good half-hour strolls.

Walk (or drive) all the way down the Pinegrove group campground access road to the old campground whose attractive setting on a rocky bluff overlooking the confluence of Jumpingpound and Bryant Creeks entices you into spending some time exploring the environs before travelling on. The cabin out on the point was built by Calgary Correctional Institute inmates and serves as a more cozy alternative for lunch than the newfangled picnic shelter nearby.

The route resumes behind the toilets. A grassed-over road at this point, it runs out into the big meadow behind the campground, turns left and crosses a corduroy bridge over a sluggish stream which is Bryant Creek. A little farther on, an ill-defined road heads south across Jumpingpound Creek. Keep right here, aiming for the west end of the meadow which is filling up with charcoal-colored bushes known as the black birch or greasewood, one of nature's more unpleasant creations which unless controlled by fire quickly smothers grazing land. The road, well defined now, enters forest and in less than half a kilometre comes to an abrupt end above Homestead Road, severed by a road cut. A trail to your left joins the road close to the bridge over Jumpingpound Creek.

Cross Homestead Road to a former campground access road opposite. As soon as you've slipped through a gap in the gate, turn right and follow the fence trail up the bank into a young pine plantation. Alternatively, turn right up the road and enter the plantation via the next dirt road to left. Bikers should continue along this road all the way to Thomas Road. Hikers and equestrians are strongly advised to use a grassed-over road — obviously a continuation of the road you followed earlier —which wanders pleasantly along the bank top. After 1 km it comes within spitting distance of the dirt road, touches the parking lot for christmas tree cutters briefly, then swings away again. Disregard an access road and intersecting N.W.-S.E. cutline descending to Jumpingpound Creek. A few metres on, it joins the dirt road at a 4-way junction and follows it around every inundation of the bank top to the junction with Thomas Road.

337 JUMPINGPOUND LOOP — Map 21

Half-day hike, equestrian
Easy ski
Distance 9 km
Height gain 140 m
Maximum elevation 1433 m
Topo map 82 O/2 Jumpingpound Creek

Access: **1. Sibbald Creek Trail (Hwy. 68) at Pinetop day-use area.**
Access: **2. Sibbald Creek Trail (Hwy. 68) at Jumpingpound day-use area.**
Access: **3. Sibbald Creek Trail (Hwy. 68) at Pinegrove group campground.**

Connecting 2 day-use areas and a group camp, Jumpingpound Loop is an excellent choice for the short days of spring and fall; often you can hike here right through the winter. Skiers might find sufficient snow on sheltered sections along the river bank.

Starting behind the picnic tables at Pinetop day-use area, the trail parallels the big loops of Jumpingpound Creek to Jumpingpound day-use area which is identified by picnic tables and a gravelled trail to right leading to the parking lot. (If you want to cut 4 km off the loop, a shortcut trail leaves the far side of the parking lot, crosses the highway and climbs uphill to join the return leg in the dip east of the exploration road.) The main trail continues along the top of the river bank, dipping steeply in 2 places to cross side creeks on logs. Keep left after a third creek crossing in a small clearing and arrive shortly afterwards at Pinegrove group campground access road by the side of the newest campground loop. Turn right and walk up the access road to the highway.

The return trail — initially a logging road — starts from the north side of the highway a little east of the access road. A little way in make 2 right turns in quick succession; first onto a S.W.-N.E. cutline and then onto a new trail which traverses predominently aspen hillsides 45 m above the highway, dipping 5 times into densely-wooded side creeks and rising occasionally onto open slopes which, though of modest height above the highway, offer clear views of Moose Mountain to the S.W. Bisect an exploration road, the shortcut trail from Jumpingpound day-use area, various cutlines and a logging road running north from Jumpingpound Ranger Station. Shortly after passing the ranger station, the trail returns you to your starting point on the highway opposite Pinetop day-use area access road.

Close to the aforementioned S.W.-N.E. cutline, the trail passes underneath some magnificent specimens of white spruce growing in a damp hollow. The trees may look like Englemann spruce, but if you examine the cones, you'll find the scales are fan-shaped with completely smooth margins. Farther east, between the exploration road and the junction with the shortcut trail from Jumpingpound day-use area, look for a stand of douglas firs which are easily recognizable by their massive girth and deeply-seamed bark.

KEY MAP

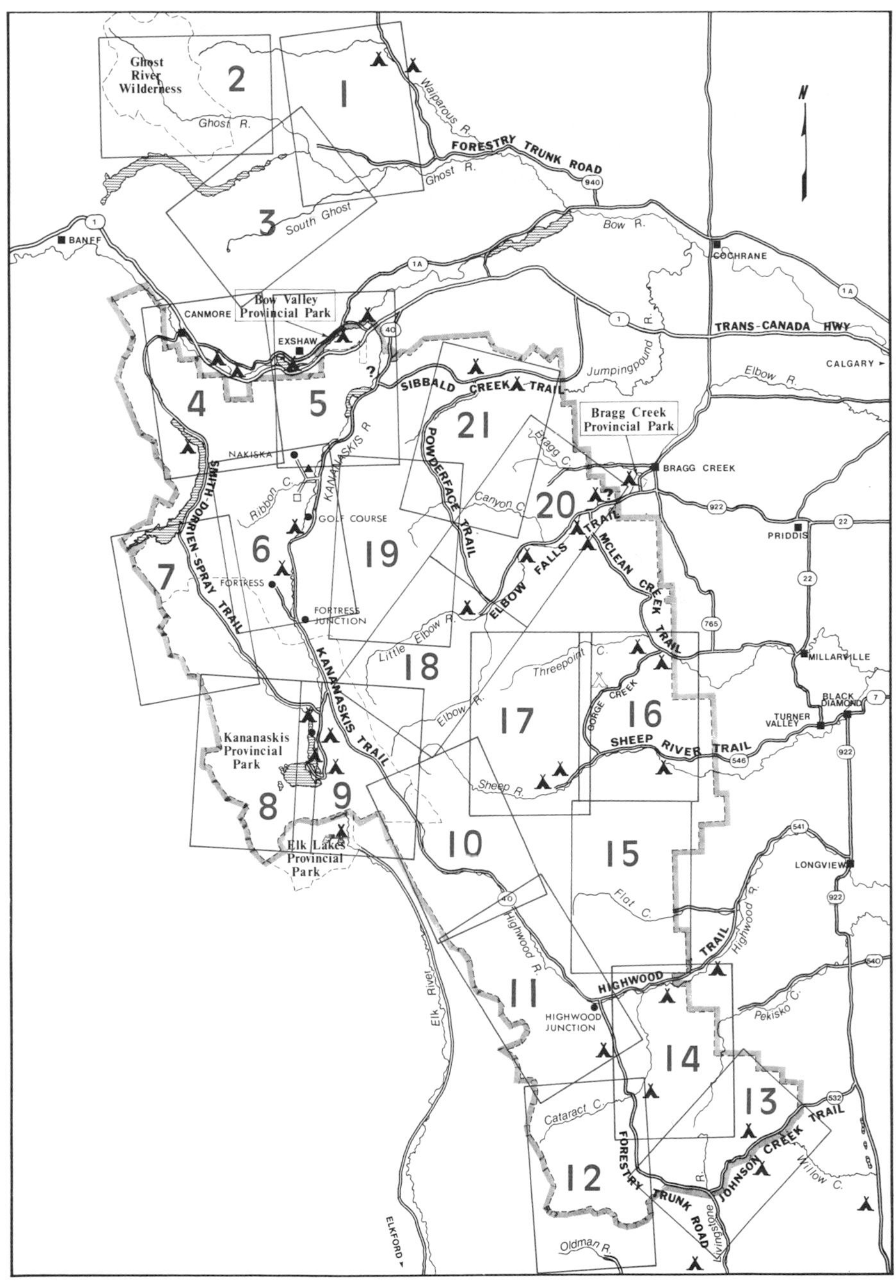

Ghost River Wilderness
Ghost R.
South Ghost
Waiparous R.
FORESTRY TRUNK ROAD
BANFF
CANMORE
Bow Valley Provincial Park
EXSHAW
COCHRANE
TRANS-CANADA HWY
CALGARY
Bow R.
Jumpingpound R.
Elbow R.
SIBBALD CREEK TRAIL
POWDERFACE TRAIL
Bragg Creek Provincial Park
BRAGG CREEK
PRIDDIS
NAKISKA
KANANASKIS R.
Ribbon C.
GOLF COURSE
Canyon C.
Bragg C.
ELBOW FALLS TRAIL
McLEAN CREEK TRAIL
SMITH-DORRIEN-SPRAY TRAIL
FORTRESS
FORTRESS JUNCTION
Little Elbow R.
KANANASKIS TRAIL
MILLARVILLE
BLACK DIAMOND
TURNER VALLEY
Threepoint C.
GORGE CREEK
SHEEP RIVER TRAIL
Elbow R.
Sheep R.
Kananaskis Provincial Park
Elk Lakes Provincial Park
LONGVIEW
Flat C.
Highwood R.
HIGHWOOD TRAIL
HIGHWOOD JUNCTION
Elk River
Pekisko C.
Cataract C.
JOHNSON CREEK TRAIL
Willow C.
Livingstone R.
Oldman R.
ELKFORD

MAP 1 — WAIPAROUS

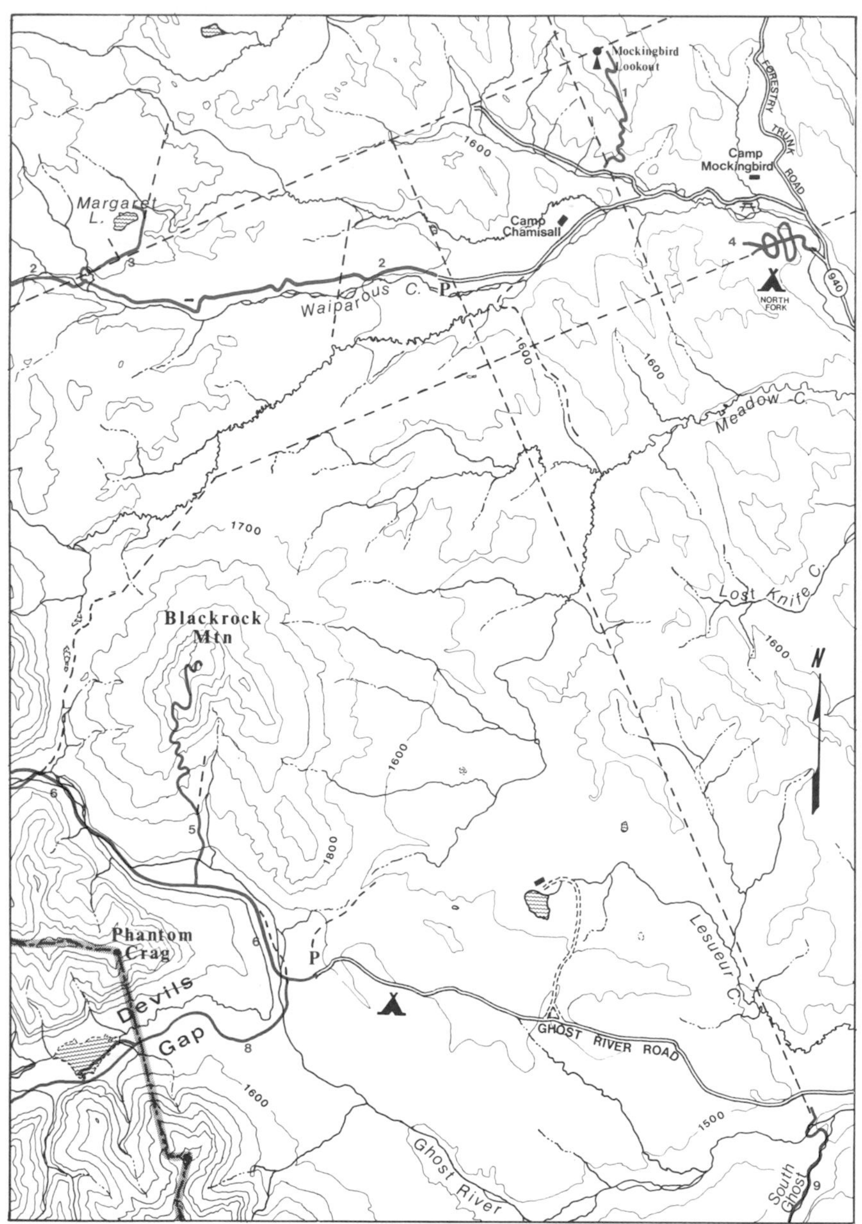

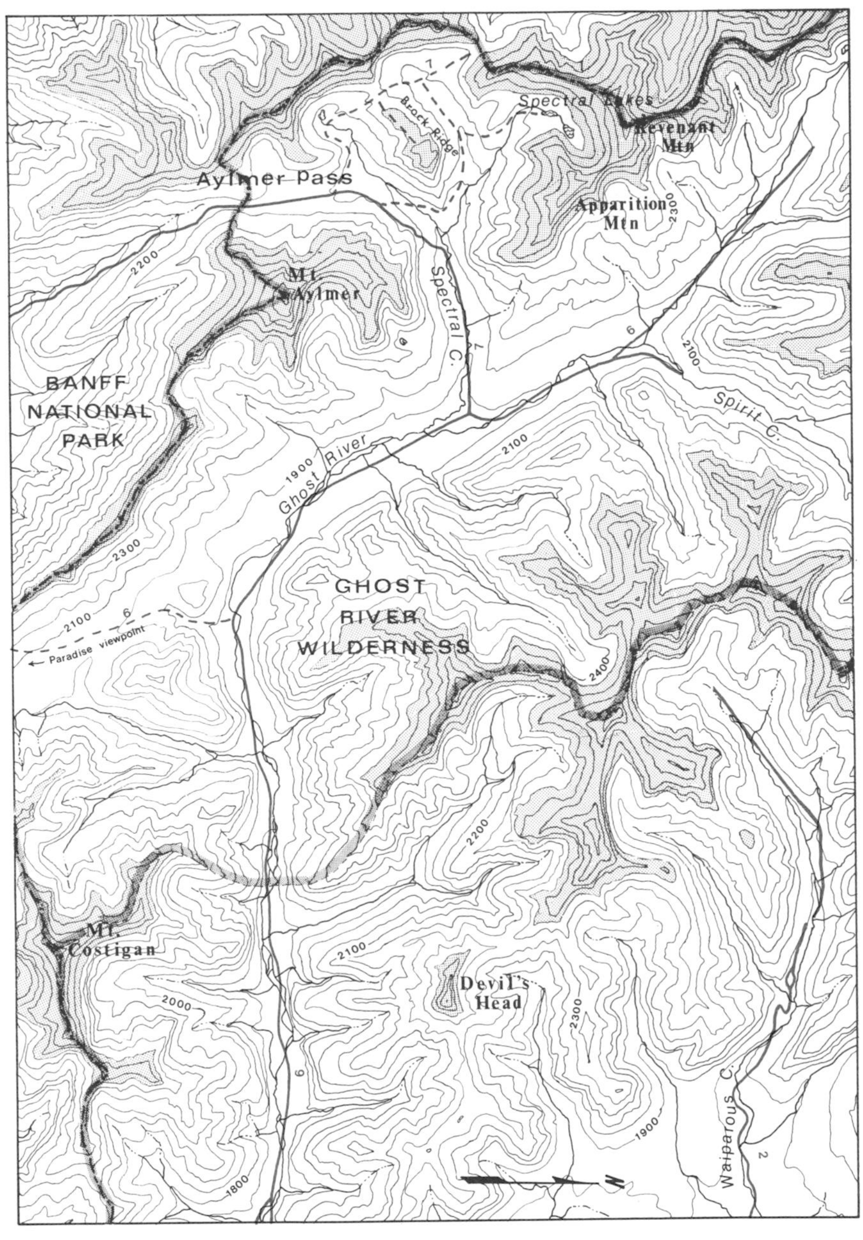
Aylmer Pass
Brock Ridge
Spectral Lakes
Revenant Mtn
Apparition Mtn
Mt. Aylmer
Spectral C.
BANFF NATIONAL PARK
Ghost River
Spirit C.
GHOST RIVER WILDERNESS
Paradise viewpoint
Mt. Costigan
Devil's Head
Waiparous C.

MAP 3 — SOUTH GHOST

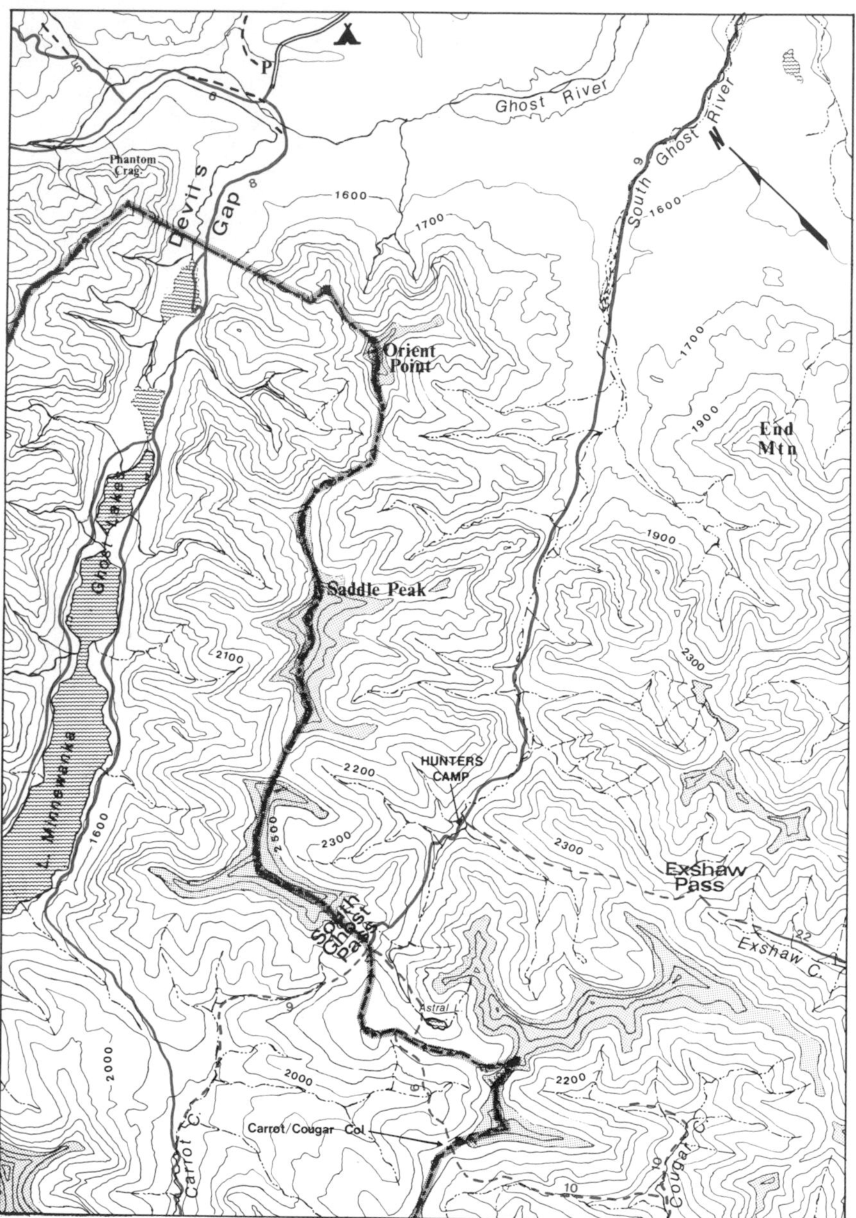

WEST CANMORE — MAP 4

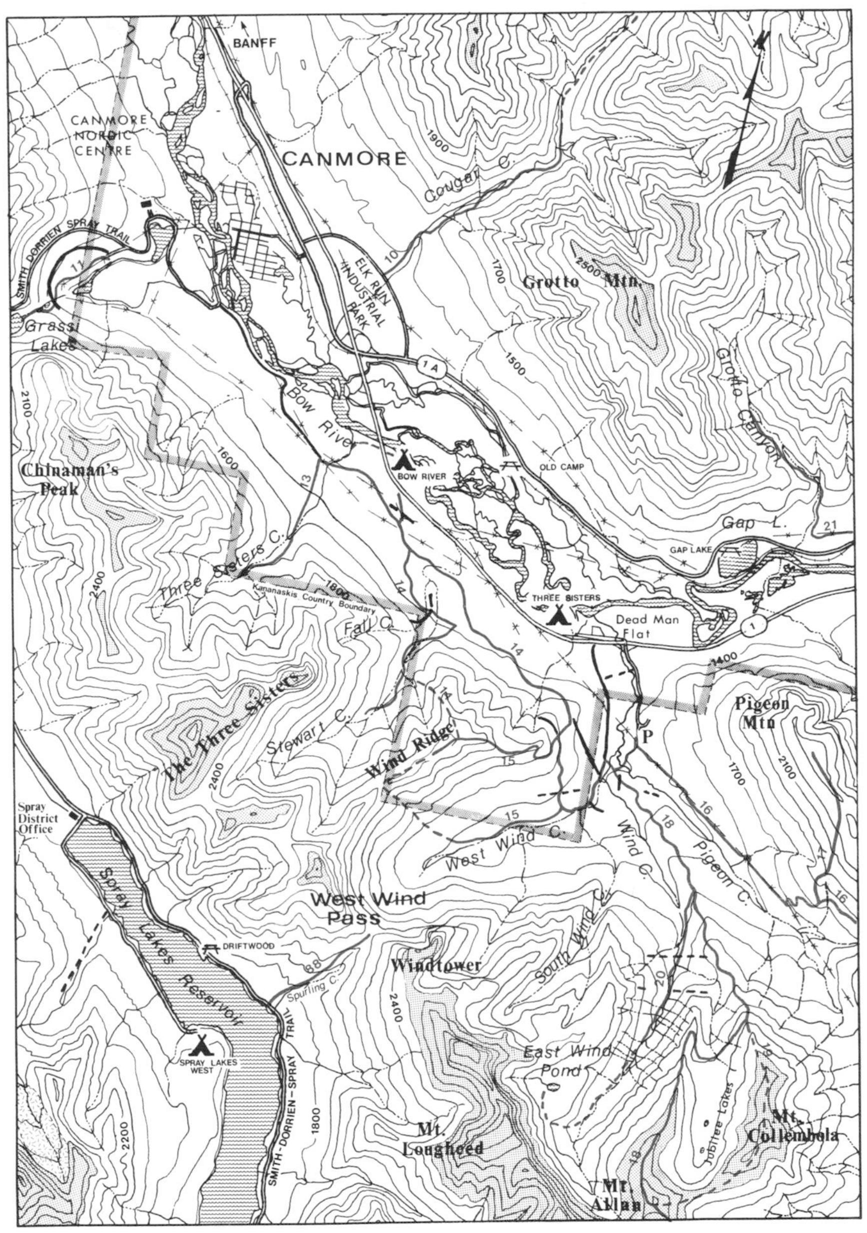

MAP 5 — EAST CANMORE

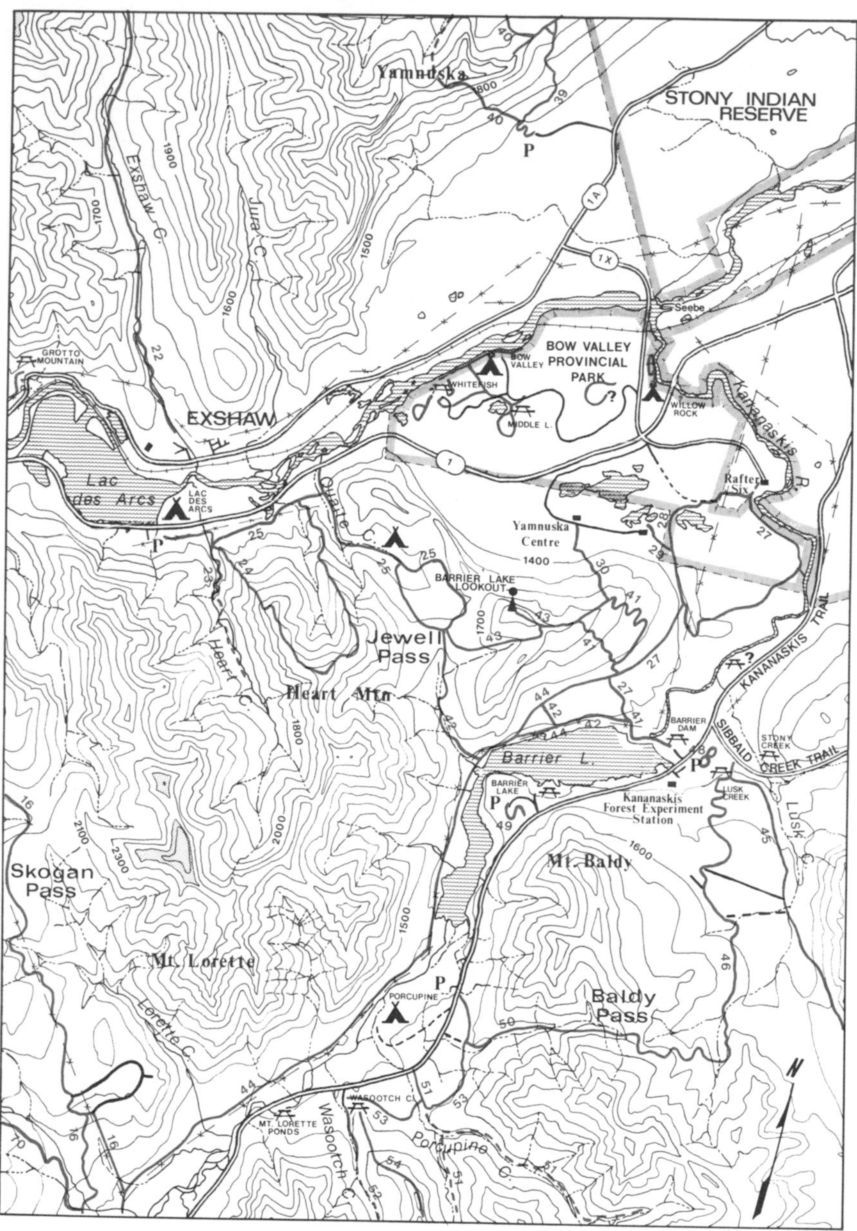

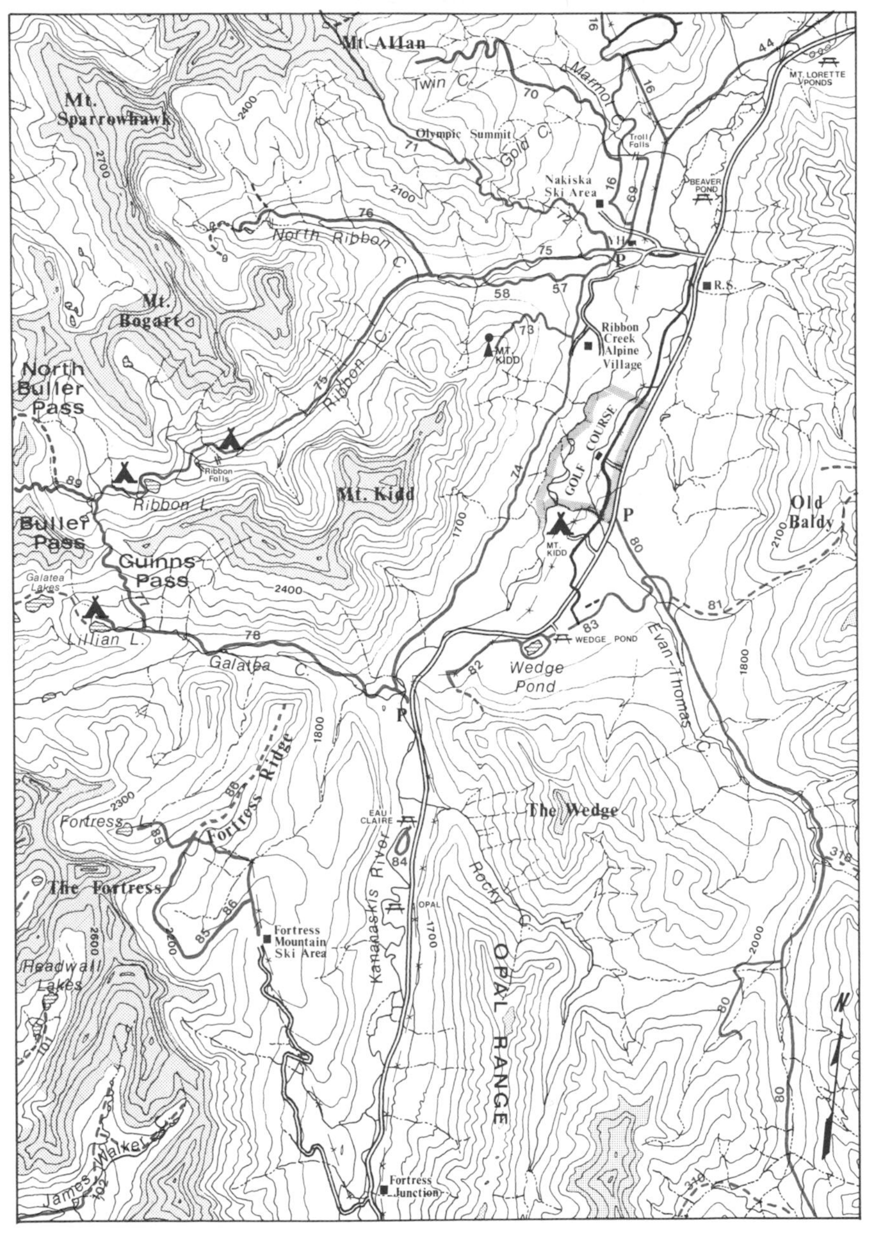
Mt. Allan
Mt. Sparrowhawk
Twin C.
Marmot C.
Olympic Summit
Gold C.
Troll Falls
MT. LORETTE PONDS
BEAVER POND
Nakiska Ski Area
North Ribbon C.
R.S.
Mt. Bogart
Ribbon Creek Alpine Village
MT. KIDD
North Buller Pass
Ribbon C.
GOLF COURSE
Ribbon Falls
Mt. Kidd
Ribbon L.
Old Baldy
Buller Pass
Guinns Pass
Galatea Lakes
Lillian L.
WEDGE POND
Wedge Pond
Galatea C.
Evan-Thomas C.
Fortress Ridge
Fortress L.
The Wedge
EAU CLAIRE
The Fortress
Kananaskis River
OPAL
Rocky C.
Fortress Mountain Ski Area
OPAL RANGE
Headwall Lakes
James Walker C.
Fortress Junction

MAP 7 — SMITH-DORRIEN—SPRAY

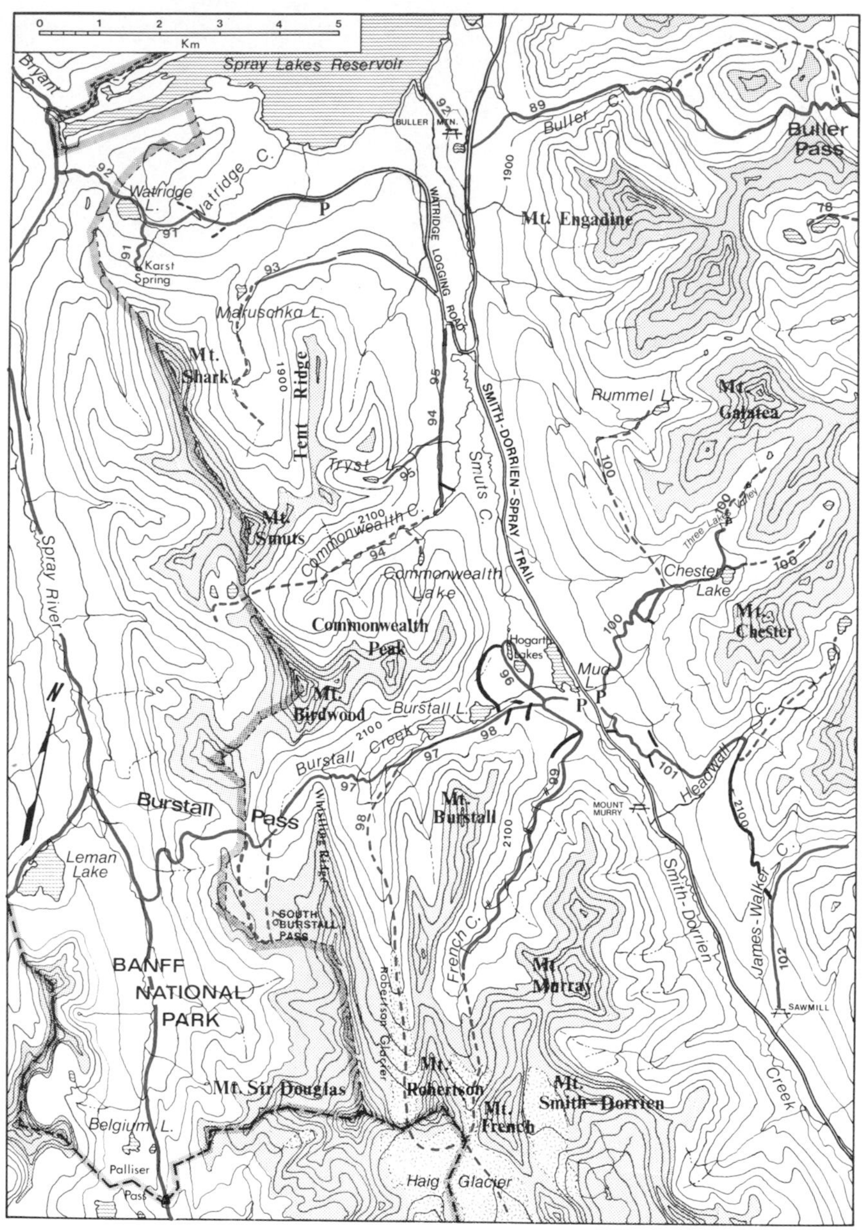

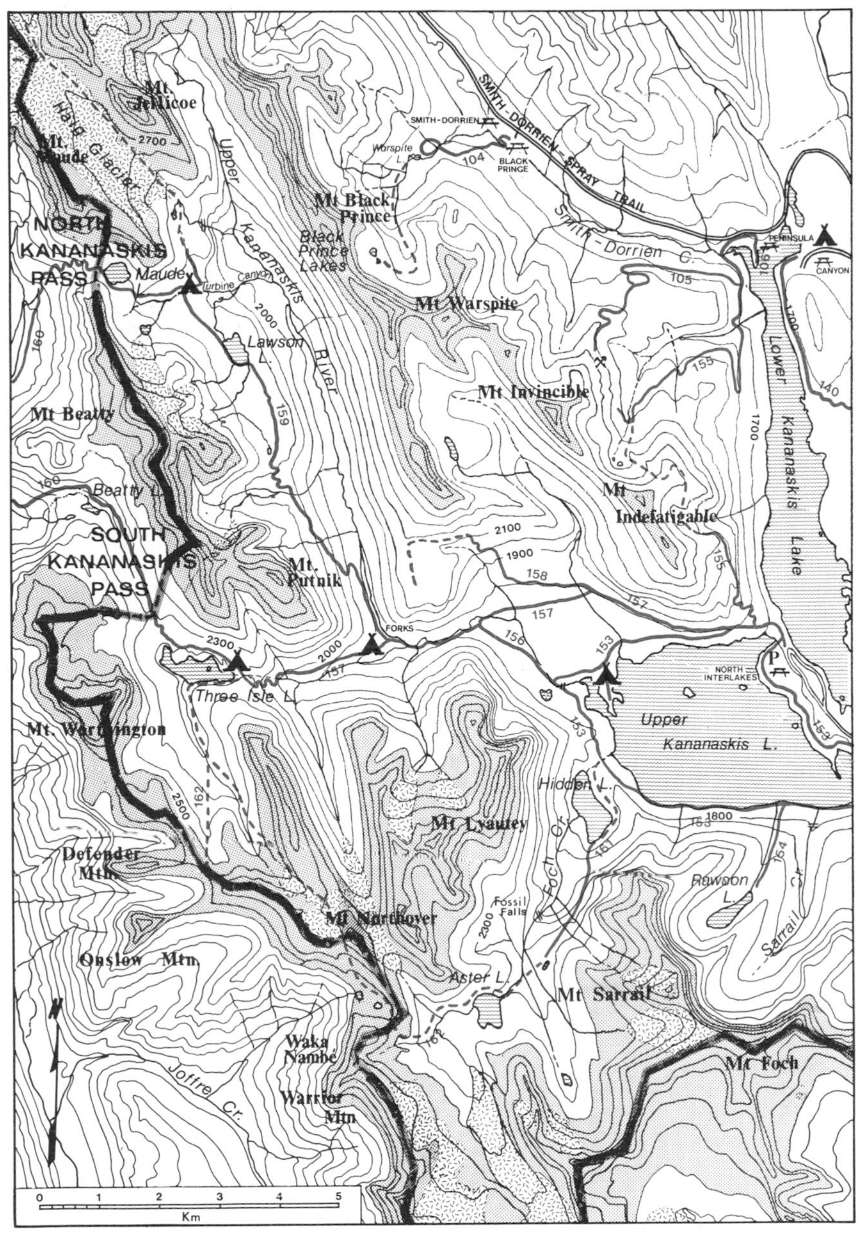
Mt. Jellicoe
Haig Glacier
Mt. Maude
NORTH KANANASKIS PASS
Maude L.
Turbine Canyon
Upper Kananaskis River
Lawson L.
Mt Black Prince
Black Prince Lakes
Warspite L.
SMITH-DORRIEN
BLACK PRINCE
SMITH-DORRIEN-SPRAY TRAIL
Smith-Dorrien C.
PENINSULA
CANYON
Mt Warspite
Mt Invincible
Mt Indefatigable
Lower Kananaskis Lake
Mt Beatty
Beatty L.
SOUTH KANANASKIS PASS
Mt. Putnik
FORKS
Three Isle L.
NORTH INTERLAKES
Upper Kananaskis L.
Mt. Worthington
Hidden L.
Foch Cr.
Mt Lyautey
Defender Mtn.
Fossil Falls
Rawson L.
Sarrail Cr.
Mt Northover
Onslow Mtn.
Aster L.
Mt Sarrail
Waka Nambe
Warrior Mtn
Joffre Cr.
Mt Foch
Km

MAP 9 — LOWER KANANASKIS PROVINCIAL PARK

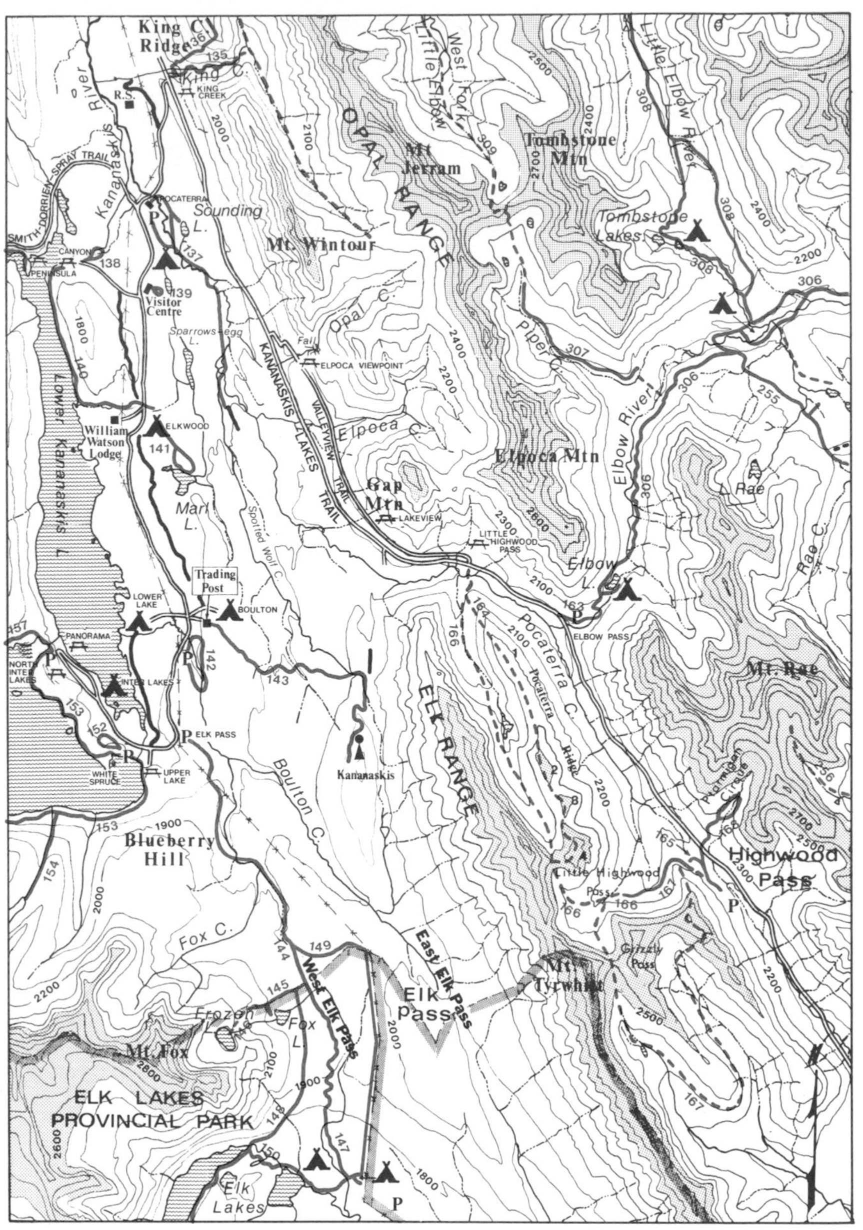

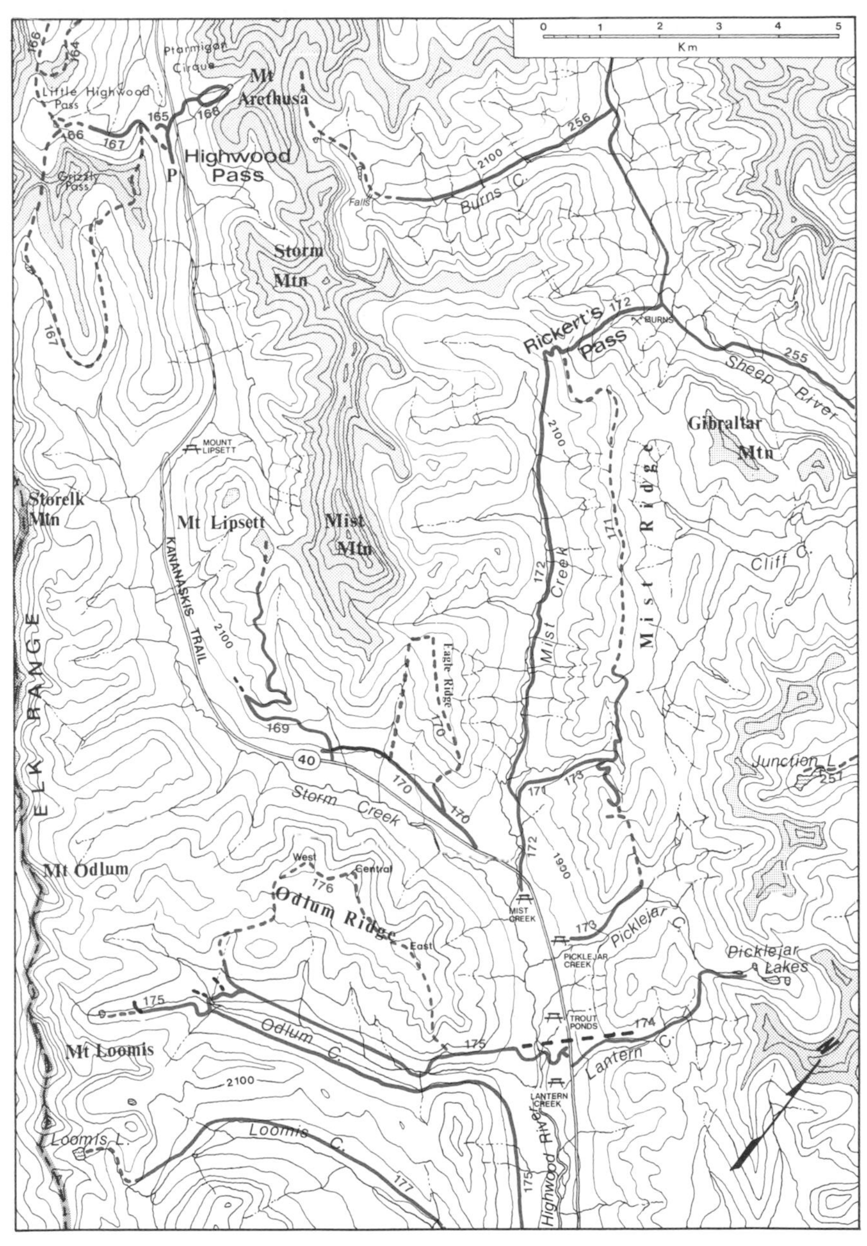

0 1 2 3 4 5
Km
Ptarmigan Cirque
Mt Arethusa
Little Highwood Pass
Highwood Pass
Grizzly Pass
Falls
Burns C.
Storm Mtn
Rickert's Pass
BURNS
Sheep River
Gibraltar Mtn
MOUNT LIPSETT
Storelk Mtn
Mt Lipsett
Mist Mtn
KANANASKIS TRAIL
Mist Creek
Mist Ridge
Cliff C.
Eagle Ridge
ELK RANGE
Junction L.
Storm Creek
Mt Odlum
West
Central
East
Odlum Ridge
MIST CREEK
PICKLEJAR CREEK
Picklejar C.
Picklejar Lakes
TROUT PONDS
Odlum C.
Mt Loomis
Lantern C.
LANTERN CREEK
Loomis L.
Loomis C.
Highwood River

MAP 11 — WEST HIGHWOOD

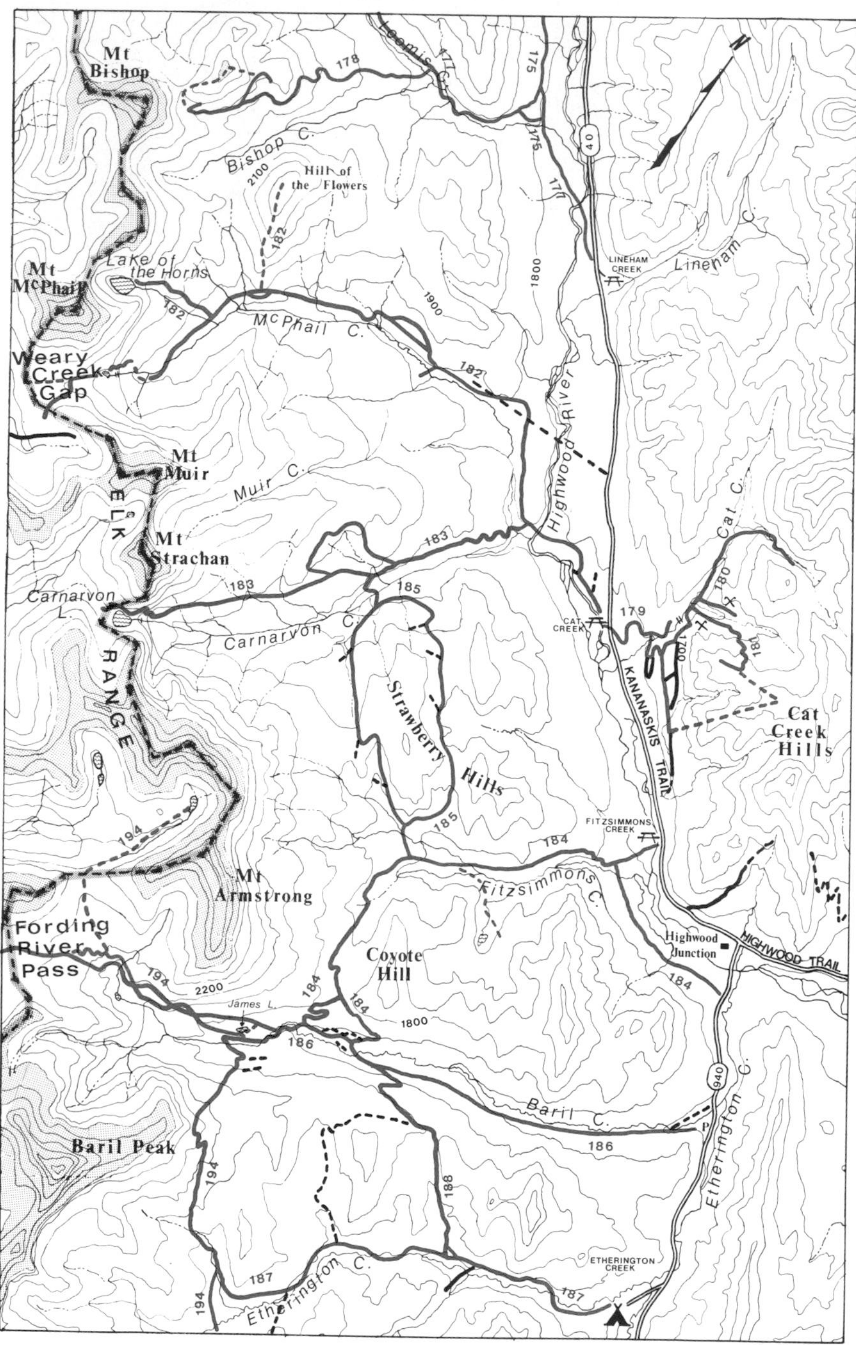

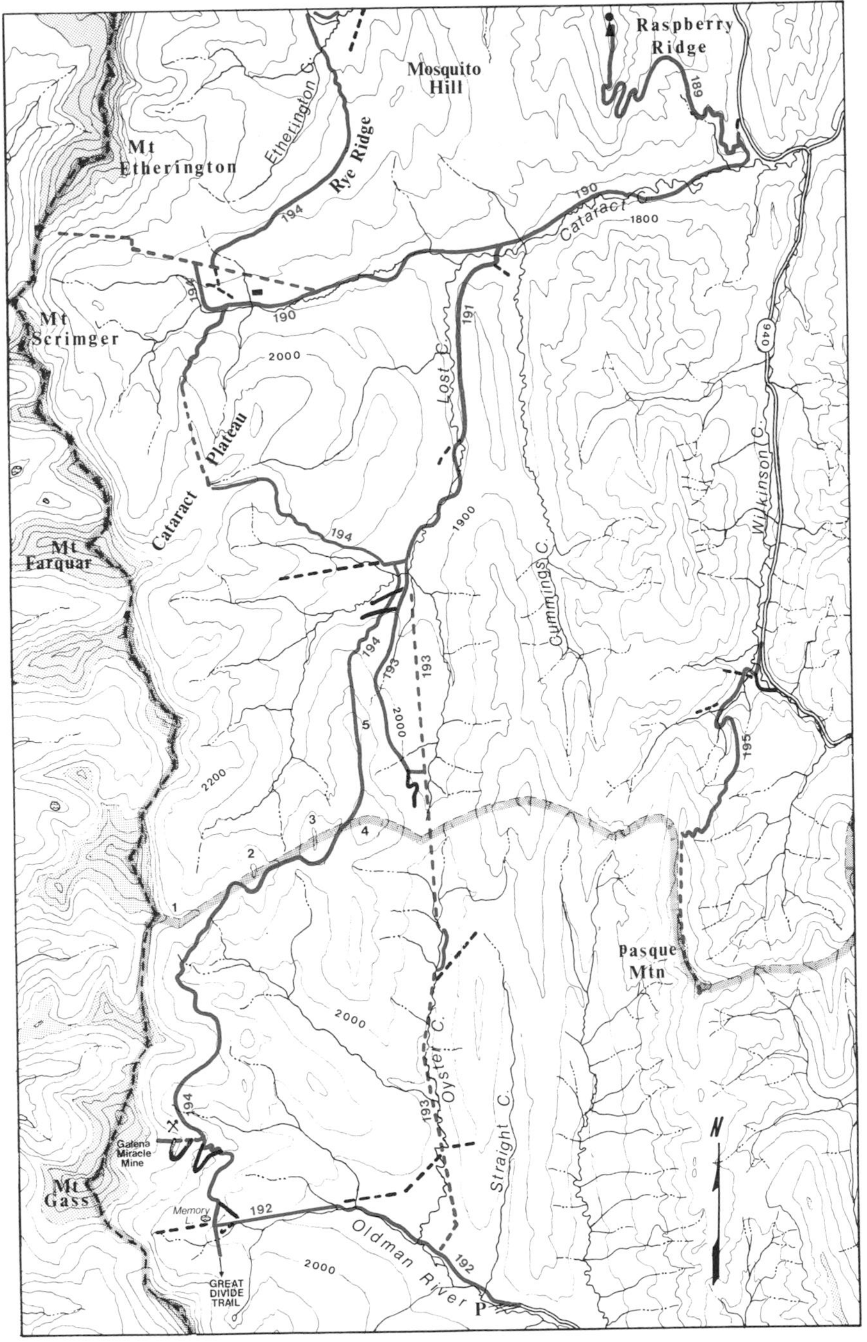
Raspberry Ridge
Mosquito Hill
Etherington C.
Rye Ridge
Mt Etherington
Mt Scrimger
Cataract Plateau
Cataract C.
Lost C.
Mt Farquar
Cummings C.
Wilkinson C.
Pasque Mtn
Oyster C.
Straight C.
Galena Miracle Mine
Mt Gass
Memory L.
GREAT DIVIDE TRAIL
Oldman River
P
N
189
190
191
192
193
194
195
940
1800
1900
2000
2200
1
2
3
4
5

MAP 13 — LIVINGSTONE

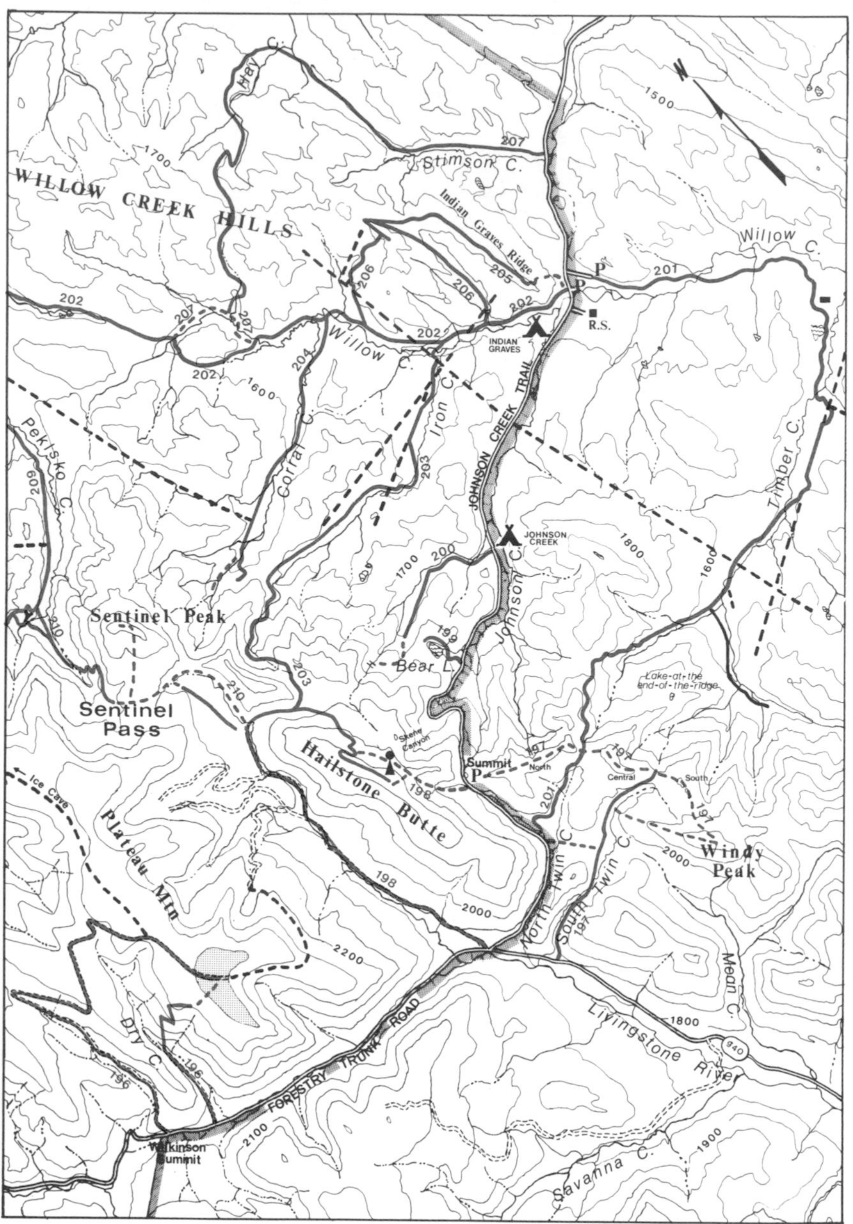

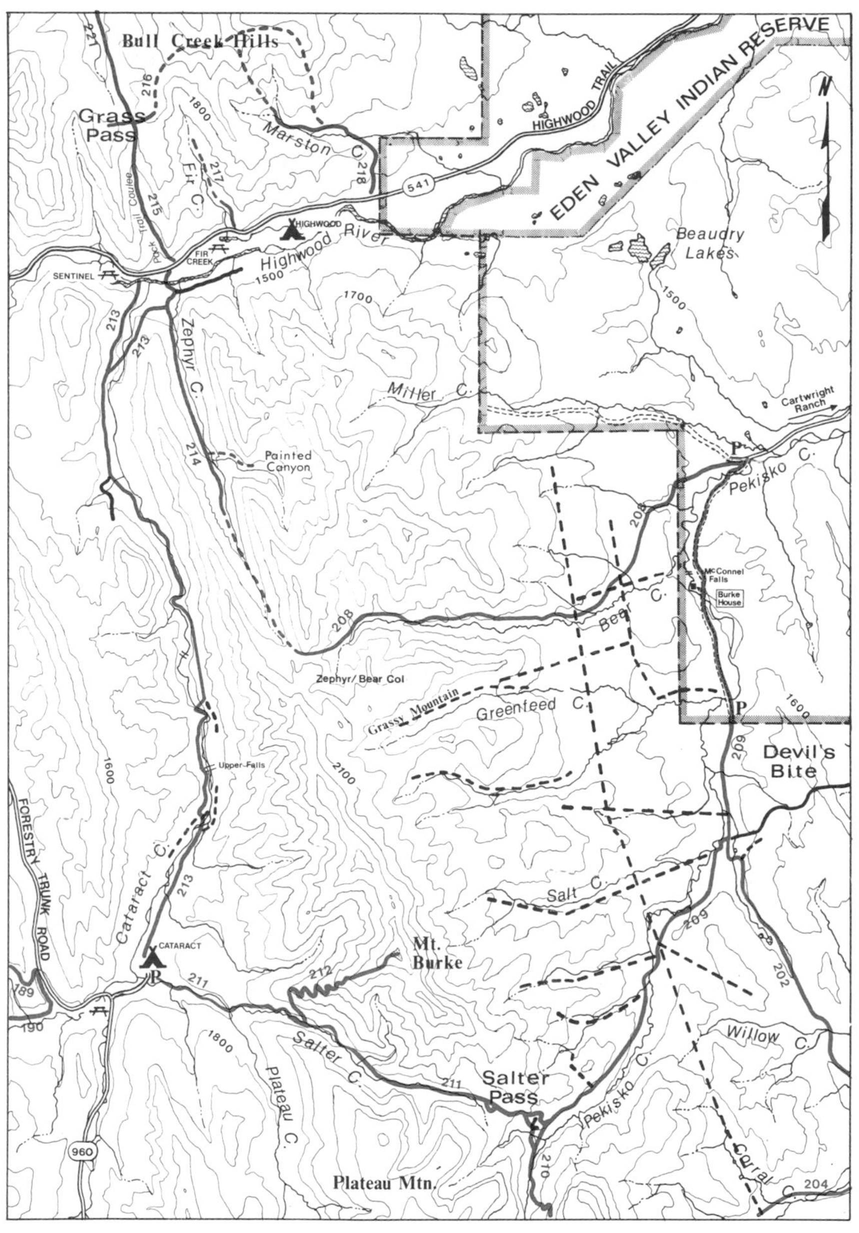
Bull Creek Hills
Grass Pass
Marston C.
Fir C.
Trail Coulee
Pack
HIGHWOOD TRAIL
EDEN VALLEY INDIAN RESERVE
N
HIGHWOOD
Highwood River
FIR CREEK
SENTINEL
Beaudry Lakes
Zephyr C.
Miller C.
Cartwright Ranch
Painted Canyon
Pekisko C.
McConnel Falls
Burke House
Bear C.
Zephyr/Bear Col
Grassy Mountain
Greenfeed C.
Devil's Bite
Upper Falls
FORESTRY TRUNK ROAD
Cataract C.
Salt C.
CATARACT
Mt. Burke
Willow C.
Salter C.
Plateau C.
Salter Pass
Pekisko C.
Corral C.
Plateau Mtn.
541
960

MAP 15 — FLAT CREEK

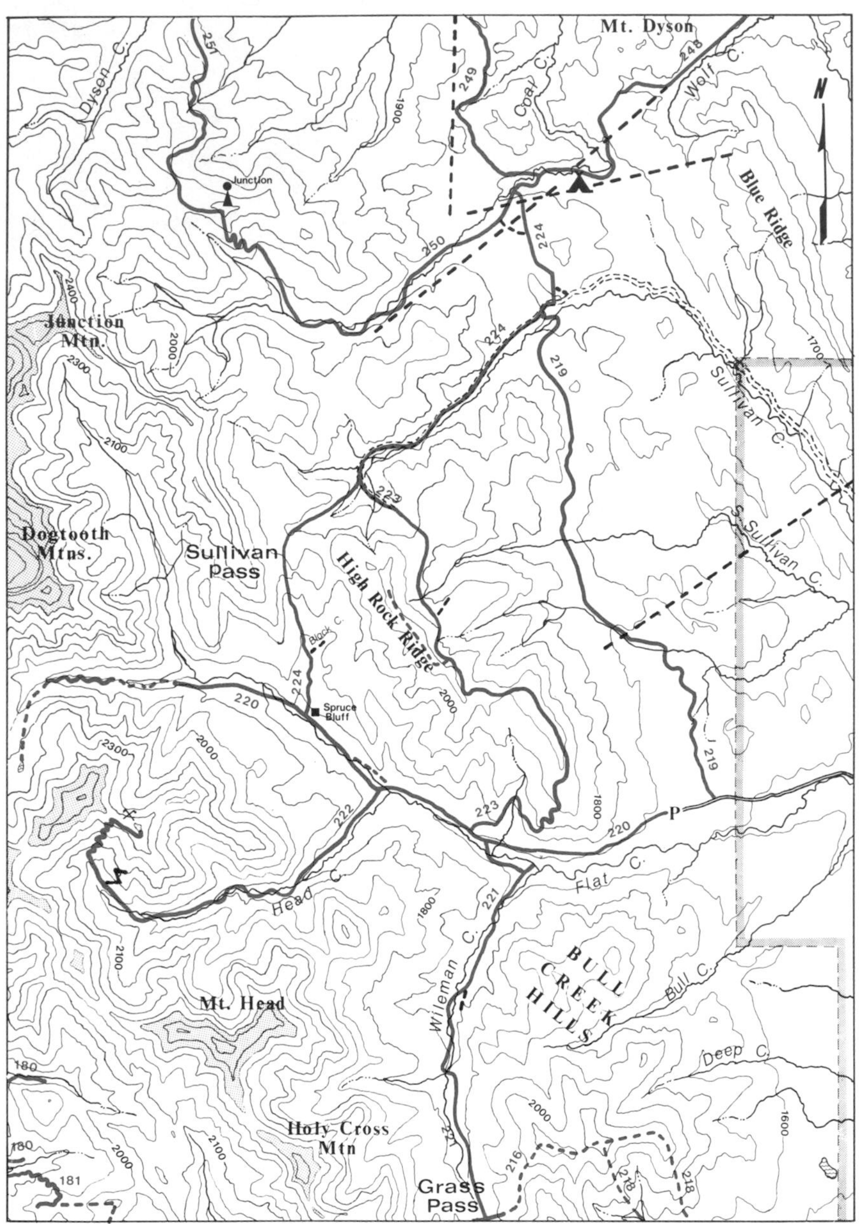

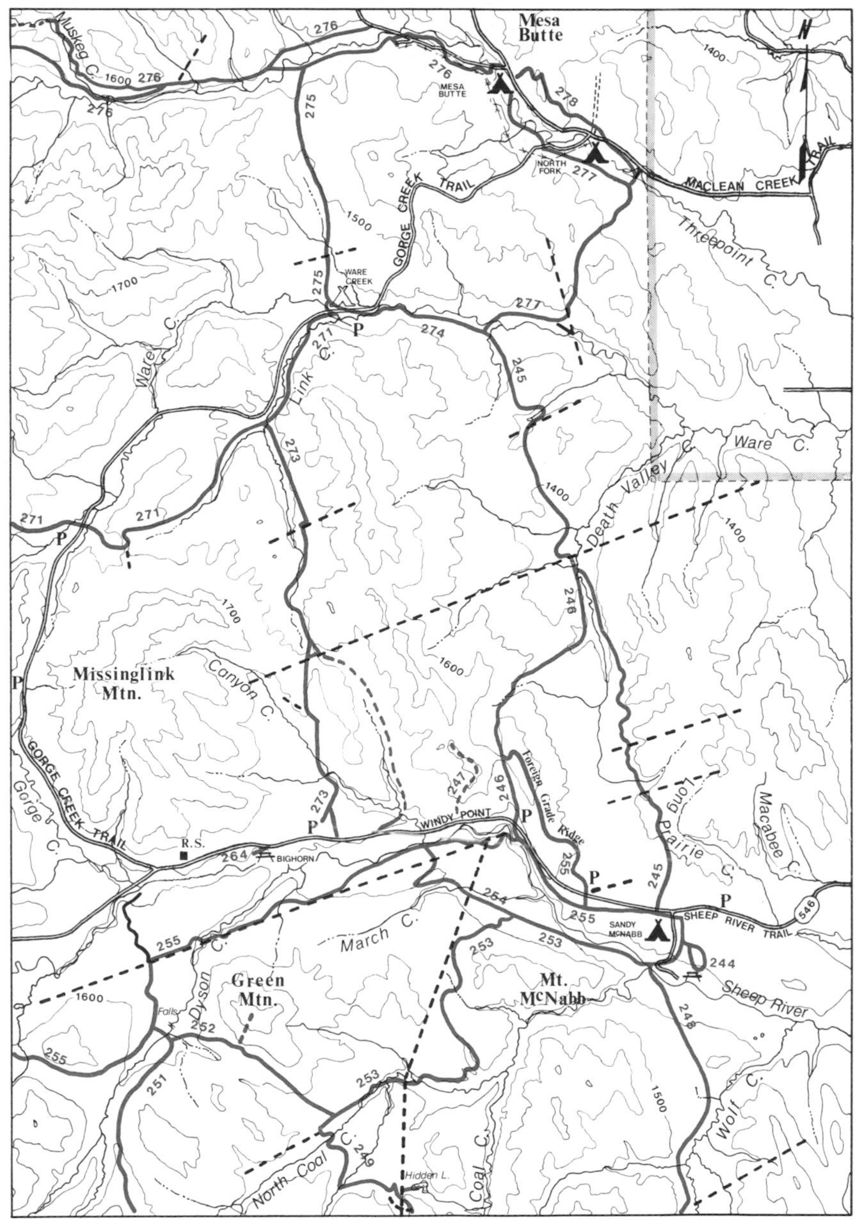

Mesa Butte
Muskeg C.
276
1600
275
MESA BUTTE
278
NORTH FORK
277
GORGE CREEK TRAIL
MACLEAN CREEK TRAIL
1400
Threepoint C.
1500
1700
WARE CREEK
Ware C.
271
Link C.
274
245
273
Ware C.
Death Valley C.
P
1400
Missinglink Mtn.
Canyon C.
1600
248
GORGE CREEK TRAIL
Gorge C.
Forgetmenot Ridge
Long Prairie C.
Macabee C.
247
246
WINDY POINT
R.S.
264
BIGHORN
255
254
SHEEP RIVER TRAIL
546
SANDY McNABB
253
March C.
Dyson C.
Green Mtn.
Mt. McNabb
244
Sheep River
Falls
252
251
1500
Wolf C.
North Coal C.
249
Hidden L.
Coal C.

MAP 17 — WEST SHEEP

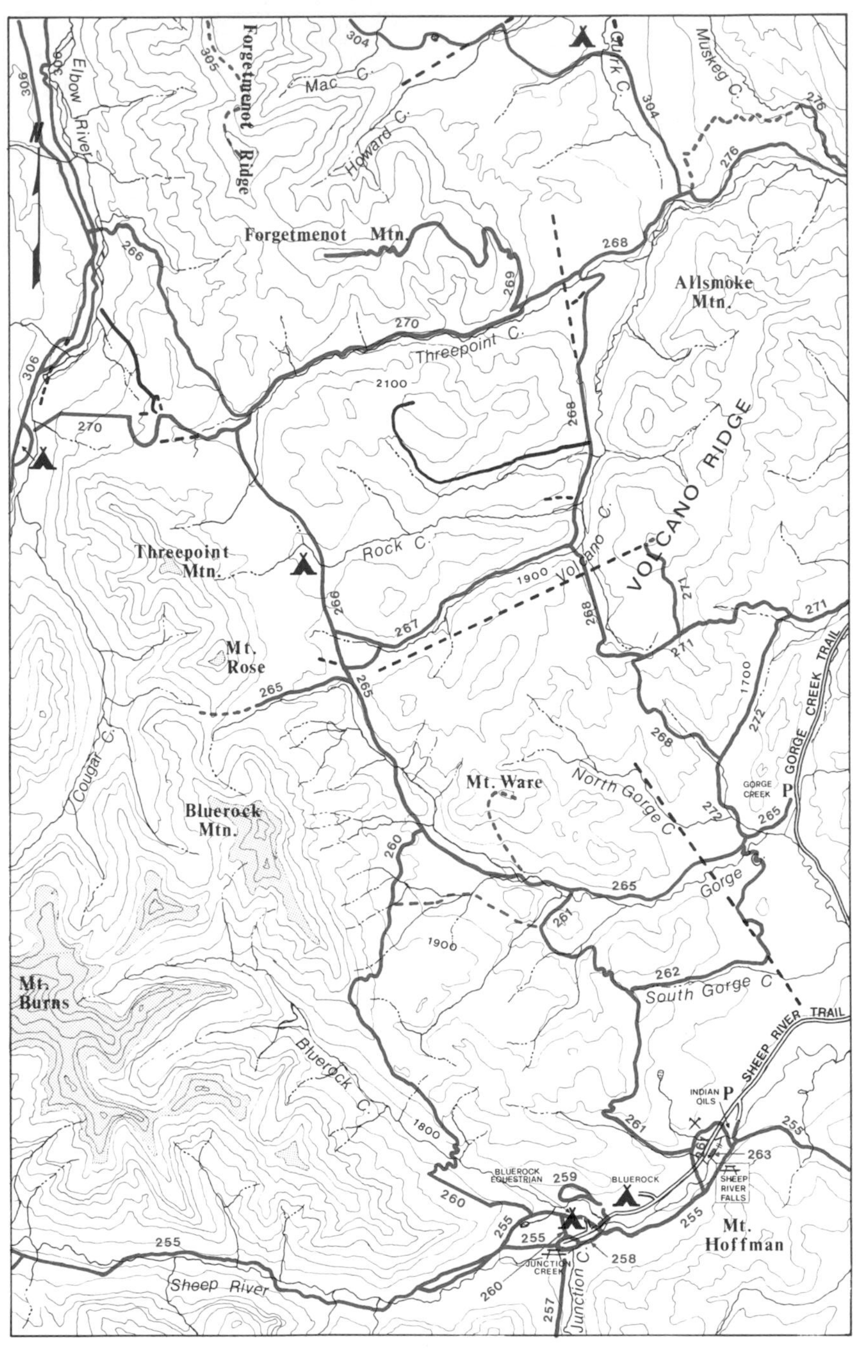

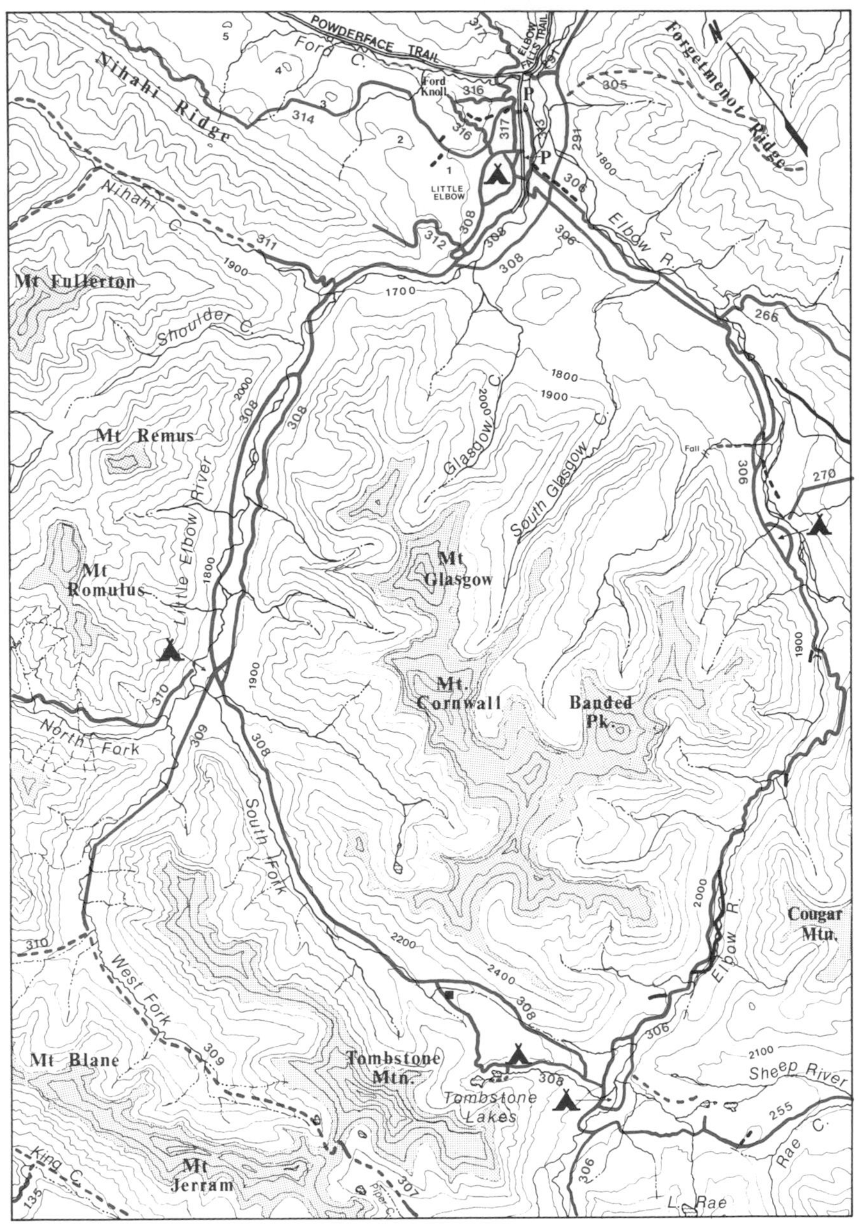
POWDERFACE TRAIL
Ford C.
Nihahi Ridge
Forgetmenot Ridge
Ford Knoll
LITTLE ELBOW
ELBOW FALLS TRAIL
Nihahi C.
Elbow R.
Mt Fullerton
Shoulder C.
Glasgow C.
South Glasgow C.
Mt Remus
Little Elbow River
Mt Glasgow
Mt Romulus
Fall
Mt. Cornwall
Banded Pk.
North Fork
South Fork
Cougar Mtn.
West Fork
Mt Blane
Tombstone Mtn.
Tombstone Lakes
Sheep River
Rae C.
King C.
Mt Jerram
Piper C.
L. Rae

MAP 19 — FISHER RANGE

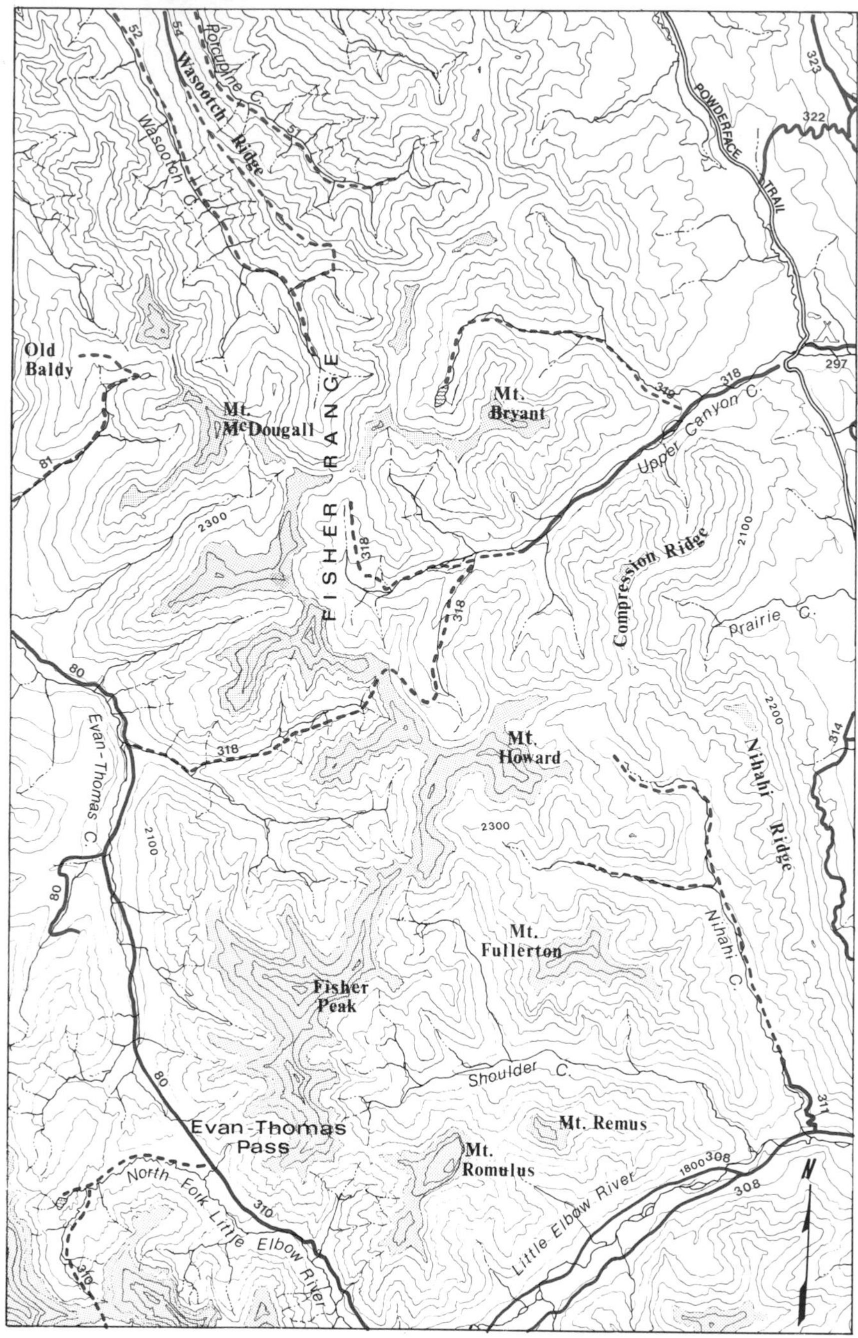

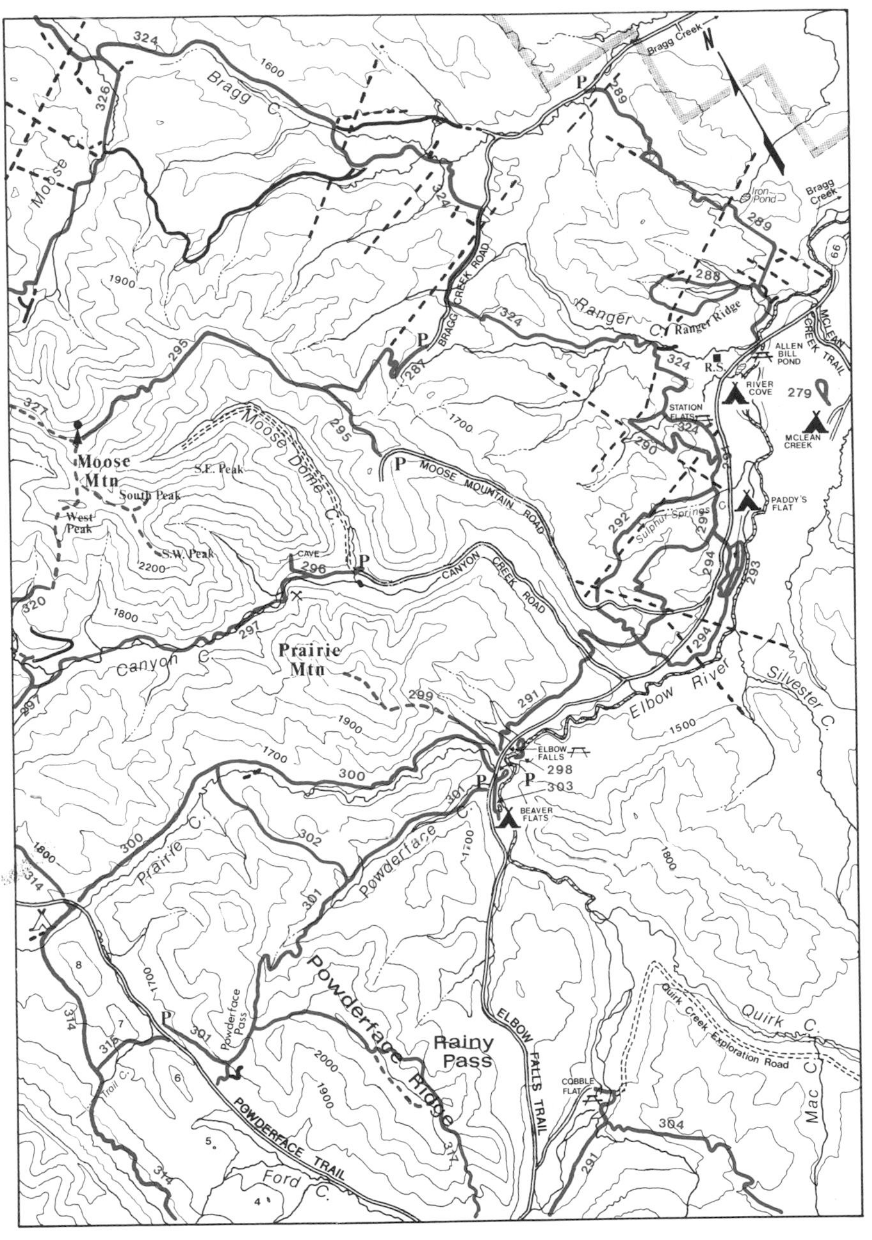
Bragg Creek
N
Bragg C.
Moose C.
Iron Pond
Bragg Creek
BRAGG CREEK ROAD
Ranger C.
Ranger Ridge
ALLEN BILL POND
R.S.
RIVER COVE
MCLEAN CREEK TRAIL
MCLEAN CREEK
STATION FLATS
Moose Mtn
S.E. Peak
South Peak
West Peak
S.W. Peak
Moose Dome C.
MOOSE MOUNTAIN ROAD
Sulphur Springs C.
PADDY'S FLAT
CAVE
CANYON CREEK ROAD
Canyon C.
Prairie Mtn
Elbow River
Silvester C.
ELBOW FALLS
BEAVER FLATS
Prairie C.
Powderface C.
Powderface Ridge
Powderface Pass
Rainy Pass
ELBOW FALLS TRAIL
Quirk C.
Quirk Creek Exploration Road
COBBLE FLAT
Mac C.
Trail C.
POWDERFACE TRAIL
Ford C.

MAP 21 — JUMPINGPOUND

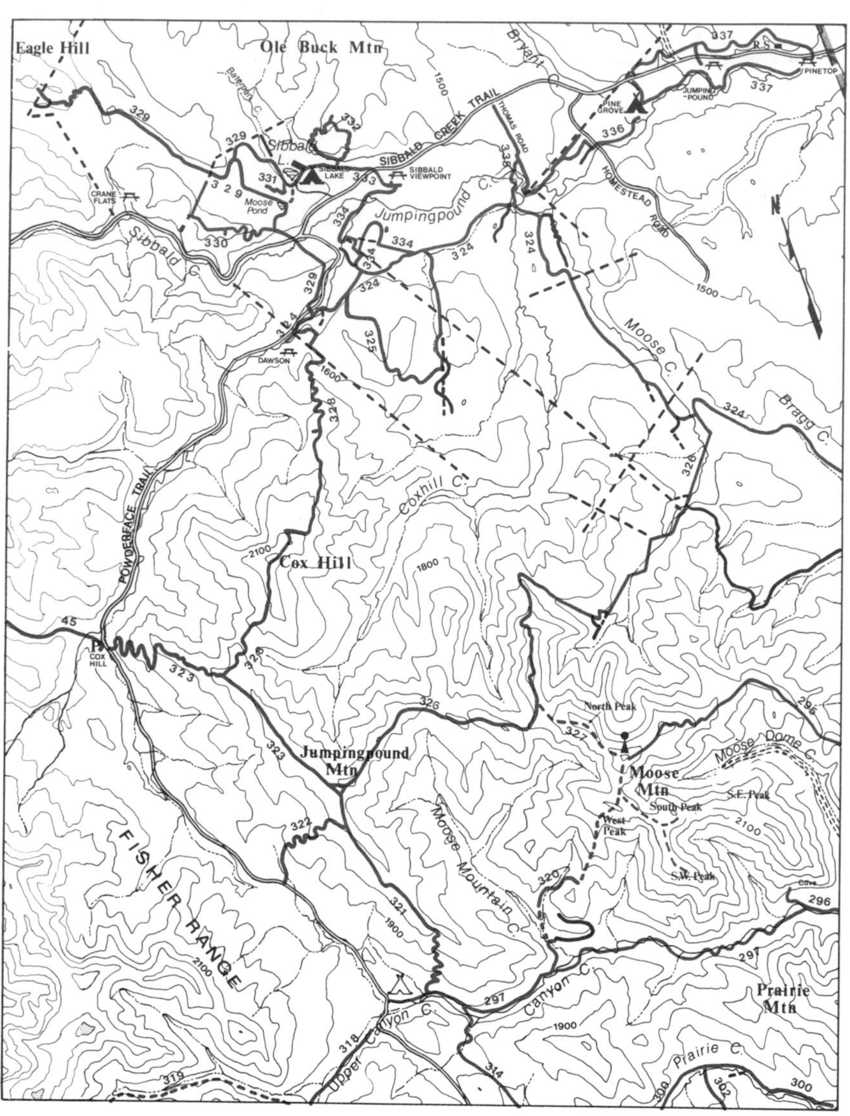

ALPHABETICAL INDEX

THIS IS GODS COUNTRY
WHY MAKE IT
LOOK LIKE HELL